Multicultural Counseling With Teenage Fathers

MULTICULTURAL ASPECTS OF COUNSELING SERIES

SERIES EDITOR
Paul Pedersen, Ph.D., *Syracuse University*

Volumes in This Series

Multicultural Counseling With Teenage Fathers

A Practical Guide

Mark S. Kiselica

Multicultural Aspects of Counseling Series 6

SAGE Publications
International Educational and Professional Publisher
Thousand Oaks   London   New Delhi

For information address:

 SAGE Publications, Inc.
2455 Teller Road
Thousand Oaks, California 91320
E-mail: order@sagepub.com

SAGE Publications Ltd.
6 Bonhill Street
London EC2A 4PU
United Kingdom

SAGE Publications India Pvt. Ltd.
M-32 Market
Greater Kailash I
New Delhi 110 048 India

Printed in the United States of America

Library of Congress Cataloging-in-Publication Data

Kiselica, Mark S.
Multicultural counseling with teenage fathers: A practical guide/
Mark S. Kiselica.
p. cm.—(Multicultural aspects of counseling series, v. 6)
Includes bibliographical references and indexes.
ISBN 0-8039-5336-4 (cloth: alk. paper).—ISBN 0-8039-5337-2
(pbk.: alk. paper)
1. Teenage fathers—Counseling of—United States.
2. Multiculturalism—United States. I. Title. II. Series.
HQ756.7.K57 1995
362.7'0835'1—dc20   95-12232

This book is printed on acid-free paper.

95 96 97 98 99   10 9 8 7 6 5 4 3 2 1

Sage Production Editor: Tricia K. Bennett
Sage Copy Editor: Gillian Dickens

This book is dedicated to the memory of the late Joseph P. Smyth (1933-1974)—my dear "Uncle Buddy"—whose legacy of paternal love continues to impress and inspire me more than 20 years after his untimely death.

Contents

Foreword

The prophet Hosea, in speaking to the children of Israel, said, "My people are destroyed for lack of knowledge. . . ." In a like manner, current literature on teenage fathers would suggest that they too are being destroyed for lack of an in-depth, practical guide for dealing with their concerns and concomitantly a framework for addressing simultaneously the common and culturally distinct needs of any given unwed teenage father. Although practitioners have substantial knowledge regarding unwed adolescent paternity, they do not always know how to put this knowledge into practice to effect a positive change in the lives of teenage fathers and their children.

Multicultural Counseling With Teenage Fathers: A Practical Guide, however, provides a refreshing and welcome solution to this unsatisfactorily state of affairs. It not only ameliorates the frustration of practitioners who want to help and do not always understand how, but it also gives teen fathers the best chance for therapeutic outcomes by equipping practitioners with an easily understood guide and framework for meeting the material and nonmaterial needs of teenage fathers that vary within and across cultures.

What is exciting about this book is that it will help practitioners improve their skills in helping teenage fathers to reshape their lives and act responsibly irrespective of their cultural background. The author explains in clear, concise terms how to attend to the common and culture-specific concerns of teenage fathers. This knowledge enhances the practitioner's ability to select and implement interventions that are appropriate for each teenage father's specific need situation.

Moreover, the timeliness of the author's book is underscored by President Clinton's 1995 State of the Union Address, in which he declared "the epidemic of teen pregnancies and births where there is no marriage" to be "our most serious social problem." His desire to combat teenage pregnancy is shared by many of us in the field. Thanks to Mark Kiselica's book, we now have a weapon that would please the president and at the same time help practitioners win the battle of keeping teenage fathers in school, in counseling, and in a positive relationship with their children.

In no small way, this book provides the best help possible for practitioners working with unwed adolescent fathers and helps future generations avoid the pitfalls and tragedies that create unmarried paternity.

Leo E. Hendricks, Ph.D.
Washington, D.C.

Acknowledgments

Over the past several years while I worked on this manuscript, I benefited from a wellspring of support provided by a host of people. It is my privilege to acknowledge the many ways that each of these individuals contributed to the development and completion of this project.

Writing this book has been a labor of love that was inspired by many adolescent men and women whose troubled lives have touched me profoundly. I thank these youngsters for their trust in me and I hope that this book adequately expresses my gratitude for the meaning their struggles have brought to my life.

More than any other persons, my wife, Sandi, and my precious sons, Andrew and Christian, deserve credit for the successful completion of this book. Without their ongoing patience, love, and understanding during the many hours I was sequestered away researching and writing, this project would not have been possible. I also am deeply indebted to my parents, Sandi's parents, and our brothers and sisters for their support of my work on this book.

This book was written during my tenure at two fine institutions of higher education, Ball State University and Trenton State College. Various forms of support from each institution were crucial throughout the time I worked on this project. The Office of Academic Research and Sponsored Programs of Ball State University awarded me a summer research grant in 1992 that

supported my writing the initial prospectus for this book. While I was
employed at Ball State University, Sharon Bowman, Richard Brosio, Ken
Dimick, Dave Dixon, Lonnie Duncan, Larry Gerstein, Roger Hutchinson,
Paul Spengler, and Roy Weaver willingly shared their scholarly materials
and advice during the initial research for this project. Steve Capps, Mark
Hurst, and Cassie Nichols faithfully located library resources for me; Tyrone
Powell graciously reviewed the first draft of the chapter on African American
teenage fathers (Chapter 9); and Teresa Story kindly offered secretarial support.
Suzanne Pasch, Dean of the School of Education at Trenton State College,
generously granted me release time from teaching that enabled me to see this
undertaking achieve its fruition. My current faculty colleagues at Trenton
State College—Marion Cavallaro, Bill Fassbender, Mary Lou Ramsey, and
Roland Worthington— offered me their wisdom, scholarly consultation, and
companionship while I revised and expanded my initial version of this book.
Carolanne Lowrie and Nancy Morrell cheerfully obtained numerous articles
for me from the library, and Kathleen Underwood and Gloria Valeri addressed a number of my clerical needs with the utmost care and consideration. Omayra Rivera diligently typed the author index for this book. I am
sincerely grateful for these many forms of support.

I also thank a variety of colleagues from an assortment of institutions for
their contributions to my ongoing research on teenage fathers and their input
regarding and support of this project: Jill Scheckel, Dawn Kessler Murphy,
James Stroud, and Judith Stroud, Ball State University; Anne Miller, Federal
Correctional Institution, Cumberland, Maryland; Larry Beymer, Indiana
State University; Catherine Hill, Louisiana State University; Joan Pfaller,
Michigan State University; Stan Baker, North Carolina State University; Alex
Hall, Saint Joseph's College, Rensselaer, Indiana; Andy Erkis, The Pennsyl-
vania State University; David Joliff, Phoenix Associates, Fort Wayne, Indi-
ana; Donna Bookout, Planned Parenthood of Muncie, Indiana; Kevin Kelly,
Purdue University; Paul Sturmer, State University of New York—Albany;
Andrea Rotzien, Texas A&M University; Andy Horne, University of Geor-
gia; Jennifer Clark, University of Oklahoma; Christine Weaver, University of
Pittsburgh; Skip Niles, University of Virginia; Louise Silverstein, Yeshiva
University; and Steve Scheckel, Youth Opportunity Center, Muncie, Indiana.

A special thanks is extended to the reviewers of this book, Sally Brown of
the Philliber Research Associates and Harold Cheatham of The Pennsylvania
State University, whose careful, thought-provoking comments were invaluable as I crafted my final version of this book. I also thank Harold for his
many years of personal and professional support.

I am grateful to Joe Ponterotto of Fordham University, who, as the Action
Editor of this book, warmly guided me through the revision process, and to

Paul Pedersen of Syracuse University, the Series Editor of the **Multicultural Aspects of Counseling Series**, who in recent years has mentored my interests in multiculturalism. I also thank Marquita Flemming, Dale Mary Grenfell, Tricia Bennett, Gillian Dickens, Yvonne Könneker, and their colleagues at Sage for their friendly and competent assistance during the production of this book.

Last, but not least, I am deeply honored that Leo Hendricks wrote the Foreword to this handbook. His pioneering research on teenage fathers produced some of the classic publications on the subject, which enhanced my understanding about the joys and hardships experienced by teenage fathers and taught me how to help them. His writings and conference addresses have inspired me and his kind encouragement has affirmed my endeavors as a scholar. He is an admirable role model whom I hope to emulate.

I welcome readers' comments about this book and can be reached at the Department of Counseling and Personnel Services, 332 Forcina Hall, Trenton State College, Hillwood Lakes—CN 4700, Trenton, New Jersey 08650-4700.

Mark S. Kiselica

1

Multicultural Counseling
With Teenage Fathers

AN OVERVIEW

Throughout my 17 years of counseling adolescents, I have encountered many teenage fathers from diverse cultural backgrounds. Any reader who has worked with this population can empathize with the joys and difficulties I have experienced through my efforts to help these young men master the developmental crisis of unplanned fatherhood. In my early work with teenage fathers, I enjoyed a number of successful therapeutic outcomes with inspirational boys who accepted their responsibilities as parents, often against great odds, while juggling the demands of both work and school. However, I also must admit that I struggled through many frustrating periods with some adolescent fathers who dropped out of school and gradually distanced themselves from their children and from continued counseling. I now realize that some of these "failures" might have been avoided had there been more accurate information to guide me in my work with this easily misunderstood and often elusive population.

This book is an attempt to provide such a guide and it represents the culmination of years of clinical practice and scholarly research on the subject of teenage fathers. When I started counseling adolescents and their families during the early 1980s, I turned to the mental health literature for resources that might direct me toward a counseling process and interventions that were beneficial to adolescent males involved in unplanned out-of-wedlock pregnancies. Most of the literature on teenage parents that was published at that time focused on the important challenge of effectively responding to the needs of teenage mothers. Unfortunately, the paucity of information then available on teenage fathers for the most part reinforced harmful stereotypes about this population, emphasized punitive responses, and did little to promote a compassionate understanding of the teenage father's experience. Consequently, I was forced to rely on my general counseling skills, my knowledge of adolescents, and my instincts, all the while wishing that I could refer to some handbook that specifically suggested an approach to counseling that was sensitive to the needs of teenage fathers.

In the absence of such a resource, I attempted to improve my skills as a counselor of teenage fathers by learning from my experiences with my clients and by reading articles on adolescent fathers that appeared in the mental health literature. During the mid- to late 1980s, I discovered an emerging literature that provided useful, though scattered, information on the subject. New evidence reported in this literature challenged old, simplistic stereotypes that had depicted teenage fathers as psychologically maladjusted males who first exploited adolescent girls and then callously abandoned them and their children. For example, in contrast to this stereotypical view, findings reported in a series of ground-breaking studies conducted by Leo Hendricks and his colleagues at Howard University (Hendricks, 1980, 1982, 1983, 1988; Hendricks, Howard, & Caesar, 1981; Hendricks & Montgomery, 1983; Hendricks & Solomon, 1987) indicated that many teenage fathers do experience genuine concern for their children and the mothers of their children but that a complex set of factors could contribute to their gradual withdrawal from their responsibilities as fathers. These researchers also discovered that African American, Anglo American, and Hispanic American teenage fathers have diverse needs that vary within and across their cultures. These needs include information, practical help, and counseling. Hendricks and his colleagues recommended that helping professionals provide these services so as to empower adolescent fathers to become responsible parents. Moreover, outreach counseling, to be effective, should include a variety of strategies that are sensitive to the cultural backgrounds of teenage fathers.

The work of Hendricks and his colleagues represents a growing body of research directly targeting teenage fathers. This recent research has been reviewed and organized in two landmark books, *Adolescent Fatherhood* (Elster & Lamb, 1986) and *Teenage Fathers* (Robinson, 1988a). In both, a comprehensive profile of the adolescent father as well as an overview for addressing his counseling needs are provided. By advancing our understanding of and sensitivity toward teenage fathers, these books are major contributions to the social sciences literature.

Nevertheless, there still are two major gaps in the literature on teenage fathers. First, no books provide counselors, social workers, psychologists, psychiatrists, ministers, nurses, early childhood professionals, high school teachers and administrators, and health care educators and practitioners with an in-depth, practical guide for their dealings with teenage fathers. Second, the literature on counseling teenage fathers lacks a framework for addressing simultaneously the common and culturally distinct needs of any given teenage father. Instead, either universal (e.g., Robinson, 1988a) or culture-specific (e.g., L. A. Smith, 1988) approaches to counseling have been proposed and advocated. In brief, universal counseling approaches are based primarily on principles that apply to all counseling contacts, but culture-specific counseling approaches focus on counseling processes and techniques that are effective with particular cultural groups. To date, no one has attempted to organize the literature on teenage fathers from a multicultural perspective that combines the universal and culture-specific points of view.

In this practical handbook, the extremes of the universal and the culture-specific viewpoints are synthesized in a generic approach to multicultural counseling with teenage fathers. Thus, the purpose of this book is to prepare helping professionals to effectively respond to the common and unique needs of adolescent fathers from different cultural backgrounds. As such, this book expands on the existing literature on how to help young men who face unplanned out-of-wedlock pregnancies during their teenage years.

Specifically, the following questions are raised and addressed in this book: What are the common and unique views of fatherhood and teenage fatherhood in our multicultural society? What are the shared and different needs of young fathers from varying cultural backgrounds? How should helping professionals generally and specifically respond to the counseling concerns of the culturally distinct adolescent father?

In addition to these questions, this book tackles a commonly asked question confronting the professional with an interest in helping teenage fathers: Why focus on teenage fathers? A brief response to this challenge follows.

Why Focus on Helping Teenage Fathers?

A book on helping teenage fathers is needed because these youth historically have been understudied by researchers (see Barret & Robinson, 1982;

Robinson, 1988a; Chapter 13, this volume) and underserved by the helping professions. Some scholars (e.g., Allen-Meares, 1984; Robinson, 1988a) observed that societal responses to teenage fathers traditionally have been limited to punitive measures, such as denying adolescent fathers counseling services unless they were seriously intent on marriage. These authors also suggested that biases against teenage fathers are manifested in programs for teenage parents that tend to include medical, educational, and psychological services for teenage mothers but not for teenage fathers.

Data from qualitative, national reports (Children's Defense Fund, 1986a; Smollar & Ooms, 1987; U.S. Congress, 1986) and quantitative studies (Kiselica, 1992; Kiselica & Sturmer, 1993b, 1995) on the status of services for teenage parents support these contentions, indicating that most federal, state, and local social service programs for adolescent parents have been focused almost exclusively on the needs of teenage mothers, but only a few programs with limited services have been provided to teenage fathers. Thus, in spite of the expressed concerns of teenage fathers (see Chapter 2) and the repeated assertions by numerous authorities on teenage parents (e.g., Ascher, 1985; Children's Defense Fund, 1988a; McGee, 1982; Robinson, 1988a; Smollar & Ooms, 1987) that teenage fathers are an at-risk group who require many of the same services deemed to be essential for teenage mothers, it appears that the needs of teenage fathers go largely unnoticed by service providers. According to Kiselica and Sturmer (1993b), these findings suggest that society is giving teenage fathers a mixed message: We expect you to become a responsible parent but we won't provide you with the guidance for how to become one.

The failure of society and the helping professions to assist teenage fathers can be tolerated no longer. An unplanned adolescent pregnancy occurring out of wedlock often represents a crisis for the teenage mother *and* the teenage father, their extended families, and society—a crisis that warrants a variety of interventions, one of which is counseling teenage fathers. Although the needs of teenage fathers are accentuated in this book, multisystemic issues as they relate to the adjustment of the teenage father, such as his relationship with his parents, his child(ren), the mother of his child(ren) and her parents, and his peers also are addressed. Therefore, this book will be of value to *all* professionals who work with teenage parents, including those whose primary mission is to assist teenage mothers and their children.

The central thesis of this book is that the therapeutic goal of helping teenage fathers can best be achieved through the use of process and intervention skills that are embedded in Pedersen's (1991b) model of multiculturalism as a generic approach to counseling. A brief history of multicultural counseling is presented to fully describe this perspective.

Multicultural Counseling:
A Brief History

Multicultural counseling in the United States has a relatively brief history. Although a few early pioneers (e.g., Du Bois, 1903; Frazier, 1939/1966; Horney, 1937; Sanchez, 1932; Stonequist, 1937) recognized the importance of cultural factors in understanding human behavior, until the 1960s most psychological theorists, researchers, and practitioners rarely acknowledged culture as playing a major role in personality dynamics or influencing the psychotherapeutic process. Instead, during the first half of this century, psychology became a source of tools for educators and mental health professionals in the United States to force conformity on the "different" (see Ramirez, 1991), perpetuate inaccurate stereotypes regarding minority groups (see Sue & Sue, 1990), and attempt to demonstrate the intellectual, cultural, and racial superiority of the dominant White Anglo culture (see Guthrie, 1976; Ramirez, 1991; Sue & Sue, 1990).

These practices reflected the prevailing societal view that the United States was a melting pot of cultures. A basic assumption of this thought was that cultural homogeneity (assimilation) was a success and cultural heterogeneity was a failure. Mainstream society expected the culturally different to forsake their unique cultural identities and "melt in" with the dominant culture (Vacc, Wittmer, & DeVaney, 1988). Consistent with this assumption, the goal of psychotherapeutic interventions with clients experiencing cultural conflicts was to promote their acculturation to the values and customs of the majority culture (Ramirez, 1991).

During the 1960s, however, the mental health professions witnessed and participated in a number of dramatic sociocultural changes spawned by the civil rights movement (Pedersen, 1991a) and the feminist movement (Kelly & Hall, 1992; Pedersen, 1991a). These movements challenged the melting pot perspective by recognizing that the United States is a multicultural society and by promoting a tolerance for cultural diversity. During this era, the concept of cultural pluralism, the ideal that "the dominant culture benefits from coexistence and interaction with the cultures of adjunct groups" (Axelson, 1993, p. 14), was embraced. According to Axelson (1993), the goal of a culturally pluralistic society is "unity in diversity" (p. 14), that is, the creation of a cohesive society in which multicultural communities are permitted to live according to their own styles, customs, languages, and values without penalty to their members. Thus, a pluralistic society is one in which cultural groups merge while maintaining their distinct identities.

Cultural pluralism has had an important impact on the research, training, and clinical practice of the mental health professions. A new approach to counseling, first referred to as cross-cultural counseling and more recently as multicultural counseling, evolved in response to the promotion of cultural pluralism as a societal goal (Lee & Richardson, 1991; Pedersen, 1991a; Vacc et al., 1988) and to the rising population of ethnic minorities in the United States (Lee & Richardson, 1991; Pedersen, 1991a; Sue & Sue, 1990). Although there are a variety of definitions for multicultural counseling, all definitions are based on the assumption that the cultural background of both the counselor and the client are factors that could influence the process and outcome of counseling and psychotherapy. Multicultural researchers in the mental health fields have examined such topics as ethnic group use of mental health services, client preferences for counselor race and ethnicity, counselor prejudice and stereotyping, cultural influences and biases on the diagnosis of client problems, the impact of cultural variables on the counseling process, and differences in treatment strategies and outcome as a function of race and ethnicity (see Atkinson, 1985). Recently, these topics have been incorporated into the training experiences of mental health professionals (Casas, 1984) and into several texts on multicultural counseling (e.g., Axelson, 1993; Ivey, Ivey, & Simek-Morgan, 1993; Lee & Richardson, 1991; Locke, 1992; Pedersen, 1985, 1988; Ramirez, 1991; Sue & Sue, 1990; Vacc et al., 1988).

These developments have helped to shape several different paradigms of multicultural counseling, each representing a different approach to counseling. Although it is beyond the scope of this book to furnish an in-depth review of these paradigms, a succinct summary of three major models is provided.

The Culture-Specific Model

The culture-specific, or *emic,* model of multicultural counseling is based on the premise that cultural, racial, and ethnic differences between people can affect the relationship and interactions between counselor and client. In a culture-specific approach to counselor training, counselors are taught about a particular nationality, ethnicity, or cultural group in terms of its special perspective (Pedersen, 1988).

The merits and limitations of the culture-specific model have been debated in the literature. Proponents of the culture-specific model have argued that informing counselors of the unique outlooks of particular cultural groups prepares them to use process and intervention skills that are sensitive to the cultural perspective of the client. Under such conditions, clients who are culturally different from their counselor are likely to accept their counselor's behavior and respond favorably in treatment (Marsella & Higginbotham, 1984). Opponents of the culture-specific model have suggested that this approach has resulted in a multicultural "cookbook," with each group receiving a "recipe" that includes a checklist of the group's characteristics and some instructions regarding how the counseling should proceed (Speight, Myers, Cox, & Highlen, 1991). Culture-specific counseling also might result in within-group stereotyping and a consequent failure to recognize within-group differences (Pedersen, 1991b; Speight et al., 1991). With an emphasis on the acquisition of knowledge about various groups, the training process can seem an insurmountable task, considering the many possible groups that one could study (Speight et al., 1991). Finally, Pedersen (1991b) warned that culturally defined special interest groups could pressure the counseling profession to overemphasize their culture-specific perspectives, thereby diverting attention away from the needs of other culturally distinct groups.

The Universal Model

Similarities rather than the differences between people are emphasized in the universal, or *etic,* model of multicultural counseling (Pedersen, 1991b). The universal model is based on the assumption that unifying themes bind people of different cultures together (Patterson, 1986). By focusing on universal issues and characteristics that are shared across cultures, such as existential dilemmas, advocates of the etic model believe that cultural differences can be transcended (Vontress, 1988) and that the counseling profession can avoid overemphasizing the interests of a particular cultural group (Pedersen, 1991b). Some critics of the universal model point out that more specific information about the client's culture often is needed to effectively intervene in individual situations (see Pedersen, 1991b). For example, Lum (1992) argued that ethnic minority groups in the United States share distinctive cultural issues, such as the effects of discrimination on one's worldview, that are overlooked when a universal framework is practiced. For multicultural counseling to be effective, Lum added, it must include an understanding of the unique themes and issues of ethnic minority groups. According to Pedersen (1991b), an additional potential problem of widespread adherence to a universal approach is that it might result in the continued domination by the more powerful majority culture at the expense of minority cultures.

Pedersen's Generic Model

Pedersen (1990, 1991b) proposed a model of multicultural counseling in which the culture-specific and universalistic perspectives are combined, culture is defined broadly, and multiculturalism is viewed as a generic approach to counseling.

Recognizing the pros and cons of adhering strictly to either a culture-specific or a universal model, Pedersen (1991b) suggested a new, multilevel theory that acknowledged "the complex diversity of a plural society while, at the same time, suggesting bridges of shared concern that bind culturally different persons to one another" (p. 7). Using the terms *multiculturalism* and *multicultural perspective* to describe his model, Pedersen (1991b) argued that his theory weaves the extremes of the culture-specific and universal models by explaining behavior in terms of culturally unique perspectives and common-ground universals that are shared across cultures.

A central tenet of Pedersen's model is a broad definition of culture that was suggested to replace earlier, more narrow conceptions of culture. According to these prior views, culture was defined as being synonymous with ethnicity and nationality. Such a restricted definition of culture had limited cross-cultural counseling to a consideration of the similarities of religion, history, and ancestry that were shared by ethnic groups. Although Pedersen (1991b) acknowledged that ethnicity and nationality are important to individual and familial identity as one subset of culture, he argued that the construct of culture goes beyond national and ethnic boundaries:

> Persons from the same ethnic or nationality groups may still experience cultural differences. Not all Blacks have the same experience, nor do all Asians, nor all American Indians, nor all Hispanics, nor all women, nor all old people, nor all disabled persons. No particular group is unimodal in its perspective. (p. 7)

A broad definition of culture includes demographic variables (e.g., age, sex), status variables (e.g., educational, economic), and affiliations (formal, informal), as well as ethnographic variables such as nationality, ethnicity, language, and religion (Pedersen, 1990, 1991b).

An important implication of a broad conception of culture is that, to some extent, *all* counseling is multicultural. If one considers age, lifestyle, socio-economic status, and gender differences in addition to ethnic and national differences, it quickly becomes apparent that there is a multicultural dimension in every counseling relationship (Pedersen, 1990). For example, any individual client "may change his or her cultural referent group during the course of an interview—from emphasizing gender, to age, to socioeconomic status, to nationality or ethnicity, to one or another affiliation" (Pedersen, 1991b, p. 8). By using a broad definition of culture as a lens to interpret these behaviors, helpers will be skilled enough to understand that each of these referents represent salient cultures for the client, each having a number of possible meanings. Employing a broad definition of culture in all counseling endeavors transforms multicultural counseling from a counseling subspeciality to a generic approach that can be used with all clients (Pedersen, 1990, 1991b).

How Can a Generic
Multicultural Counseling Approach
Enhance Counseling With Teenage Fathers?

Both universal and culture-specific strategies for helping teenage fathers have been recommended in the literature, each somewhat limited in its clinical utility. Although universal approaches, such as those proposed and described by Kahn and Bolton (1986), Klinman, Sander, Rosen, and Longo (1986), and Robinson (1988a), are designed to address the common conflicts that confront adolescent males facing fatherhood, they lack guidelines for how helpers should modify the counseling process and interventions in order to respond effectively to the needs of teenage fathers from different cultural backgrounds. And although culture-specific counseling tactics, such as those advocated by L. A. Smith (1988) for counseling African American teenage fathers and by Zayas, Schinke, and Casareno (1987) for assisting Hispanic American teenage fathers, may facilitate the work of practitioners with African American and Hispanic American young fathers, respectively, they may not be helpful in counseling conducted with adolescent fathers from other cultural groups. In addition, overreliance on culture-specific models could result in overlooking within-group variations among teenage fathers from the same cultural group. It follows that a clinician versed in both universal and culture-specific approaches will likely enhance his or her effectiveness in supporting adolescent males confronting an unplanned pregnancy. By using Pedersen's generic multicultural model as an approach to counseling with teenage fathers, counselors will be better equipped to respond to the needs of teenage fathers that vary within and across cultures.

Counselors who use a generic multicultural approach would attend to both the common and culture-specific concerns of the teenage father. By employing this approach, the counselor will ask him- or herself a complex set of questions that serves as a framework for exploring, interpreting, and understanding the perspective and behaviors of the teenage father: What are the joys and challenges awaiting any adolescent boy who is about to become a father? What are the developmental conflicts of adolescent males facing an unplanned pregnancy and impending parenthood? How might the cultural background of the client, including his ethnicity, socioeconomic level, religiosity, and living environment influence his risk for premature paternity, his conception of fatherhood, and the manner in which he and his partner resolve the pregnancy? By attempting to answer these and other questions, the counselor can formulate and test a rich array of hypotheses with each new teenage father until a clear understanding of his unique, yet multidimensional, perspective has been established. Based on this extensive assessment, the counselor can select and implement interventions that are appropriate for each teenage father's given situation.

Overview of the Book

To assist the reader in developing general and culture-specific hypotheses about teenage fathers involved in unplanned out-of-wedlock pregnancies, this book has been divided into four parts. Throughout Part I (Chapters 2 through 7), universal counseling considerations are reviewed. In Chapter 2, important background information about teenage fathers is supplied to sensitize the reader to the common problems experienced by this population and evoke the reader to evaluate his or her attitudes regarding teenage boys responsible for an adolescent pregnancy. Program development issues, strategies for conducting outreach and establishing rapport, and case management issues with teenage fathers are highlighted in Chapter 3. The complicated pregnancy-resolution process and associated legal considerations are explored in Chapter 4. The challenges of addressing the teenage father's issues with his and his partner's families and his peers are discussed in Chapter 5. Chapter 6 is dedicated to the task of helping young fathers to prepare for the responsibilities of parenthood. Part I of this book concludes with Chapter 7, in which short-term and long-term educational and career counseling considerations are suggested.

In Part II (Chapters 8 through 11), culture-specific ideas for counseling teenage fathers are emphasized. In Chapters 8 through 10, variations in counseling that are sensitive to the particular issues and needs of Anglo American, African American, and Hispanic American teenage fathers, respectively, are proposed. These three chapters are organized according to each of the universal issues covered in Part I. The counseling implications of other cultural variables, such as social class, religion, and rural and urban environments are considered in Chapter 11.

In Part III (Chapter 13), the reader is provided with a concise review of the material covered in the first two parts of the book. Three case studies also are presented. In each of these cases, the generic multicultural model was employed. This part of the book demonstrates for the reader how to integrate and apply the general and culture-specific counseling considerations mentioned earlier in the book. Thus, Part III is designed to assist the reader in "putting it all together" in actual counseling situations.

This book concludes with Part IV (Chapter 14), in which implications for training and research are discussed. The prior research on teenage fathers is critiqued and suggestions for future research are offered. Recommendations for integrating research and practice are provided and ethical principles pertaining to research with adolescents and multicultural research are reviewed.

It is hoped that this book provides the reader with a better understanding of the experiences of teenage fathers and an effective framework for helping this population. Perhaps this book will also inspire more professionals to engage in the challenging and complicated but profoundly fulfilling mission of sensitively guiding adolescent fathers during their transition to parenthood.

PART I

Universal Considerations

Regardless of his particular background, every teenage father in the United States faces some common issues precipitated by his participation in an unplanned out-of-wedlock pregnancy. The purpose of Part I is to acquaint the reader with these issues and suggest counseling considerations that apply to all adolescent fathers.

Counselors assisting teenage fathers face many challenges. Prior to working with this population, counselors need to learn accurate information about adolescent fathers and clarify their feelings about working with young men whose entry into paternity was unplanned and launched by premarital conception. It behooves counselors to understand the mechanics of program development and case management and use effective strategies for recruiting and engaging adolescent fathers in counseling. During the prenatal period, the teenage father and his partner need help resolving the pregnancy. Thus, helpers are obliged to know the pros and cons of each option associated with the pregnancy-resolution process and the legal implications of these options. Finally, practitioners are challenged to address the family and peer issues of young fathers, help prepare teenage fathers for their critical role as parents, and assist them in their educational and career adjustments. Each of these therapeutic objectives is covered in Part I.

2

A Profile of the Teenage Father

Girl, 17, Delivers Baby, Concocts Story

Tustin, Calif. (AP)—A 17-year-old girl gave birth at home by herself, then helped concoct a story about how her boyfriend bought the newborn in a parking lot for $10 from a man who wanted drugs, police said.

The baby, a boy, was fine.

The tale fooled police for a day before the father, Robert Garcia, 18, confessed Monday that it wasn't true.

"As most young people, they were simply afraid to tell their parents," said Police Chief Doug Franks.

Garcia initially told police he was walking through a shopping center parking lot Saturday night when a man in a car offered to trade the baby for drugs. Garcia told police he didn't have drugs but gave the man $10 to get the baby away from him.

The child was being cared for Monday at a children's home.

Authorities were considering whether to file charges against Garcia, which could include child abandonment, sex with a minor and filing a false report with police. But none seemed likely, Franks said.

The mother, a junior in high school, hid her pregnancy by telling her father she was gaining weight, Franks said. While her father was at work Saturday, she delivered by herself in her bedroom.

Social workers were counseling the couple about whether to put the child up for adoption or keep him, Franks said.

—Associated Press (January 26, 1993, p. D2)[1]

When we found out my girlfriend was pregnant I was emotionally very scared
and upset. At first I wanted to run but was scared and couldn't leave my new
family behind. I loved them very much. I wasn't sure what my parents would
say and how they would react. I found myself always looking for a fight. I
was depressed because I realized that I would have to grow up and take
responsibility for my actions. Although I wanted to party with my friends and
wanted to be free, I realized that I desired a good life for my upcoming family
and would be forced to make many sacrifices.

Behaviorally, I took responsibility by getting a full-time job and graduating
from high school. I refinished the basement of my parents' house so we could
live down there after the baby was born.

Excerpt from Kahn's (1986) interview
with a teenage father named Elwood (p. 193)

*   *   *

How does the reader feel about each of the teenage fathers depicted above?
Does either adolescent fit the reader's image of the teenage father? Which
young man is the reader more inclined to help? To condemn? How representative are these reactions of adolescent males to an unplanned pregnancy? What factors contribute to their unexpected route to fatherhood?
What difficulties are they, their partners, and their children at risk to
experience? What transitional challenges are they likely to encounter?
How might they be viewed by our society? How likely are they to receive
compassionate, professional guidance?

Answering these questions is a critical task for any helper responding to
the problem of unwed adolescent pregnancy and parenthood in the United
States. The purpose of this chapter is to assist the reader to address these
questions by providing a profile of the teenage father in the United States.
The following subjects are reviewed: trends in adolescent sexual behavior
and teenage parenthood, the causes of premarital adolescent pregnancy, the
challenges and opportunities for growth experienced by teenage fathers, the
service needs of teenage fathers, and societal treatment of young fathers. It
is hoped that this information will prompt the reader to acquire a complex
understanding about teenage fathers, question stereotypic thinking regarding
this population, and clarify his or her feelings and attitudes about working
with these youth.

Trends in Adolescent Sexual Behavior
and Teenage Parenthood

Sexual activity among adolescents in the United States is increasing. Nationally, levels of premarital sexual activity have risen since the 1920s, although premarital intercourse did not gain social acceptance until the 1970s (Brindis, 1990). The proportion of teenage females 15 to 19 years old who reported ever having sexual intercourse rose from 28% in 1971 to 42% in 1982 (see Brindis, 1990), to 47% in 1985 (see Children's Defense Fund, 1988b), and to 51% in 1991 (Centers for Disease Control, 1992). According to data reported by Pleck (cited in Beymer, 1995), the percentage of adolescent males reporting sexual intercourse also has risen from 65% in 1979 to 76% in 1989. Increases in the levels of sexual activity were greater among younger teenagers than older teenagers. At every age, adolescent boys are more likely to report being sexually active than are adolescent girls (Centers for Disease Control, 1992).

The majority of sexually active teenagers do not consistently use contraceptives. Boys are slightly less likely than girls to report having used some form of contraception, whether the occasion is first intercourse, last intercourse, or during the past month (Sonenstein, 1986). For example, at first intercourse, 44% of boys and 49% of girls report using some form of contraception (Brindis, 1991). Thus, at least half of all sexually active teenagers are at risk for conceiving a baby during their first experience of sexual intercourse. In addition, they are at risk for contracting sexually transmitted diseases.

The United States has the highest teenage pregnancy rate of any industrialized nation (Jones et al., 1985). Due to the large number of teenagers engaging in unprotected sexual intercourse, approximately 1 million adolescent girls became pregnant each year between 1980 and 1988. During that same time period, nearly half a million teenage girls gave birth to a child annually (Ventura, Taffel, Mosher, & Henshaw, 1992). The vast majority of these births were reported to be unintended (Moore, 1992).

Contrary to popular thinking, teenage pregnancy is not a new phenomenon in the United States. In support of this conclusion, Males (1993) noted that national records indicate hundreds of thousands of births among teenage girls every year during this century. What *is* a new trend in this country is the growing number of adolescent girls having children outside of marriage. The number and rate of children born out of wedlock to teenage parents has risen steadily over the past three decades, from 68,000 in 1960 (12% of all births to teenagers) to 361,000 (68% of all birth to teenagers) in 1990 (Moore,

Snyder, & Halla, 1992). According to the Vera Institute of Justice (1990), "This trend has heightened public concern, since young, unmarried mothers and their children are at so much risk of being poor and dependent on public welfare" (p. 4).

Variations among different racial and ethnic groups regarding the number of teenage pregnancies, births to teenagers, and rates of out-of-wedlock adolescent childbearing have been noted in the literature. According to recent national statistics reported by Henshaw (1993), about two thirds of all pregnant teenagers are White and about one third are of other races. White adolescent girls account for about two thirds of the births to teenage mothers. Most of the remaining births occur among Black teenage mothers. According to Brindis (1991), although the teenage pregnancy rate is higher among Blacks than Whites, the rate for both groups climbed during the 1970s. Between 1980 and 1988, the pregnancy rate for White teenagers declined slightly, but the rate for non-White teenagers increased by about 6% (Henshaw, 1992). Among ethnic groups, births to teenage mothers happen most often among Anglo Americans, followed by African Americans and then Hispanic Americans, but the teenage birth rates for African Americans and Hispanic Americans are twice as high as that for Anglo Americans (Children's Defense Fund, 1988b). Rates of out-of-wedlock childbearing among teenagers are higher among disadvantaged racial and ethnic minorities than among Whites, although the sharpest increases have been among Whites (Vera Institute of Justice, 1990). In summary, teenage pregnancy and out-of-wedlock childbearing in the United States are phenomena that cut across socioeconomic, racial, and ethnic lines.

According to Sonenstein (1986), although there is fairly accurate information regarding the numbers and characteristics of teenage mothers in this country, precise demographic data on teenage fathers are unavailable because the age of the father is often not listed on birth registration forms. Therefore, Sonenstein hypothesized that government statistics regarding the number of teenage fathers are probably underestimates and warned researchers to interpret those statistics with caution.

This warning notwithstanding, the best available data seem to indicate that teenage fathers "are demographically a heterogeneous group—they come from all regions of the country, and all income and racial groups" (Smollar & Ooms, 1987, p. 3). Adolescent males who are African American, have educational deficiencies, and come from poor economic circumstances are disproportionately represented among those who become fathers at an early age (Marsiglio, 1987).

Official data also show that most teenage pregnancies involve 18- or 19-year-old females and males in their early 20s. For example, data reported by the National Center for Health Statistics (cited in Beymer, 1995) indicated that only 29% of 309,819 babies born to teenage mothers in 1988 had teenage fathers. Other data cited by Males (1994) regarding a 1990 analysis of 60,000 births to teenage mothers in California showed that senior high school boys fathered only 24% of all births to school-age girls. The Children's Defense Fund (1988a) estimated that approximately 30% of the children born to adolescent mothers nationally are fathered by teenage boys. Thus, although it would appear that there is a substantial number of teenage fathers in this country, the majority of adolescent pregnancies are caused by male adults, not teenage boys.

This book is focused on helping teenage boys who are partners to an unmarried adolescent female experiencing an unplanned pregnancy, rather than adult males. Although both populations deserve the compassionate attention of the helping professions, the counseling concerns of these younger males are emphasized for two reasons. First, males who father a child as a teenager are much more likely than males who delay fatherhood until their 20s to experience emotional distress, truncated educations, reduced occupational attainment, lower incomes, greater job dissatisfaction, and divorce (Buchanan & Robbins, 1990; Card & Wise, 1978; Furstenberg, Brooks-Gunn, & Morgan, 1987; Marsiglio, 1987). Counseling interventions targeting younger fathers may help to prevent many of these difficulties. Second, in the words of Beymer (1995), "Teen fathers are the victims of massive misunderstanding and discrimination from nearly everybody who comes into contact with them. They are simultaneously rejected and ignored, disparaged and excluded, condemned and punished" (p. 26). A book concerning teenage fathers may help to clear up erroneous impressions of this population and prompt practitioners to reexamine the manner in which they view and treat teenage boys who father children out of wedlock.

Causes of Premarital Teenage Pregnancy

What can account for the large numbers of children having children? Many of the proposed causes of premarital teenage pregnancy have been summarized by Brindis (1991). A brief overview of these follows.

Some experts believe that early sexual activity reflects a lack of *family and moral values* in our culture. Others suggest that a *lack of knowledge* about reproductive processes, pregnancy prevention measures and the consequences of early childbearing play a major causative role in teenage pregnancy. *Skills deficits* in important interpersonal (e.g., assertiveness) and cognitive (e.g., decision making) coping skills have been hypothesized to explain why some teenagers engage in sexual relations before they are emotionally prepared to do so. *A lack of access to contraceptive and abortion services* has been suggested as a reason why some teenagers do not prevent and terminate unplanned pregnancies. Some pregnancies might represent reactions to a sense of a *lack of opportunity and power.* That is, poor teenagers drift into parenthood as a means to enhance an existence devoid of promising life opportunities. *Welfare* has often been cited as an economic system that rewards young women for becoming mothers. The *media* have been charged with contributing to increased unprotected sex among teenagers by depicting sexually explicit behavior in the absence of birth control.

Several other explanations for premarital adolescent pregnancy have been suggested. According to the *generation recidivism hypothesis* (alternatively referred to as the *intergenerational hypothesis*), the tendency to become teenage parents runs in particular families and is passed on through observational learning and socioenvironmental constraints (Burton, 1990; Robbins & Lynn, 1973). The central thesis of the *transitional object theory* is that the adolescent unconsciously attempts to re-create through a pregnancy the pre-Oedipal transitional object to meet needs for symbiosis and individuation (Miller, 1986). Proponents of the *dysfunctional family model* hypothesize that some teenagers become parents as a mechanism for escaping from an unstable and hostile family (see McKenry, Walters, & Johnson, 1979). Finally, *deviancy models* are based on the assumptions that teenage parents lack internal controls to inhibit the expression of sexual impulses or that adolescents with poor self-esteem engage in sexual activity in an attempt to bolster their personal worth (see McKenry et al., 1979).

Each of the many postulated causes of premarital teenage pregnancy has some empirical support (see McKenry et al., 1979; Miller & Moore, 1990; Stiffman & Feldman, 1990). Based on such findings, Brindis (1991) concluded that teenage pregnancy probably results from some combination of these proposed causes. Similarly, Stiffman and Feldman (1990) have argued persuasively that simple cause-and-effect relationships are inadequate explanations for adolescent pregnancy. Rather, examination of the complex interplay of multiple socioeconomic and psychological factors must be the direction of future research and interventions.

Challenges and Opportunities for Growth

The reactions of the two teenage fathers described in the beginning of this chapter illustrate that an unplanned pregnancy can precipitate a crisis for unmarried adolescent males. It is imperative that professionals who work with teenage fathers become aware of the many problems associated with unplanned adolescent fatherhood so that interventions can be tailored to the needs of this population. But as Kiselica and Pfaller (1993) noted, it is equally important that helpers understand that teenage parenthood presents many opportunities for growth, joy, and fulfillment, such as learning new skills and bonding with one's baby. Counselors who maintain this balanced perspective will help young fathers view the unplanned pregnancy as a challenge to develop their potential and appreciate the positive aspects to parenthood that might be overlooked during the crisis.

Consistent with this point of view, common events that have been described in the literature solely as "problems" are presented in the following subsections as challenges for teenage fathers to master. These challenges pertain to their emotional reactions to the unplanned pregnancy, abortion and adoption decisions and denied access to the baby, parenting skills, the children of teenage fathers, relationship issues, and educational and career considerations. An examination of these challenges provides the reader with a profile of the experiences of teenage fathers.

Emotional Reactions to the Unplanned Pregnancy

Findings from several studies indicate that adolescent fathers report a wide range of reactions to an unplanned pregnancy, including happiness and acceptance, depression, anger, and denial of responsibility for the pregnancy (Achatz & MacAllum, 1994; Elster & Panzarine, 1983a; Fry & Trifiletti, 1983; Vaz, Smolen, & Miller, 1983). According to Robinson and Barret (1985), these reactions are similar to those reported by young, unwed, expectant mothers. The following account illustrates how difficult, confusing, and lonely a unmarried young man can feel during the crisis of an unexpected pregnancy:

> To tell you the truth I didn't know how I was s'posed to act. . . . My girlfriend was going through her own little emotions and couldn't be bothered with me. . . . And it just seemed like her mom was doin those things I wanted to do and there wasn't no place for me. . . . In fact I think . . . [my girlfriend's mother] hated me at first cuz of what I did to her daughter. . . . And like I felt responsible and I wanted somebody to tell me what I needed to do. . . . I was so downed out and there was no one, NO ONE, I could talk to. . . . I was scared to tell my parents and friends. (Achatz & MacAllum, 1994, p. 38)

Although an unplanned pregnancy clearly is a trying event for teenage fathers, they can use the empathic support of caring professionals to learn how to manage their emotional reactions and, in the process, clarify their conceptions of fatherhood. The process of mastering this challenge was described by a youth who had benefited from Public/Private Venture's Young Unwed Fathers Pilot Project:

> I didn't know what to do, but I had to do something before I . . . well, I don't know what I mighta done. . . . I was so depressed. So I knew like I had to get a job. I had to get money. So I started working myself to death. . . . I worked the third shift and first shift for nearly three months because I thought that it was money that made you a father. You know, I was sayin' he gonna have this, he gonna have that and you know it was just too much pressure that I was puttin on myself. Finally, I decided that I better tell somebody about all of what I was going through because I just couldn't cope with it on my own. So like I started talkin to my older brothers who had kids and they gave me some good support . . . tellin me how it is and to calm down. So as time went on, especially after my son was born, I thought to myself that I don't need to have lots of money to be a good father. The main thing I need to give him is love and spend a little time with him you know. That's when things really changed because I didn't know how it was until I became a father. I thought it was all a money thing, but now to this day, I see it's not a money thing. It's the time and love you give to the child. (Achatz & MacAllum, 1994, pp. 37-38)

Abortion, Adoption, and Denied Access to the Baby

Research by Barret and Robinson (1982) and Hendricks (1988) suggested that many teenage fathers want to be involved with their female partners in decision making and planning concerning their babies (Barret & Robinson, 1982; Hendricks, 1988). Yet young fathers often are not told when the baby is born and have little input when their children are turned over for adoption or foster care (Robinson & Barret, 1985). In addition, they are often excluded from participating in the mother's decision to have an abortion (Robinson, 1988a). In other situations, they may be in favor of their partner having an abortion but the young mother decides to give birth and keep the baby.

Young fathers who are involved in their partners' decisions regarding abortion and adoption can experience agonizing distress. Teenage fathers who are left out of such important decisions regarding their children report experiencing intense rejection, anxiety, and sadness (Robinson, 1988a). In either case, teenage fathers require counseling interventions to help them with these painful experiences, regardless of our personal views on premarital pregnancy, adoption, and abortion.

Even if the mother decides to keep the baby, the teenage father might still be denied opportunities to bond with his child. The relationships between adolescent parents frequently are tenuous due to the many strains associated with unplanned parenthood and the unrealistic expectations of adolescents regarding relationships. Although teenage fathers typically maintain contact with the mother during the pregnancy and after childbirth (Barret & Robinson, 1982; Rivara, Sweeney, & Henderson, 1986; Vaz et al., 1983), they commonly report relationship difficulties with the mother of the child (Elster & Hendricks, 1986). During periods of estrangement between an adolescent father and his partner, the mother, who in most cases has legal custody of the child, might prevent the father from visiting the baby (Achatz & MacAllum, 1994; Kiselica, 1993). Some parents of teenage mothers are angry at the father for impregnating their daughter, have little contact with him (Cervera, 1991), and deny him access to their daughter or his child (Achatz & MacAllum, 1994; Kiselica, 1993). When he is shut out from interacting with his child for extended periods of time, important opportunities for father-child bonding are lost (Kiselica, Stroud, Stroud, & Rotzien, 1992). In such cases, the teenage father who cares about his child can feel angry, rejected, and violated. Unfortunately, he may perceive himself to be powerless to do anything about this treatment except to resign himself to the situation, become depressed, and, worst of all, shut off his feelings for his child.

These predicaments regarding adoption, abortion, and visitation illustrate the naivete of teenage fathers regarding their legal rights and indicate that they may benefit from legal advice and counseling to address issues with their partner and her family. Through the process of confronting these hardships, young fathers can develop effective decision-making and interpersonal skills and learn how to understand and beneficially use the legal system.

Developing Effective Parenting Skills

Conventional wisdom suggests that because teenage parents enter parenthood prematurely in the face of economic and psychosocial stresses, they are likely to have inadequate parenting skills and might be at risk for physically abusing their children. Although there is limited empirical support for the former of these hypotheses, there is virtually no support for the latter.

Most of the research on the parenting skills of teenage parents has been conducted with teenage mothers. The findings of this research indicate that adolescent mothers may provide less appropriate forms of stimulation and care for their young children than do adult mothers (see Lamb & Elster,

1986). Only meager data regarding the parenting skills of adolescent fathers are available. In their review of a few early studies with very small samples of adolescent fathers, Parke, Power, and Fisher (1980) concluded that, although there is considerable diversity in the amount and quality of father-child involvement, father participation can have direct positive influences on the social and cognitive development of the children of adolescent parents. The results of a more recent study of the parent-child interactions between 15 pairs of adolescent parents and their infants indicated that the fathers were less sensitive than the mothers to their infants' communications and tended to demonstrate less reciprocity (McGovern, 1990). Thus, although teenage fathers can have a positive influence on their children's development, at least some young fathers may not know how to respond consistently to their infants' cues in a sensitive manner.

The hypothesis that teenage parents are at high risk to abuse their children appears to have been overstated. In their critique of the literature addressing the issue of child abuse by teenage parents, Bolton and Belsky (1986) reported that the data indicate that adolescent mothers may be only slightly more likely than adult mothers to abuse their children. The authors also noted that, although teenage fathers often share many of the same psychological, contextual, and offspring characteristics as those that are typical of maltreating adults (e.g., role confusion, employment difficulties, financial stress), no data suggest that young fathers are more likely than adult fathers to maltreat their children.

What are we to make of these findings? Probably that teenage fathers might benefit from parenting programs through which they are given information on child development, child care skills, and parent-child relationships. Promoting his involvement with his child represents the potentially greatest reward in working with teenage fathers, for it provides both the young man and the helper the opportunity to focus on what could be one of the most enriching experiences of the teenage father's life: giving and receiving love from his child.

The Children of Teenage Fathers

The child born to teenage parents is at a higher than average risk for prenatal complications, premature births, birth defects, mental retardation, and other health problems. These medical difficulties occur in part because young mothers have not reached their full biological maturity prior to conception and because they have poor diets and receive inadequate prenatal care (Field, Widmayer, Stringer, & Ignatoff, 1980; Phipps-Yonas, 1980; Simkins, 1984).

In addition to the risk of health problems, the children of teenage parents are more likely than the offspring of adults to experience emotional and behavioral problems and academic difficulties, particularly if they are born to teenage parents from lower socioeconomic levels (Klerman, 1982). These problems may be attributable to poor prenatal and postnatal care and inadequate parenting (Robinson, 1988a).

Not all children of teenage parents have these difficulties, however. Effective outreach designed to provide high-risk expectant mothers with quality prenatal and postnatal care has prevented many health problems for their children (Institute of Medicine, 1985). In addition, strong social support networks for the teenage mother can have a positive bearing on the child, especially if the father provides emotional support and child care assistance. His encouragement can foster the teenage mother's use of health services, thereby potentially preventing medical complications. His social support of the mother can indirectly enhance his child's development by bolstering her positive influence on the child, and he can directly promote his child's competence through father-child interactions (Furstenberg, 1976; Unger & Wandersman, 1985).

These findings suggest that the teenage father can contribute positively to the physical and emotional adjustment of his partner and his child. Although fulfilling these responsibilities may be a source of stress for the youth, it also represents a chance for him to learn the value of contributing to the well-being of others.

Relationship Issues

Although some of the relationship problems between the teenage father and his partner, his partner's parents, and his child were mentioned earlier, other facets of his relationships with others must be discussed to understand more fully the potential emotional turmoil he might experience. In addition, he may experience some positive changes in his relations with others.

Relationship Issues With the Adolescent Mother. Teenage parents often have ambivalent feeling toward one another. Although adolescent parents typically were involved in what they had perceived to be a caring, meaningful relationship prior to the pregnancy (Elster & Panzarine, 1983a), both parents might harbor a desire to date other people, feelings that could create conflicts between the couple. Disagreements regarding child-rearing responsibilities, financial hardships, and tensions between the young father and his partner's parents could strain the couple's relationship further. These negative forces explain, in part, why most teenage parents do not marry and why most who do marry experience significant discord and eventually divorce (Children's Defense Fund, 1987a). At times, the child is caught in the middle. In order to act in the best interests of the child, an amicable relationship must be negotiated. Unfortunately, often it is not.

With compassionate assistance, teenage fathers can cope with these uncomfortable experiences. Counseling designed to clarify his feelings for his partner can help him to decide if he wants to marry his partner. Whether or not he chooses to marry, he can be taught how to negotiate a cordial, supportive relationship with his partner that will permit both of them to have a quality relationship with their child.

Relationship Issues With Extended Family Members. Preto (1988) observed that a common fear of the parents of adolescent girls is that their daughter will be sexually exploited, whereas the parents of adolescent boys worry that their son's sexual interests might jeopardize his future. Clinical experience supports this observation. In light of the fears preoccupying parents, it is often the case that their child's participation in an unplanned adolescent pregnancy represents "a nightmare come true" for both sets of parents.

Given these fears, it is understandable that teenage fathers are likely to encounter a range of supportive and hostile responses from his and his partner's parents. Though angry with the teenage father initially, in time some parents place their indignation aside in an attempt to help him and his partner develop constructive plans regarding the pregnancy. Often, these productive reactions are fueled by his and her parents' love for the expected grandchild. In other instances, however, the anger of one or both sets of parents can take the form of outrage, prompting them to blame and punish the young father for his role in the pregnancy. He might never be forgiven, and the status of his relationship with both sets of parents can be tainted with resentment forever. According to Elster and Hendricks (1986), dealing with these varying reactions represents a significant concern of teenage fathers.

Even if the adolescent father is accepted in a supportive manner by some or all of the grandparents involved, his relationship with these adults will still be altered as he attempts to renegotiate his role as both a son and an emerging parent. Throughout this process, role confusion and boundary issues are likely to develop, even among the most well-adjusted families. The task of addressing these family issues can be a source of strain. However, it can also result in the fulfilling experience of developing adult responsibilities and a sense of gratitude to those family members who rally to assist the teenage father.

Relationship Issues With Peers. Teenage fathers experience stressful changes in their relationships with their peers (Achatz & MacAllum, 1994; Elster & Hendricks, 1986; Hendricks, 1988; Robinson, 1988a). Dropping out of school and/or demands to work or care for the baby diminish opportunities to socialize with other adolescents. Important experiences, such as relating with other teenage boys and experimentation at dating, might be curtailed. For many adolescent fathers, this is a difficult change to accept and they report a sense of loss and isolation from their peers (Achatz & MacAllum, 1994; Fry & Trifiletti, 1983). Nevertheless, the teenage father can be taught with guidance how to maintain contacts with his peers and be encouraged to seek and discover new friends who also have children. Through the support of others who are parents, he can receive advice and encouragement on how to become a fulfilled and effective father.

Educational and Career Considerations

Compared to their nonfather peers, teenage fathers are at higher than average risk to drop out of school. Approximately one third of teenage fathers are dropouts, compared to 13% of males who father a child when they are 20 years old or older. Adolescent fathers are also less likely than their nonfather peers to receive a GED by age 20 (Marsiglio, 1986).

It is unclear whether early fatherhood precedes or follows school dropout (Furstenberg, Brooks-Gunn, & Chase-Lansdale, 1989). Brindis (1993) reported that some children who have dropped out of school subsequently drift into parenthood in an attempt to add a meaningful purpose to their lives. Other youth enrolled in school at the time of conception appear to have been poor achievers or disconnected from the school environment. It seems that these youth are at risk to drop out and the pregnancy serves as the culminating event to leave school (Brindis, 1993).

The abbreviated educational experiences of teenage parents are associated with long-term educational and career difficulties. Because teenage parents tend to receive less education, they are apt to earn lower salaries, work in less prestigious jobs, and have less fulfilling work experiences than their nonparent peers over time (Card & Wise, 1978; Kerckhoff & Parrow, 1979). Not surprisingly, many teenage fathers doubt that they are capable of financially supporting a family and express a variety of educational, career, and employment worries (Achatz & MacAllum, 1994; Elster & Hendricks, 1986; Elster & Panzarine, 1983b; Furstenberg et al., 1987; Hendricks, 1988; Hendricks et al., 1981).

These findings support Robinson's (1988a) observation that the educational and economic pressures of becoming a teenage father can be wrought with "hard truths and tragic consequences" (p. 39). But the crisis also can prompt the youth to learn about the world of work, become an effective planner, and master the art of juggling responsibilities in life. Because these can be imposing tasks, teenage fathers need educational and career counseling to assist them in becoming economically self-sufficient parents.

The Service Needs of Teenage Fathers

This review has shown that teenage fathers have a variety of needs. The following services have been recommended to help this population realize its many positive potentials when facing the crisis of unplanned parenthood: child care; relationship counseling to address issues with their partners and their families of origin; assistance with housing, employment, job training, transportation, and education; instruction in parenting skills and financial planning; health care for their children; and emotional support regarding the sudden loss of freedom and ambivalent feelings regarding parenthood (Ascher, 1985; Children's Defense Fund, 1988a; Hendricks, 1988; Hendricks & Montgomery, 1983; Hendricks & Solomon, 1987; Klinman & Sander, 1985; Lindsay & Rodine, 1989b; McGee, 1982; Robinson, 1988a; Smollar & Ooms, 1987).

Societal Treatment of Teenage Fathers

Many teenage fathers acknowledge that they need and want help, especially training in the responsibilities of being a father and caring for a child (Elster & Panzarine, 1983b; Hendricks, 1988). Yet it appears that the needs of teenage fathers go unheeded. Service programs purported to target teenage *parents* tend to consist of medical, educational, and psychological assistance for teenage *mothers* but not teenage *fathers* (Children's Defense Fund, 1986a; Kiselica, 1992; Kiselica & Sturmer, 1993b, 1995; Smollar & Ooms, 1987; U.S. Congress, 1986). Why? Three explanations are suggested.

The Influence of Societal Stereotypes

Some scholars (e.g., Allen-Meares, 1984; Parke & Neville, 1987; Robinson, 1988a) have argued that the bias against serving teenage fathers is a manifestation of societal stereotypes about this population. Robinson (1988a, 1988b) has been most vocal in charging that myths about teenage fathers abound in our society. Specifically, he suggested that erroneous depictions of adolescent fathers could be traced to some early writings from the 1940s (Futterman & Livermore, 1947; Kasanin & Handschin, 1941; Reider, 1948) in which all unwed fathers, regardless of age, were lumped together for analysis and discussion. In his critique of these writings, Robinson (1988b) observed that anecdotal data had been used to make inaccurate profiles of teenage fathers that were later popularized by the media in the form of the following five myths:

1. *The Super Stud myth:* He is worldly wise and knows more about sex and sexuality than most teenage boys.
2. *The Don Juan myth:* He sexually exploits unsuspecting and helpless adolescent females by taking advantage of them.
3. *The Macho myth:* He feels psychologically inadequate, has no inner control, and, unlike other adolescent boys his age, has a psychological need to prove his masculinity.
4. *The Mr. Cool myth:* He usually has a fleeting, casual relationship with the young mother and has few emotions about the pregnancy.
5. *The Phantom Father myth:* Absent and rarely involved in the support and rearing of his children, he leaves his partner and offspring to fend for themselves. (p. 47)

According to Robinson (1988a, 1988b), these five myths have no scientific basis and, in fact, are dispelled by a growing body of research. Unlike the adolescent males described in the myths, today's teenage father knows little more than his partner or nonfather peers about sexuality and reproduction (Barret & Robinson, 1982; Brown, 1983; Finkel & Finkel, 1975). Psychologically and intellectually, teenage fathers are more like than unlike their nonfather peers and older fathers (McCoy & Tyler, 1985; Nakashima & Camp, 1984; Rivara, Sweeney, & Henderson, 1985; Robinson, Barret, & Skeen, 1983). Furthermore, teenage fathers tend to remain involved, physically and/or psychologically, throughout the pregnancy and childbirth experience (Achatz & MacAllum, 1994; Panzarine & Elster, 1983; Rivara et al., 1986), maintain intimate feelings toward teenage mothers and their babies, and contribute financial support (Achatz & MacAllum, 1994; Furstenberg, 1976; Rivara et al., 1986; Vaz et al., 1983).

These recent findings compel practitioners to examine carefully their assumptions about young men participating in out-of-wedlock pregnancies. Although some adolescent males do fit negative societal images of the teenage father, the tendency to rigidly view all adolescent fathers in this manner is a harmful stereotype that can block many young fathers from receiving desperately needed help.

Social Service Policy Tends to Ignore Fathers in General

The tendency to underserve the teenage father as a client may be an indication of cultural biases about fathers in general. According to Lamb (1983), our society historically has defined men as the instrumental and economic leaders of the family but has viewed women as expressive figures responsible for child rearing and the socialization of children. Based on the unfounded theoretical notion that mothers are more biologically prepared than fathers to raise children, the mother-infant relationship also has been emphasized in psychological theory and research (Parke & Neville, 1987). Jaffe (1983) argued that these assumptions have influenced social service policy so as to create a pattern of de facto discrimination concerning fathers as social service clients. Because mothers have been socially assigned a preeminent role in their children's lives and fathers have been deemed to play a different role in child development, policy regarding social services for families and children has devalued the father's involvement through the following practices: (a) a large number of social services were created specifically for the purpose of helping mothers and their children but not fathers and (b) the working hours of the majority of helping professionals conflict with men's work schedules, thereby making it more difficult for men to receive services (Jaffe, 1983). These practices have discouraged both adult and teenage fathers from using social services.

A different but frequent criticism of social service policy for its negative influence on father involvement pertains to the welfare system in the United States. Historically, according to regulations regarding Aid for Families With Dependent Children (AFDC), the benefits awarded to AFDC recipients have been reduced as family earnings begin to increase. A working-class father who acknowledges his paternity and lives with his partner jeopardizes the family's AFDC benefits, including food stamps and Medicaid, if he earns an income above the poverty line. If this same father continues to acknowledge his paternity but resides apart from his partner and family, his families' AFDC benefits could still be reduced as a function of the amount of child support he contributes to the family (Garfinkel, 1992). Many families cannot survive the forgoing of these benefits. Thus, it is financially advantageous to mothers and children from lower socioeconomic levels to conceal the identity of the biological father from authorities and have the father leave home, rather than remain with his family (Wolins, 1983). Thus, among the poor the father is a potential financial liability whose freedom to live with his family is constrained by public policy. Because teenage fathers are overrepresented among the poor, public policy has negatively influenced the involvement of many with their families.

A final criticism regarding social service policy, expressed by Jaffe (1983), concerns the effects of the female-dominated helping professions on the provision of services to fathers. Jaffe argued that because the majority of social workers and counselors are women, services tend to be geared toward females because women social workers may be more comfortable working with female rather than male clients.

I offered a similar argument in reviewing the history of the helping professions in responding to the problem of unwed adolescent childbearing in the United States (Kiselica, 1993). The predominant strategy practiced during the late 1970s and the early 1980s attempted to address the needs of pregnant girls and adolescent mothers. Although this was a vital development, the concerns of teenage fathers were largely disregarded. I suggested that this neglect might not have been intentional and could be related, in part, to the fact that most social service personnel are women. I hypothesized that adult women can easily empathize with another female facing a crisis pregnancy. In addition, I noted that many women express an awkwardness at relating to adolescent boys whose relational styles are often very different from those of females. Consequently, women are likely to feel more comfortable and skilled at responding to the concerns of young mothers than to those of young fathers. Because most early service programs for teenage parents were provided by women, it makes sense that services were more commonly offered to teenage mothers than to teenage fathers.

In addressing this issue further, I noted that both female and male service providers commonly become more receptive to and confident at working with teenage fathers once they understand the difficulties and complexities of this population and are taught strategies for helping young fathers (Kiselica, 1993). In support of this last argument, I cited findings reported by Barth, Claycomb, and Loomis (1988), which indicated that in-service training on issues of paternity and on procedures for engaging male clients improved the counselors' commitment to serve young fathers. In addition, the training boosted the performance of both male and female counselors in conducting outreach and ongoing counseling with these youths.

Teenage Fathers Do Not Use Services Even When They Are Available

Many professionals across this country express frustration with teenage fathers who do not use existing services. In reaction to these discouraging setbacks, it is common for practitioners to conclude that young fathers rarely care about their responsibilities as parents and will therefore discontinue programs for young fathers, whereas those for teenage mothers, who are more likely to seek help, are maintained. Such unfortunate outcomes can be avoided if clinicians understand five reasons why teenage fathers underuse services. Each of these reasons are, in varying degrees, a function of how adolescent males in general and young fathers in particular are treated by society.

Fears of Being Judged and Punished. Hendricks's (1988) research has shed some light on the reluctance of adolescent fathers to use services. Through interviews conducted with African American, Anglo American, and Hispanic American teenage fathers, Hendricks found that most of the young fathers he interviewed wanted help with the challenges of fatherhood. Yet many of these youths expressed a belief that they would be negatively evaluated by employees of social service agencies. The young fathers reported that they were more likely to turn to their mothers and friends than to professionals for help.

In addition to a fear that they will be judged, some teenage fathers perceive counseling and health care professionals as players in a system designed to punish rather than to help them. As I noted (Kiselica, 1993), because teenage fathers are overrepresented among lower socioeconomic levels, many face difficulties in providing financial support to the mothers of their children. Consequently, they frequently are the target of investigations conducted by the child support divisions of local prosecutors' offices. Because these fathers worry that they will be reported by any professional for legal prosecution, they avoid educational, social service, and health care settings.

Considering these fears, counselors are challenged once again to examine the manner in which they view teenage fathers. Judgmental attitudes must be replaced by nonjugmental acceptance. Furthermore, teenage fathers may need reassurance that participation in counseling will result in no legal harm to them.

Teenage Fathers and Helpers: Mismatch of Relational Styles? Another explanation for why teenage fathers do not avail themselves of services pertains to the potential mismatch between the relational style of many males and that of most helping professionals. Borrowing Holland's (1973) typology, Bruch (1978) suggested that the helping environment is best suited for individuals who would be classified as having a "social" personality type (p. 27). That is, clients who are skilled at and comfortable with self-disclosure of thoughts and feelings and who are introspective can easily relate to helping professionals because the latter use the same relational style. However, many males, especially traditional males (and many females, for that matter) are not social types. Instead, Bruch (1978) argued, traditional males tend to be "realistic" and "conventional" (p. 27) types whose relational styles are not congruent with the social environment of counseling. These individuals avoid less structured interpersonal and exploratory activities, such as counseling, and prefer activities involving the manipulation and organization of data and objects. Consequently, they are likely to feel ill at ease with counseling as it is customarily practiced.

These considerations suggest that perhaps some teenage fathers avoid counseling and other services because they are uneasy with the manner in which helpers typically relate to them. Counselors can adapt their relational styles to the unique personality of the teenage father so as to make the helping process more appealing. This issue is addressed in detail in Chapter 3.

Becoming Overwhelmed and Discouraged to Seek Help. Unplanned parenthood can overwhelm some teenage boys. The process of telling both sets of parents and dealing with their respective reactions; the emotional decisions regarding abortion, adoption and marriage; the dual pressures to complete an education and yet be a provider; the sometimes competing desires to interact with the baby and the mother and socialize with peers; the relationship difficulties and the educational, career, and financial hardships associated with unplanned parenthood; and the potential legal complications of the male's paternal behavior—all of these stressors can make the teenage father's head spin. In the face of such confusion, he may recognize that he needs help but feels too burdened to seek the very assistance that could enable him to get a handle on things.

But even if the teenage father is ready to accept help, the odds are that he will have difficulty finding it, for most pertinent service programs are geared toward teenage girls (Children's Defense Fund, 1986a; Goldstein & Wallace, 1978; Kiselica, 1992; Kiselica & Sturmer, 1993b, 1995; Smollar & Ooms, 1987; U.S. Congress, 1986). This can be very disheartening. Consider the painful experience of a young father who had searched for a program but had trouble finding one:

> I found out . . . there was nothing for us, just a lot of counseling and help for women. Men are left out on their own to deal with it and like if your girlfriend or your wife is pregnant, sometimes men be goin through some depression, you know, you be thinkin about certain things and you ain't got nobody to talk to. But if a lady's goin through that, she got all kinds of pregnant women groups to go to and they can help them and stuff like that. But for a man, you ain't really got nobody. You all alone by yourself. (Achatz & MacAllum, 1994, p. 38)

If the teenage father's early efforts to receive professional guidance are frustrated, then he may become discouraged from looking elsewhere. Sometimes he might persevere after such initial disappointments and successfully identify a setting that serves teenage fathers, only to find that the employees do not understand his issues or know how to relate to him, thereby discouraging him further. Worse yet, should he encounter a professional who automatically judges him, he likely will grow leery of helpers and avoid them altogether.

Tragically, when the teenage father encounters the full range of these frustrating experiences in the face of the many overwhelming stressors mentioned previously, he can become depressed (Elster & Panzarine, 1980; Vaz et al., 1983) and hopeless that fatherhood can ever be a pleasant experience (Kiselica, Doms, & Rotzien, 1992). Because of these feelings, some fathers gradually reduce their involvement with their children, even though they may have initially wanted to be caring fathers (Kiselica et al., 1992). As a society, we cannot allow this to happen to such well-intentioned fathers.

The Influence of Traditional Societal Standards for Masculine Behavior. Traditionally, males in our culture have been socialized to act tough, aggressive, confident, and self-reliant. Doyle (1989) observed that, from a very early age, a boy is given the message to be a "real man" who is not dependent on anyone else and willing to survive on his own. According to Beymer (1995), these expectations imbue adolescent boys with the belief that one should never be emotional and share private feelings.

The emotional constraint implied by traditional societal conceptions of masculinity can deter many teenage fathers from seeking help during the crisis of an unplanned pregnancy. Yet several investigators have discovered that at least some of these fathers *do* want help (Achatz & MacAllum, 1994; Elster & Panzarine, 1983b; Hendricks, 1988). Thus, a common challenge for counselors is to be persistent in reaching out to young fathers, even whey they appear disinterested in receiving help during initial contacts. Over time, most adolescent fathers who are traditional in their expression of masculinity will confide in caring, committed counselors who understand the needs of unmarried male youths confronting an unexpected pregnancy.

Some Boys Never Intended to Accept Responsibility. A final reason why some teenage fathers disregard services is that they *do* fit the stereotypic picture of the exploiting, callous male. It cannot be emphasized strongly enough, however, that the research indicates that these males represent the minority of teenage fathers (see reviews by Robinson, 1988a, 1988b). Nevertheless, clinical experience indicates that some boys do not conscientiously entertain the idea that they have responsibilities as fathers, either prior to conception, during the pregnancy, or after the birth of the child. These youth typically are antisocial in nature and are often involved in gangs ruled by delinquent norms of behavior. For example, the "Spur Posse," a self-proclaimed gang of adolescent boys residing in Lakewood, California, recently received national media attention in response to the boys' cavalier sexual attitudes toward girls. Gang members espoused a group norm that awarded "points" for every girl engaged in sexual relations. Furthermore, the members expressed neither remorse for their actions nor any concern for possibly having caused a pregnancy.

Disdainful sexual behavior by teenage boys is not always a group phenomenon, however. Some males without strong ties to gangs view girls merely as sexual objects for their pleasure. This attitude is illustrated graphically in the film *Not Me* (Production People, Ltd., 1990). This captivating video contains actual interviews with a teenage boy who unabashedly describes his shallow feelings for girls, the ploys he uses to seduce them, the manner in which he dumps them, his total disinterest in considering that he may have fathered a child, and his belief that it is solely the girl's responsibility to worry about the baby.

The behavior of the members of the "Spur Posse" and other boys disinterested in the well-being of girls raises very serious questions about how some males are socialized to view and treat females. Addressing this issue is paramount in the effort to end the exploitation of women in a patriarchal culture. Men can take the lead in this effort by redefining masculinity to include those valuable aspects of traditional masculinity and eliminating those that are obsolete and dysfunctional (Levant, 1992). As a part of the reconstruction of manhood, adults must teach impressionable boys to value and practice socialized, nonsexist ways of relating to women. Clearly, this undertaking has tremendous potential for training males to act with responsibility and consideration toward the mother and baby should they discover that they have become parents as adolescents.

In addition to this initiative, counselors are challenged to evaluate their attitudes and feelings toward delinquent boys who sexually exploit girls. As Reid (1986) noted, a tendency among mental health professionals is to turn their backs on antisocial clients whose behavior angers and alienates others, including practitioners. It must not be forgotten, however, that delinquent youth *are people* who require sensitive and committed counseling in order for them to become more socialized in their relations with their women partners and their children. To accomplish this task, clinicians can integrate the counseling recommendations contained in this book with interventions that are designed for remediating conduct disorders. Appropriate treatment strategies are described in several excellent resources addressing the clinical challenge of working with antisocial adolescents (Henggeler, 1989; Horn & Sager, 1990; McCord & Tremblay, 1992; Stumphauzer, 1986).

Conclusion:
Let's Focus on How We Can Help

To adequately assist teenage fathers, we must move beyond simplistic, knee-jerk stereotypes about this population, think complexly about their behavior, empathize with their difficulties, stop rejecting them, and ponder the question, "What exactly does it take to engage in counseling a teenage boy facing fatherhood?" In the next chapter, I address this question by describing the mechanics of developing and conducting outreach service programs tailored to adolescent fathers and by reviewing rapport-building and case management strategies that have been successful with this population.

Note

1. Reprinted with permission from the Associated Press.

3

Program Development,
Outreach Considerations,
and Case Management Issues

Historically, social service programs for teenage parents have failed to address the needs of teenage fathers. Many initial programs targeted teenage mothers only (see Children's Defense Fund, 1986a; Goldstein & Wallace, 1978; Smollar & Ooms, 1987; U.S. Congress, 1986). Other programs, which had opened their doors to young fathers, were unappealing to and underused by males because the programs were geared toward mothers. Thus, the designs of many teenage parent service programs either excluded or inadvertently discouraged the father's participation (Robinson, 1988a).

In response to the failure of social policy to promote the involvement of young fathers in service programs, a handful of researchers (e.g., Barth et al., 1988; Brindis, Barth, & Loomis, 1987; Hendricks, 1988; Hendricks & Montgomery, 1983; Hendricks & Solomon, 1987; Klinman & Sander, 1985; Klinman et al., 1986; Sander & Rosen, 1987) conducted investigations designed to identify effective strategies for working with the male partner in adolescent childbearing. Perhaps the most famous of these efforts was the Teen Father Collaboration (see Klinman & Sander, 1985; Klinman et al.,

1986; Sander & Rosen, 1987), a 2-year national research and demonstration project developed to determine the most effective ways to assist teenage fathers in contributing to their children's social, emotional, and financial well-being. The findings from this and other investigations have indicated that successful programs were tailored toward the needs of males, rather than being mechanical duplications of programs for adolescent mothers. In this chapter, these findings are incorporated into a review of several program development tasks and outreach and case management considerations. It is hoped that this information will assist counselors in starting effective programs and recruiting and retaining young fathers in counseling.

Program Development Considerations

This section highlights several key aspects to program development. Because this section represents an overview of program development, the reader may wish to consult several resources that provide in-depth coverage of the subject (e.g., Baker & Shaw, 1987; Bloom, 1981; Brindis, 1991; Cowen, 1984). In addition, the reader is referred to Brown (1990) for her thorough description of the development and implementation of the Maine Young Fathers Project.

There are six steps to program development: (a) forming a service coalition, (b) designating a lead agency and a coordinator, (c) conducting a needs assessment, (d) developing an implementation plan, (e) conducting and monitoring the implementation process, and (f) evaluating the effects of the interventions. Each of these steps is discussed in terms of developing programs for teenage fathers.

Forming a Coalition
of Services for Teenage Fathers

Several writers (e.g., Ascher, 1985; Hackney, 1991; Kiselica & Pfaller, 1993; Mitchell, 1991; Schinke, 1989) have maintained that teenage parenthood is a complex societal problem that can be solved only through committed, collaborative, professional interventions. Speaking specifically about teenage fathers, Kiselica et al. (1992) argued that because adolescent fathers are an at-risk group with a multitude of needs, effective interventions will require the efforts of different professionals working alone and in concert. Therefore, it is recommended that program development begin with the formation of a coalition of agencies interested in helping teenage fathers. The strength of such coalitions is that a wider range of services can be provided through collective action than through uncoordinated service efforts.

Prior to the creation of a new coalition, however, existing services for pregnant and parenting teenagers should be identified. If other pertinent coalitions have been formed already, then a duplication of services should be avoided. In the absence of an existing coalition serving teenage fathers, a new coalition can be formed consisting of a board of directors (alternatively referred to as a steering committee or a planning group), one or more lead agencies, and a program coordinator.

The Board of Directors

According to Brindis (1991), the board of directors sets policy, makes suggestions, and provides guidance for the service coalition. Some writers (e.g., Brindis, 1991; Lindsay & Rodine, 1989b) warned that well-intentioned programs are doomed to failure unless they muster a true sense of community ownership through the actions of the board of directors. To achieve this support, Brindis (1991) recommended that a board of directors consist of 6 to 10 members. Potential board members may include teenage and adult fathers; representatives from the community school system, nearby colleges, and universities; local agencies and organizations serving youth (e.g., Boys Clubs, the Urban League); health professions; Planned Parenthood; local churches; the juvenile justice system; the media; and local, county, state, and federal departments responsible for programs and activities in the areas of health, social services, child welfare, and public assistance (Brindis, 1991; Lindsay & Rodine, 1989b). In addition to these considerations, board members should reflect the community in terms of sex, race/ethnicity, and socioeconomic background (Brindis, 1991).

Although it is desirable to have a board membership that is representative of the community, Lindsay and Rodine (1989b) cautioned coalitions against creating designated seats on the board (e.g., one for the health department, another for the PTA). With this plan, someone often gets assigned to the coalition as part of their job responsibility and not because he or she wants to be part of the coalition (Lindsay & Rodine, 1989a). Sander and Rosen (1987) noted that leaders who are not committed to serving young men can undermine the work of others who are positive about serving adolescent fathers. Thus, recruiting leaders who are genuinely interested in the well-being of teenage fathers is crucial.

Although the board of directors can benefit from having both men and women members, it is recommended that at least half of the board membership and the president or director of the board be men. Frequently, groups initiating coalitions to assist teenage fathers primarily consist of professional women who already serve teenage mothers. Although the good intentions and participation of such women should be encouraged, it is important to ensure that men, at least one of whom is currently a teenage father, are involved in the coalition leadership to incorporate a male perspective and provide male role models. In the absence of representation by males, service coalitions run the danger of unintentionally repeating the mistake of developing programs that are not sensitive to teenage fathers' issues and the relational styles of males.

A focus on male involvement should not negate the potentially important contributions of women on the board, however. All too often discussions of gender differences have promoted the concerns of one gender at the expense of another (see Scher, 1993). This problem can be avoided by forming coalitions to help teenage fathers not forget the important needs of the mother and the couple's child. Having women on the board can help the program developers to envision strategies that not only promote the development of the teenage father but also enhance the adjustment of the mother and the baby. In addition, as Brindis et al. (1987) suggested, females who are committed to extending services to fathers can be effective advocates for this population.

Finally, Lindsay and Rodine (1989a) recommended that the head of the board be a "community catalyst" (p. 77), that is, a well-known and respected member of the community who has the clout and connections to make things happen. In addition, Lindsay and Rodine (1989a) offered numerous guidelines regarding administrative issues the board establishes for the coalition, such as incorporating and developing coalition bylaws and a constitution.

Designating a Lead Agency
and a Coordinator

The Lead Agency

The lead agency conducts the needs assessments and program evaluations and provides the services of the program (Brindis, 1991). Ideally, the lead agency should have several characteristics. It is recommended that the lead agency's service mission is to help teenage boys. Brindis (1991) advised that the lead agency should have an in-house staff or subcontract consultants skilled at collecting and analyzing data, designing and conducting assessments, reviewing plans and preparing reports, and serving as a liaison to the media. Kiselica and Pfaller (1993) suggested that faculty from colleges and universities be approached as potential consultants because they are often required to conduct research and provide services to communities to receive promotion and tenure. Because teenage fathers are an at-risk group with a variety of needs, ideally the lead agency should be a site capable of providing multifaceted services. Hospitals and schools are good examples. Having such settings as the lead agency enables teenage fathers to do "one-stop shopping" for services. In addition, according to Duggan, DeAngelis, and Hardy (1991), comprehensive service programs offered at the same setting facilitate efficient case management and continuity of care.

When service projects target adolescent fathers from vast geographic regions, several lead agencies may be required. For example, Brown (1990) reported that the planning group for a statewide service program for young fathers in Maine selected three sites as lead agencies for the project, two in rural areas of Maine, a third in an urban area of the state.

The Program Coordinator

The daily decisions regarding the management of the program should rest with a program coordinator at the lead agency. The program coordinator supervises the staff and serves as a liaison to the public and the many service providers and agencies comprising the coalition (Brindis, 1991).

Careful considerations should be given to the selection of the program coordinator. Brindis (1991) recommended that the program coordinator be housed administratively in the lead agency. Ideal qualities of the program coordinator include the following: technical competence, political savvy, strong interpersonal skills, high energy, and commitment (Brindis, 1991). In addition to these qualities, it is recommended that the program coordinator be a male who is already trusted and respected by community leaders or has the skills to engender such trust. Also, it is preferable that he have a working knowledge about the stereotypes regarding teenage fathers and the problems and needs of this population. Finally, the program coordinator should be capable of working as an active advocate for teenage fathers (Brown, 1990).

In working as an proponent for teenage fathers, the program coordinator must be prepared to manage controversy. Although he may be assisted with this difficult task by members of the board, he is likely to be the target of opposition to the coalition because he is responsible for the day-to-day activities of the program. Opposition is common because many people have biases against teenage fathers. Therefore, it is imperative that the program coordinator knows how to respond to challenges commonly raised during the development and implementation of the program.

Effectively Dealing With Opposition. Many adults in the community, including a number of prominent and forceful individuals, may object to services
for teenage fathers on three grounds. First, opponents often argue that
programs for teenage parents actually promote irresponsible sexual behavior,
unplanned pregnancies, and teenage parenthood. Fueling this argument is the
belief that the provision of services, such as free child care and health
programs, rewards the creation of out-of-wedlock children. A second accu-
sation is that, because teenage parenting programs often include training in
sexual education, they encourage promiscuity that places the participants at
risk for repeat teenage pregnancies. These two common objections are raised
whether proposed programs target teenage mothers, fathers, or both. A third
complaint specifically targets teenage fathers, namely, that young unwed
fathers are an exploitative, callous lot who should be punished rather than
helped in response to their role in fathering children. According to S. Brown
(personal communication, November 1, 1993), a fourth objection sometimes
is raised by providers of services for teenage mothers who fear that the
creation of programs for young fathers will result in a loss of funds for
adolescent mother programs.

   Several counterarguments can be directed toward each of these charges.
First, although it is possible that the decisions of some current teenagers to
have out-of-wedlock children may have been influenced by the availability
of services, it is important to note that the teenage pregnancy rate in the
United States rose sharply during the 1970s (Ventura, Taffel, & Mosher,
1985), *prior to the widespread development of service programs for teenage
parents.* Thus, service provision is a response to and not the cause of the
teenage parent phenomenon in this country. Second, data from several
studies have demonstrated that teenage parents who participate in comprehensive service programs are less likely to play a role in repeat teenage
pregnancies than those young parents who fail to receive those services (see
Children's Defense Fund, 1987a). Third, the conclusion that all adolescent
boys who become fathers are exploitative and callous can be countered by
providing an overview of the profile information discussed in Chapter 2 of
this book. Fourth, perhaps turf issues over funding can be avoided by the
development of parenting programs through which services for adolescent
mothers and fathers are combined.

   This information will prompt some critics to earnestly reevaluate their
attitudes about service provision to teenage fathers. These counterarguments
might cause some other objectors to refrain from posing any further public
opposition to the coalition, even though their private attitudes toward the
coalition may remain the same.

   Some skeptics might raise their own counterarguments, however. No
doubt, every community has teenage fathers who *do* fit the stereotypes about

this population. When citizens point this out, they question the appropriateness of serving young fathers who are not motivated to act responsibly. In response to this concern, it is helpful to report that research findings indicate that most teenage fathers respond positively to helping strategies tailored toward their needs (see Klinman & Sander, 1985; Klinman et al., 1986; Sommerfeld, 1992). This challenge also can be addressed by assuring critics that a major purpose of the coalition is to promote responsible behavior among young fathers. In addition, it can be emphasized that the provision of services for teenage fathers can have potential benefits for the community, such as fewer repeat pregnancies, the prevention of sexually transmitted diseases, increased involvement of fathers with their partners and their children, reduced drop-out rates, and greater economic self-sufficiency of teenage parents.

In responding to opposition, diplomacy is the key. In advocating for teenage fathers, the program coordinator must tactfully assert himself without further alienating the opposition. Remembering that most objections are raised by people who have good intentions can help one to not feel attacked and prevent responding in a hostile, defensive manner. Adopting a *win-win* attitude and empathizing with the other's position can be beneficial. Sometimes it is productive to respond to challenges by stating, "I think you've raised an important concern to address before we proceed any further with this subject." Making this statement acknowledges the legitimacy of the opinion and prevents an escalation of tensions. Therefore, the critic is more likely to be receptive to listening to a counterargument, which should be stated with an air of conviction and authority so as to increase its persuasiveness.

Should all of these measures fail, the vocal support of board members, other community leaders, and concerned parents can provide power to override even the staunchest of opposition.

Finally, in some instances community opposition can be so strong that it may be prudent to cancel plans for program implementation in certain locales and concentrate one's efforts on providing services in other communities that are more receptive to the idea of helping teenage boys responsible for an out-of-wedlock pregnancy. Such was the case in the Maine Young Fathers Project. Brown (1990) reported that one of the three lead agencies pulled out of the service coalition because its administrators found the project to be too progressive for their rural community.

Conducting a Needs Assessment

The purpose of a needs assessment is to document the extent of teenage fatherhood in a particular community and the degree to which that community responds to the needs of those fathers. Program developers can use the information acquired through a needs assessment to determine what new interventions are necessary and as baseline data to evaluate the effectiveness of those interventions. Key aspects of the needs assessment follow. For a more detailed account of conducting a needs assessment, consult the Children's Defense Fund's (1987b) *Childwatch Manual* and discussions of the subject by Bloom (1981), Barclay (1984), Brindis (1991), and Lindsay and Rodine (1989a).

Determine the Target Community

An initial task in conducting a needs assessment is to decide who constitutes the target community (Bloom, 1981; Brindis, 1991). Does the community refer to a state, a county or city, or a particular section or population within a city (Brindis, 1991)? The answer to this question will be determined by the service missions of the agencies and schools forming the coalition.

What Information Should Be Gathered?

The next step is to determine what information needs to be gathered (Bloom, 1981; Brindis, 1991). Obviously, an estimate of the number of teenage fathers in the community is needed. It is difficult to obtain precise estimates, in part because many mothers do not indicate the name of the father on official birth records. It should be noted that birth records used for this assessment purpose probably underestimate the number of teenage fathers in a community.

Demographic data are needed to understand how teenage fatherhood is distributed in the community according to such factors as age, race, ethnicity, socioeconomic level, and religious affiliation. These data also are necessary to consider cultural variations in the design of the intervention program. Brindis (1991) suggested that estimates of demographic data can be developed by carefully integrating data from birth records, census data, school district offices, and the local chamber of commerce. Professionals who work closely with teenage mothers in different areas within a community and local legislative representatives also might have demographic information (Brindis, 1991).

As part of the assessment, it is recommended that schools and agencies be surveyed regarding existing services. The survey should ask respondents to indicate whether or not these services are offered to teenage mothers, teenage fathers, or both, or to teenagers in general. The information obtained though such an assessment will inform program developers about current efforts to help teenage fathers and other existing services that might be used for such purposes. An example of a comprehensive Teenage Parents Services Survey, based on one developed by Kiselica and Sturmer (1993b), is provided in Appendix 3.1.

Brindis (1991) recommended that the needs assessment identify the sources of funding used by schools and agencies that serve teenagers. This can provide ideas for financing new programs or for the reallocating of funds among organizations.

In addition, it is recommended that the assessment garner qualitative data from teenage boys in the community to establish how they learn about sources of help (Brindis, 1991) and which sources they are most likely to use (Hendricks, 1988). With regard to the former, adolescent males should be asked to rank the most popular media sources in the community, including television shows, radio stations, and publications. This information will determine outlets for the advertising of services (Brindis, 1991). The boys also should be asked, "If you suddenly learned that your girlfriend was pregnant, to what school or agency would you most likely turn for help?" Responses to this question should be considered in determining the lead agency for an intervention program.

Prepare a Needs Assessment Report

Finally, it is advisable that all of these data be organized in a needs assessment report, in which the unmet needs of the community are documented. Resources that can be used to help teenage fathers, statements regarding the need for additional resources, and descriptions of those areas in the community having the highest concentrations of teenage fathers not yet receiving help also can be included in the needs assessment report.

Developing an Implementation Plan

Based on the information contained in the needs assessment report, an implementation plan can be developed (Brindis, 1991). According to Cowen (1984), the plan translates the broad conceptual program into a specific, step-by-step itinerary of events. The plan indicates the lead agency for the coalition (Brindis, 1991) and the goals and the specific target population of the program (Bloom, 1981; Brindis, 1991; Cowen, 1984). The plan also includes a description of the overall program (Brindis, 1991) and an outline of the specific activities the coalition will pursue over a period of time (Brindis, 1991; Cowen, 1984), usually 3 to 5 years (Brindis, 1991). In addition, the plan accounts for how the program will be administered and funded (Brindis, 1991).

The activities of the coalition should be stated in clear, measurable terms. The specific objectives and projected timetable for each activity must be delineated. The intervention strategies and resources used to accomplish the objectives should be outlined, as should the plans for monitoring and evaluating progress toward meeting those objectives (S. B. Baker, 1992; Bloom, 1981; Brindis, 1991). It is recommend that the plan specify any training workshops the staff will receive to prepare them to work with teenage fathers. According to Brindis (1991), the means of advertising the program also should be specified.

Policies are another feature of implementation plans. Considering that coalitions depend on interagency cooperation, program policies should define who will be responsible for individual case management, how referrals will be handled, and how confidentiality will be ensured, given that client information is to be shared among different agencies (Brindis, 1991).

Finally, the plan should address how the program is to be funded (Brindis, 1991). Most plans use some existing services that already are funded. However, new services require additional sources of support.

Potential Sources of Funding

Multifaceted service programs typically necessitate multiple sources of funding made up of a combination of private and public sources. Private sources include local and national foundations that provide support for research and service related to adolescent pregnancy and parenthood. For example, the William T. Grant Foundation is a national foundation that supports studies and community service projects related to preparing youth for the transition to adulthood (William T. Grant Foundation, 1993). Local private sources include churches and county divisions of charitable organizations (e.g., the United Way). Public sources consist of funds allocated through federal and state governments. At the state level, departments of education, social services, and workforce development typically fund programs serving teenage parents, provided the programs are consistent with the mission of the state agency. For example, state departments of education are likely to support special educational programs for teenage parents offered in the public schools. Specific state offices should be contacted to learn the types of programs those offices will support. Multifaceted service programs can rely on a variety of state sources of support. For example, a comprehensive program—based at a public school where parent skills training, academic and vocational instruction, health care, and child care services to teenage parents are offered—might be eligible for multiple sources of support at the state level. The same considerations apply for federal monies designated for education, youth and family services, and maternal and child health care.

Several strategies can be used to identify the many potential sources of private and public funding. The legwork in finding grants can be reduced by recruiting board members who are active in the community, particularly in a capacity of serving youth, for they tend to be knowledgeable about funding sources. Another easy method is to contact other professionals offering services to teenage parents to learn about the funding sources they have used, especially local and state funds. Members of the state legislature who serve on committees addressing the needs of children, youth, and families are excellent authorities on state funding, as are administrators from pertinent state agencies. The Foundation Center, located in New York City, assists potential applicants in identifying appropriate foundations and publishes annual listings of active grantmaking foundations (see Appendix 3.2). The National Organization on Adolescent Pregnancy, Parenting and Prevention (NOAPPP) publishes two newsletters—*Quick Notes* and *NOAPPP Network* (see Appendix 3.2)—that provide updates on both federal and private sources of funding.

To learn specifically how to apply for pertinent federal support, it is recommended that program developers first contact the Office of Adolescent Pregnancy Programs (OAPP; see Appendix 3.2), a branch of the Department of Health and Human Services. OAPP provides federal monies to support adolescent pregnancy prevention programs and/or comprehensive service programs for pregnant and parenting teenagers. In addition, OAPP staff can advise potential grant applicants of OAPP funding procedures and can recommend other federal offices to contact for additional support. Besides contacting OAPP, the reader may wish to consult Moore's (1981) comprehensive review of government programs that might affect teenage parents. These programs range from welfare assistance, such as Aid to Families With Dependent Children and health care programs such as Medicaid, to social services, school lunches, public housing, job training, family planning, and parent education.

Appendix 3.2 provides information related to funding, including addresses and phone numbers of key organizations and government offices, and references for publications that identify potential sources of grants and provide tips for writing grant proposals.

**Conducting and Monitoring
the Implementation Process**

After funding has been secured, the implementation plan must be put into action (Bloom, 1981; Brindis, 1991; Cowen, 1984). The program activities should be monitored throughout the implementation process to ensure that the plan is enacted properly (Bloom, 1981; Brindis, 1991).

The program coordinator is advised to schedule meetings periodically to assess the ongoing implementation of the program. At these meetings, the coordinator should foster communication between representatives from coalition agencies to evaluate successes, failures, and solutions to difficulties in carrying out the objectives of the implementation plan. As a result of these interchanges, the coordinator can determine if the program is achieving its objectives and whether or not a revision of the original implementation plan is necessary (Brindis, 1991).

Brindis (1991) suggested that the following questions serve as useful probes during the process evaluation:

- Are appropriate personnel, equipment, and financial resources available in the right quantity, in the right place, and at the right time to meet program needs? If not, what barriers are preventing these activities from taking place?
- Are expected "products" of the program actually being provided? Is the program providing the expected services and reaching the target population?
- What key ingredients contribute to the results being achieved?
- Are the activities being completed on time? Is the time line adequate to reach the established objectives? (pp. 214-215)

The results of these assessments should be reported to the board of directors. Their approval of changes in the implementation plan is vital if revisions are to be accepted by the community.

Evaluating the Effects of the Interventions

Process evaluations represent just one step in the evaluation process. Several writers (e.g., S. B. Baker, 1992; Baker & Shaw, 1987; Barclay, 1984; Bloom, 1981; Brindis, 1991; Card, Peterson, & Greeno, 1992; Cowen, 1984) have suggested that program developers should also evaluate the effects of their interventions. Card et al. (1992) used the term *impact evaluation* (p. 18) to distinguish this type of evaluation from process evaluations.

Impact evaluations can include several types of assessments. S. B. Baker (1992) recommended that impact evaluations include a blend of enumerative, opinion, and outcome assessments. Data regarding such facts as the hours of service provided and the number of individuals served are gathered in *enumerative assessments.* In *opinion assessments,* consumer satisfaction with the services rendered are measured. *Outcome assessments* are evaluations of the effectiveness of a program. Outcome data answer such questions as the following: Did the program work? For whom? Under what circumstances? In addition to these assessments, cost-effectiveness evaluations should be conducted (S. B. Baker, 1992; Bloom, 1981; Brindis, 1991).

Obviously, impact evaluations that include all three of these assessments require considerable skill, time, and funding. According to Card et al. (1992), the type of assessment undertaken should match the available resources and the size and complexity of the program. They argued that no reason exists why every service program for teenage parents should complete or even aspire to conduct a full impact evaluation. They recommended that complete impact evaluations are appropriate for demonstration projects that have the prerequisite funding and resources for such ambitious endeavors. Nevertheless, they encourage all programs to conduct some form of impact evaluation, especially because funding resources typically require programs they support to carry out some form of program evaluation.

No matter which type of impact assessment is chosen, program developers can refer to several helpful resources on the subject. S. B. Baker (1992) and Baker and Shaw (1987) provided numerous suggestions for developing enumerative and opinion assessment instruments. Kiselica et al. (1992) recommended a number of outcome measures appropriate for research with teenage fathers. The *Sourcebook of Comparison Data for Evaluating Adolescent Pregnancy and Parenting Programs* by Card, Reagan, and Ritter (1988) contains thorough coverage of the subject of evaluating adolescent pregnancy and parenting programs. Other resources (Brindis, 1991; Heppner, Kivlighan, & Wampold, 1992; Kazdin, 1992) include information on treatment research designs and their relative effectiveness in evaluating the impact of intervention strategies and on methods for analyzing and reporting the results of impact evaluations. Finally, in *A Basic Bibliography on Adolescent Sexuality, Pregnancy Prevention and Care Programs and Program Evaluation* by NationalNet (1990), a number of resources on program evaluation are cited.

Once the effects of the program have been determined, it is important to act on the findings. This entails deciding which components were critical to the program's success and what needs to be added or deleted from future programs. The final task is to make recommendations to the board of directors and the funding source to assist those bodies in making decisions about the future of the coalition (Brindis, 1991; Cowen, 1984).

Outreach Considerations

A common complaint heard from frustrated practitioners is, "It's no use trying to help teenage fathers. We offered a program for them but they just didn't come. It's clear they just don't want to be helped or to be responsible fathers." It is easy to empathize with these professionals, for they had made genuine efforts to assist teenage fathers but were unsuccessful in recruiting participants. Yet on close examination of their outreach work, it is often the case that their well-intentioned missions were doomed from the start: They had not incorporated into their service programs strategies especially designed for enlisting and retaining teenage fathers. The failure of these endeavors teaches us that developing a program specifically for young fathers is not enough. Program development must be followed by persistent and patient outreach.

In this section, methods of identifying, recruiting, establishing, and maintaining rapport with teenage fathers are summarized. But first, some comments are offered regarding the tone of outreach with this population.

Commitment and Nonjudgmental Caring: The Essential Tone of Outreach

All outreach work can be sabotaged even before it starts by a true lack of commitment to helping young fathers. Klinman and Sander (1985) and Sander and Rosen (1987) reported that one of most insurmountable obstacles hindering outreach work with teenage fathers is agency ambivalence, such as an implicit lack of support by the board of trustees and the administrator of the service agency. Sometimes top-level members of an organization who pay lip service to helping teenage fathers for public relations reasons give a disguised message that teenage mothers are the ones who should be getting help. According to Sander and Rosen (1987), these antimale sentiments can permeate the agency and ultimately undermine the staff ostensibly hired to work with the male teenagers. Similarly, Kiselica and Sturmer (1993b) suggested that some agencies purporting to help teenage fathers may do so in name only. Unless services are truly "available," the needs of teenage fathers will continue to be ignored.

These observations underscore the importance of the commitment to serving teenage fathers before outreach is considered. As Sander and Rosen (1987) put it, a teenage father program must be seen "not as an appendage to the rest of the agency, but as an integral part of the entire operation" (p. 109).

Another important prerequisite to outreach with the teenage father is an understanding of potentially loaded subjects, such as the issue of male responsibility. Given the prospect of an automatic assumption by some adults that he is oversexed, irresponsible, and uncaring, it is understandable that he can become leery of adults, including service providers. Thus, societal stereotypes, even when they are encountered by the adolescent father on an infrequent basis, can engender in him a hypersensitivity toward the reactions of others regarding the pregnancy. He may feel overwhelmed by the pressures of teenage parenthood, as well as some regret about his role in fathering a child. In his mind, what he most needs from others is empathic support rather than discussions about responsibility. Well-intentioned professionals overlook this point and alienate the young father without intending to do so by inviting the teenage boy to participate in a program designed to teach him the duties associated with fatherhood and responsible sexual behavior. When this approach is used, the potential client typically backs away. For this reason, Allen-Meares (1984) recommended that the issue of responsibility, especially as it pertains to family planning, should not be raised until a strong rapport has been established with the teenage father.

An additional vital quality to the tone of all outreach activities is a nonjudgmental and supportive attitude. Many teenage fathers are suspicious because they fear that contact with program staff could result in trouble with the authorities regarding child support payments. Thus, would-be helpers should make it clear from the start that they will not report the boy to officials from the child support divisions of the local prosecutor's office. Nevertheless, "over time young fathers should be encouraged to contact authorities, with the support of the counselor, to establish legal paternity and have reasonable child support set" (S. Brown, personal communication, November 1, 1993).

The bottom line is this: Outreach can only be effective when the agency is perceived as one committed to addressing the needs of adolescent boys, and its workers are seen as nonpunitive helpers dedicated to focusing on the immediate concerns of young fathers. With this philosophy in place, the nuts and bolts of outreach can begin.

Identifying and Recruiting Teenage Fathers

Outreach with teenage fathers begins with two challenges. First, young fathers need to be identified, and then they must be enticed to come in for services. Both require an involved referral process.

Strategies for Identifying Teenage Fathers

A variety of strategies are necessary for identifying teenage fathers. An important resource is their female partners (Barth et al., 1988; Brown, 1990; Sander & Rosen, 1987). Thus, many teenage fathers can be located by tapping into existing services for teenage mothers, such as obstetrical-gynecological clinics, Planned Parenthood clinics, and pediatric services (Robinson, 1988a). Formal networks among physicians, school counselors, teachers, coaches, administrators, clergy, and staff at vocational training centers, GED programs, and recreational centers might lead to many referrals for counseling (Huey, 1987; Kiselica, Stroud, et al., 1992; Sander & Rosen, 1987). Informal networks between professionals and teenage boys, especially teenage fathers already engaged in counseling, might result in other referrals (Barth et al., 1988; Huey, 1987; Kiselica, Stroud, et al., 1992). To establish these informal networks, helpers may have to spend time on the basketball courts, in poolrooms and on street corners where adolescent males "hang out" (Klinman & Sander, 1985; Sander & Rosen, 1987).

The media are another proven mechanism for reaching teenage fathers. "Public service announcements on television and radio that feature males talking realistically about their experiences as fathers and the help they have received from programs may increase the likelihood of participation" (Robinson, 1988a, pp. 107-108). Television, radio, and newspaper advertisements also inform other professionals about the program and can prompt them to make referrals (Sander & Rosen, 1987).

Rosenbaum (1985) suggested that the words and vocabulary used for written advertisements and materials regarding service programs for teenage parents be tailored to young adults. With this consideration in mind, it is recommended that program developers contact educational psychologists and special educators and ask for their assistance in reviewing the reading level of all written materials.

Finally, program developers can consult Lindsay and Rodine (1989b) for dozens of suggestions for creating marketing materials and managing the media.

Recruitment Strategies

Identifying teenage fathers can be a relatively easy task. Getting them to come in for services, even for an initial meeting, is another matter requiring the use of a number of the tricks of the trade.

Key people in the teenage father's life can be instrumental in convincing him to set up and keep an initial appointment. Several writers (e.g., Barth et al., 1988; Sander & Rosen, 1987) reported that teenage mothers were willing to encourage, coax, and even nag their partners to join service programs. The parents of the young father, at times, can convince him to participate in services (Brindis et al., 1987). Hendricks (1988) noted that the mothers of teenage fathers might be the most useful ally in promoting service use because these males commonly report close relationships with their mothers.

In some cases, a counselor must make the first contact without help from others. Hendricks (1988) noted that the chances of arranging a first meeting improve when it can be held at the young father's residence or some mutually agreed-on site. Sometimes, the initial encounter may have to occur on a bus, at a park, or on a basketball court (Barth et al., 1988).

During the initial contact with the teenage father, whether it be face-to-face or over the phone, he will need to be convinced that his involvement in a program will provide him with some tangible benefit. Although vocational counseling and training are the most common services used to attract teenage fathers to service programs (Brown, 1990; Brindis et al., 1987; Hendricks, 1988; Klinman & Sander, 1985; Sander & Rosen, 1987; Sommerfeld, 1992), other forms of practical help can be used to recruit young fathers, including the following:

1. Legal advice regarding paternity issues (Barth et al., 1988; Hendricks, 1988)
2. Specific information about and ways to become involved in the pregnancy, delivery, and parenting (Barth et al., 1988; Brindis et al., 1987; Hendricks, 1988; Klinman & Sander, 1985)
3. Free transportation to and from the service site (Barth et al., 1988)
4. Free medical services, such as physical examinations and diagnosis and treatment of sexually transmitted diseases (Hendricks, 1988)

It should be reiterated that the teenage father must be assured during the initial contact that his involvement in the service program will not result in legal punishment.

Establishing and Maintaining Rapport

The teenage father can be a very wary and elusive client. Promising him some practical help and reassuring him that he will not be punished might get him to step inside your door to check you out, but it is no guarantee that he will return. The practitioner must prove time and time again that he or she is worthy of the young man's trust. This is no easy task. The helper must be adept at a number of process and case management skills to establish and maintain rapport. A strong rapport with the teenage father is necessary to sustain a relationship that can weather the many crises precipitated by the experience of unplanned parenthood. Yet many professionals, especially women, have expressed anxiety about how to relate to young men. The purpose of this section is to equip helpers with an understanding of effective rapport-building strategies that are sensitive to the relational styles of adolescent fathers.

Rapport can be established with many young fathers by having the initial interactions outside the office setting. The professional can conduct much of the early information gathering in a gym or outside where the clinician and teenage boy take turns shooting baskets or tossing a football while they talk (Kiselica, 1993). Or the two might go for a walk to a store, share a snack and a soda, and chat about the young man's interests as they walk side by side (Kiselica, 1993).

During initial contacts, heavy reliance on open-ended questions such as, "How are you feeling?" tends to be ineffective. Instead, Barth et al. (1988) recommended that the counselor conduct issue-specific discussions centered on how the counselor can help the young father find job training and legal advice or address issues with his partner. Counselors are advised to proceed carefully and follow the father's cues regarding his comfort level with any topic. After the youth grows more comfortable and trusting, counseling can be more direct and less tentative.

Empathy, availability, honesty, and persistence are essential to the development and maintenance of rapport (Brindis et al., 1987; Kiselica, Stroud, et al., 1992). The teenage father needs to know that he can count on the counselor during times of crisis. Therefore, it is essential early on to assure him of one's availability for as long as it is needed and empathize with his feelings about unplanned parenthood. The counselor is advised to provide his or her business card, which should list the counselor's name, work address, and phone number, and the hours during which the counselor can be contacted. Also, it is recommended to obtain his name and address and his preferred procedure for getting in touch with him. Expressing a willingness to make an occasional home visit might also be beneficial (Hendricks, 1988).

These measures will help many adolescent fathers feel comfortable visiting a counselor in his or her office. Additional tactics are recommended for making office visits a success. Hendricks (1988) stated that the dos and don'ts of counseling teenage fathers in office settings begin with a careful consideration of the selection of appointment times. He pointed out that, to the extent possible, the time for meetings with a young father should be convenient for him. Setting up rigid, specified meeting times tends to be unsuccessful. It is better to be more general. For example, the worker can ask, "Can you come in the morning between the hours of 9 and 11, or is the afternoon better for you between the hours of 3 and 6?"

Brown (1990) offered some other suggestions regarding office appointments. First, she recommended that practitioners be available in the evenings and weekends if possible. Second, she found that the young fathers who participated in the Maine Young Fathers Project were not very good at following through on making and keeping appointments. Thus, she advised counselors to be persistent in their efforts to serve young fathers, even though they may feel frustrated at times. She also noted that patience and persistence frequently prove successful in engaging this population in counseling.

According to Hendricks (1988), the clinician can do many things to put the teenage father at ease once he arrives at his or her office:

1. During interview sessions . . . address the young father as mister until such time as you have gained his permission to call him by his first name.
2. Relax him by offering a soft drink prior to the start of the session.
3. Have all calls held during the interview. This contributes to his sense of importance.
4. Have magazines displayed with which the father can identify, especially sports publications.
5. Be knowledgeable about the slang he may use.
6. Be prepared to discuss events going on in the community.
7. Keep interview sessions brief—a maximum of 45 minutes. (p. 719)

The manner in which one talks to the teenage father can greatly influence his response. During the early stages of counseling, it is advisable not to ask too many questions because young fathers often associate such questioning with being in trouble. Instead, be prepared to do a lot of listening and follow the boy's lead about what topics he is ready to discuss. This communicates to the youth that the counselor is there to address the youth's own pressing needs (Hendricks, 1988). "Moreover, trust, rapport, and constructive communication are likely to be established more rapidly . . . when the young father and clinician sit side-by-side rather than opposite each other" (Hendricks, 1988, p. 719). This seating arrangement tends to reduce suspicion (Hendricks, 1988). Kiselica (1993) recommended that the counselor wearing a long-sleeved shirt should role up his or her shirtsleeves, thereby conveying to the youth that the counselor is ready to work for him.

Another critical task during the initial stages of counseling is to explore the teenage father's view about counseling. Through this process, misconceptions about the purpose of counseling can be corrected. In addition, the counselor can prepare the client for some of the problems that might lie ahead (Kiselica, Stroud, et al., 1992).

Case Management Strategies and Issues

A dialogue regarding potential future difficulties is an opportune time for the helper to establish himself or herself as an advocate for the teenage father (Kiselica, Stroud, et al., 1992). In their discussion of the advocacy role, Brindis et al. (1987) recommended that counselors serve as brokers of services. In this capacity, counselors work as active advocates in securing services, such as family-life education, parenting training, and family counseling. As a broker, the counselor maintains an ongoing relationship with the teenage father, guiding him or her through the process of identifying and obtaining needed services. By offering the teenage father key emotional support throughout this process, the counselor can help the youth to successfully navigate the counseling services system. In addition, this support typically fortifies the client's trust in the counselor.

Besides pursuing services for teenage fathers, the role of advocate/broker involves several unique case management strategies that have been described by Brindis et al. (1987). With regard to making referrals, the counselor is advised to respond to the client's hesitation and ambivalence by presenting service options as being attractive and obtainable while allowing the client to make the final choice. Initially, the counselor can call to set up referral appointments with the client in the office. The counselor should have the youth make the phone call himself from the counselor's office; this empowers the young father to become more self-sufficient. Other effective brokering strategies include arranging for the teenager to meet the service provider so that services can be explained, assisting in setting up initial appointments so that the client can try out the service, following up with the client to see whether or not he had tried the service, communicating with other service providers to monitor the client's progress, and coordinating case conferences with professionals from the agencies helping the young father. Periodic phone calls and home visits to the teenage father may be necessary to keep him engaged in counseling. A relationship with the teenage boy's parents should be developed, not only to enlist their support of the counseling efforts, but also to respond to their issues regarding their son's role as a father and his use of services (Brindis et al., 1987).

A controversial issue related to the brokering of services regards the gender of the case manager and how it affects the counselor-client relationship. In reviewing the outreach performance of counselors employed in the Teenage Father Collaboration, Sander and Rosen (1987) reported that case managers assigned to work with teenage fathers had to be able to go into the community to relate to young men on an one-to-one basis. They concluded that a man in his 20s or 30s from the same ethnic and cultural background as the teenage clients usually succeeded best as a counselor. Yet findings from the Teenage Pregnancy and Parenting Project (TAPP) in San Francisco suggested that women counselors who were committed to extending services to young fathers were effective case managers with this population (Brindis et al., 1987). Similarly, I have known several female colleagues from around the country who have been invaluable helpers to teenage fathers. In addition, I have encountered a few ineffective male counselors with backgrounds similar to the teenage fathers they have been hired to serve. Based on these data, it can be concluded that indigenous male counselors who are skillful case managers might have a slight initial advantage in establishing rapport, but background differences can be transcended by any dedicated counselor, *male or female,* who assertively advocates for teenage fathers with caring, persistence, sincerity, patience, a sense of humor, and a sensitive understanding of the fathers' cultural backgrounds.

A second case management issue concerns case assignment when the teenage father and his partner are unmarried and both are receiving services at the same site. Relationships between teenage parents tend to be rocky and stormy and can pose potential problems during service delivery. Hendricks (1988) advised against having a joint session during the initial meeting with the teenage father, cautioning that the relationship might not be stable enough for such a meeting. Sander and Rosen (1987) recommended that joint sessions should occur during the first appointment only if the relations between the couple are amicable. Barth et al. (1988) suggested that both parents be assigned to different case managers if the partners are involved in a long-term service program. This arrangement ensures that each parent has a supportive advocate and prevents a conflict of loyalties for the counselor should problems arise over custody, visitation, support payments, and the demise of a romantic relationship between the teenagers.

Conclusion

Dedicated outreach with the teenage father can win his trust and open the door to assisting him with the pregnancy resolution challenge, relationship issues with his partner, extended family and peers, preparation for fatherhood, and the exploration of his educational and career concerns, each of which are discussed in the remaining chapters of Part I.

APPENDIX 3.1

Teen Parent Services Survey

Agency/School: _____

Address: _____ County: _____

Phone: _____ Contact Person: _____

Do you offer a special program specifically for teen parents?   Yes   No

If yes, what is/are the name(s) of the program(s)? _____

Please write **M** next to each service offered at your agency/school to teen mothers, **F** next to each service offered to teen fathers, or **MF** next to each service offered to both teen mothers and teen fathers.

1. *Health Services*
1.01_____pregnancy testing
1.02_____prenatal care
1.03_____postnatal care
1.04_____pediatric care
1.05_____birth control counseling
1.06_____abortion counseling
1.07_____sexual responsibility counseling
1.08_____home health care
1.09_____nutritional counseling
1.10_____family health education
1.11_____first aid training
1.12_____sex education
1.13_____breast-feeding training

2. *Services for Children*
2.01_____child care
2.02_____adoption services
2.03_____foster care

3. *Parent Training*
3.01_____parent education/training
3.02_____early childhood development

4. *Basic Living Needs*
4.01_____food
4.02_____clothing
4.03_____financial aid
4.04_____housing
4.05_____WIC (food supplements for
women/infants/children)

5. *Life Skills Training*
5.01_____homemaking
5.02_____consumer education
5.03_____budgeting
5.04_____assertiveness training

6. *Academic Education*
6.01_____regular school curriculum
6.02_____special/remedial curriculum

7. *Counseling Services*
7.01_____bibliotherapy (information
on teen parenthood)
7.02_____individual, personal
adjustment counseling
7.03_____couples counseling
7.04_____family counseling
7.05_____teen parent support groups
7.06_____grandparent support group
7.07_____psychiatric services

8. *Employment Assistance*
8.01_____vocational skills training
8.02_____job-seeking skills
(e.g., résumé and letter-writing,
interviewing skills)
8.03_____job-keeping skills
(e.g., employee responsibility)

9. *Social/Recreational*
9.01_____informal gatherings
9.02_____field trips

10. *Requirement/Outreach Services*
10.01_____public service announcements
10.02_____use of other media
10.03_____hotlines
10.04_____transportation
10.05_____drop-in centers

11. *Other Services*
11.01_____legal assistance
11.02_____other (please specify below)

58

APPENDIX 3.2

Information Related to Grants
Office of Adolescent Pregnancy Programs

4330 East West Highway
Bethesda, MD 20857
(301) 594-4004

Historically, this office has awarded grants to support adolescent pregnancy prevention programs and comprehensive service programs for pregnant and parenting teenagers. OAPP also funds studies investigating adolescent contraceptive use and societal causes and consequences of adolescent premarital sexual relations. In addition, OAPP staff can advise program developers about other federal monies that might be used to support programs related to teenage pregnancy and parenthood.

Resources for Identifying Grants

Annual Register of Grant Support: A Directory of Funding Sources. Wilmette, IL: National Register Publishing. Annual.

Brief entries detail grant support programs of more than 2,800 government agencies, public and private foundations, corporations, community trusts, unions, educational and professional associations, and special interest organizations.

Catalog of Federal Domestic Assistance. Washington, DC: Government Printing Office. Annual.

A government-wide summary of financial and nonfinancial federal programs, projects, services, and activities that provide assistance or benefits to the American public.

Corporate 500: The Directory of Corporate Philanthropy. San Francisco: Public Management Institute. Annual.

Lists nearly 600 corporations that give approximately $500,000 or more per year.

The Foundation Directory. New York: The Foundation Center. Annual.

Perhaps the single most important reference book on grant-making foundations in the United States. Includes brief entries on more than 5,000 foundations whose assets exceed $1,000,000 or whose annual giving exceeds $100,000.

59

Foundation Grants Index. New York: The Foundation Center. Annual.

Lists 500 foundations that have given grants of more than $5,000. Entries include a statement of limitations on grants and a list of recipients for the previous year, including amounts awarded.

Guide to United States Department of Education Programs. Washington, DC: Government Printing Office. Annual.

Contains an overview about the process of applying for funding from individual federal education programs.

National Data Book (2 Vols.). New York: The Foundation Center. Annual.

Comprehensive listing of 23,578 active grant-making foundations.

National Foundations. New York: The Foundation Center. Annual.

Includes more than 24,000 U.S. foundations regardless of assets or annual total of grants awarded.

National Organization on Adolescent Pregnancy, Parenting and Prevention (NOAPPP). 4421-A East-West Highway, Bethesda, MD 20814. Phone: (301) 913-0378.

NOAPPP is a national network focused on adolescent pregnancy care and prevention issues. NOAPPP publishes *NOAPPP Network* and *Quick Notes,* which are newsletters providing legislative updates regarding congressional acts related to adolescent pregnancy, parenting, and prevention.

Shellow, J. R. (Ed.). (1985). *Grantseekers Guide: Funding Sourcebook.* Mt. Kisko, NY: Moyer Bell.

Contains information on a variety of funding sources for community-based programs and social and economic justice projects.

Guides to Writing and Applying for Grants

Baron, R. A. (1987). Research grants: A practical guide. In M. P. Zanna & J. M. Darley (Eds.), *The Complete Academic: A Practical Guide for the Beginning Social Scientist* (pp. 151-169). New York: Random House.

Written for academics interested in applying for research grants, this chapter describes the grant review process and the mechanics of submitting a grant proposal.

Bauer, D. G. (1988). *The "How To" Grants Manual: Successful Grant-seeking Techniques for Obtaining Public and Private Grants* (2nd ed.). New York: American Council on Education.

An excellent source on how to prepare for grant-seeking, including needs assessment, proposal evaluation, market research, and government and private funding sources.

Ezell, S. (Ed.). (1981). *Proposal Writer's SWIPE FILE III: 15 Professionally Written Grant Proposals . . . Prototypes of Approaches, Styles and Structures.* Washington, DC: Taft Corporation.

Contains grant proposals written by seven professional proposal writers. Includes proposals in the areas of social welfare, education, science, arts, and humanities.

Gooch, J. M. (1987). *Writing Winning Proposals.* Washington, DC: Council for Advancement and Support of Education.

Discusses several areas of proposal writing, including organizing material, budgeting, form, style, editing, follow-up, and "tools of the trade."

Margolin, J. B. (1983). *Individual's Guide to Grants.* New York: Plenum.

Written for individuals seeking grants who are not affiliated with an institution and who have little or no experience in grantsmanship.

4

Pregnancy Resolution
and Legal Considerations

A teenage boy who has impregnated an adolescent girl is faced with some of the most important decisions of his life. Should he persuade his partner to have an abortion, or should he urge her to carry the baby to term? If the child is born, should the couple keep the baby or give the infant up for adoption? If they keep the child, should they marry? If they marry, should they live on their own or with parents or relatives? If they do not marry, who should have custody of the baby? If the father is excluded from decisions regarding abortion and adoption, or if he chooses or is placed in a noncustodial role, what are his legal rights and obligations? What does unmarried custodial fatherhood entail?

Clearly, these significant and potentially agonizing dilemmas can overwhelm the adolescent who struggles to face them alone. Young fathers need help in making these decisions so that they can decide on a course of action that will help them to manage the crisis of an unplanned pregnancy successfully. The challenge of resolving the pregnancy is filled with legal considerations and ramifications that teenage fathers often overlook. The purpose of this chapter is to review the many emotional and legal issues associated with pregnancy resolution and recommend counseling interventions designed to support adolescent fathers during this stressful period. Because so much of the work involves helping expectant fathers to make decisions regarding the pregnancy and paternity, this chapter begins with a brief overview of the basics of decision-making counseling. Because these decisions are laden with moral dilemmas, some important ethical issues also are considered. This chapter concludes with a review of the options of abortion, adoption, marriage, noncustodial fatherhood, and unmarried custodial fatherhood.

Decision-Making Counseling

In his provocative and scholarly volume, *Counseling for Effective Decision-Making: A Cognitive-Behavioral Perspective,* Horan (1979) observed that the most frequent and perhaps the most important concerns of clients are problems of choice. Therefore, one of the primary responsibilities of counselors is to render assistance to clients with decision making.

There are a variety of decision-making and problem-solving paradigms. In his review of these models, Horan (1979) concluded that all share four common components represented by different phases of counseling. During the conceptualization phase, the counselor helps the client to define the problem as one of choice. In phase two, the counselor assists the client in enlarging the response repertoire by generating alternatives, first from the client's perspective, then from the counselor's vantage point. In the next phase, information regarding the advantages and disadvantages for each alternative is gathered. In the final phase, alternatives are ranked and a tentative decision is made by the client. Throughout this process, it is critical that the counselor not make the decision for the client. Instead, the client should accept full responsibility for making the decision (Horan, 1979).

Much of this chapter contains a wealth of information that can be shared with young parents during the pregnancy-resolution counseling process. Counselors can incorporate these details into Horan's (1979) paradigm to assist expectant fathers with their decisions regarding the pregnancy and parenthood. In phase one of pregnancy-resolution counseling, the counselor helps the client to define the problem as one of choice. In phase two the counselor ensures that the teenage father has considered all options (i.e., abortion, adoption, marriage, etc.) before making a rash decision. Next, the helper shares information and explores the client's perspective regarding the pros and cons of these options. Finally, the counselor helps the young father to make a decision and take ownership for whatever choice he finally selects.

Several curricula can be used to teach expectant teenage parents decision-making and problem-solving skills. Whipple's (1987) *Career Orientation and Preparation for Teen Parents Curriculum* and the *Adolescent Parent Resource Guide,* published by the Ohio State Department of Education (1989), contain decision-making modules that have been designed specifically for training with teenage parents. Several writers (e.g., Elias & Clabby, 1982; Schinke, Blythe, & Gilchrist, 1981; Schinke, Blythe, Gilchrist, & Burt, 1989; Spivack, Platt, & Shure, 1976; Weissburg, Gesten, Leibenstein, Doherty-Schmid, & Hutton, 1980) have developed very thorough problem-solving training curricula for use with children and adolescents in general that can be adapted to the decision-making concerns of teenage fathers.

Because a decision-making paradigm provides a road map for counseling during crisis pregnancies, it can leave counselors with the erroneous impression that pregnancy-resolution counseling is straightforward and easy. It is neither. Many young expectant parents suffer considerable anguish that can render them indecisive, even if they have been hooked up with a professional who is knowledgeable about decision-making counseling. Other more impetuous youth are ready to plow ahead with a decision with total disregard for the counselor's efforts to discuss the available options. Many who would like help with their decision making, especially youth from multiproblem communities, are detoured from counseling by other difficulties in their lives. Working with teenage parents requires ongoing patience, persistence, emotional fortitude, and the artful craft of responding to unanticipated surprises. This goes with the territory and should not be forgotten. Furthermore, ethical issues abound, a subject that warrants separate and special consideration.

Moral and Ethical Considerations

Like it or not, unplanned out-of-wedlock pregnancies create moral dilemmas for clients and counselors alike. No doubt, much of the conflict centers around how to resolve the pregnancy, especially regarding the issue of abortion, one of the most controversial and emotionally charged subjects of our time. Some counselors, arguing for the sanctity of conception, may decide that their moral opposition to abortion necessarily restricts them from presenting this as an option to any client. Others may forcefully steer expectant parents toward abortion or adoption because of convictions that teenage parenthood places adolescents and their children at risk for lifelong hardships. A handful of counselors will deny the young father services unless he commits to marrying the mother of his child.

Behavior of this kind, though perhaps morally correct for the individual counselor, is inappropriate in decision-making counseling for two reasons.

First, these actions rest on the assumption that there are absolute "right" answers for dilemmas of choice. As Herr (1970) correctly observed,

> the problem is that judgments about whether or not a decision is a "good" one are typically made not by the chooser but by some external expert. Consequently, such judgments may have no relationship to anything that the decision-maker himself values. (p. 3)

Based on this reasoning, Horan (1979) concluded, "Problems of choice permit few if any 'right' answers" (p. 83). Therefore, counselors should give "all viable alternatives in a choice problem a fair hearing" and should deliberately withhold "any reinforcement for implementing a particular alternative until after the client makes the decision favoring that alternative" (Horan, 1979, p. 88). Second, imposing one's values on a client and coercing clients to select a choice preferred by the counselor violate the ethical guidelines of the helping professions. For example, the *Ethical Principles of Psychologists and Code of Conduct* (American Psychological Association, 1992) states, "Psychologists strive to be aware of their own belief systems values, needs, and limitations and the effect on these on their work" (Preamble, Principal B) and "In their work-related activities, psychologists respect the rights of others to hold values, attitudes, and opinions that differ from their own" (Ethical Standard 1.09). Section A of the *Ethical Standards of the American Counseling Association* (American Counseling Association, 1988) states,

> In the counseling relationship, the counselor is aware of the intimacy of the relationship and maintains a respect for the client and avoids engaging in activities that seek to meet the counselor's personal needs at the expense of that client.

Finally, according to the *Code of Ethics* for the National Association of Social Workers, social workers are delegated to "act in accordance with the highest standards of professional integrity and impartiality" (National Association of Social Workers, 1990, Section D).

These ethical considerations have two implications for pregnancy-resolution counseling. First, professionals need to clarify their own values and attitudes about abortion, adoption, adolescent marriage, and out-of-wedlock births before they begin to advise teenagers on how to respond to an unplanned pregnancy. Second, when counselors find themselves strongly believing in or opposing a particular alternative, they are obliged to discuss their biases with their clients, and, if necessary, refer the client to another counselor.

Abortion and Adoption

Abortion is frequently considered and used by young expectant mothers as a method to resolve an unplanned pregnancy. In 1988, 26% of the women who had abortions in the United States were under age 20 (Henshaw, 1992) and approximately 40% of all teenage pregnancies ended in induced abortions (Ventura et al., 1992). Although adoption is a less popular option among this population, it nevertheless is used by some pregnant adolescents (Hofferth, 1987b).

Teenage fathers may or may not be included by expectant mothers in their decision making regarding the pregnancy. Counseling considerations for each possibility are provided.

Helping Boys Who Are Excluded From
Decisions Regarding Abortion and Adoption

Since the landmark ruling by the U.S. Supreme Court in *Roe v. Wade* in 1973, the practice of abortion has been legal in this country. According to Steinfels (1981), subsequent judicial and regulatory decisions have favored a policy that would require public agencies, and many private ones as well, to treat adolescents from puberty (at the age of 11 or 12) through the age of majority (18 or 19) as if they were adults for the purpose of providing contraceptive services and performing abortions. (For an extensive review of these precedents, see Steinfels, 1981.) Consequently, in some states minors now may consent to health care as it relates to family planning, sexually transmitted disease, pregnancy care, and abortions without parental notification. However, the expectant adolescent girl is not legally mandated to notify the father should she decide to terminate the pregnancy (Johnson, 1991; Steinfels, 1981).

According to Robinson (1988a), many teenage fathers are not included in their partners' decisions to have abortions. There are several possible explanations for this exclusion. First, as was indicated earlier, women are legally not required to inform the father of this decision (Johnson, 1991; Steinfels, 1981). Second, expectant mothers who turn to their parents for guidance early on in the pregnancy often are urged and sometimes coerced by family members into having an abortion without consulting the father (Kiselica, 1993). Third, agencies and institutions that provide family planning services historically have tended to devalue the male role in the pregnancy resolution process (Hendricks et al., 1981; Kiselica & Sturmer, 1993b; Scales, 1977). Fourth, during a period of estrangement from her partner, the young mother, in a state of anger, may proceed with the abortion without alerting the father.

When teenage fathers learn that they have been ignored in the decision to abort, they feel angry and violated. Fry and Trifiletti (1983) found that the greatest rejection experienced by adolescent fathers occurred in cases in which babies were aborted. Similarly, Redmond (1985) reported that young men excluded from the decision-making process felt confused and neglected.

Expectant fathers who are excluded from decisions to place a child for adoption also experience hurt and loss. When this occurs the father's legal rights may have been violated. The law generally requires adoption agencies to contact the father to obtain his consent for relinquishment and adoption (Baum, 1980; Robinson, 1988a; Schwartz, 1986). However, there is considerable variation in the application of these guidelines (Schwartz, 1986).

In other instances involving adoption, the father "participates" in the decision to give up the baby only to the extent that he is ordered by his partner's parents to accept their decree that the child will be placed for adoption. Fathers placed in this circumstance typically feel coerced to cooperate with this decision. Thus, in some situations, a child may be placed for adoption against the father's wishes even though he has ostensibly approved of the plan.

How can professionals intervene so as to prevent the exclusion of young fathers from abortion and adoption decisions? Also, how should counselors respond to a young father for whom abortion/adoption is a fait accompli without his input?

Preventing Male Exclusion

Involving young fathers in the decision-making process begins with an examination of one's attitudes about this issue. This is an especially important step for professionals who work with expectant mothers. Many employed in the service of young women hold steadfastly to the belief that the right to determine the course of a pregnancy ultimately should rest with the expectant mother. I agree with and support this belief. What is disconcerting, however, is the practice of counseling young women *without encouraging them to even consider the father as a factor in this decision.* Sometimes it is assumed automatically by the helper, on learning that the father is a boy, that he is an unworthy candidate to support the mother. Based on this stereotype, counseling proceeds without any exploration of the individual father's unique character, his willingness and ability to take on parental responsibilities, and his feelings regarding abortion. In response to this type of behavior, Robinson (1988a) urged that counseling services for adolescents need to be expanded so that boys who impregnate girls are included in programs of abortion and adoption counseling. The first step is to carefully monitor any personal prejudices that characterize young fathers as aloof, unconcerned, and eager to avoid responsibility for involvement in that pregnancy. (p. 109)

In addition to reevaluating one's attitudes about teenage fathers, counselors should bear in mind that Redmond (1985) found that the more the adolescent male is involved in the decision-making process, the more active he is during and after the pregnancy. Thus, a consideration of the father's feelings might promote responsible male behavior.

Thus, the counselor assisting the young expectant mother with a crisis pregnancy is urged to balance a respect for her needs and legal rights with a sensitive and complex understanding of the male role. Besides helping the woman to clarify her own values regarding abortion and adoption, it is recommended that counselors examine the female's relationship with her partner. Throughout this process, a priori assumptions about the young man should be avoided. As information is gathered, thought-provoking questions can be posed: How supportive has your partner been to you in the past? To what extent have you discussed his feelings about abortion? How willing and able is he to support you emotionally and financially? Although responses to these questions can give the counselor an impression of the expectant father, practitioners are cautioned to remember that the mother's self-report of the male's behavior and attitudes is often greatly different from his perception of himself (see Braver, Fitzpatrick, & Bay, 1991; Robinson & Barret, 1982). Counselors need to gently discuss this issue with the woman, explore her feelings about involving her partner in the counseling, and be sure that she has carefully considered the implications of involving and excluding him. In the end, it is critical that the counselor support her decision. If these suggestions are followed, then more women may find that they need not face crisis pregnancies without the support of their partners, and more expectant fathers might feel that their potential paternity has been respected.

Direct work with the teenage father also can promote his inclusion in the expectant mother's decision making. At times, he may report that he has expressed his feelings to his mate, when, in fact, he has done a poor job of communicating with her. Some males may be indecisive and/or afraid to face the situation during the crisis and, consequently, avoid discussing their preferences with their partners until it is too late. Thus, as soon as an expectant unmarried young man tells a counselor that his girlfriend is pregnant, the counselor needs to quickly evaluate the nature of the boy's contact with his partner regarding pregnancy resolution. If he has not attempted to help his partner with her concerns and/or if he has failed to address his preferences with her, then the counselor should encourage the boy to do so immediately. Otherwise, the outcome of the pregnancy may be determined prior to his input. If the youth has attempted to contact his partner and her family but has been ignored, then the counselor is advised to ask the youth for his permission (and if he is a minor, his parent's permission) to contact those parties on his behalf.

Reaching out to a family with an expectant daughter while serving as an advocate for the young father is an extremely tricky business. The odds are that this initiative will be unsuccessful. Nevertheless, the counselor must attempt to somehow connect with the parents in spite of their hostile feelings toward the male client. The goal is to help the family be sure that they have carefully considered all options before they follow through with an abortion or place the child for adoption. At the same time, the counselor should not impose a decision on the family. During the initial phone conversation, it is useful mainly to listen empathically to the parents' concerns. It is important that the parents feel they have been heard and use the counselor as an outlet for their worries regarding their daughter. Usually, the parents have some legitimate concerns about the young man. In addition, they often are unaware of the many resources in the community that might be of assistance to them. Immediately informing them of these services sometimes alters their plans about an abortion or adoption. For example, the counselor might share information about child care options, supportive school programs for young mothers, and so on. Afterward, the parents might regard the counselor as a caring individual. Occasionally, this foundation of trust enables the family to use the counselor as a mediator between them and the teenage father. Consequently, the young man will have an opportunity to discuss his opinions about the pregnancy with his partner. Clinical experience suggests that some teenage boys who were initially opposed to an abortion become supportive of their partners' decisions to abort once the boys' perspective on the matter has been understood and acknowledged by the partner.

When the issue involves placing the child for adoption, and the family has continued to disregard the father's preferences, the father may have to resort to legal action if he wishes to obtain custody of the child. Although this happens rarely, it can lead to complicated and vexatious proceedings. For example, in May 1985, the ABC television program *20/20* featured the story of a legal dispute between the family of a 16-year-old boy and the family of a 12-year-old girl he had impregnated. On delivery of the baby, the child was placed with a couple who were eager to adopt the child. Although the father sought custody of the child so that he could raise the baby, the California

Supreme Court resolved the case in favor of the adoptive parents (Schwartz, 1986).

Cases like these indicate that in some instances counselors must seek legal counsel on the youth's behalf. Legal precedents in many states protect the father's right to give his consent or veto the granting of an adoption (Schwartz, 1986). It may be necessary to assist the young man in obtaining legal counsel, which is often available free of charge or at reduced rates at local legal aid societies or legal clinics provided by schools of law, to ascertain the particular legal regulations in his state.

If it has been determined that the father's legal rights are being violated, he will need decision-making counseling regarding the dilemma of whether or not he should pursue the matter legally. If he decides to oppose the mother's desire to place the child for adoption, he must be prepared for a potentially drawn-out and nasty battle that he may well lose. Is he ready for this? Also, there is the remote possibility that he will be granted custody of the child. Is he truly capable of taking on this responsibility? Another likely scenario in response to his opposition is that the mother and her family may opt to keep the child and resent the father for asserting himself. In preparation for this possibility, he will need to consider whether or not he wants to petition the court for custody of the child. If he considers a noncustodial role, he must anticipate the potential ramifications of dealing with a family that views him as a thorn in their side.

Counseling Teenage Fathers Who Have Been Excluded From Decisions Regarding Abortion

In spite of all efforts to include males in the pregnancy-resolution process, some young men will be denied any say in the outcome of an unborn child. Others may have their opposition to abortion go unheeded by a partner who decides to terminate the pregnancy. For the youth who truly was ready to accept his responsibilities as a parent, these decisions can be a source of turmoil. Consider, for example, the experience of a 17-year-old boy named Quawie, whose girlfriend was whisked away by her mother to a clinic for an abortion before the couple could discuss their feelings regarding the pregnancy. In outrage, he punched a cinder block wall, scraping and spraining the knuckles and fingers on his right hand. Another adolescent male, David, spent a year recovering from the bitterness he experienced after his girlfriend opted for an abortion against his wishes.

In counseling teenage boys such as these, the goal is to help them mourn the loss of a child and foster an empathic understanding of the mother's decision to abort. Although the client typically is more amenable to working on the first task, helping him to appreciate the mother's perspective can facilitate the mourning process and prompt him to be a source of support to the woman as she recovers from the abortion. Thus, it is recommended that counselors first concentrate on helping the youth to ventilate and understand his pain and confusion and then focus on building his sensitive awareness for the mother's predicament.

Many of the techniques used in grief counseling are effective in addressing these issues. For example, the *empty chair,* a gestalt therapy technique developed by Fritz Perls, is a commonly used method to help clients to mourn the loss of a loved one. This technique employs an empty chair to which the client expresses fantasy dialogues or learns to experience polarities of experience (Young, 1992). As applied in work with a boy who has lost a child to abortion, the counselor would suggest to the youth that he try a technique designed to help him recognize and resolve powerful, unexpressed feelings associated with the loss. In one variation of the empty chair, the counselor would instruct the client to imagine that his unborn child is sitting in the chair across from him. Next, the adolescent is encouraged to express to the child his feelings about the abortion. Afterward, the client moves to the empty chair and imagines that he is the unborn child talking back to the client. Several rounds of switching may follow, as the client conveys the many emotions associated with the lost opportunity to bond with a child. In another version of the empty chair, the client verbalizes to his partner his hurt and angry feelings about the abortion. When he switches chairs, he expresses the side in him that understands her reasons for terminating the pregnancy. Both of these variations of the empty chair can be used to move the boy beyond his pain while promoting his sympathy for his partner's decision.

Clinical experience suggests that teenage fathers are receptive to participating in the empty chair procedure only after they have a well-established relationship of trust with the counselor. Therefore, practitioners are cautioned against using this tactic prematurely with their clients. Furthermore, prior to employing the empty chair technique, counselors are advised to read Young's (1992) lengthy discussion regarding several potential problems and precautions associated with this technique.

In addition to learning how to use the empty chair procedure, counselors might wish to read other books on grief counseling (e.g., Chapin, 1991; James & Cherry, 1988; Kalish, 1985; Mannion, 1986; Worden, 1982) to learn other strategies for helping grieving adolescent boys.

Recovery from grief can be expedited by sharing with the youth information about the difficulties experienced by young mothers. This can be conveyed verbally or via the viewing of *A Different Family . . . Our Teenager*

Has a Baby (Planned Parenthood Association of Cincinnati, 1991), an excellent film that depicts actual young mothers and the joys and hardships they encountered as parents. After watching the movie, it is recommended that counselors ask the client the following: How might the situations of the mothers in this film be like that of your partner? Can you appreciate how frightening impending parenthood might have been to her? How clearly did you express to her your readiness to support her emotionally and financially? If you did communicate these intentions, were you being realistic about your ability to follow through on those promises? Can you comprehend the many pressures she might have faced? Can you forgive her? Probes like these can help the young man empathize with his partner's position and, in the process, moderate his anger and hurt at her decision.

Once this work has been completed, it is helpful to encourage the boy to have a face-to-face meeting with his partner to express his new perspective on the issue and see if the two can work out an amicable relationship in the aftermath of the abortion. When these tasks are accomplished, young men report a feeling of recovery, wholeness, and a readiness to move on with their lives.

Helping Boys Who Are Involved in
Decisions Regarding Abortion and Adoption

Counseling expectant fathers who are included by their partners in pregnancy-resolution decision making is less complicated than the challenge of helping boys who are excluded from the process. Nevertheless, advising young couples about the pros and cons of abortion and adoption requires a thorough knowledge of these options and sensitive information-giving skills. Each of these options is considered in turn. Helpers who can use this information in counseling adolescents might also want to arrange a consult with professionals from a local Planned Parenthood office to tap their expertise on pregnancy-resolution counseling. In addition, counselors might peruse *Family Planning Perspectives,* a periodical that has updated information pertaining to family planning and pregnancy-resolution issues.

Abortion Counseling

In a national study of adolescent knowledge and attitudes about abortion, Stone and Waszak (1991) found that most teenagers lack accurate knowledge about abortion and the laws governing it. In addition, most of the participants expressed erroneous beliefs about abortion, describing it as medically dangerous, emotionally damaging, and widely illegal. Stone and Waszak (1991) and other researchers (e.g., Fischman, 1977; Zelnik, Kantner, & Ford, 1981, cited in Moore & Burt, 1982) found that adolescents in general are personally opposed to abortion.

These findings may explain, in part, why abortion is such a torturous consideration for young expectant parents. As teenagers scurry to deal with impending parenthood, they realize that abortion is a possible way out from a crisis situation. At the same time, however, they may be misguided by unfounded fears and filled with self-reproach because of their personal distaste for abortion. In addition, they find themselves in a pressure cooker once they realize that a decision to abort must be made especially quickly, because an abortion after the first trimester of pregnancy has increased dangers and, in some states, is illegal. Furthermore, as they wrestle with their dilemma, they may receive very strong, conflicting advice from others.

In response to these many stressors, expectant teenagers often waver on the abortion question, an indication that assistance with the decision making is warranted. Even when the couple decides expeditiously and with confidence, counseling is called for to make sure that they have carefully considered all of their options. Specifically, they need to know the legal issues related to abortion, the medical risks involved, the reasons why adolescents abort or keep their babies, and the pros and cons of abortion versus giving birth.

Legal Issues. Three important legal considerations involve the issue of patient consent, parental consent, and the legal time limits for termination of a pregnancy. Although some general legal guidelines pertaining to these issues are discussed here, counselors are urged to contact the local Planned Parenthood Association or Legal Aid Society to learn about specific legal parameters because they vary from state to state.

State variations in legal requirements pertaining to abortion help to explain, in part, why adolescents have misconceptions on the subject. Clarifying local requirements for the young couple can help reduce their confusion about the subject. Acting as an advocate on the couple's behalf in the event that their legal rights have been violated can be a vital means of support as they attempt to resolve the pregnancy. What are their legal rights?

It is generally accepted that doctors must receive patient consent, even if she is a minor, before performing an abortion. However, in some states the doctor also must acquire the consent of the girl's legal guardian, who is typically the custodial parent. In several states where parental consent is required, the pregnant adolescent may petition the court to bypass parental notification by demonstrating that parental knowledge of the girl's pregnancy and intention to abort would place the girl in imminent danger.

Couples who choose to pursue this option when it is available will need emotional support to deal with the anxiety of awaiting a judge's decision on the matter. In those rare instances in which the court intervenes on the girl's behalf, the counselor may need to address the guilt that the couple experiences for having acted "behind our parents backs."

Even if a girl is not legally required to inform her parents, the counselor is advised to discuss with the couple the possibility of seeking their parents' input for the assistance these adults might offer. Support for this idea comes from studies indicating that many parents are positively involved in the pregnancy resolution. For example, in a study of the pregnancy-resolution strategies of adolescent girls, Rosen (1980) found that most of the girls interviewed in her study initially were hesitant to involve their mothers in the process. However, approximately half of the pregnant adolescents eventually included their parents in their decision making and perceived their parents to be supportive. Hendricks (1988) asked 54 teenage fathers who they would go to first with a problem. Seventy percent of the young men reported that they would most likely go to their families for assistance. A series of reports on a longitudinal study of teenage mothers and their families by Furstenberg and his colleagues (Furstenberg et al., 1987; Furstenberg et al., 1989; Furstenberg & Crawford, 1989) indicated that most of the parents provided emotional comfort and financial support to their daughters. Commenting on the potentially positive role of parents, Moore and Burt (1982) stated,

> Counseling oriented to encourage family involvement seems like a reasonable . . . strategy. Most parents do have resources to share with their children, most parents care about their children, and most parents would be affected by the decision their child makes. Counselors can encourage teenagers to recognize this strong natural interest, without forcing the issue for those who are unwilling. (p. 120)

In addition to issues related to consent, the law varies with regard to the stage of the pregnancy during which an abortion can be performed. Many states limit legal abortions through the first trimester, and some permit the procedure during the early part of the second trimester. There are exceptions to these rules. For example, some abortions during the second and third trimester are permissible if it can be demonstrated that not performing the abortion would seriously damage the girl's health.

The fact that abortions tend to be restricted to the early stages of the pregnancy complicates matters for many adolescents. Data on the realization of pregnancy among expectant teenagers indicate that many miss a period or two without suspecting they are pregnant, and approximately one quarter do not know that they are pregnant until the second trimester (Miller, 1983). On learning of the pregnancy, they may have little time to consider abortion as an option. In these instances, swift but thorough and competent counseling is called for.

In spite of the fact that abortions conducted during early pregnancy have been legalized in the United States, illegal abortions still are performed by doctors and nonprofessionals who are willing to break the law. Desperate teenagers whose pregnancy has passed the legal time constraints sometimes conspire to arrange for illegal abortions, even performing abortions themselves. Expectant adolescents, both girls and their partners, should be warned of the grave dangers associated with abortions conducted by nonmedical personnel. For example, in New York City during the 1960s—when abortion was still illegal—half of the maternity-related deaths among Black and Puerto Rican women and a quarter of such deaths among White women were attributed to criminal abortion procedures (Dickman, 1981).

Public policy may be a contributing factor to the continued practice of illegal abortions in this country. Federal funding for health care does not support abortion services, except in cases of rape, incest, or life endangerment. According to Rubin (1988), the average price of an abortion in 1986 was about $1,000, a prohibitive amount for people with limited incomes. Although some states and some private clinics provide support for these services out of their own funds, many do not. Legal abortion might not be a viable option for many expectant teenage parents who are poor. For those who want to terminate a pregnancy but cannot afford the procedure, illegal abortion sometimes is the only alternative to bringing the pregnancy to full term. For this reason, it is particularly important to warn economically strapped youth about the dangers of illegal abortions.

Medical Risks of Abortion. Examining the potential medical complications associated with abortion is a crucial aspect to reviewing the abortion option. According to Baum (1980), abortion is a less risky event than is childbirth for teenage parents. However, the dangers vary according to the type of procedure that is called for at different stages of the pregnancy. Abortions are least risky, physically and psychologically, during the first trimester when menstrual extraction is performed (Baum, 1980; Group for the Advancement of Psychiatry, 1986). This method involves neither anesthetic nor dilation of the cervix. A plastic cannula is inserted into the uterus and a suction procedure takes place (Baum, 1980). Abortions conducted during the second trimester involve the pumping of saline into the womb, causing a miscarriage. The death rate associated with this procedure is higher than that related to menstrual extraction but lower than that occurring at childbirth (Baum, 1980). In addition, women who have later abortions experience higher rates of postabortion emotional complications (Group for the Advancement of Psychiatry, 1986). Abortions performed during the third trimester are the most risky (Baum, 1980).

Reasons Why Adolescents Abort or Keep Their Babies. Chilman (1988) conducted a review of studies examining the characteristics of young women who do not choose to terminate a pregnancy versus those who elect an abortion. Chilman concluded that the following factors were associated with decisions by adolescent women to carry the pregnancy to term: high religiosity (especially fundamental Protestant and non-Caucasian Catholic); low education of parents; low educational-occupational goals; low educational achievement; having dropped out of high school; mother opposed to abortion; peer group, including boyfriend, opposed to abortion; teenage friends and/or siblings who are parents; wanting to have a child; access to financial aid from family and/or the government; and traditional conservative attitudes, including "abortion is murder" and "a woman's place is in the home." In counseling young mothers who have these characteristics, helpers are cautioned that the client quickly may write off abortion as an option. Conversely, clients lacking in these features may be more likely to rush ahead with a decision to abort. In light of these possibilities, it may be particularly important to explore with these girls and their male partners how carefully they have considered the pros and cons of the option that is opposite to the one they tentatively have chosen. This does not imply that the counselor pushes the couple in any given direction. Rather, the counselor ensures that the expectant parents have been thorough in their decision making to minimize the chances that they will regret their final decision.

The Pros and Cons of Abortion Versus Giving Birth. The potential advantage of abortion is that the procedure is a single time-limited trauma. It avoids the increased sense of loss and guilt associated with giving an infant up for adoption after 9 months of anticipated attachment (Group for the Advancement of Psychiatry, 1986). It precludes the many burdens of premature parenthood (Group for the Advancement of Psychiatry, 1986) and might increase the life opportunities of young people (Hayes, 1987).

The potential disadvantages of abortion are noteworthy. For some, consent to an abortion might represent a moral transgression that induces guilt (Group for the Advancement of Psychiatry, 1986). For example, highly religious expectant parents and their families might view abortion as murder and a "sinful act" that will result in punishment in the afterlife. Those who legally obtain the abortion without parental consent or knowledge may have guilt at having not informed their parents. In addition, the young parents may grieve the loss of the unborn child as they forgo the opportunity to know a baby that they had conceived.

Again, there is no "right" or "wrong" answer when it comes to abortion. The counselor's role is to help the expectant parents to consider these pros and cons, clarify their values, and make a decision that is best for them. The more the clients "can understand their choices and take the responsibility for them, the more their sense of maturity will have been earned" (Group for the Advancement of Psychiatry, 1986, p. 63).

Obviously, the counselor will need to do follow-up with teenagers after they have made the decision. Those who choose to keep the child can be helped by the many suggestions contained throughout the rest of this book. For those who do decide to abort, some separate counseling considerations are warranted. Data from postabortion interviews with males (Robinson, 1988a; Shostak, 1979) and females (Bedger, 1980) indicate that they find the experience to be painful and difficult to forget. In addition, a study of adolescent mothers by Bedger (1980) indicated that participants who had an induced abortion or other fetal or infant loss were likely to plan the second pregnancy soon after the termination of the first. Based on this finding, Bedger recommended counseling to help young parents "work through" this loss so that they may understand and resolve this experience and postpone the next conception. The techniques and resources for grief counseling, which were mentioned earlier in this chapter, can help young parents avert a second pregnancy designed to fill the void that is often felt subsequent to an abortion. In addition, counselors also can ask the young man to read *After Her Abortion* (A. Baker, 1992), a pamphlet that provides the male partner with suggestions for how he can help the women to adjust after an abortion. This resource also is designed to address the male partner's feelings about the abortion.

Adoption Counseling

Although adoption once was the preferred method of resolving a teenage pregnancy, it is seldom used today. During the 1950s, approximately 80% of teenage mothers gave their children to be adopted (Baum, 1980). By 1976, it was estimated that 3% of teenage mothers used adoption as an option (Dickman, 1981). Data from the 1980s indicated that adoption remained an infrequently used alternative by young mothers (Hofferth, 1987b). The increasing prevalence of abortion services and the willingness of many mothers to keep their children because of the decreasing stigma of unmarried parenthood have been proposed to account for the declining use of adoption (Baum, 1980; Rubin, 1988).

Kiselica (1994) recommended that counselors be skilled at adoption counseling for four reasons, in spite of the fact that adoption is rarely used by young parents. First, the minority of expectant adolescent parents who *do* choose the adoption option need guidance from professionals who are knowledgeable about adoption procedures and issues. Second, in recent years the Office of Adolescent Pregnancy Programs has funded programs whose purpose is to increase the proportion of pregnant teens who opt for adoption over abortion or keeping their children (Hofferth, 1987b). These efforts may lead to a rise in the use of adoption services by teenage parents. Third, the decreased availability of "suitable" children placed through adoption agencies has prompted frustrated adoptive parents to seek nontraditional adoption services, such as independent adoptions (e.g., adoptions arranged by lawyers who serve as intermediaries between biological and adoptive parents) and illegal "black market" adoptions (e.g., kidnapped babies who are sold to nonbiological parents; DeWoody, 1993). Expectant young parents, who may be at risk for exploitation by unsavory characters working in the adoption business, need to be taught what are legitimate and illegal adoption operations. Fourth, the emerging practice of "open adoption," an arrangement by which the biological parents relinquish their legal child-rearing rights to the adoptive parents but retain opportunities for continuing contact with the child (Rompf, 1993), may make adoption a more appealing option for adolescent parents. However, teenage parents may be unaware of open adoption because it is a relatively new practice. Therefore, counselors should appraise expectant parents of this option during the pregnancy-resolution process (Kiselica, 1994).

Kiselica (1995) noted many of the potential advantages to adoption in general and open adoption in particular. Adoption may represent the best alternative for expectant parents who are morally opposed to abortion but lack the motivation and resources to care for a child (Hayes, 1987). Adoption might ensure a better quality of life for the child and the parents if the parents are uneducated and unemployed (Burgess, 1981). Open adoption reassures biological parents that they have provided a loving and secure home for their child, gives them an opportunity to know their child in the future, and does not cause them to feel excluded or rejected because of agency or legal stipulations (Baran, Pannor, & Sorosky, 1976). Studies examining reactions to open adoptions indicate that both biological and adoptive parents respond favorably to this form of adoption (see Gross, 1993). Children placed through open adoption report minimal feelings of rejection and a more complete picture of who they are because of their contact with their biological parents (Groth, Bonnardel, Devis, Martin, & Vousden, 1987).

Kiselica (1995) advised that all forms of adoption have potential disadvantages that should be considered during decision-making counseling with teenage parents. For example, placing the child with an agency for adoption is no guarantee that the child will be adopted. Generally, state laws require disclosure of information regarding the child's medical history and the biological family's medical history and social and educational background (DeWoody, 1993). Ross (1982) noted that adoptive parents typically want a healthy child. Sometimes, when the adoptive parents learn that the child was born to teenage parents, they become suspicious that the birth mother may have been a victim of poor prenatal care. Hence, many babies, particularly children of mixed races, are left with agencies and never adopted (Ross, 1982).

Other disadvantages to adoptions were reviewed by Kiselica (1995). With traditional adoptions, once the biological parents give their consent to the adoption, they are denied any further contact with the child. In these cases, the privacy of the adoptive parents is protected by the law (Schwartz, 1986). Consequently, the birth parents often experience a lifetime sense of loss along with a desire to search for their child so they can let their children know they still care and discover how they turned out (Baum, 1980; Schwartz, 1986). At the same time, the biological parents may worry that they will be rejected by the child should they attempt to make contact. In addition, they may fear complicating the child's life (Baum, 1980). Their children also may grow up with a sense of rejection that interferes with their personal development and their relationships with their adoptive parents (Bertocci & Schechter, 1991). Thus, traditional adoption might pose a variety of emotional hardships for some biological parents and adoptees.

Although open adoption appears to mitigate some of the difficulties associated with traditional adoption, open adoption can also pose problems. Open adoption stipulates some form of contact between adoptees and their birth parents, ranging from occasional exchanges of letters to periodic, formal, supervised visits or frequent, informal, and unsupervised visits (Argent, 1987). In spite of this contact, some birth parents still experience grief after each separation from their children and also have a desire for more frequent contact. In addition, birth parents sometimes have difficulties in arranging for contact with their children and feel awkward toward the adoptive parents (Gross, 1993).

The pros and cons of traditional and open adoptions should be carefully reviewed with young expectant parents to help them anticipate the potential consequences of choosing either option. As a stimulus to this process, Schwartz (1986) recommended that counselors ask their clients to imagine themselves as the child 10 or 20 years hence and ask what might be the child's response to the decisions being made in the present. "For example, would a continuing pattern of visits by the biological father to the child in the adoptive parents' home be a source of pleasure or provocative of a loyalty dilemma in the long run?" (Schwartz, 1986, p. 353). Similarly, the Group for the Advancement of Psychiatry (1986) advised that counselors should help young parents entertaining the adoption option to "evaluate what they want for their babies, what their babies will need, what they might and might not be able to provide for their babies were they to keep them, and what they want and need for themselves" (p. 63).

In addition to examining the pros and cons of adoption, exploring the motives of the parents involved in their decisions is recommended. For example, Schwartz (1986) hypothesized that biological fathers oppose adoption for a variety of reasons that have implications for their suitability as parents. Schwartz suggested that the expectant father who has genuine affection for the child may be a better candidate for keeping the baby than those fathers who oppose adoption simply because they see the child as their property, are angry at the child's mother, or are interested in extorting money from would-be adoptive parents.

Additional counseling considerations are warranted when the decision has been made to place the child for adoption. First, it is essential that the young mother obtain high-quality health care throughout the pregnancy and afterward (Rubin, 1988). Teenage fathers should be encouraged to support their partners in receiving this care and in following through with medical advice. Second, counselors need to safeguard young parents from potentially unsavory characters on the hunt to exploit desperate couples for financial gain. Planned Parenthood and the local office of the state department pertaining to child protective services usually can provide counselors with the names of credible adoption services. The state bar association and the legal aid society can refer counselors to trustworthy lawyers who arrange independent adoptions. Counselors can pass this information on to couples who are sure they want to use adoption services. Third, the biological parents should be appraised of what occurs during the adoption process so they know what to expect. For example, they need to understand that they will be required to provide background information about themselves and the baby. When traditional adoption is arranged, they should be prepared for the finality of their contact with the baby. When open adoption is used, they should be advised to clearly define the type and level of openness they desire in a written agreement that is signed by them and the adoptive parents to maximize their future satisfaction with the agreement (Etter, 1993). Finally, after arrangements have been completed and the birth parents say good-bye to their flesh and blood, whether through traditional or open adoption, they will need supportive grief counseling to mourn their sense of loss.

Traditional and Common-Law Marriages

A traditional assumption in American society is that "legitimate" pregnancies occur within the confines of marriage. Consequently, young couples historically have resolved unplanned out-of-wedlock pregnancies by marrying and "legitimatizing" the pregnancy. The expectant adolescent father who goes this route is viewed as settling the crisis through responsible male behavior. However, as Marsiglio (1987) noted, a father can express responsibility and commitment to his partner and child in other significant ways. For example, when a young couple lives together in a nonmarital union and shares child-rearing responsibilities, the consequences are similar to those related to marriage (Marsiglio, 1987). This latter arrangement sometimes is referred to as common-law marriage or cohabitation.

Traditional and common-law marriages/cohabitation appear to be frequent choices made by adolescent fathers and their partners when the decision has been made to bring the pregnancy to term. Analyzing nationally representative data from the National Longitudinal Survey of Work Experience of Youth, Marsiglio (1987) found that 50% of those teenage fathers responsible for a nonmaritally conceived first child (and therefore were assumed to be unplanned) lived with their child after the child's birth. Of these, 22% lived with one or both of their parents or in-laws. It is unclear from Marsiglio's report whether or not the mother also resided with the father when he lived with the child. However, because mothers typically have custody of their children (see Montemayor, 1986), and because absentee motherhood is rare compared to absentee fatherhood (see Greif & Pabst, 1988), it is likely that most teenage fathers who live with their children also live with the biological mothers. Based on these considerations, it is estimated that approximately half of those adolescent males responsible for an unplanned pregnancy initially live with their partner in either a traditional or common-law marital arrangement, and that a minority of these couples reside in the home of either the mother's or father's parents.

Factors Related to the Marriage Dilemma

The decision to marry or consider some other arrangement appears to be related to a number of factors that are considered by teenage parents, with economics being a primary consideration. Data from several studies suggest that teenage fathers lack the financial resources to support a family. For example, through their interviews with 20 teenage fathers, Elster and Panzarine (1983b) learned that all the young fathers worried that they were able to support a family financially. In his classic longitudinal study of unplanned adolescent parenthood, Furstenberg (1976) found that only 46% of the adolescent fathers for whom employment data were available were working full-time when the pregnancy occurred. More recent data, reported by Hardy and Zabin (1991), indicated that the majority of the 211 teenage fathers in their sample were unable to provide sufficient financial support to their partners. Among the subjects from these latter two studies, the limited earning power of the fathers appears to have been a major factor in the couple's decision not to marry. For example, Furstenberg (1976) found that most of the adolescent mothers in his study wanted to marry the father of the child *if* and *when* they thought he would be capable of supporting a family. The fact that couples who have the financial resources to support a family appear to prefer marriage as a form of pregnancy resolution is further evidence of the importance of economic factors in considering marriage (O'Connell & Moore, 1980).

Additional considerations, such as the maturity and educational goals of fathers, and the father's prior commitment to and feelings for the mother, also enter into decisions regarding marriage (Furstenberg, 1976). Pregnant teenagers with high educational aspirations and ability were least likely to marry, and those under strong family pressure to marry in order to avoid social embarrassment were generally more willing to wed (Furstenberg, 1976). Other findings suggest that young women who marry forgo much of the assistance they might have received from their parents (Furstenberg, 1976); if pregnant teenagers are made aware of this trade-off, some may decide to avoid marriage (Moore & Burt, 1982). Similarly, some expectant mothers may decline to marry because their welfare benefits might be reduced as a result of this decision. The increased social acceptability of unmarried motherhood and the legalization of abortion may also contribute to the decision not to marry (Moore & Burt, 1982). Finally, the decision may not be up to the couple if their parents choose to prevent the marriage (Moore & Burt, 1982).

The Quality of Adolescent Marriages

Unfortunately, the majority of adolescent marriages prompted by an unplanned pregnancy are highly unstable (Hayes, 1987). Furstenberg and his colleagues found high rates of divorce from his urban sample of adolescent parents. Eighty percent of his sample at the 17-year follow-up had been married, but two thirds of the first marriages had ended in divorce, half of the second marriages had dissolved, and the dissolution of cohabitational arrangements was even greater. The divorce rates were higher than those found in a comparable sample of women who had their first child after age 19 (Furstenberg et al., 1987). Nye and Lamberts (cited in Robinson, 1988a) found that the divorce rate is greater for school-age couples with premarital pregnancies than for those who conceive after marriage. Hardy and Zabin (1991) found that the relationships between the parents in their study tended to be unstable and deteriorated over an 18-month period, even when the couple was married or cohabitated. Nakashima and Camp (1984) and deLissovoy (1973) noted that adolescent marriages have greater discord than do adult marriages.

Why do so many of these relationships erode and crumble? Nakashima and Camp (1984) suggested that unrealistic expectations of the marital relationship may contribute to the demise of marriages among adolescent couples. In her review of the literature on adolescent parents, Chilman (1988) concluded that forced marriages to legitimate a pregnancy are particularly apt to end in divorce and are especially prone to be unhappy and characterized by low income. In addition, Chilman (1988) noted that many young parents may have a number of social, psychological, familial, and economic problems that predispose the couple toward distress, and that the responsibilities of parenthood can exacerbate these difficulties. Fulfilling these responsibilities might impede the educational progress of teenage parents, thereby worsening their economic prospects and further stressing the couple's relationship. For example, Furstenberg (1976) observed that adolescent mothers who left their families to reside with the father were less likely to fulfill their educational aspirations than those mothers who remained with their families. Marsiglio (1987) reported that living with the child (and presumably with the child's mother) is directly related to adverse educational consequences for the teenage father. Finally, welfare policies might undermine marriage for some young couples. As noted in Chapter 2, in certain circumstances, an employed father who decides to marry or live with his partner can hurt his family financially if the mother is receiving public assistance; according to welfare policies, his marriage to the mother or his presence in the home could result in the reduction or termination of AFDC and Medicaid benefits (Chilman, 1988). Consequently, some couples who decide to live apart for economic reasons report a withering away of the bond between them because they "can't live like a normal family."

A minority of adolescent marriages do succeed. Several characteristics of these marriages might explain their success. Furstenberg's (1976) data indicated that marriages among teenage parents are likely to survive when the couple had a long-standing and exclusive relationship prior to the pregnancy and married soon after conception. The most important factor related to marital stability, however, was the father's ability to support a family (Furstenberg, 1976). Some successful marriages may be related to the ability of either or both extended families to provide financial assistance to the young couple.

Marriage also can have positive benefits for the couple and the baby. Infants born to teenagers who are married at the time of birth have more favorable outcomes (e.g., less likely to have low birthweights, more likely to be breast-fed) than those of unmarried mothers (Hayes, 1987). The supportive involvement of the father can heighten the mother's sense of security after delivery (Earls & Siegel, 1980) and enhance the parenting efforts of the young mother (Furstenberg, 1976). Adolescent mothers who marry and remain married and live with their spouses typically achieve somewhat higher socioeconomic levels than women who separate and set up independent households or return to the homes of their relatives (Furstenberg & Crawford, 1989). Marriage may reduce stress and some of the role ambiguities associated with unwed adolescent fatherhood. For example, Fry and Trifiletti (1983) found in their study of 35 married and 60 unmarried adolescent fathers that fathers who married or planned to marry felt less stress, anxiety, guilt, and rejection and reported more confidence about their responsibilities to themselves and others than did unwed fathers.

In summary, the data show that although teenage marriages might provide some benefits to the young couple and the child, and that a minority of these unions are successful, most adolescent marriages are characterized by a variety of stressors that culminate in separation and divorce. Given these findings, how should the counselor advise the teenage father considering marriage?

Implications for Counseling

Again, the potential pros and cons of marriage should be discussed with the young man and his partner. The couple who are rushing toward a "shotgun" wedding especially will need to be appraised of the data that have been reviewed here. All couples should be encouraged to contemplate their compatibility and emotional commitment to each other, their economic resources, the potential for financial support from their families, theirs and their families' values regarding marriage, their educational plans, and how each of these factors can make marriage a positive reality or a hardship doomed for failure. Also, the legal implications of formal and common-law marriages need to be considered. For example, in many states, the legal ramifications of common-law marriages are similar if not identical to those associated with formal marriages. However, in some states, such as California, common-law marriages are not legally recognized (S. Brown, personal communication, November 1, 1993). It is recommended to involve the couple's parents in the decision-making process to the extent that is possible to be sure that the expectant parents have perceived their parents' views on the subject accurately. By carefully considering these variables, and by sensitively exploring the potential ramifications of marriage with the couple's family, those who eventually marry will be more likely to succeed, and others might avoid a marriage that was never meant to be.

Noncustodial Fatherhood

Because at least half of all teenage fathers do not live with their children, and because many who do live with their children are not legally married, the vast majority of adolescent fathers legally take a noncustodial role in their children's lives. As young fathers grope to resolve the pregnancy, they need to be aware of their legal rights and responsibilities associated with the option of noncustodial fatherhood. Males who choose noncustodial status may need to be encouraged and taught how to be helpful to their partners and their children. Finally, noncustodial fathers, particularly those who are forced against their wishes into a noncustodial role, need supportive counseling measures to help them cope with the situation. These considerations are woven into the following sections on establishing paternity, child support, and visitation.

Establishing Paternity

No uniform standards across the states deal with the establishment of paternity (Everett, 1985). In some states, paternity is determined when the father's name is listed on official birth records. According to Horowitz and Dodson (1984), paternity may be recognized by other means: (a) the natural father's formal acknowledgment of paternity, (b) conduct tending to show the father's voluntary acceptance of the child, or (c) a subsequent marriage of the parents.

Findings from research on the concerns of young fathers indicate that many of these youths want advice regarding their legal rights regarding paternity (Hendricks, 1988). Thus, counselors are challenged to assist young fathers to learn about the legal process of establishing paternity or refer them to a qualified consultant who can advise them on this matter. Once young fathers are appraised of this process, they need help evaluating the costs and benefits of legally establishing paternity. In brief, through legally recognized paternity the father is required to pay child support but also is ensured access to his child either through the awarding of custody or, more commonly, visitation privileges.

Generally, paternity is socially recognized and respected by mothers who sense that the father will be a supportive parent, even when no formal legal measures have been taken to establish paternity. However, paternal rights can become an issue for teenage fathers who have not married the mother or have taken other steps to formally establish paternity. For a variety of reasons, the mother may attempt to deny the paternity of the true biological father. For example, during periods of estrangement, a young mother might disavow the paternity of the biological father. This decision may or may not have anything to do with his performance as a parent. At times, the mother may use access to the child as a ploy to coerce the father to remain romantically involved with her. In these instances, fathers who are unaware of their legal rights may give in to the mother's wishes or abdicate the right to visit the child.

Fathers mired in this situation need supportive counseling, legal advice on how to formally establish paternity, and an appraisal of the financial and emotional costs involved. In an attempt to avert a legal battle, counselors should attempt to engage the mother in counseling so as to mediate the dispute and work toward an agreement that is in the best interests of the child. When this proves unsuccessful, the counselor should contact the mother's family to see if any headway can be made there. Legal avenues should be explored but with caution when these measures fail. If the father legally was an adult (i.e., at least 18 years old) and the girl was a minor at the point of conception, then the father may run the risk of facing statutory rape charges if the legal system is involved. Although the odds of this happening are rare, considering that many prosecutors are not inclined to charge statutory rape under certain circumstances (e.g., when the boy is 18 and the girl is 16 at the time of conception, and the girl voluntarily had consented to sexual intercourse), I have observed some girls and their parents use the threat of statutory rape charges as a measure to scare young fathers away. In these situations, it is useful to contact the local prosecutor's office to ask what would happen "hypothetically speaking" to a young man in this predicament. When it is clear that the father will face no rape charges, the youth can proceed onward. The legal aid society can advise the father on procedures for petitioning the court to recognize his paternity and set up visitation arrangements.

Fathers need to be aware that establishing paternity, even when free legal counsel is available, could amount to significant expenses. For example, blood and genetic testing might be necessary to establish paternity. In some states, once paternity is established, the father is usually expected to pay not only the fee for the blood tests and child support but also a "lying-in fee," which is the medical fee for the delivery of the child (Everett, 1985, p. 87). Because this is such a financial burden, some states refuse to collect lying-in fees when the father is under age until such time as he is capable of paying (Everett, 1985).

In other cases, the mother's denial of the father's paternity may represent an expression of her frustration with him for failing to support the child. As one teenage mother once complained to the author, "He doesn't give us a dime or ever visit his child. Why should I admit that he's the child's father when he don't act like one?" When it is true that a young man neglects his paternal responsibilities, counselors need to explore the motivations behind the father's behavior. Is he punishing the mother for some reason? Does he understand the self-defeating nature of his behavior and the potential damage to his child? Is he aware that he could face prosecution should the mother suddenly decide to acknowledge his paternity and solicit child support? Sensitively addressing these questions typically prompts the father to act in a more supportive manner.

Child Support

Statistical data provided by the U.S. Bureau of the Census (cited in Bovee, 1991) for child support payments in 1989 indicated that just over half of all fathers required to provide child support paid the full amount that was due. Data for 1981 (cited in Everett, 1985) revealed that 40% of single mothers did not have child support orders, and less than half of the 60% who actually received support got the full amount of support to which they were entitled. A substantial number of these women were teenage mothers whose children's paternity rights had not been established (Everett, 1985). Thus, it appears that many of the fathers involved in adolescent childbirth are unable or unwilling to provide child support payments. The percentage of these fathers who are teenagers is unknown due to difficulties in determining the age of the father (see Chapter 2). However, findings from studies that have been able to identify the father as an adolescent demonstrate that many teenage fathers are unable to furnish adequate financial support to their partners (Bolton, 1987; Furstenberg, 1976; Hardy & Zabin, 1991). These latter findings should be interpreted with caution, however, because they are based on the mothers' reports of payments received. As Braver et al. (1991) demonstrated, fathers' reports of compliance (i.e., the percentage of what they owned that they actually paid) is higher than mothers' reports. In addition, court records may underestimate monetary support provided by noncustodial fathers because those records do not include payments made directly to mothers, therefore bypassing the courts (Braver et al., 1991).

Many teenage fathers avoid using formal measures to financially support their families. For women who are dependent on AFDC, child support collections may result in either a reduction or the termination of Medicaid and cash benefits (Garfinkel, 1992). Some young parents collude to hide the paternity of the father from officials so that he can continue to contribute money to his family without jeopardizing their welfare and Medicaid benefits. Although this is illegal behavior, some parents feel they have no other recourse when it is virtually impossible to survive on either government assistance or the father's meager salary alone. Other young fathers may prefer informal measures of support because their employment opportunities are limited and erratic. They worry that they will be unable to abide by court-ordered support levels and strive to provide assistance when they can.

The fact that many fathers feel pressure to take these measures raises questions about the utility of government policies that had been designed to strengthen families. According to Marsiglio (1987), public policies have the effect of making adolescent fathers accountable for their actions through the enforcement of child support payments while discouraging them from taking central roles in family formation and functioning. Rather than promoting father involvement, welfare policies and the legal system tend to treat young fathers as "walking wallets" (Sander & Rosen, 1987, p. 107) who should provide child support even though their employment opportunities are limited and sporadic.

Policies that narrowly conceive father involvement as his willingness and ability to provide financial support fail to recognize that teenage fathers tend to support their partners in a number of ways, even if they are unable to do so financially. The father may live with his partner and provide child care for periods ranging from a few days to a few months (Stack, 1974; Sullivan, 1985). Two thirds of the young fathers studied by Klerman and Jekel (1973) and the vast majority of those interviewed by Achatz and MacAllum (1994) reported contributing informal support in the form of cash or necessary living items to both mother and child. Vaz et al. (1983) noted that approximately 76% of the teenage fathers in their sample helped the mother by giving her money and 85% helped her in other ways, such as providing transportation and gifts while she was pregnant. After the baby was born, these figures rose to 88% and 92%, respectively. Hendricks (1980) also found teenage fathers willing to provide emotional and financial support. It has been suggested that these many forms of support contribute positively to the well-being of the mother and the child (Furstenberg, 1976; Parke & Neville, 1987).

Given the economic limitations of adolescent fathers and the many nonfinancial ways that they can assist their families, new policies with a broader perspective on child support need to be developed. In addition, policies should address the economic problems of unemployment and underemployment that complicate the child support picture for teenage fathers. An example of a such innovative thinking at work is the On Track program, operated by the Child Support Enforcement Division of the Marion County Prosecutors Office in Indianapolis, Indiana. On Track provides young fathers with economic incentives to be involved with their partners and children. Levels of support are lowered for impoverished fathers who enroll in child care classes and take an active roll in their children's lives. The philosophy of this program is that father-child bonding is an important process that should be encouraged. In addition, the program recognizes that many young fathers need assistance finding gainful employment and, through referrals, provides them with employment counseling.

Although research findings confirm that most adolescent noncustodial fathers provide some form of financial and emotional assistance to their partners, in spite of flawed policies, other data indicate that this support decreases over time (Furstenberg, 1976; Lerman, 1985). Several explanations for this trend are offered. The pattern of support may be related to the degree of commitment that once characterized the relationship between the couple, in that divorced fathers were more likely than never-married fathers to continue child support payments (Lerman, 1985). Some fathers might intend to provide continued support but are unable to do so because of their own economic hardships (Braver et al., 1991; Sander & Rosen, 1987). Others may stop payments as part of an attempt to cut ties with the mother and child because of the emotional pain associated with noncustodial fatherhood (especially the visitation experience) or because they want to focus solely on a new family (see Loewen, 1988; Tedder & Scherman, 1987).

In light of these possible explanations for the decline in child support over time, counseling during the pregnancy-resolution phase should address the importance of the father-child relationship. Fatherhood involves a commitment to one's child for life, regardless of the financial and emotional costs involved. Young fathers need to understand this as well as the potentially positive effect of the father and child on each other's development (see

Chapter 6). In addition, teenage fathers may need assistance in coping with the often painful experience of visitation.

Visitation

Visitation by the noncustodial, adolescent father can have positive benefits for his child, his partner, and himself. Visitation can provide children with a sense of heritage, family identity, and emotional support (Everett, 1985). Involvement by the father is associated with enhanced self-control, self-esteem, sense of trust, and social competence among the children of adolescent parents (Furstenberg, 1976). Access to one's children on a regular basis appears to encourage the father's support. For example, in 1990, 80% of fathers with visitation rights but less than half of fathers without visitation rights or joint custody paid child support (Bovee, 1991). The young father's support of the family can bolster the confidence and competence of adolescent mothers in caring for their children (Unger & Wandersman, 1985). Teenage fathers who are included in decisions regarding their children tend to be more involved with their children and experience less stress and greater self-esteem than those who are excluded from such decisions (Redmond, 1985; Robinson, 1988a).

Unfortunately, adolescent fatherhood can become an experience that is solely biological and without apparent psychological significance for many noncustodial teenage fathers who are denied access to their children. The mother and her family may discourage or forbid his visiting with the child when there is hostility between the mother's family and the father (Belsky & Miller, 1986). In these instances, the father's role is devalued and important father-child bonding is lost. This treatment can prompt many fathers to discontinue child support (Everett, 1985). As one young father once angrily proclaimed to the author, "They tell me, 'Stay away but send money.' But I ain't sendin' nothin' if I can't see my baby boy!"

A multifaceted counseling approach is called for in these situations. Obviously, the young father will need supportive counseling and advocacy work on his behalf. The tactics for contacting the mother's family, described earlier in this chapter, might help the family to recognize and honor the father's paternal rights to visitation. However, it is more likely that the father will have to resort to legal interventions to protect his rights. Again, the Legal Aid Society can be of assistance to the majority of adolescent fathers who lack the financial resources to hire a lawyer. In addition, local divisions of organizations such as Fathers United for Equal Rights and Parents' and Children's Equality can advise noncustodial fathers about the procedures for petitioning the court to establish and enforce visitation agreements. In addition, these organizations often have support groups for noncustodial parents.

Once visitation has been arranged between hostile parties, fathers might confine their contact with their ex-partners to the mechanics of passing the kids back and forth so as to minimize further conflict (Anderson-Khleif, 1982). A detailed agreement also can deter discord. In his review of the literature on visitation agreements, Loewen (1988) concluded that several characteristics of visitation avoid strife and promote cooperation. Both parents should have access to school records, social security numbers, and other documents; be informed about school functions and health problems; and have a say about where their children attend school or church and what medical treatments they receive. The agreement also should spell out visitations that are frequent and routine (Loewen, 1988).

Whether or not there is a formal visitation agreement, the young father can take several steps to maximize the joys and minimize the emotional strains of visitation. He can regard himself as "having a family," even when his children are not staying with him; his children are "home" at his house, not "visitors" (Loewen, 1988). He can establish a homelike setting for his children by establishing some space in his home for them, even if it is merely a toy chest (Gatley & Koulack, 1979), and by keeping a permanent supply of their clothing, games, and other belongings (Keshet & Rosenthal, 1978). Family rituals and traditions, such as an annual fishing trip together, and the recording of special events through photographs and videotapes, can give the children a sense of continuity with their father (Newman, 1981). I have found it beneficial to encourage young fathers to talk with their children over meals so that they are "feeding" their children nutritionally and emotionally at the same time. Rather than spoiling his children during each visit, the father can balance fun-filled and costly outings with periods of resting, working, and just "hangin' out" together (Gatley & Koulack, 1979). Reassuring hugs (Newman, 1981) and quiet times for conversations (Loewen, 1988) can help to address the children's emotional needs during visits, especially if the father faces the tasks of introducing the children to the father's new girlfriend or integrating them into a blended family after the father has married or remarried.

Unmarried Custodial Fatherhood

Very few unmarried teenage fathers have custody of their children. Data on the living arrangements of teenage mothers (e.g., Bolton, 1987; Furstenberg, 1976; Hardy & Zabin, 1991), who typically have custody of their children, indicate that most live with their parents. Nevertheless, Marsiglio's (1987) findings revealed that a minority of teenage fathers reside with their children in their parent's home. Other research by Stack (1974) and Sullivan (1985) showed that the families of both the mother and the father might share in the care of the child, thereby establishing "folk" or socially recognized forms of joint custody among unmarried couples. Through these arrangements, fathers may be "given" custody of the child during periods of hardship for the mother and her family. Thus, although the degree of responsibility for child rearing may vary for the young father over time, this sort of informal arrangement requires him to be prepared to take on a custodial role from time to time. Some judges are inclined to view the father who behaves in this manner as a custodial parent should the custody of the child become a legal issue.

Fathers considering the possibility of unmarried custodial fatherhood need to assess his and his family's capacity to financially support and care for the child. If these combined resources are inadequate to the needs of raising a child, then the father may need to use some of the previously discussed options for resolving the pregnancy.

In addition to exploring the potential support of his family, the teenage boy who is considering unmarried custodial fatherhood can benefit from learning about the coping mechanisms and hardships of adult men who are lone fathers. For example, O'Brien (1987) studied the patterns of kinship and friendship among 56 lone fathers. Although many of these fathers relied heavily on their families for support, many others were disengaged from their families. Fathers from both groups coped with the challenges of single fatherhood by developing significant platonic relationships with women (both single and married) who had children. The supportive friendship of these women helped to mitigate the limitations that parental responsibilities placed on the social lives of the men. Based on these findings, it is suggested that the young father be forewarned that single fatherhood may bring hardships socially for the teenager, but that family and peer support can help allay his loneliness.

Family members and friends can play significant roles during and after the pregnancy-resolution crisis of adolescent fathers. Therefore, family and peer relationship issues are addressed in the next chapter.

5

Addressing Issues With
the Extended Family and Peers

For the teenage father, the developmental transition to parenthood occurs within the context of two existing families: his and his partner's family of origin. After the pregnancy is revealed, both families are faced with a crisis that requires decision making to resolve the pregnancy. If a decision is made to deliver and keep the baby, new adolescent-parent conflicts can emerge and old ones may resurface as the young father copes with parenthood. The roles and responsibilities of the expectant parents, their parents, and their siblings and the composition of one or both households may change. The economic resources of both families are likely to be strained and redistributed. The precious baby will be a source of pride and joy, as well as frustration and worry, and possibly resentment and shame for some or all of the members of both families.

The families of adolescent parents can benefit from supportive counseling designed to assist them in addressing these issues. The purpose of this chapter is to provide practitioners with suggestions for engaging, understanding, affirming, and empowering the families of adolescent parents in counseling. A discussion of the impact of each family of origin on the teenage father's entry into and progress toward parenthood is provided. Strategies for helping both families to achieve a lasting, cooperative relationship that best serves the needs of the new child are described. Because the young father's attitude toward sex and paternity and his response to the demands of fatherhood are influenced by his friends, this chapter also includes recommendations for addressing the peer issues of teenage fathers.

The Extended Families:
Considerable Resources Untapped by Counselors

A wealth of data suggests that the parents of adolescent parents are, in the majority of cases, a vital source of support to their children's efforts to cope with unplanned parenthood. The parents of the young mother typically help the daughter adjust to her new parenting role and responsibilities in the following ways: sharing their input in the pregnancy-resolution process; providing financial support and a residence for the mother and child, and sometimes the father, typically in her parents' home; offering assistance with child care while the adolescent mother works or completes school; and serving as a means of emotional support to the young mother during this challenging period of her life (Furstenberg, 1976, 1979, 1981; Furstenberg & Crawford, 1989; Lindsay, 1990; Sullivan, 1985; Williams, 1991). Likewise, the parents of the teenage father have been known to be useful sources of support by entering into negotiations with the mother's family regarding the outcome of the pregnancy and the care of the child; supporting the father's acceptance of paternal responsibilities; providing him and, at times, his child and partner a place to live and financial assistance; working full- or part-time as the child care provider for the baby; and assisting the boy with his problem solving (Allen-Meares, 1984; Robinson, 1988a; Sullivan, 1985). Teenagers receiving these various forms of support are more likely to complete school, enter the labor force, and secure employment and economic independence than those young parents who do not receive assistance from their families (Furstenberg & Crawford, 1989; Sullivan, 1985).

   In their efforts to help teenage parents, families typically experience many hardships. The news of the pregnancy is one of shock for the adolescents' parents. Obtaining medical care for the mother and child and providing food and clothing for the baby represent new expenses that the families must meet. Personal space must be reallocated in the home to make room for the child. As the child grows older and more difficult to manage, child care arrangements may break down, authority and boundary issues among multiple caretakers can cause conflict, and the young parents may increasingly resent their dependency on their families (Furstenberg, 1979; Lindsay, 1990; Sullivan, 1985).

The extended families also can hinder the development of the young parents in a variety of ways. The parents of the adolescents may intentionally or inadvertently foster risk-taking sexual behavior by their children (Ooms, 1984; Sullivan, 1985). By having been teenage parents themselves, many parents and siblings of adolescent parents may communicate an implicit message that unwed adolescent parenthood is acceptable (Hendricks, 1983; Rivara et al., 1985; Sander, 1991; Sullivan, 1985; Williams, 1991). In highly dysfunctional families, socially isolated adolescents must attempt a transition to parenthood while dealing with parents who are substance abusers, antisocial, or suffering from some other form of mental illness (Ooms, 1984).

Other behaviors by family members can cause considerable emotional harm to adolescent fathers. The parents of the teenage mother may express their hostility to the young father by denying him access to his child (Achatz & MacAllum, 1994; Allen-Meares, 1984; Furstenberg, 1979; Robinson, 1988a), and they may threaten the mother with expulsion from their home unless she joins them in rejecting the father (Furstenberg, 1979). Thus, some maternal family members may force the mother to chose between the father or her family of origin, thereby coercing her into ignoring the father's rights to paternity and visitation (Furstenberg, 1979).

Together, these findings suggest that the families of teenage parents can be sources of support or liability for the young parents and that these families, themselves, may have a variety of service needs. Yet results from studies by Forbush (1981) and Kiselica and Sturmer (1993b) indicated that agencies rarely involve the parents of adolescent mothers and fathers in service programs for pregnant and parenting teens. Allen-Meares (1984) argued that the parents of the adolescent father particularly are apt to be overlooked by professional helpers. In light of such findings, Ooms (1979, 1981, 1984) has repeatedly criticized service providers for treating adolescent parenthood as an individual phenomenon devoid of a family context. Considering the significant influence of the extended family on the response of teenagers to an unplanned pregnancy, several writers (e.g., Allen-Meares, 1984; Forbush, 1979, 1981; Furstenberg & Crawford, 1989; Hendricks, 1992; Kiselica et al., 1992; Ooms, 1981, 1984; Robinson, 1988a) have recommended that involving families may be more effective and efficient than individual approaches to helping pregnant adolescents and teenage parents.

Addressing Issues
With Family Members

In response to these recommendations, a five-stage approach to counseling that involves both sets of parents of adolescent parents is suggested and described: (a) establishing rapport and facilitating cooperation between the two families, (b) negotiating a plan of action, (c) managing ongoing problems, (d) preparing the young parents for adulthood, and (e) addressing prior unresolved family issues.

Stage 1: Establishing Rapport and
Facilitating Rapport Between the Two Families

A key to establishing rapport is for the clinical coordinator or counseling administrator to assign both families their own counselor, rather than assigning both families to the same counselor. This practice avoids a conflict of interest for the counselors involved. It also conveys to the families that their respective counselors will advocate for their particular concerns.

Once a counselor has been assigned to a family case involving an unplanned adolescent pregnancy, it is critical that the counselor understand the emotional ramifications of the crisis for the adolescent's parents. A virtually universal reaction of the parents of teenage parents, on learning of the pregnancy, is shock, accompanied by a variety of emotional responses. Through her work with hundreds of teenage parents, Allen-Meares (1984) observed that many maternal grandparents express to the daughter their outrage for the father by exclaiming, "Look what he has done to you and your life!" and "I never want you to see him again!" (pp. 32-33). The paternal grandparents may view the mother as "promiscuous" or "easy" (Allen-Meares, 1984) and resent the girl for having "ruined our son's future!"

Although such sentiments unfortunately can prolong the initial crisis and delay the necessary decision making associated with adolescent pregnancy, they tend to dissipate after the parents recover from the initial surprise (Allen-Meares, 1984). However, in some cases the resentment can continue and the maternal grandparents may force their daughter to sever contact with the father (Allen-Meares, 1984; Furstenberg, 1979; Robinson, 1988a) and the paternal grandparents may pressure their son to deny being the father (Allen-Meares, 1984). Moreover, unplanned adolescent parenthood implies an early onset of grandparenthood at a time when the parents may be unwilling to accept this new role (Parke & Neville, 1987).

Frequently, the maternal and paternal grandparents experience dismay, anger, and resentment about the pregnancy and anxiety about their children and grandchildren's future. These feelings must be validated before these family members can be expected to contribute constructively to a plan of action.

During initial contacts with either set of grandparents, counselors are advised to meet with each family separately. During these early sessions, it is therapeutic to listen and allow the adults to ventilate, all the while affirming their concerns. After the grandparents have discharged many of their negative emotions, they can be steered toward a consideration of their hopes and dreams for their grandchild. Usually, this tactic will prepare most grandparents to enter negotiations about how to resolve the pregnancy and care for the baby. With some families, it also may be necessary to listen carefully to and attempt to address what the grandparents identify as their needs unrelated to this particular crisis. For example, one maternal grandfather had glaucoma that had caused his vision to deteriorate in recent months. Referring him to a free eye clinic at a nearly medical school solidified his and his family's trust in the counselor. Hendricks (1992) stated that measures such as these are necessary because families need to know "What's in it for us?" should they agree to participate in counseling.

Another way to establish rapport with the family is to work as an advocate for their child. Parents who perceive the counselor to be someone who has gone the extra mile for the teenage parent will be viewed as a person whom the family can trust with their concerns and needs.

Eventually, the counselors working with both families will have to coordinate their strategies and encourage the two families to enter into negotiations about how to resolve the pregnancy if the families have not yet done so on their own. It is important that the counselors be up front about this objective from the onset of counseling. Clinical experience suggests that when this agenda is hidden from the family initially, they sometimes feel deceived and manipulated by the counselor when the idea finally is disclosed. This was especially true with one pair of maternal grandparents, who responded to their counselor by saying, "We thought you were here to help us but this whole time all you really wanted was to get us to help *him* [the teenage father] and *his* family."

Although it is preferable to meet with the entire family of the teenage father prior to negotiations with his partner's family, research findings (e.g., Furstenberg, 1976; Hendricks, 1988) indicate that teenage parents are more likely to turn to their mothers for assistance than any other family member. Therefore, contacting the maternal or paternal grandmother may be the most fruitful strategy for starting a dialogue between the two families.

In some cases the grandparents may need persuasive information to get them involved in working toward a solution with the other family, such as gently warning them that sooner or later they will have to deal with the other family, so it is better to try to establish a working relationship with them now with the help of an experienced "family negotiator." In addition, based on research findings by Redmond (1985), it is beneficial to inform the maternal grandparents that the father is likely to be more supportive if he and his family are involved in decision making regarding the baby. It also is helpful to describe to the paternal grandparents research findings by Sullivan (1985), which indicated that the rights of the father and his family were likely to be recognized by the mother and her family if the paternal family offered their support. Sharing these two forms of information can help both sides feel encouraged about what they can hope to gain through negotiations.

As a final strategy to devise a cooperative venture between the two families, before they actually meet it is advisable to ask both sets of grandparents and the two young parents to withhold any blaming messages during their meetings together. The families are asked instead to promise to arrive for the meeting prepared to suggest how each party involved is ready to help the young couple and their child. With this *win-win* attitude in place, the two families amicably can work toward an arrangement that is in the best interests of the child. To facilitate such arrangements, Ooms (1984) recommended that counselors conduct an intake interview with the adolescent and his or her parents, grandparents, and siblings to assess the family's ability to offer assistance. Specifically, the interviewer should gather information regarding their ability to provide shelter, economic assistance, and infant care; to what extent other family members can share in the care of the baby; and whether the sharing of responsibilities creates much stress and conflict or is relatively harmonious.

Stage 2: Negotiating a Plan of Action

To help families adjust to adolescent parenthood, Lindsay (1990) suggested that they develop formal written contracts that spell out the roles and responsibilities related to the care of the child. Sullivan (1985) learned that informal agreements with a similar purpose often are worked out between the maternal and paternal families. Such arrangements help to distribute the financial and child care obligations across the two families so that no one family is overwhelmed. In addition, formal and informal contracts define the role boundaries between the two families so as to minimize confusion. In effect, they provide the family with a plan of action for how to manage the crisis of unplanned adolescent parenthood.

The specifics of an interfamily contract will vary from situation to situation, depending on such factors as when the contract is established (e.g., pre- or postnatally) and the quality of the relationship between the young couple and between their respective families. When the arrangement is decided during the prenatal stage, and abortion or adoption is the agreed-on course of action, then the contract should detail who will finance the medical care associated with either option. In addition, both families should be coached as to how they can emotionally support the young parents during the potentially stressful aftermath of abortion or adoption. In those instances in which the couple marries and sets up an independent household, the contract can outline how the maternal and paternal families plan on supporting the young couple and what, if anything, the couple owes their families in return. Through other arrangements, both teenage parents and the baby will live with one set of grandparents, or one parent and the child will live with one set of grandparents. For these latter types of arrangements, Lindsay (1990) recommended a formal written contract, signed by all interested parties, that addresses the following questions: Who will do the housecleaning, laundry, preparation of meals, and cleanup of bottles and dishes associated with child care? Who will take care of the baby on which days? Who is in charge of disciplining the baby? How will each family contribute to the medical bills and financial costs associated with child care? On what nights of the week will the teenage parents be permitted to go out for social activities and what curfews will they need to follow? What are the procedures of changing the contract?

Stage 3: Managing Ongoing Problems

Although contracts, whether written or unwritten, can help to prevent some intra- and interfamily conflict, tensions are inevitable. The resources and needs within and between families can change over time (Furstenberg, 1979; Lindsay, 1990). The adolescent parents may resent their continued dependence on their own parents (Scherman, Korkames-Rowe, & Howard, 1990) and rebel against prior agreements. The grandparents may lose patience with the adolescent parents and "take over" in areas that previously had been the domain of the young parents (Lindsay, 1990). A breakdown in the father's ability to financially support the child can strain relations between his and his partner's family (Sullivan, 1985).

Thus, counselors are challenged to help young fathers and their families to manage ongoing difficulties. Several common problems and strategies for managing them are described. These ideas were gleaned from my clinical experience counseling adolescent parents and their families and from Lindsay (1990).

The Father Cannot Keep His End of a Financial Agreement to Support the Child. The teenage father tends to have consistent difficulties in financially supporting his child (Achatz & MacAllum, 1994; Bolton, 1987; Furstenberg, 1976; Hardy & Zabin, 1991; Sander & Rosen, 1987). Not only does he worry about a lack of money (Elster & Hendricks, 1986; Elster & Panzarine, 1983b; Hendricks, 1988; Hendricks et al., 1981), but his limited financial resources can jeopardize the willingness of the mother's family to respect his paternity and allow him access to his child (Sullivan, 1985). Thus, if this problem is not addressed quickly, the father could be shut out by his partner's family.

To address this problem, counselors can provide the young father with career and educational counseling (see Chapter 7). In addition, it may be necessary to encourage the youth to express other means of support to his partner and her family. For example, during periods of unemployment he can assist with child care and with transporting the mother to and from school, work, or a doctor's appointment. He can offer to help his partner's parents with their duties, such as running to the store for them or assisting with household chores. He can listen nondefensively to concerns his partner's parents have about their burdens. Through these gestures, he can communicate to the family his dedication as a father, express his concern for the family's needs, and increase the chances that his paternity will be respected.

The Teenage Father Is Unsure of How to Comfort His Partner. Coping with a pregnancy, delivering a baby, and caring for a child can be stressful for any woman even under the best of circumstances. In response to this stress, the young mother may explode at her partner and he may be at a loss for how to deal with her. His inability to respond could lead to a permanent break-up and potential problems in terms of his access to the baby.

Many males have difficulty communicating and comforting a distressed female. As an expression of this difficulty, some teenage fathers complain in exasperation, "I don't know what to do or say when she gets upset!" These youths need to be taught that the young mother wants an understanding ear from her partner to hear and empathize with her worries and frustrations, and simply sitting quietly and listening carefully to the mother's concerns can provide her with tremendous comfort. If a teenage father cannot find the precise words to console his partner at any given moment, he can address her emotions through sensitive actions that communicate his support for her. For example, if she is crying, he might take her in his arms and hold her, gently stroke her hair or her back or arm, and offer her a tissue. If she or the baby has a doctor's appointment, he can accompany her to the doctor's office. If the baby is sick, he can go to the pharmacy to fill a prescription. If the mother is out of diapers or formula he can pick up these items for her at the grocery. If the mother feels overwhelmed by a fussy baby, he can offer to take the baby for a while. By making these efforts, he will not only reassure his partner of his concern for her, but he may further earn the admiration of the mother's family.

One or Both Sets of Grandparents Dictate How the Young Father Should Parent. Grandparents often support the child-rearing efforts of teenage parents by directly teaching them how to care for a child (Furstenberg & Crawford, 1989). In some instances this tutelage can be reassuring to young parents unsure of their parenting skills. In other situations, however, adolescent parents longing for independence may resent the grandparents' guidance on child care matters. For example, adolescent parents interviewed in studies by Barth, Schinke, Liebert, and Maxwell (cited in Montemayor, 1986) and Lindsay (1990) reported that they found the unsolicited advice of parents and relatives to be more stressful than helpful.

To alleviate these tensions, it is recommended that counselors educate the grandparents about the developmental desire of teenagers to feel autonomous from their parents. This information may help the grandparents feel less defensive if the adolescents are offended by advice. It also is helpful to encourage the grandparents to "suggest" rather than "order" or "dictate" how the adolescent should parent. Finally, the counselor can employ cognitive restructuring with the teenager to help him or her interpret the grandparents' behavior as well-intentioned rather than intrusive and offensive. Cognitive restructuring is a cognitive-behavioral, coping-skills training procedure that teaches clients to replace maladaptive thoughts with adaptive ones. For a thorough description of this technique and some of the clinical issues associated with its use, see Meichenbaum (1977), Cormier and Cormier (1991), and Kiselica and Baker (1992).

A Family Member Feels Overwhelmed by Child Care Responsibilities. Raising the child of teenage parents typically requires a juggling act for at least one or more people. Even though an initial contract may identify several people from both families as part-time child care providers, over time one individual may "inherit" the bulk of the burden in caring for the child. This can be overwhelming if the family member also is employed outside of the home or attending school, particularly when the infant is sick, fussy, or getting into everything through exploration during the toddler stage.

To reduce the pressure on the overtaxed person, the counselor can mediate family meetings designed to reassign responsibilities so that there is a greater sharing of the work load. For extremely stressed families, the extended families may be available to rally to the rescue. For example, aunts and uncles, the great-grandparents, and other family members might have time in their schedules to give the two immediate families a break from the sometimes wearisome responsibility of raising the child. If no support is available through the extended family, then the counselor might explore community child care services or other resources (e.g., volunteer baby-sitters from the church) that can be of assistance to the family.

Someone Feels Left Out. The redistribution of time and energy prompted by the addition of a new child can leave some family members feeling that their needs are being neglected. For example, siblings might be envious of the attention devoted to the teenage parent or the grandfather may not feel bonded to the child.

In these instances, it helps to affirm everyone's importance in the family. This can be accomplished by assigning each family member some special role in the care of the child. For example, the grandfather may have the pleasure of bathing the baby each morning. A sibling could read the baby a story every night after dinner. In addition, each family member can reserve particular nights of the week as a special time to address his or her unique needs. For instance, the adolescent parent may choose Friday night as his or her night out with friends, whereas the grandparents might reserve Saturdays as their time together and Sunday church and brunch as celebrations that the entire family can share.

The Teenage Parent Is Becoming Sloppy Around the House. Most parents complain that keeping a tidy room is a low priority for a teenager. This is particularly true among some teenage fathers. As they attempt to adjust to their new responsibilities as parents, their room can look like it has been hit by a hurricane. Also, the presence of a toddler can add to the messiness in the home. This can annoy the grandparents and lead to many arguments.

Reframing the sloppiness of the teenager can help to dissipate the anger of some grandparents. For example, disorder could be a sign that the teenager is attending to other important duties, such as comforting the baby, assisting the child's mother, working to earn money, and/or completing schoolwork. Sometimes, this reinterpretation of the adolescent's behavior can help the grandparents to be more accepting of an unkempt room. Disarray also could be a sign that the teenager is overwhelmed, too tired to clean, and in need of assistance with his responsibilities. Again, the ability of other immediate and extended family members to step in and lend a hand should be explored. Finally, the teenager may be using his status as a young parent as an excuse to not even try to keep a tidy abode. In these instances, the counselor may have to support the grandparents' confrontation of irresponsible behavior and devise a behavior modification program to alter the boy's behavior. For example, the grandparents can establish a system of rewards earned only for orderliness. For additional ideas of behavior modification, see Craighead, Kazdin, and Mahoney (1981) and Lanyon and Lanyon (1978).

There Is a Lack of Family Support. Ooms (1984) noted that there are times when a teenage parent is estranged from his or her family. The adolescent may be fleeing from a home with serious abuse, alcoholism, or mental illness. For example, Sullivan (1985) described a dysfunctional family experienced by a teenage father, named Lucky, and his partner:

> Lucky's wife was living with her mother. . . . Her mother drank and beat her sometimes, which was part of the reason she and Lucky got married. Lucky's wife and her child were enrolled for public assistance at the time. His wife's mother, angry at the prospect of losing that welfare budget in her own household, reported their marriage to the welfare office. Lucky then had to enroll on their welfare budget. They found their own apartment, also in some rundown tenements near the projects where they had both grown up. (p. 65)

Teenagers facing parenthood under such stressful and socially isolated conditions are unlikely to complete school and achieve economic stability (Furstenberg & Crawford, 1989) and are at risk to develop inadequate parenting skills (Lamb & Elster, 1986) and maltreat their children (Bolton & Belsky, 1986). To assist these youth, Ooms (1984) recommended assessing whether extended family or other adult friends in the community can serve as a possible resource to the young couple. For example, some communities have developed Mentor Mother and Mentor Father programs and Foster Grandparent services that link isolated teenage parents with caring adults who provide guidance and support during the parenting experience. Some alienated youth may need more comprehensive assistance that can be provided through foster care or group home placements (Ooms, 1979).

Stage 4: Preparing the Young Parents for Adulthood

All adolescent fathers face common challenges involved in the developmental transition to adulthood. For example, eventually all teenage fathers and their partners need to know how to adequately parent a child, how to earn a living and manage a budget, and how to set up and maintain a household. Counselors can encourage family members to impart their wisdom in these areas to the adolescent parents. If the young parents are involved in service programs providing instruction in these areas, the counselor can recruit the grandparents, when they are able, to review these topics with the adolescents to reinforce the skills that have been taught.

A common barrier to the young father's ability to develop competency as an adult and parent is the difficulty that some maternal or paternal grandparents have in "letting go" of the child after they have assisted with child care and the teenager is ready to set up his or her own household. This problem is understandable, considering the special place that the baby might take in the grandparents' lives. Furstenberg (1976) and Sullivan (1985) reported that the families of the teenage parents they studied almost universally considered the baby to be a source of pride and joy, in spite of the families many negative reactions to the unplanned pregnancy. Furstenberg (1976) found that the baby helped to pull the family closer together in some of the families he studied, and Lindsay (1990) reported that the baby filled a void that existed in a few of the families she interviewed. Given the many needs that a child can fulfill in a family, it is understandable that there may be some resistance to letting the young parents move on with their lives. The grandparents may discourage the adolescents from establishing their own abode and taking a more central role in the rearing the child.

These sorts of reactions can be forestalled by predicting their possible future occurrence. Counselors can help the grandparents and siblings to prepare for the eventual departure of the young parent and child by having them agree to establish traditions between the baby and the extended family. For example, one afternoon per week the siblings or grandparents might share a special treat, such as ice cream, with the child. The adolescent parents can promise to allow these traditions to continue after a separate household is established. As a result, the family members will be assured of continuity in the bond experienced between them and the child.

Several scholars (Allen-Meares, 1984; Ooms, 1984; Robinson, 1988a; Sullivan, 1985) have argued that another important issue for families in preparing teenage parents for adulthood is the potential role of the grandparents in preventing a second unplanned pregnancy. Secondary prevention is considered necessary because research suggests that a repeat pregnancy can further complicate the young parent's transition to adulthood. For example, Furstenberg's (1976) findings indicated that the unexpected birth of a second child strained the resources of the adolescent mother's family such that she was forced to prematurely set up her own independent household. Typically, this move reduced her chances to complete school, work, and achieve economic self-sufficiency. Family involvement in secondary prevention has been recommended because of the impact parents have on the sexual activity of their children and the mediating influence they also have on their children's response to sex education. Ooms (1984) reviewed research that indicated that there is little direct communication about sex between children and parents and that parents tend to provide unclear messages and guidance regarding the teenager's sexual activity. Such influences can undermine the sexual education provided in schools. In comparison, when parents *do* communicate openly and honestly with their children about sex, regardless of the content of the discussion, this communication seems to delay the start of sexual activity (Ooms, 1984). Sullivan (1985) reported similar findings in his research regarding the sexual knowledge and behaviors of 11 teenage fathers.

On the basis of such findings, these scholars (Allen-Meares, 1984; Ooms, 1984; Robinson, 1988a; Sullivan, 1985) have suggested that the grandparents can play a key role in preventing repeat pregnancies by participating in family-life education. In brief, family-life education involves teaching students about dating, human sexuality, contraceptives, family life, and human communications and feelings. According to Brindis (1991), family-life education is designed to deter unplanned pregnancies while providing trainees with a variety of skills to develop a strong family life. Robinson (1988a) recommended that practitioners conduct groups composed of parents and their teenagers to establish honest, straightforward communication about sexuality and contraception. According to Allen-Meares (1984), these cross-generational exchanges might help the parents to better understand adolescent sexuality, and Ooms (1984) hypothesized that the inclusion of the grandparents in the training might enhance its effectiveness in preventing unplanned pregnancies among the targeted adolescents.

Stage 5: Addressing Prior Unresolved Family Issues

Teenage fathers hail from a variety of families who represent a continuum of adaptiveness and mental health. The purpose of this section is to briefly detail how to work with those families whose relations have been characterized by significant, ongoing dysfunction. Addressing maladaptive conflicts within these unfortunate families is important because, if left unresolved, they might negatively influence the adolescent father's response to the pregnancy and fatherhood.

Wounds in the Father-Son Relationship. According to Green (1976), a boy has a natural inclination to identify with his father, that is, to appreciate his existence, to want to be like him, to be willing to learn from him, and to be wanted and accepted by him in return. Thus, the manner in which a father relates to his son can have a profound impact on his son's adjustment and his son's performance as a father (Green, 1976).

A boy can be helped by the presence of an involved father. A warm and loving father, Green argued, encourages his son to continue in the father's path, to be like him. The teenage father who has been blessed with a father who lives and talks with him, takes an interest in him, expresses affection to him, helps him with decision making, and sets limits on his behavior is likely to receive continued support from his father and emulate his father's nurturant ways. Typically, the young man who has been raised by such a positive force in his life has little unfinished business with his own father as the youth, himself, tackles the challenges of parenthood for the first time.

Sadly, a boy can be hindered by the absence of a father or by the influence of an ineffectual one. In their review of the literature on the effects of fathers on their son's development, Horie and Horie (1988) concluded that inadequate fathering is associated with low intellectual achievement, poor self-control, and sexual confusion in sons. Klinman (cited in Stengel, 1985) suggested that poor fathering skills can be passed from father to son and from generation to generation in families. Green (1976) hypothesized that the boy who lacks a father or a significant adult male role model in his life is likely to suffer from an inability to know his place in the world. In an effort to define his "maleness," he may imitate the behavior of other males, including other boys from the streets who may communicate a message that he must become aggressive, violent, and sexually exploit women to be considered masculine.

Although systematic data evaluating the quality of the relationship between teenage fathers and their own fathers are not available, considerable evidence suggests that many teenage fathers were raised in father-absent homes and that this absence had a detrimental impact on these boys. Debra Klinman, the project director for the Bank Street Collaboration study of approximately 400 teenage fathers nationwide, reported to Stengel (1985) that teenage fathers involved in the study tended to have phantom fathers, although no precise figures were given. In an investigation by Hendricks (1981), 35% of 20 unwed adolescent fathers reported living in father-absent homes. In a later study by Hendricks (1988), 40% of 40 teenage fathers were raised in father-absent homes and about 70% of this sample reported that they felt closer to their mothers than to their fathers when they were growing up. Hardy and Zabin (1991) reported that the majority of the 72 teenage fathers from their study who were not living with the mother and child resided in single-mother households. Sullivan (1985) discovered that only 2 of the 11 adolescent fathers from his study had grown up in households with father figures present, none had lived with their fathers for any extended period of time, two had been completely abandoned by their fathers, and one boy's father had murdered the boy's mother. Ballard (1993), a community worker in Cleveland who has focused on helping teenage fathers, feels that the kids he works with are profoundly affected by the absence of their fathers. They feel angry, hurt, and unimportant due to what they perceive to be parental unconcern and disinterest. Similarly, I reported that the young fathers I had served in a number of clinical settings, including psychiatric hospitals, mental health centers, and prisons, mourned the absence of a caring father in their lives (Kiselica, 1993).

Because the samples of teenage fathers used in the above studies are not necessarily representative of all teenage fathers, the reader is cautioned not to make any unwarranted generalizations about the quality of the father-son relationships experienced by this population. Nevertheless, the reader is encouraged to consider the potential impact of father-son wounds on the adjustment of adolescent males facing an unplanned pregnancy. Data reported by Panzarine and Elster (1983) demonstrate that the prospect of becoming a father can cause the adolescent to reflect on how he was raised and evaluate his parents' parenting abilities. For the boy who lacked a positive father figure in his life, these recollections can stir unresolved issues and ambivalent feelings about his own father's treatment of him while he was growing up. For example, consider Sullivan's (1985) description of the following teenage father's thoughts about his own father:

> Stan's son was born when he was 19. . . . He had had some part-time work, but most of his employment while he was in school was in his father's "numbers store" where he took illegal bets and also sold some marijuana. Stan's father had abandoned his mother and children some years before and Stan still resented it, admitting that his father probably gave him work to make up for having abandoned them but insisting that he treated his father like "the boss" rather than like his father. (p. 67)

Clinical experience suggests that young fathers who were abandoned by their own fathers experience significant emotional pain and have difficulty demonstrating responsible paternal behaviors. Consequently, they may need psychotherapy to address the unresolved issues and ambivalent feelings about their own fathers and intensive but sensitive training in parenting skills (see Chapter 6).

Therapeutic measures for addressing the father-son wounds of teenage fathers include individual and group procedures. The group counseling process, first described by Kiselica et al. (1992) and later refined by Kiselica (in press-b) and Kiselica, Rotzien, and Doms (1994), is reviewed in a discussion regarding group preparation of fatherhood in Chapter 6. The individual psychotherapy process is described here and represents an integration of ideas from my clinical experience with suggestions by Fine (1988), Frankl (1959), Gordon (1990), Silverberg (1986), and Vogt and Sirridge (1991).

According to Vogt and Sirridge (1991), the first step in healing father-son wounds is to help the son acknowledge his feelings of hurt. The authors suggested several strategies designed to identify and ventilate pent-up emotions, including the following: talking to the counselor about past disappointments; writing a journal about one's feelings; and composing a letter that is completed but never actually mailed, in which the son expresses his anger and disenchantment. These tactics can help teenage fathers to unravel the confusion and ambivalence felt toward their own fathers. In addition to these methods, the empty chair technique, described in Chapter 4, can be used to encourage the son to engage in a fantasy dialogue with his father, disclosing to the father the lingering issues that exist between the two. Also, a standardized format for constructing family genograms (see McGoldrick & Gerson, 1985) or a family tree is a useful tool for helping the boy to review and examine past generations in his family. This can help the son to understand how transgenerational forces influenced the manner in which his father had treated him. As Gordon (1990) observed, an intergenerational review also can help some sons to see that since childhood, they have mistakenly blamed *themselves* for their fathers' rejection. With these insights, some sons are able to forgive their fathers and become determined not to repeat the pattern of dysfunction with their own children.

Vogt and Sirridge (1991) argued that the healing process involves a second step: directly working on the relationship between father and son. The authors stated that this step is important because of the son's remaining desire to connect with his father in spite of the difficulties between the two. Although this wish should be respected, Vogt and Sirridge (1991) and Gordon (1990) cautioned that the son must guard against setting himself up for new disappointments by expecting the father to give more than he is able. For example, the authors questioned the fantasy entertained by some sons of confronting and shaming their fathers with the expectations that the father will repent and suddenly shower the son with the affection the son longs for. It is unlikely that many dysfunctional fathers will be able or willing to respond in such an idealistic manner. Instead, Vogt and Sirridge (1991) and Gordon (1990) recommended that the counselor help the son abandon his childhood fantasies, learn to view the father in realistic terms, and work toward establishing some sort of relationship with the father, even if it is a very limited one.

Clinical experience with boys who have been abandoned or abused by their fathers supports these recommendations. Some of these sons are able to build relationships with their fathers that are characterized by the type of special closeness for which the youth has yearned. In these cases, the transformation in the adult father was precipitated by some significant event in his life, such as the recent death of his own father, which caused him to reevaluate how he has related to his own son. When this occurs, the father typically is amenable to counseling through which grieving takes place and some very touching father-son bonds are established. In many other cases in which the teenage father has had a very dysfunctional father, however, there is little change in the boy's father. In these situations the son needs assistance in forgiving his father for his shortcomings and appreciating whatever good qualities his father may have. At the same time, if the father has been an abusive man, the adolescent needs to be taught how to assert his right to be treated with respect. In addition, when child abuse has occurred the counselor may be legally compelled to contact child protection agencies to ensure that the boy is protected. It is imperative that the boy receive supportive counseling when this latter course of action is taken, for the investigations and decisions of child protective services can be very disruptive to the youth's family life. Also, counselors are recommended to urge officials to provide the abusive father with treatment to address his dysfunctional behavior. In some instances, the father is ready and able to try to forge a new relationship with his son after he receives counseling himself. In other instances in which it is clear that the adolescent has little hope of having any positive contact with his father, the support of a positive male role model recruited through Big Brother, Mentor Father, and Mentor Grandfather programs can ease the pain of father absence.

Father-son wounds also can be related to the messages fathers give their sons about masculinity. For example, some adult fathers have been good providers and a steady presence in their son's lives, but they have imbued their boys with the hypermasculine qualities of aggression, emotional constriction, and domination. Worse yet, the hypermasculine father may promote a shallow regard for women as sexual objects to be conquered. The adolescent may begin to question these values as he suddenly finds himself having difficulties maintaining an intimate relationship with the mother of his child. The son may begin to resent his father for having discouraged the son from being emotionally expressive, and the son may become angry at his father's failure to have been an affectionate parent. In addition, the son may be at a loss for how to respond to his female partner in a manner that suits her needs.

As numerous writers have noted (e.g., Balswick, 1982; Levant, 1992; McGuire, 1991; Scher, 1993; Silverberg, 1986), this form of socialization encourages the male to hide his emotionally expressive and nurturant qualities, thereby denying fundamental aspects of the self. According to Balswick (1982), this denial can become an obstacle to the development of healthy heterosexual relationships. Levant (1992) has been a leader in challenging men to redefine masculinity in a way that values the expressive and tender sides of males. Silverberg (1986) has written eloquently about how to achieve this goal in counseling, stating that counseling can be a safe environment for promoting the nurturant capabilities of men and helping men to forgive their fathers for relating to them in an emotionally restricted fashion. In addition to this goal, Gordon (1990) recommended that counseling should help the son to see the connection between how his father related to him and how the son now relates to others.

Consistent with the suggestions of Levant (1992) and Silverberg (1986), recommendations were offered earlier in this chapter for how the teenage father can express his sensitive, gentle side to his partner. In addition to employing these measures, I (Kiselica, in press-a) advise that it may be necessary to help the client address his feelings toward his father regarding this issue of emotions and affection. Using a family genogram and discussing the powerful influence of society on male roles can help a young man to understand and accept his father better and recognize the father's influence on the son's current behavior. Also, exploring connections between father-son wounds and the adolescent father's current manner of relating to his child is probably warranted (Kiselica, in press-a).

Although these strategies can help the son to reconcile his past, it is important to not get bogged down lamenting old heartaches. The son must be confronted to move forward with his life and commit himself to being a responsible father, no matter how inadequate his own father had been. Using Adler's notions of creating a constructive "guiding fiction" (Ansbacher & Ansbacher, 1956, p. 88) and "life plan" (Ansbacher & Ansbacher, 1956, p. 334), the counselor can assist the teenage father to paint a positive vision of the future, of seeing himself as sharing happily with one's child over the years, of giving of himself to his child and supporting his partner, whether the couple marry or not.

Therapeutic approaches suggested by Fine (1988) and Frankl (1959) can be used to inspire the young father to adopt this future-oriented, optimistic frame of reference. Fine (1988) has argued that perhaps the most fundamental way that a counselor can help a troubled male is to teach him to love and to work. That is, healing occurs by tapping the creative energies in men to give of themselves to others and to meaningful activity. These ideas are reminiscent of Frankl's (1959) assertion that psychological health is achieved by creating meaning in one's life through love, work, and suffering. Applying these concepts with the teenage father, the counselor challenges the youth to view disappointments as opportunities to become stronger persons and convert their sorrows into productive caring for their children and partners through loving behavior and hard work. In short, the therapeutic objective is to impress on the client that by giving freely to his loved ones he will fill the painful void within himself.

Reciprocal Wounds in the Mother-Son Relationship. Data from studies examining the living arrangements of teenage fathers have indicated that most live either with both of their parents or in a single-mother household (Hardy & Zabin, 1991; Hendricks, 1988; Marsiglio, 1987; Sullivan, 1985). Findings from other research investigating the problems and coping strategies of teenage fathers have demonstrated that the majority of adolescent fathers identify their mothers as the person they are most likely to turn to for assistance with the unplanned pregnancy (Hendricks, 1988; Sullivan, 1985). Together, these findings suggest that the mothers of teenage fathers are consistent sources of support for their sons. In spite of the positive characteristics of the mother-son relationship, however, the members of this dyad have been known to have significant issues with each other.

Dysfunctional mothers have contributed to conflicts with their sons and reacted pathologically in response to the boy's fatherhood. For example, Sullivan (1985) and Dash (1989) reported some tragic stories of single mothers who were unable to provide any reliable supervision to their children because of the mothers' addiction to drugs and/or involvement in prostitution. Both Sullivan and Dash surmised that this lack of structure contributed to the children's risky sexual behavior that frequently culminated in unplanned pregnancies. Many teenage fathers have described to me their deep resentment toward their mothers for not making better choices in their lives and for "allowing all sorts of jokers to take advantage of her." Horie and Horie (1988) described case examples of single mothers who responded to their loneliness by clinging to their sons and making them dependent and captive to the mothers' emotional needs. Clinical experience suggests that such mothers experience an irrational sense of betrayal on learning about the boy's role in an adolescent pregnancy and, in response, give him a choice of denying his paternity or leaving the mother's home. In other instances, mothers have communicated to their sons an implicit message that "You can do no wrong." For example, in a recent ABC television news interview, the mother of an adolescent boy expressed her support for her son who was a member of the "Spur Posse." Members of this gang espouse a cavalier sexual attitude toward adolescent girls (see Chapter 2). The mother denied any wrongdoing on the part of her son and accused the girls who were sexually involved with gang members of willful seduction and promiscuity. Essentially, by making this statement this mother gave her son permission to exploit girls and not worry about the consequences of his behavior.

Helping boys to address these sorts of problems is similar to, and yet different from, addressing father-son wounds. The counseling is similar in that the boy may need help in addressing his unfinished business with his mother. Thus, the many counseling techniques suggested for resolving father-son issues apply here as well: The client must grieve his losses, forsake childhood-idealized fantasies regarding his mother, learn to understand that complex familial and societal forces may be factors contributing to her dysfunction, forgive her, redefine his relationship with her, perhaps find "surrogate mothers" to ease his pain, and move on with his life in a constructive fashion by focusing his energies on giving and receiving love from his child. The major difference between counseling for father-son and mother-son issues is that the counselor is much more likely to engage the mother than the father in the counseling process. This conclusion is supported by both systematic empirical research indicating that women are more likely than men to use counseling services (see Wilcox & Forrest, 1992) and by my own experiences in counseling teenage fathers and their families.

When the mother participates in counseling, the counselor can support the boy to directly address issues with his mother. The counselor also can use this opportunity to enhance the mother's adjustment by helping her resolve her family of origin issues, empowering her to protect herself from abusive men, teaching her parenting skills, and providing her with the necessary resources to become an emotionally and economically self-sufficient woman. As is the case with extremely dysfunctional fathers, if the mother is abusive or neglectful to the son, child protective services may need to get involved.

The mothers of teenage fathers are more likely to participate in the counseling process. Thus, it is possible to observe *the ways that the sons have hurt their mothers* and how that can affect the mother's reaction to the son's fatherhood. Frequently, this hurt has its roots in the developmental process through which sons emotionally distance themselves from their mothers during adolescence. Data from McGuire's (1991) empirical study of mother-child relationships and Arcana's (1986) qualitative interviews with mothers about their sons suggest that mothers tend to experience physical and emotional intimacy with their sons until the boys reach adolescence, at which time fathers appear to exert a greater influence than mothers over their sons and the sons begin to behave in more traditionally masculine ways. In response to this change, although mothers may still desire to remain close with their sons, they also may feel uncomfortable relating to their sons as the boys display the traditional male qualities of aggression, competition, and emotional inexpressiveness. Thus, although many sons maintain close ties with their mothers, albeit in a different way than they had during childhood (e.g., sons may replace physical affection with doing things as a sign of caring for mother), males and their ways of relating can gradually replace the centrality of the mothers in the boys' experience during adolescence. In the words of Arcana (1986), these "outside factors" can interfere with mother-son closeness (p. 59). Many of the mothers of teenage fathers I have counseled have reported their sadness at this change, followed by resentment when the boy suddenly turns to his mother for help during the pregnancy-resolution phase. One mother said, "For the past 2 years he's put up walls between us and now that he's in trouble because his girlfriend's pregnant, the first person he runs to for help is dear old mom!" When this sentiment is expressed by the boy's mother, her feelings must be addressed by empathizing with her sense of loss and insult, helping the son to understand how his mother feels "left behind" and taken for granted, and encouraging the son to apologize to his mother and convey his appreciation for her on a steady basis.

In some cases, the emotional separation between mother and son can grow worse in response to other factors, such as the influence of a delinquent peer culture. For example, many single mothers from impoverished neighborhoods struggle to exert a positive influence over their adolescent boys and report feelings of frustration and helplessness in trying to counter the overwhelming appeal of gangs. The caring mother who has watched her son gradually drift into the culture of the gang, by whom he may be encouraged to be reckless in his sexuality, typically feels profound disappointment and bitterness when he fathers a child out of wedlock. In these situations, as the practitioner attempts to counsel the family regarding the many issues associated with the boy's fatherhood, once again attention must be focused on the mother's hurt, and the boy will require the interventions designed to remediate his delinquent lifestyle.

Sibling Tensions. Although little has been written about the siblings of the teenage father and their reactions to the pregnancy, data from a few studies (e.g., Elster & Panzarine, 1980; Hendricks, 1980, 1983; Robbins & Lynn, 1973; Sullivan, 1985) indicate that it is common for teenage fathers to have a sibling who is an unwed parent. Data from Sullivan's (1985) research and my own clinical experiences with teenage fathers indicate that siblings, especially those who also are a parent, often are significant sources of help to the young father by offering their emotional support and practical assistance, such as serving as child care providers.

Nevertheless, teenage fatherhood can be a disruptive and upsetting experience for some of the young father's siblings. His child may be a source of pride that can cause a sibling to feel displaced in terms of his or her relative importance to the parents. Also, siblings can envy the attention devoted by the family to the needs of the adolescent father and his child. In some instances, the young father's new position in the family, prompted by the pregnancy and fatherhood, exacerbates old sibling rivalries.

This latter issue was illustrated in the powerful movie *Boyz 'N the Hood*. One of the central families featured in this highly acclaimed film consisted of a single mother, Mrs. Baker, and her two sons, Ricky and Darren. (The latter was frequently referred to by his nickname "Doughboy.") Over the course of the boys' lives, the mother bestowed a favored status on Ricky but projected negative attributes onto Darren, treatment that Darren gradually grew to resent. After Ricky fathered a child, his girlfriend and the baby moved in with the family, further alienating Darren from his mother. Eventually, Darren's resentment toward Ricky spills out and the two have a fistfight on the front lawn.

In response to sibling problems such as these, it is recommended that counselors explore with the family the reason for the sibling's resentment, his or her role in the family, how the family projection process (see Bowen, 1978) contributed to this role, and how the family can adjust so that the sibling's needs are met. The siblings also might participate in a sibling support group to deal with their feelings of jealousy, anger, and resentment.

In some dysfunctional families, it is the sibling who has held the position of favored child and the teenage father has filled the role of the scapegoat for the family. In these families, the son's participation in an out-of-wedlock pregnancy is seen as further evidence of his "good-for-nothing" character. For example, during a family session, Don, the brother of a teenage father, David, acidly described his reaction to David's role in an unplanned pregnancy, "Well, I wasn't surprised. . . . Once a screw-up, always a screw-up!" In situations like these, the parents typically have given the sibling implicit permission to have a field day at the young father's expense. Again, how the boy was placed into the scapegoat position must be understood and he must be supported in his efforts to demand respect from his family. The use of a genogram might reveal to the family the reason behind their treatment of the youth (e.g., he may resemble a much-hated grandparent). Confronted with this understanding, some families acknowledge their transgressions against the son and redefine how they relate to him. With severely maladjusted families, these sibling tensions may not be resolved, and the young father may need to be taught how to emotionally distance himself from the family's destructive treatment.

Peer Relationships

Generally speaking, during adolescence dependence and involvement in the family declines, but participation in peer activities increases and the attitudes of peers exert an growing influence on adolescent behavior (Montemayor, 1986). According to Elster and Hendricks (1986), the normal adolescent desire of the teenage father to socialize with other adolescents may conflict with the social obligations of parenthood. Demands from one of these theaters in his life can interfere with his satisfactory acclimation to the other. For example, the desire to date and socialize may distract him from fully investing himself in his child and partner and retard his growth as a father. Conversely, his dedication to his child and partner may limit his peer interactions and leave him missing peer events and feeling out of place when he actually attends them. These developmental dilemmas must be addressed in counseling to help the teenager strike a balance between fulfilling his responsibilities as a parent and meeting his peer-affiliated needs.

In addition to addressing these problems, counselors need to understand the potential influence of peers on the teenage father's attitudes toward sex and paternity. Even though parents can play a significant role in delaying the sexual behavior of their teenage children, peers have a greater influence than do parents on the sexual activity of adolescents (see Ooms, 1984). Teenagers rely on one another for information and misinformation about sexuality and contraception (Thornberg, 1981). Among youth ages 12 to 17 surveyed in a national poll conducted by Harris and Associates (1986), social pressure was identified by 50% of the boys participating in the survey as a reason why they do no wait until they are older to have sexual intercourse. The 11 teenage fathers interviewed by Sullivan (1985) revealed that they had received pressure from their peers to engage in sexual relations with girls and avoid using condoms because condoms were perceived by the boys to inhibit sensual pleasure during sexual intercourse. However, the peer group of these fathers also expected a young man to accept the responsibilities of paternity, should he father a child, and they held no respect for a male who did not at least try to support his children in some way. Similar values were reported by teenage fathers studied by Hendricks (1982).

In addition to being influenced by peer norms, it appears that many teenage fathers want the support of their peers during the fatherhood experience. For example, 23% of the 56 teenage fathers surveyed by Hendricks (1988) indicated that they were likely to turn to their peers when they needed help with a problem. In spite of this need for peer support, however, teenage fathers may be unlikely to receive it. In their review of studies examining the stresses experienced by adolescent fathers, Elster and Hendricks (1986) concluded that teenage fathers consistently report feeling socially isolated from peers, perhaps because the social limitations imposed by parenthood preclude sufficient peer interactions. The loneliness of young fathers may also be related to an unwillingness or inability of peers to offer their support, a finding that was reported in a study by Fry and Trifiletti (1983).

In summary, peers play a major role psychologically in the teenage father's life before, during, and after the pregnancy. Yet little has been written about how to use the powerful influence of peers in preventing repeat unplanned pregnancies and in promoting the father's role as a parent. Recommendations to deal with this gap in the literature are made regarding individual and family counseling with the father to address peer-related issues and outreach with the young father's peer group to solicit their support.

Individual and Family Counseling to Address Peer-Related Issues

When the teenage father has been deeply involved and committed to his partner and child while juggling other demands from school or work, he may need a sympathetic ear to hear about his sorrow and frustration at reduced contact with peers. Through supportive individual counseling these feelings can be aired and his desire to socialize with other boys and girls can be affirmed. Family sessions can be conducted through which the young father can request the assistance of his family in assuring him that he has time to be with other youth his age. For example, his parents might agree to watch his child on Saturday nights while he and his partner and/or friends spend an evening together. In exchange, he can do a favor for his parents, such as helping them with a special chore or project.

Although the counselor should confirm the importance of peer involve-ment, the counselor also is advised to educate the young father about the potentially negative influence of other teenagers. For example, they may still intentionally or unintentionally encourage him to engage in risky sexual behavior. He may find excuses to avoid his paternal responsibilities to spend more time with friends. Training him to apply coping self-statements with peer-related dilemmas is recommended to prepare him for these possibilities. For example, he might learn try telling himself, "If I stick to my responsi-bilities during the week, then I can really have a great time this weekend when I get out with the boys." Or, "I had better be very careful when it comes to sex again, no matter what these guys may think." For additional ideas on using cognitive self-instructional strategies, the reader is referred to several pertinent resources (Baker & Butler, 1984; Cormier & Cormier, 1991; Meichenbaum, 1977).

Outreach With the Peer Group
of the Young Father

It is highly recommended that the counselor become well acquainted with the adolescents in his or her community. By having a strong rapport with local teenagers, the counselor can "get the word from the streets" about boys who are expectant fathers. In addition, establishing oneself as a respected advocate for young people enhances the likelihood that these youth can be called on to assist the counselor in helping youngsters in crisis.

A counselor who is well known among a teenage father's peer group can reach out directly to the boy's friends to solicit their support. Alternatively, the counselor can recruit the assistance of the young father's friends by asking the father to invite a few of his buddies to meet the counselor. Both male *and* female acquaintances of the father can be valuable allies to the counselor.

Recruiting the Support of Other Teenage Boys

Most adolescent boys know someone who is a teenage father. However, they may not comprehend the complexity of the situation for the young man. For this reason, reaching out to the friends of the father, fully explaining to them his situation, and asking their assistance to help the father cope with the many demands placed on his life are recommended.

Teenage boys can help a young father behave as a caring parent in many ways. Surprising as it may sound, teenage boys can assist the adolescent father with child care from time to time and enjoy themselves in the process. The trick is to integrate the task at hand into activities that boys naturally use to experience camaraderie between them. For example, groups of boys can be persuaded to invite a young father and his baby to accompany them to the park for a game of football. Once at the playing field, each male can take 15-minute breaks on the sidelines to play with the baby. In this way, the father can enjoy an hour or so of carefree physical exertion and fun with his friends while his baby enjoys fresh air and stimulation from people. Boys also can stop by the young man's home and help attend to and entertain the baby while they all hang out and listen to music on the stereo or watch videos.

Teaching friends how to be supportive listeners is another way that the counselor can indirectly help the teenage father. Although many boys are up to the task of mixing child care with football, some may find it difficult to respond to the father when he appears preoccupied. Instructing his buddies to use empathic listening and responding skills can go a long way in helping them ease the emotional burdens of the young father. The counselor also might pull the friends aside and use informal language and slang expressions to suggest how they might incorporate supportive statements into recreational activities with the adolescent father. For example,

> "Look guys, you know Jim here is having a rough time trying to keep it all together with his girlfriend and the baby. Later today when you guys walk to the park to play football, try saying to him, 'Hey man, how's things going with your lady and your baby?' When he starts to tell you, if he seems to get a little upset and you don't know what to say, just walk up to him, give him a little tap on the back, and say, 'That's rough man . . . hang in there. . . . Let's see if we can give you a break from it all at the park.' Then, after you're done playing football and taking turns watching the baby and you're on your way home, joke around about the game you just had. This way, you'll give him a break from his worries for a while. What do you say?"

When other boys respond to a teenage father in this manner, they help the young man to ventilate his feelings, release pent-up energy, have a mental break from his anxieties, and care for his child in the process.

In addition to these indirect measures, it may be necessary to address the sexual attitudes and behaviors of the father's peer group, especially if his friends are a sexually active group. In these circumstances, a well-respected counselor can encourage the boys to support the father's need to act in a sexually responsible manner while telling them to be cautious too. In doing so, the counselor must be careful to not come on too strong or else the message may come across as moralistic and preachy and could alienate the youngsters. At times, it helps to phrase the advice in the vernacular used by adolescent boys. For example, consider this statement offered to the friends of one teenage father named Fred:

> Now remember guys, Fred's got enough to worry about without having pressure on him to do the nasty [i.e., have sex]. Cut him a break and help him to be careful next time. And while you're at it, think about yourselves too. There's deadly stuff going around out there and you guys don't want to mess with it or to find yourselves being fathers when you're not ready. If you're going to do it, remember to use a condom, OK?

Finally, some teenage fathers lack a circle of peer support prior to the pregnancy and/or their relationships with old friends gradually fade after he becomes a father, in spite of the efforts of the counselor to help maintain these ties. In these situations, teenage father support groups can place young fathers in touch with others who share their concerns. Through these groups, adolescent fathers can socialize together, help each other with their responsibilities, and receive crucial emotional support.

Recruiting the Support of Teenage Girls

Teenage boys represent only half of the potential pool of peers who might be able to support an adolescent father. In a variety of ways, teenage girls can be of assistance to him, too. Because of the traditional way in which many males are socialized to deal with their emotions and problems, some young fathers find it easier to talk about their feelings to girls than to other boys. Therefore, the counselor might encourage the significant female friends of the young father to check in on him from time to time to see how he is doing and praise him when he demonstrates responsible parenting behavior. The emotional support of an empathic girl can temporarily relieve a troubled young father from his many worries. When a teenage father has decided that he will not marry his female partner, he typically wants to date a girl who is understanding about his situation. His current female friends might be willing to date him on a casual basis, or they might be able to recommend a friend for a blind date. Finally, girls who have had no prior romantic relationship with the young father but who themselves are teenage mothers through a relationship with another male might form a friendship with the young father through which they assist one another with child care and emotional support.

A word of caution is warranted, however. Before a girl gets too involved with a troubled young father, both should be warned about their potential vulnerabilities in such a relationship. Any normal boy will have a need to have relationships with girls his age. The potential problem is that he must avoid seeking a female savior for his problems. The teenage father tends to experience significant confusion and acute depression at various times before and after the birth of the child. Consequently, he is likely to be extremely needy and subject to becoming infatuated with a girl who can respond sensitively to his concerns. Likewise, the girl who is in this position may find herself developing feelings for the boy as the two of them experience emotional connections during conversations regarding his hardships. She needs to understand how her desire to help someone in distress might get confused with true love. Meanwhile, the boy should be told that his need to be cared for may cause him to rush into an exclusive relationship with someone who might not be compatible with him. In short, it is recommended that the counselor forewarn both the boy and the girl that feelings between them are likely to develop and encourage the couple to take things between them slowly and contact the counselor for help in clarifying their feelings in the event that their relationship becomes serious too quickly.

Conclusion

The focus of this chapter was on providing suggestions for using the support of family and peers in helping the teenage father during the transition to parenthood. Because fatherhood represents one of the most important experiences of a young man's life, the next chapter is devoted entirely to this subject.

6

Preparation for Fatherhood

MARK S. KISELICA
JAMES C. STROUD
JUDITH E. STROUD

Becoming a caring, committed, and effective parent during the adolescent years is arguably the most significant challenge that teenage fathers face. Because they are in a process of transition from adolescence to adulthood, teenage fathers experience epic biological/physical, cognitive, and socio-emotional changes, including the following: puberty milestones (e.g., the growth of facial hair, a deepening of the voice, a rise in testosterone secretion, and the development of pubic hair), shifts in cognitive capabilities (e.g., from concrete operational to formal operational thinking), and a preoccupation with questions pertaining to identity development (e.g., Who am I?) (Montemayor, 1986). Because this developmental transition parallels parenthood, many questions invade the teenage father's psyche, such as: How will my relationship with my parents change? How will my relationship with my partner's parents change? How will my relationship with my friends change? How will I support my partner and child? How will my plans to finish high school and/or college change? Am I ready to

121

be a father? What is a father? Pondering these questions can prompt a variety of emotions, including fear, loneliness, frustration, helplessness, anger, and denial. Because teenage fathers "have many problems, . . . are young, are capable of sexual reproduction but not considered adults, are cognitively and psychologically immature . . . and are out of life-cycle synchrony with their peers" (Montemayor, 1986, p. 14), unplanned parenthood represents a developmental crisis.

On the whole, adolescent fathers acknowledge their developmental dilemma by expressing an interest in receiving preparation for fatherhood (Achatz & MacAllum, 1994; Elster & Panzarine, 1983a; Hendricks, 1988). Yet programs designed to teach adolescent fathers parenting skills have problems recruiting participants (Sommerfeld, 1992). Why is this the case?

A teenage father can be turned off to fatherhood training immediately if it is presented as a means to show him how to fulfill his paternal obligations. Helpers should bear in mind that young fathers tend to be defensive about the subject of "responsibility" and with good reason. After the news of the pregnancy is revealed, the teenage father commonly is castigated by adults for his "irresponsible" behavior. Often, he is berated for his role in the pregnancy and warned that he had better not repeat his "mistake" in the future. Authorities might be after him to pay child support, even though his financial resources may be severely limited and in spite of the possibility that he may be providing various forms of informal support to his partner and child. Guarded against similar reactions from other adults, he is likely to avoid anyone who approaches him with the intention of teaching him how to act responsibly. Therefore, it is essential that parenting skills training be focused on helping teenage fathers with *their* concerns and that it be presented in a nonjudgmental manner. Otherwise, young men will be alienated from participating.

Another factor that subtly discourages father participation is that parenting programs historically have been directed toward females and have emphasized the mother's role in child rearing. Parenting skills training for teenage fathers must be "male friendly," that is, provided in a manner that males will find comfortable and attractive. In addition, the important role of fathers in child development must be emphasized (Kiselica et al., 1992).

Even if the training is geared toward males, however, it may still discourage participation if traditional teaching methods (e.g., didactic lectures) are relied on as the sole means of instruction. This issue is relevant to parent education with both teenage mothers and teenage fathers. Streett (1991) noted that many youngsters who become parents too soon have poor reading skills. Consequently, parent skills training with teenage parents is likely to be unsuccessful unless a variety of educational strategies and materials (e.g., easy-to-read handouts, audiovisual materials, role-plays, and discussions) are used.

A final and often overlooked reason for the avoidance of parent skills training and responsible parenting by some teenage fathers is that the subject of fatherhood might touch too close to home for boys whose own fathers were negligent or abusive parents. Impending fatherhood for these youth can trigger painful memories and feelings stemming from unresolved conflicts with their own fathers. Parent educators are advised to remain sensitive to this issue and address it early on in the training or some boys might be frightened away (Kiselica et al., 1992).

The purpose of this chapter is to describe a course on fatherhood, which was designed with these issues in mind, that would appeal and respond to the specific needs of teenage fathers. This course is an expanded and refined version of a similar course that was originally developed by Kiselica et al. (1992) and revised by Kiselica et al. (1994) and Kiselica (in press-b). This course also reflects and extends ideas suggested by Carrera (1992), Klinman and Kohl (1984), and Levant (1988).

A Fatherhood Training Course
for Teenage Fathers

An essential feature of this course is that it has been designed to engage and retain teenage fathers. The sequence of the modules reflects a movement from exploring personal issues that teenage fathers are ready to face (e.g., sharing reactions to the unplanned pregnancy) to a discussion of more upsetting topics (e.g., reactions to one's own father, safe sex). Specifically, in Module 1, participants develop group cohesion, share their reactions to the unplanned pregnancy, and then clarify their attitudes about fatherhood and masculinity, including their feelings about their own fathers. Through training provided in Module 2, group members learn about child development, the father-child relationship, and child care. Strategies for practicing safe sex are taught in Module 3. Using male-oriented activities and male consultants and a variety of instructional materials and methods, this course is designed to provide a "male-friendly" and "teenager-friendly" learning environment. Teaching the modules in this manner increases the likelihood that the participants will be receptive to the training.

Note that the subject of safe sex is covered within the domain of fatherhood training. Thus, the issues of preventing repeat unplanned pregnancies and sexually transmitted diseases are addressed as part of a supportive training process through which teenage fathers learn how to be loving, competent parents.

Although this course can be taught to teenage fathers on an individual basis, it was fashioned to use a group psychoeducational format. Streett (1991) recommended teaching parenting skills to teenage parents in small groups for several reasons. First, group sessions are cost-effective and time efficient. Second, teenagers are comfortable learning with and from their peers. Third, through group education, trainees can readily observe differences in child-rearing styles and evaluate the advantages or disadvantages of these styles.

Because this course is designed to provide the participants with a therapeutic experience, it is recommended that it be taught by a professional who has received solid training in group counseling and has acquired a sensitive understanding of the complicated developmental challenges that adolescent fathers face. Furthermore, in order for the training to be successful, the trainer must be attuned to the concerns of teenage fathers throughout the training.

This course can be taught in a variety of formats. Trainers can offer the entire three-module course as presented here, or they can teach any of the modules separately. In addition, this course can be modified according to the varying needs and values of different cultural groups. For example, particular cultural conceptions of fatherhood (e.g., Anglo, African, and Hispanic) can be incorporated into the first module on clarifying attitudes about fatherhood when it is used with specific cultural groups of teenage fathers. Or, discussions regarding birth control can be replaced with information on abstinence strategies in the third module when the trainees have strong religious convictions against contraception use.

Before any of the modules are taught, however, the idea of fatherhood training must be proposed to the young father. This requires a very tentative, sensitive approach, a description of which follows.

Introducing the Idea of
Group Parenting Skills Training

Teenage fathers tend to be hesitant to participate in any service program unless they already have a strong relationship of trust with some professional associated with the program. Typically, the influence of this individual plays a crucial role in a young father's decision to give the service a try. Therefore, creating a very positive individual relationship with a teenage father is paramount before broaching the subject of his joining a parenting skills training group. Even after this trust has been achieved, the idea of group participation must be introduced tentatively, for practitioners who come on too strong with their promotion of a young fathers group can scare some potential clients away (Kiselica et al., 1992). In addition, the adolescent father needs to be convinced that the program has something concrete to offer, that it really will help him (Hendricks, 1988; Sommerfeld, 1992).

Because group training programs tend to employ a variety of consultants, it is recommended that the teenage father be assigned an individual case manager who has the responsibility of assuring continuity of care for the client. Through his relationship with the case manager, the young father can process his reactions to the group experience and receive additional encouragement and support to continue his participation. Throughout the group training period, the case manager can attend to any issues that require supplementary individual counseling or client advocacy work.

It is a good idea for the case manager to introduce the teenage father to whomever is in charge of leading the fatherhood training group. This introduction can serve as a passing of the reins of trust from one caring adult to another and foster the client's acceptance of the group leader.

As a final preparatory measure, it is recommended that the group leader inform the youth that he will receive many educational materials throughout the training. Because some adolescents have a tendency to misplace handouts and readings, the group leader is advised to provide the client with a folder and ask him to bring the folder to each training session and store it in a safe place between sessions. Having taken these measures, the training can begin by helping the youth to clarify his attitudes about fatherhood.

Module 1: Clarifying Attitudes About Fatherhood

Module 1 begins with the creation of a therapeutic environment through which group members can explore their reactions to unplanned fatherhood. Module 1 varies in length from four to six sessions, the exact number of sessions determined by how much time is necessary to respond to the initial concerns of the participants.

The Role of Recreational Activities

According to Bergin (1993), a standard practice in group work with adolescents is to employ "icebreaker activities" (p. 201). Icebreaker activities for adolescents consist of interactive games or assignments that are designed to create cohesion among group members.

Although a number of icebreaker exercises specifically designed for counseling has been developed (see Corey & Corey, 1992; Corey, Corey,

Callanan, & Russell, 1992; Devencenzi & Pendergast, 1988; Kottler, 1983; Napier & Gershenfeld, 1993), Barber and Munn (1993) and Kiselica (1993) found that teenage fathers tend to report feeling awkward with traditional icebreaking activities. Consequently, Kiselica et al. (1994) recommended that professionals conducting group training with teenage fathers employ the strategies suggested by Barber and Munn (1993) and Kiselica (1993), such as sporting activities and field trips for meals. Barber and Munn (1993) reported that participation in recreational activities, such as basketball, is an effective mechanism for helping teenage fathers interact and feel comfortable with each other. In addition, the physical exertion helps the boys discharge some of their presession anxieties. Free meals provided by the training program, such as a trip to McDonalds, can mean a lot to many adolescent males who tend to come from economically depressed neighborhoods and consequently are apt to be malnourished. The provision of a meal communicates to the boys that meeting *their* basic needs is an important goal of the training. In addition, eating together provides the participants with additional opportunities to know each other on an informal basis.

These types of activities can be used not only as icebreakers, but also as the initial activity for each subsequent group session. It is recommended that the recreation segment last about 45 minutes to an hour, followed by a 30- to 40-minute educational section for each session throughout the course.

Informality and Responding
to Immediate Needs

Because teenage fathers tend to be turned off by formal counseling and educational experiences (Barber & Munn, 1993; Hendricks, 1988) and strict adherence to time schedules and a predetermined agenda (Brown, 1990; Hendricks, 1988), it is recommended that the trainer create a very informal but caring tone during the first session through a number of different strategies. For example, after the young fathers have exchanged introductions and participated in a recreational activity, it can be helpful to offer a free meal or snack, especially with young fathers from impoverished backgrounds (Barber & Munn, 1993). The group leader is advised to "mix" with the boys at this time, listening to what they have to say and trying to get to know them. It also is recommended that the group leader ask about and respond to the fathers' most immediate concerns to help them become invested in the group experience. Expressed concerns commonly involve practical matters, such as finding a job or obtaining legal advice regarding paternity matters (Achatz & MacAllum, 1994; Hendricks, 1988). By spending the first session or two focusing on these requests in an informal context, the participants are likely to maintain their trust in the group leader and be receptive to more formal structured experiences (Kiselica, in press-b; Kiselica et al., 1994).

Processing Reactions to Teenage Fatherhood

During the next session the more traditional psychoeducational work begins. After the recreation period, the group leader introduces the idea of a structured group educational activity.

As is the case during the initial stage of any group counseling process, some of the basic principles of group functioning are explained (Bergin, 1993). Confidentiality, respect, and a commitment to working together are defined and encouraged. The counselor facilitates a discussion of the purposes and rules of the group. Although the general purpose of the group is preparation for fatherhood, the group leader remains ready to adapt the overriding purpose of the course to address the particular needs of the group members as they arise. As Hendricks (1988) noted, unless such adaptability is practiced, young fathers are likely to drop out of counseling. This perspective is maintained throughout the course.

After the rules and purposes of the group have been negotiated, more substantive issues are addressed. Because the unplanned pregnancy is such a salient issue for most young fathers, it is recommended that the fathers be encouraged to share their reactions to the pregnancy (Kiselica, in press-b; Kiselica et al., 1994). A fruitful starting point is to ask the fathers to share their reactions to the pregnancy. Showing a film on teenage fathers can be a helpful tool for stimulating a discussion of these reactions. In this next section, a variety of audiovisual materials are critiqued in terms of their utility for group psychoeducational training with teenage fathers.

Audiovisual Resources. A superb 9-minute video, *Fathers Too Soon?*, features actual teenage fathers talking about their experiences (Planned Parenthood Association of Cincinnati, 1987). The brevity and realism of the production tend to capture the attention of group participants. In addition, since both Black and White teenage fathers are interviewed in the film, it appeals to a wide range of teenage fathers. Each young man featured in the film describes his reaction to the pregnancy, the impact of the pregnancy and parenthood on his family, his relationships with peers and the baby's mother, his educational and career plans, and his view of his future. In addition, the fathers talk about their participation in child rearing. Because the film captures both the joys and sorrows of teenage fatherhood, it usually prompts group members to disclose their similar experiences. This rapidly promotes an atmosphere of empathic group support that solidifies cohesion among group members.

Three other quality movies on teenage fathers are *Me, a Teen Father?* (Centron Films, 1980), *Wayne's Decision* (Memphis Association for Planned Parenthood, 1980), and *Teenage Father* (Hackford, 1978). The first film is a 13-minute production that re-creates the emotional impact of an unplanned pregnancy on a 17-year-old boy. The second is a 6-minute piece dramatizing the crisis of teenage pregnancy and the emotional repercussions of a teenage father's decision, pointing out that there can be no ideal solution. The third film, *Teenage Father,* follows a teenage couple from the time they learned that the girl was pregnant until a decision was reached as to what action to take. Because these films provide insight into the fears and feelings of teenage fathers, they are useful vehicles for prompting self-disclosure and emotional venting among group participants. One limitation of these films is that they are somewhat dated. Consequently, the style of clothing, language, and mannerisms of the featured boys can make their experiences appear foreign to some current teenage fathers.

Teenage Father (Sunburst Communications, 1989) is a widely marketed, 34-minute videotaped drama about the impact of an unplanned pregnancy on the lives of teenage couples and their extended families. The strength of this production is that it includes an instructional booklet containing probing questions that can be used to direct discussions regarding participants' reactions to the film. Although the film dramatizes some common difficulties of teenage fathers, such as interfamily conflict, disrupted peer relationships, and decision making about abortion and marriage, the actors fail to portray the realism found in other films that use actual teenage fathers. Thus, before using this film, it is important to encourage the participants to look beyond the performances of the actors and focus on the issues depicted.

As an alternative to these movies, trainers might consider using *His Baby Too: Problems of Teenage Pregnancy* (Vanderslice, 1980), a filmstrip that defines and highlights the role of the unwed father and stresses the importance of his active role in solving the problems of an unplanned pregnancy. Although this presentation also is a bit dated, it nevertheless can be used to stimulate discussions of options available to the teenage father.

No matter which audiovisual resource is used, the group leader can prompt reactions by offering probes such as, "How are the fathers in this film like or unlike you?" and "How are their experiences similar to yours?" Sometimes, two sessions are needed to adequately process the participants' responses. Typical reactions include issues involving interfamily conflict; disrupted peer relationships; father-child and father-mother relationships; legal, financial, and career worries; and concern about the child's future.

Group members who are expectant fathers are likely to express their prenatal anxieties; they can be helped when boys who already are fathers share the coping strategies they used during the prenatal period. Boys with postnatal concerns can rely on each other for support and, when possible, solicit advice from "graduates" of fatherhood groups who join current groups to offer their wisdom to other young fathers. It is through this sharing that an atmosphere of mutual support can be created, thereby conveying to the teenage fathers that they are not alone in the difficulties they face.

Clarifying Attitudes About Fatherhood and Masculinity

During the next session, films once again can be used to initiate discussions, this time with the focus on clarifying the young men's attitudes about fatherhood and masculinity. A brief review of some pertinent films follows.

Films on Fatherhood. Two films can serve as excellent stimuli for starting a dialogue among participants about their conceptions of fatherhood. *Fathers* (Steinberg & Jassim, 1980) is a 23-minute movie that provides an intimate look at three fathers whose children range in age from preschool to adolescence. Each father describes how his ways of relating to his children are in the process of change. *Dad and Me* (King Screen Productions, n.d.) is a 9-minute film portraying the loving relationship between a father and his son.

Two other films provide food for thought about different models of masculinity and gender roles. *A Man's Place* (Allan Keith Productions, n.d.) documents the lives of men who live and/or work in a setting that requires them to expand their conceptions of the traditional male role. This 23-minute video focuses primarily on five men: a homemaker, a nurse, a father raising an infant, a man sharing household responsibilities with a working wife, and a man in equal partnership with a woman. Included with the video is a discussion and activity guide focusing on dual-career families, family relationships, and planning for lifelong goals. *Fathers: Today and Yesterday* (Family Service, Inc., n.d.) is a 38-minute video of interviews with men and women about the role of fathers, now and a generation ago. It includes diverse points of view about the ideal father and the barriers fathers face.

As group members react to any of these productions, the trainer is advised to ask the participants to state their views on masculinity and their visions of themselves as fathers. Throughout these exchanges, young fathers typically express their attitudes toward their own fathers. Two or more sessions may be necessary to address the many issues that are raised. This is vital material that should be explored in depth.

Exploring Father-Son Relationships. Most men have lasting images and fantasies of their own fathers, even if their fathers were virtually unknown to them. These can influence how a young man approaches parenthood.

By discussing his own father's strengths and shortcomings, the teenage father can develop a clearer sense of the type of father he would like to be. In those instances in which his own father has been a positive male role model, the son should be encouraged to think of how he can pass on the love he received from his father to his own child. Boys whose fathers have been caring figures should be prompted to describe how their fathers have been heroes to them. In particular, participants should be encouraged to share examples of how their fathers had accepted their responsibilities as parents, nurtured their children, supported their partners, and contributed positively to their communities.

This self-disclosure is particularly helpful for boys whose fathers were negligent parents, for it provides them with a clearer sense of what characterizes a nurturant father. The discovery that there really are good, caring men may help these clients to believe that committed fatherhood is possible. Some neglected youths report a sense of healing as they listen to their peers' stories about their admirable fathers. At the same time, this experience can prompt them to get in touch with their feelings associated with unresolved father-son issues.

Helping wounded boys to process their negative reactions to their own fathers is delicate and moving work. The counselor must help the boys to mourn their sense of loss and hurt and understand how these feelings might be interfering with their relationships with their own children. This can be frightening material that some males defend against by avoiding the subject. Although the counselor is advised to tread carefully to not frighten some boys away, the counselor should not completely dismiss the subject either. When it is clear that father-son conflicts represent major unresolved issues, the youth needs to be offered adjunctive individual psychotherapy. (For a description of the individual psychotherapy process to address father-son wounds, see Chapter 5 and Kiselica, in press-a.) In addition to addressing father-son issues, particular attention should to be directed toward these boys throughout the remainder of the course, for they may have pronounced deficits in parenting skills requiring additional individualized training.

Although the resolution of father-son issues is helpful, it also is important to encourage the young men to move beyond their painful memories and consider their own roles as fathers. The group leader might ask, "How would you do things differently with your child?" and "How can you be a better father for your child?" Probes of this kind might help some boys to avert cross-generational patterns of maladaptive fathering. In addition, they place the focus on the future and serve as a bridge to the subject of parent skills training.

Wrap-Up Session

Module 1 concludes with a session in which each participant summarizes his views about fatherhood and masculinity. In addition, the fathers are encouraged to verbalize changes in their thinking, feelings, and behavior that were prompted by this module.

Module 2: Child Development Education and Parenting Skills Training

Module 2 is designed to cover from 5 to 12 class periods, the precise number of sessions determined by the degree to which pertinent resources are available.

Using Consultants

This module can be taught directly by the counselor. However, because of the trust that has been developed by this point in the course, the fathers are likely to accept instruction by an outside consultant who is introduced by the counselor. Thus, other professionals can be used as consultants to teach Module 2. Potential consultants to consider include home economics teachers, community child care workers, educators from planned parenthood, and university faculty from home economics, nursing, early childhood education, and psychology departments.

Counselors as Instructors

Counselors who decide to teach this module themselves can rely on several pertinent resources, which are described here.

Instructional Resources on Child Development and Parenting Skills. A variety of educational films on child development and parenting skills have been produced. The six-part video series *Growing Together* (American Guidance Services, 1989b) was developed specifically for teenage parents. This series covers basic parenting skills, safety tips, and topics such as building the baby's self-esteem, using proper baby-feeding techniques and nutrition, maintaining good health, and promoting the baby's physical, emotional, and social development.

The Practical Parenting Series (Research Press, 1991) is another video series advertised as specifically designed for teenage parents. Although the series does present some issues common to teenage parents, as well as information on child development and child management, it focuses almost entirely on teenage mothers, thereby largely ignoring the important role of the teenage father. Unfortunately, the few references that are made about teenage fathers tend to present these youths in a disparaging light. Thus, it is likely to offend teenage fathers.

Other films, designed for parents in general, are useful instructional media with young fathers. Early Childhood STEP: Systematic Training for Effective Parenting of Children Under Six (American Guidance Services, 1989a) is a video series that provides new parents with information on early childhood development and positive ways to discipline and communicate with young children. Both series include instructional manuals as supplements to the information presented in the films. The Developing Child (Magna Systems, 1991) is a video series focusing on all stages of child development. Caring for Infants and Toddlers (National Association for the Education of Young Children, 1985) reviews major developmental tasks of infants and toddlers and suggests appropriate caregiving behaviors for both developmental groups.

In addition to these films, trainers can use other instructional resources to develop parenting skills training courses for boys. The Bank Street College of Education has developed curricula on child development and child care that can be obtained by contacting the college. The Guide to Setting Up an Infant Care Course (The Collegiate School, n.d.) contains concrete suggestions for developing a course on child care for boys. Although this latter publication provides ideas on the structure of such a course, additional resources, such as the films already cited, should be acquired to teach the fundamentals of child development and parenting skills.

Although these resources give a good introduction to child development and parenting, the father's role in these processes are underemphasized. Therefore, it is recommended that the following section regarding the father's role and experiences be included in the training so that the young fathers can develop an understanding of the positive reciprocal influence they and their children can have on each other's lives. This particular training, more than any other, can help the father to appreciate the truly priceless and fulfilling opportunity that exists in creating a strong bond with one's child.

Fathers, Child Development, and the Experiences of Fathers With Their Children

Traditionally, research on parenting has focused on the important role of mothers in child rearing. Although this research identified the many ways that women contribute to the emotional, intellectual, and physical growth of children, for the most part it ignored the contributions of fathers to these important developmental processes. However, as gender roles were reevaluated during the 1970s, researchers began to explore the influence of fathers on their children's development. The purpose of this section is to provide an overview of this recent research, highlight the experiences of fathers, and suggest how this information can be incorporated into the group training experience.

Fathers and Cognitive Development. Numerous investigators (Blanchard & Biller, 1971; Clarke-Stewart, 1980; Honzik, 1967; Pedersen, Rubinstein, & Yarrow, 1979; Radin, 1976; Shinn, 1978; Yarrow, Rubinstein, & Pedersen, 1975) have examined the important role a father plays in his child's cognitive development. A positive relationship has been found between the amount of social stimulation (rocking, talking, looking, touching) and an infant's level of mental ability (Yarrow et al., 1975). In addition, research findings suggest that a father's presence affects the cognitive development of his son in early infancy; baby boys whose fathers live with them score higher on cognitive measures than baby boys whose fathers are absent (Pedersen et al., 1979). The amount of interaction between a baby boy and his live-in father also affects the infant's intellectual growth; more frequent contact is associated with higher scores on cognitive development scales (Parke, 1981). Research further indicates that a father's availability, as well as a father's presence or absence, affects older children's academic performance. In a study of third-grade boys, Blanchard and Biller (1971) concluded that "underachievers, who were working below grade level, came from homes where the father had left before the child was 5. The superior academic performers were the boys whose fathers were present and highly available" (p. 72). A father's absence also has a detrimental effect on his daughter's cognitive development (Shinn, 1978).

Fathers and Socioemotional Development. In early infancy, the quality of the relationship between a father and his child affects the baby's ability to socially interact with other adults. Findings from studies involving infants as young as 5 months old suggest a positive relationship between a baby boy's contact with his father and the infant's expression of friendliness toward a strange adult; baby boys who have more contact with their fathers are friendlier, more vocal, more willing to be picked up, and enjoy frolic play more than sons who have less involved fathers (Pedersen et al., 1979). Infants who experience high levels of paternal involvement and have fathers who are active caregivers are better able to cope with the potential stress associated with strangers and strange situations (Kotelchuck, 1976).

A father also influences the development of empathy in his child; the more time he spends with his child, the more opportunities he has to model empathy and respond to his son's or daughter's emotional needs (Golant & Golant, 1992). During the preschool years, a father's consistency in discipline is further related to his child's socioemotional development. In a study conducted by Baumrind (1967), paternal consistent discipline was associated with likable, autonomous, imaginative, and confident behavior in boys, and well-socialized, friendly, and dependable behavior in girls.

Fathers and Physical Development. Most studies conducted in the area of fathers and the physical development of their children have been focused on the issue of how fathers play with their children. A general conclusion from this research is that fathers are not only more likely than mothers to be an infant's play partner, but the type of play initiated by fathers is different than that provided by mothers. Fathers tend to engage their infants in physically stimulating and unpredictable or idiosyncratic types of play. Mothers, meanwhile, are more likely to initiate conventional games (like peek-a-boo and pat-a-cake) and toy-mediated play (Stevens & Mathews, 1978). Fathers' play with infants tends to be proximal, vigorous, and arousing (Yogman, 1981). In addition, fathers frequently initiate limb movement games and engage in rough-and-tumble play (Bronstein & Cowan, 1988). This paternal play style undoubtedly fosters an infant's physical competence by providing opportunities for exercise and gross motor development.

Summary and Implications for Fatherhood Training. In summary, the research indicates that fathers do indeed influence their children's cognitive, socioemotional, and physical development. Because this impact begins during infancy, it is recommended that the counselor or consultant emphasize the importance of father involvement during the early childhood years and encourage teenage fathers to be present, available, and actively involved in caregiving. As noted by Smollar and Ooms (1987), "It is generally in the best interests of the children if their fathers develop a personal relationship with them and this should be encouraged" (p. 8).

While sharing this information, it is important to process the fathers' reactions. One common response among young fathers is a sense of affirmation about the father's role, especially among boys who might have been discouraged or denied involvement with their children by the mother and her family. Another familiar response is an expressed discomfort with the non-traditional nurturing role of fathers. The advantage of the group approach is that participants tend to vary in their representation of traditional and nontraditional gender role orientation. Group members who are more comfortable with their nurturing sides can serve as role models for the more traditional instrumental peers.

The Experience of Fatherhood. Most men experience a complex series of emotional and physical reactions to fatherhood, beginning with their reactions to the pregnancy. During the prenatal period, an expectant father often experiences *couvade syndrome,* a stress-related reaction that is manifested by physical aches and pains and anxieties about the birth and delivery of the baby (Bogren, 1986). He may feel acute anticipatory anxiety about his role during labor and childbirth. At the same time, he has empathy for his partner and typically attempts to be sensitive to the expectant mother's needs (Barnhill, Rubenstein, & Rocklin, 1979).

Men appear to bond with their children immediately after birth, especially if the father is present during the delivery. During the postnatal period, fathers commonly experience a strong emotional involvement with the infant. They enjoy gazing at their babies and delight in having physical contact with their children (Greenberg & Morris, 1974).

The postnatal period is also a time of transition as both fathers and mothers struggle with the changes in their relationship and reduced free time prompted by the addition of children to the family. The typical father experiences stress in juggling the demands of being a father, spouse, and worker. Nevertheless, he tends to view his child as a source of joy that can provide a renewed sense of excitement about life (Robinson & Barret, 1986).

Summary and Implications for Fatherhood Training. In summary, although fatherhood can prompt stress and anxiety, it also can help to define the father's identity and provide him with a significant source of satisfaction. Discussing this information can prepare teenage fathers for prenatal, delivery, and postnatal experiences. Through this process, participants can identify and share their particular anxieties, expectations, and mechanisms for coping.

Child Care Experiences

Didactic training can be enhanced by field trips to child care centers through which the young fathers can obtain hands-on experiences at observing and caring for children. Alternatively, some of the participants might bring their own children to the fatherhood course at which point practical training in child care can be instituted. In either case, it is recommended that the boys be taught how to observe infants and toddlers, prepare bottles and feed preschoolers, comfort children, diaper infants, change clothes of toddlers, prepare children for bed, and play with children in an age-appropriate manner (Kiselica et al., 1992). The boys who already are competent at these tasks can demonstrate skills for fathers who are ill prepared for the direct care of children. These practical experiences can enhance the fathers' cognitive and affective learning of what child care entails.

Offering a session on infant message can further promote the nurturant side of the fathers. This exercise strengthens father-infant attachment and promotes the physical and emotional well-being of babies. Again, many of the consultants mentioned earlier might offer this training.

Finally, it is recommended that parent education conclude with infant first aid training and a review of emergency procedures. This added feature can bolster the fathers' self-efficacy for responding to their children's needs. Counselors might consider enlisting local fire/police/hospital staff to offer this training to the group as a service (Kiselica et al., 1992).

A Special Note About
Expectant Teenage Fathers

The training covered thus far in this module has covered the essentials of parenting skills. With groups consisting of expectant teenage fathers, education regarding the couvade syndrome, the birth process, and the health risks of adolescent mothers is recommended.

During the prenatal period, expectant fathers often experience the couvade syndrome. Although research on the couvade syndrome has been focused almost exclusively on the experiences of adult expectant fathers, Kiselica and Scheckel (in press) reported that some expectant teenage fathers also experience this phenomenon. The boys who were reported to suffer from this reaction recovered after they were informed that these are common experiences of men during the prenatal period and after they received training about the child birth process.

Kiselica and Scheckel (in press) recommended that expectant teenage fathers be educated about the common prenatal reactions of expectant fathers and that they be prepared in some way for the delivery of the baby. The youth who is welcomed by the mother as a labor partner might be referred to join his partner in learning about the Lamaze method or some other form of birthing training. Other boys who have unstable, conflictual relationships with their partners may not be allowed to be present at delivery. Nevertheless, it is recommended that these expectant fathers receive some training about the birthing process to help allay their fears about the event and assist them in understanding the experience of their partners during the delivery of the baby.

Expectant fathers also can benefit from education about the potential health risks associated with adolescent pregnancies. Expectant teenage mothers, especially those who lack prenatal medical care, are more likely than expectant adult mothers in their 20s to give birth to low-birthweight babies (Children's Defense Fund, 1985). Low-birthweight babies are at risk for a variety of medical complications (Baum, 1980). Most expectant teenage fathers are naive about such health risks and need to be encouraged to assist the adolescent mother in receiving adequate prenatal and postnatal medical care.

Wrap-Up Session

During the final session of Module 2, each participant summarizes and processes with other group members what he learned and the changes in thinking, feeling, and behavior that were prompted by this module. Because a wealth of information has been shared, it can help the fathers to recap what they can do during the prenatal, infancy, and early childhood stages to support the mother and the child. The following ideas, drawn from Greenberg (1985), Sears (1986), and Horie and Horie (1988), can be printed "as is" on cards for the fathers to take with them as reference guides for use after the group has been terminated.

Prenatal Period. Talk to your baby in the womb while gently laying your hands on the mother's "bulge." Provide financial support to the extent that you can. Care and feed the pregnant mother and see that she visits her doctor regularly. Understand that she may have a reduced interest and capacity for sexual relations during the pregnancy. Hold her in your arms when she is worried. Listen to her concerns. Accompany her to the delivery. Celebrate the birth of your child.

Infancy Period. Help the mother to care for the baby. Sensitively support the mother who decided to breast-feed the baby. Walk, feed, and talk to your child. Play with your child. Take turns with the mother changing the baby's diapers. Relieve the mother when she is tired. Stay in tune with her concerns and needs. Childproof your residence. Comfort your child when he or she is frightened. Encourage your child to explore his or her immediate surroundings under your guidance.

Early Childhood. Teach your children values. Be a symbol of strength, a firm but gentle guide. Express your affection. Every day, tell your child that you love him or her. Establish traditions and positive memories.

Module 3: Responsible Sexual Behavior and Pertinent Coping Skills Training

Teenage fathers tend to be uninformed about sex and sexuality (Robinson, 1988a). They also are likely to engage in high-risk sexual behavior, even after they become fathers. For example, Achatz and MacAllum (1994) concluded that the majority of the 47 adolescent fathers participating in their ethnographic survey were at high risk for additional pregnancies and sexually transmitted diseases, including HIV, and noted that young fathers need support and strategies for dealing with social pressures to engage in unprotected sex.

In light of these considerations, many practitioners consider it a duty to teach teenage fathers about human sexuality and skills for coping with pressures to have sex. Module 3 was developed with this need in mind.

Module 3 is designed to cover from 5 to 10 class periods. The number of class periods depends on the length of time that can be devoted to class discussions and practice of pertinent skills.

Setting the Stage With a Discussion of Pressures to Engage in Sexual Relations

Although the subject of safe sex can prompt defensive reactions in teenage fathers, by this point in the course sufficient trust and support have been established to enable the participants to address this issue as the training enters the third and final stage. In spite of this trust, however, the topic must be introduced delicately. A safe way to broach the subject is to begin with a discussion of "what's going on out there," that is, to what extent are teenagers in general involved in sexual relations. The boys usually are not threatened by focusing on the behaviors of peers and typically report that most of their fellow teenagers are engaged in sexual relations. Once the young fathers appear to be fully engaged in the discussion, the group leader gradually can direct the boys to discuss their own sexual experiences, particularly the pressures they face to engage in sexual intercourse.

Two films can serve as tools for facilitating this discussion. The first, *No Time Soon* (ODN Productions, 1989), is a very realistic 16-minute video interview with two inner-city adolescent boys, one African American and one Hispanic American. The boys talk frankly about how they learned about sex, their opinions of girls, pressures on guys to engage in sexual relationships, birth control, and what it means to be a man. The second film, *It Only Takes Once* (Intermedia, Inc., 1987), is presented by teenagers on the realities of sex and the issue of pregnancy. It includes a group discussion with a high school sexuality class about the feelings and pressures that accompany adolescent sexual experiences.

Challenging Unsafe Sexual Practices

As the participants react to either of these films, the counselor can ask who is comfortable in disclosing to the group an account of his current involvement in sexual relations. A discussion of such behavior provides the counselor with an opportunity to challenge any boy who is not practicing "safe sex," especially any individual having unprotected sex with serial partners, and confront him about the realistic possibility that he might father other children. Kiselica et al. (1994) suggested the following pertinent confrontations: "Given your recent experiences as a teenage father, are you ready to become a father again? Because of the topics covered in Module 1, have you thought seriously about your conceptions of fatherhood? In light of this thinking, are you acting as a responsible father by engaging in unsafe sex? Given your systematic learning of child development in Module 2, you should now more fully understand the many needs of young children. Are you capable of adequately responding to the needs of another child?" In addition to these questions, it is important to confront sexual polygamists with the question, "Do you really want to risk contracting a serious sexually transmitted disease, such as AIDS, and possibly death?"

According to Kiselica (in press-b), although the group leader can confront teenage fathers about unsafe sexual practices, it is probably more effective to have the fathers confront one another on this issue. Usually, some teenage fathers recognize that they would be placing themselves in danger of experiencing even more adjustment difficulties by risking repeated paternity. Consequently, they have decided to carefully plan for the next pregnancy. These fathers are typically the ones who confront other participants who are less cautious sexually.

I have also suggested that this is an opportune time to confront any father who demonstrates a cavalier sexual attitude toward the mother of his child

(Kiselica, in press-b). If a father remains sexually involved with the mother of his child, he needs to understand that most adolescent mothers face greater pressures after the birth of a second child (see Horowitz, 1980). To avoid making his partner's life more difficult, both he and his partner will have to practice safe sex until they are sure of their commitment to one another and of their capabilities to raise a child properly. Again, confrontations of this sort are most successful when they originate from teenage fathers in the group who are more responsive to the needs of the adolescent mother.

Counselors can capitalize on these confrontations by showing yet another film, titled *Not Me* (Production People, Ltd., 1990). Because this video is designed to discourage adolescent girls from becoming mothers, it features the difficult experiences of several actual teenage mothers from a variety of cultural backgrounds. It also illustrates how some teenage boys abide by cavalier, insensitive attitudes regarding sexual responsibility. The group leader can challenge the participants to examine their own behavior to determine if they, too, have held such attitudes at times. In an effort to promote perspective taking, the boys should be prompted to consider the experiences of the girls featured in the video and how those are similar and dissimilar to the experiences of their partners. The counselor can inform the participants that adolescent mothers face greater pressures after a second birth (see Horowitz, 1980). Following this information, it is timely to ask, "Do you truly intend to make life more difficult on your partners?" and "How can you be more supportive and considerate of your partners?"

The discussion of sexual pressures concludes with the participants considering how their attitudes regarding sexual responsibility might have been influenced by the discussion. In addition, group members are asked to describe measures they employ to deal with current pressures to have sex. The disclosure of their tactics serves as a segue into formal coping skills training.

Coping With Pressures
to Engage in Sexual Relations

Recent research evaluating the efficacy of sexual education for preventing teenage pregnancies has indicated that the effectiveness of didactic instruction on human sexuality, reproduction, and contraceptive use is enhanced when combined with training in pertinent coping skills, including assertiveness and self-instructional methods (Brindis, 1991).

A fine resource for orienting the trainer to this subject is Howard's (1991) *How to Help Your Teenager Postpone Sexual Involvement*. This book explains the developmental changes during adolescence and how those changes affect sexual decision making. This book also provides tips for understanding the adolescent's feelings and providing the youth with coping skills. Although this book focuses on postponing sexual involvement, many of the ideas contained in it are potentially helpful to teenage fathers who wish to change their sexual behavior.

The group leader also can use Rench's (1988) *Teen Sexuality: Decisions and Choices,* a book that teaches young fathers how to cope with sexual pressures. This resource provides many ideas that adolescents can use to assert themselves during sexual encounters. These include suggestions for how to respond to sexual pressure, what to say, and how to avoid repeated uncomfortable situations. An outstanding feature of this book is that alternatives to sexual intercourse as a means of expressing affection are covered. It is recommended that the counselor ask each participant to read this book and then discuss his reactions during the counseling sessions.

As a supplement to this bibliotherapy assignment, the counselor can incorporate the cognitive-behavioral, pregnancy-prevention training procedures developed by a team of researchers at the University of Washington (see Schinke et al., 1981; Schinke et al., 1989). Through these procedures trainees are first taught the facts about human reproduction and contraception. Training in cognitive problem solving follows to assist youth in recognizing problems, deriving a variety of solutions to problems, and anticipating outcomes when solutions are exercised. Nonverbal and verbal communication is taught in such a way that trainees are prepared to broach the topic of sex with a date or spouse and raise a discussion with the date or spouse about contraceptive use or postponement of sexual intercourse. Finally, group members are taught to planfully transfer rehearsed behavior to the natural environment.

During the coping skills phase of the training, the counselor again can employ the services of a consultant to teach the sexual education component. It is recommended that a male consultant be recruited so that the boys can have frank male-to-male discussions about human sexuality and contraception. Potential consultants include a physician, nurse, health educator or planned parenthood counselor (Kiselica et al., 1992).

Wrap-Up Session

Coping skills training concludes with each participant stating his views on responsible sexual behavior, as well as any changes in thinking, feeling, and behavior that were prompted by this module (Kiselica et al., 1992).

Addressing Termination Issues

Once the formal training has been completed, attention is directed toward termination issues. The group discusses their progress in becoming caring, responsible fathers. Each member shares his self-evaluation of the progress he has made and solicits feedback from other members. In addition, group members help each other in identifying work that still needs to be done. For example, one member still may feel unclear about proper child care procedures and another might continue to have a cavalier attitude toward sex. Unfinished business is defined and plans for addressing it are formulated. The group leader asks the boys to describe their anxieties related to termination and explains that some degree of anxiety is normal as groups end their work together. Boys who wish to remain in touch for peer support are encouraged to do so. In addition, the group leader assures participants that they can seek out him or her or their case manager for more help in the future.

Fatherhood training concludes with some sort of celebration through which the boys' hard work is applauded and rewarded. For example, a farewell dinner party can be organized during which the participants are awarded certificates for their participation. Afterward, the young men might engage in one last game of basketball or attend a sporting event together. The goal of this special evening is to send the boys off with a sense of accomplishment and a smile.

Combining Fatherhood Training
With Other Services

A final challenge related to fatherhood training is how to incorporate this therapeutic activity into other services for adolescent fathers. Suggestions from Chapter 3 regarding the coordinating functions of the lead agency and the case manager apply here. That is, when possible, parent skills training should be offered as a component of a multifaceted service program offered at the lead agency. It is recommended that the case manager monitor the progress of his or her individual clients throughout the fatherhood course and guide the clients to any other services they might need. In addition to applying these general guidelines, readers may wish to read Streett (1991) for an in-depth discussion of how to integrate parent education into medical services offered at health clinics for teenage parents and several pertinent chapters from Miller, Card, Paikoff, and Peterson (1992) on developing comprehensive school-based service programs. The role of schools in offering a cluster of services and the educational and career issues of teenage fathers are discussed in detail in the next chapter.

7

Educational and
Career Counseling

An inability to finish school, unemployment, and a lack of money are among the problems most frequently reported by teenage fathers (Achatz & MacAllum, 1994; Elster & Hendricks, 1986; Elster & Panzarine, 1983b; Hendricks, 1988; Hendricks et al., 1981). Adolescent fathers are more likely than their nonfather counterparts to have poor academic records (Lerman, 1985) and drop out of school (Marsiglio, 1986, 1987). Also, it is common for young fathers to be unemployed at 1 and 5 years after high school (Card & Wise, 1978), overrepresented in blue-collar jobs, and underrepresented in white-collar professions (Buchanan & Robbins, 1990; Lerman, 1985).

According to Brindis (1993) and Parke and Neville (1987), the direction of causality between early fatherhood and educational attainment is probably bidirectional. That is, early fatherhood can cause a young man to drop out of school, and termination of education can lead to early fatherhood. It follows that outreach must occur both in schools with young fathers who have not yet dropped out and in communities with adolescent males who already have left the educational system. In addition, outreach programs should offer educational and career counseling and job training. Yet although it is common for programs to offer educational services to teenage parents, relatively

143

few of these programs have offered or brokered career-related services to their clients (Kiselica & Sturmer, 1993b; Polit, 1987). This is surprising in light of the employment and financial problems experienced by teenage parents. Furthermore, this is unacceptable in "a country where one's worth is judged primarily in three arenas—school, work, and family" (Pittman, 1986, p. 8).

The purpose of this chapter is to provide counselors and educators with a theoretical framework and practical guidelines for educational and career counseling with teenage fathers. This chapter begins with a discussion of the interrelationship between career and personal issues. It is argued that schools are appropriate sites for multifaceted service programs. The philosophical controversy related to this issue is addressed. Super's (1957) model of career development is highlighted to provide the reader with a foundation for viewing career development as an ongoing process rather than a stagnant event. It is proposed that unplanned fatherhood is the precipitant and/or the consequence of a career developmental crisis. A developmental educational and career counseling process is described and the current status of career counseling with teenage fathers is critiqued. This chapter concludes with a description of comprehensive school-based service programs for teenage parents.

The Interrelationship Between
Career and Personal Issues

Historically, the helping professions have treated career issues as being quite distinct from other areas of personal functioning. Hackett (1993) charged that this is a "false dichotomy" (p. 105). She and a variety of other writers (e.g., Blustein, 1990; Herr, 1989; Osipow & Fitzgerald, 1993; Savickas, 1991; Slaney & MacKinnon-Slaney, 1990; Spokane, 1991) have argued that there is considerable overlap between career and personal issues. Work is intimately connected to the rest of one's life. Consequently, as Herr (1989) pointed out, there is a relationship between career development and mental health such that events in one domain can influence the other in an interactive fashion. For example, the school and work performance of a teenage father might suffer, in part, because of significant relationship difficulties with his partner. Eventually, the youth might drop out of school or be terminated by an employer. These latter stressors can further exacerbate tensions between the young parents.

These considerations compel us to remember that the educational and career needs of the teenage father must be considered in relation to the other spheres of his life. Thus, although this chapter focuses on educational and career counseling, the reader is encouraged to weave the suggestions contained in this chapter into the overall counseling process so that the personal and career issues of the teenage father can be addressed simultaneously. It is argued here that schools are appropriate sites for accomplishing this task.

Multifaceted Service Programs and the Role of the Schools

Meeting the many needs of teenage fathers is a complicated case management challenge. The odds of successfully helping young fathers are enhanced when a variety of services are offered for young men at the same setting. Several scholars (Flood, Greenspan, & Mundorf, 1985; Kiselica & Pfaller, 1993; Lindsay & Rodine, 1989a) have argued that schools are ideal settings for the provision of multifaceted service programs for teenage parents. This is a controversial proposal that has met much opposition.

Although many schools across the United States now house adolescent pregnancy and parenting programs, many prominent people have opposed this trend, including powerful political figures. For example, during the 1992 presidential campaign, Vice-President Dan Quayle repeatedly cited the rise in single-parent households as evidence of a decay of family values in America (see Whitehead, 1993). Central to Quayle's argument was the belief that society is harmed by parents who are too ready to divorce and/or play a role in out-of-wedlock pregnancies. Quayle pointed out that children born to such parents are more likely to suffer economic and psychological hardships than children raised in intact two-parent families. Another consequence lamented by Quayle is that the public schools have been forced to bear the burden of helping children, not because they are intellectually or physically impaired, but because they are emotionally incapacitated. An implication of Quayle's argument is that the emotional and psychological needs of children should be met at home and that schools should be left to the business of providing a quality, traditional education rather than therapeutic remediation.

Quayle is not alone in questioning what has been called "the psychologization of American education" (Whitehead, 1993, p. 77). Doyle (1993) criticized the trend of schools attempting to fill the social service needs of children and argued that schools should return to the central mission of providing academic instruction. Howe (1993) questioned an overreliance on schools to provide the stimulation and guidance young people need to mature successfully. In the future, Howe suggested, educational and social policy must address how it can strengthen families to effectively shepherd youth into adulthood. Males (1993) has questioned the appropriateness of school-based teenage pregnancy programs because schools have no control over those adults who model misbehavior. The teenage pregnancy problem can be curbed, Males recommended, if we stop trying to fix teenagers and instead focus our attention on the larger societal context that engenders teenagers to become parents out of wedlock.

These concerns highlight the burdens placed on our educational system and illuminate the role of society in the widespread problem of teenage pregnancy and parenthood. Because schools cannot, on their own, solve the problem, we must entertain how we can marshal all of our societal institutions to prevent and respond to unplanned teenage parenthood. However, as social scientists and policymakers struggle to devise a societal solution, schools cannot ignore the millions of teenage parents whose many difficulties require numerous forms of assistance. In the words of Shapiro (1990), "While rejecting a notion of social reform that sees education as the primary agent of change, it would nevertheless be wrong to exclude it entirely from the process of social change" (p. 102).

Schools are a natural setting to furnish a comprehensive range of services for several reasons. First, schools provide access to those student parents who are still enrolled (Kiselica & Pfaller, 1993; Lindsay & Rodine, 1989a). Second, except in large rural districts, schools are within commuting distance for teenage parents who have dropped out. Third, according to Brindis (1991), schools that provide needy adolescents with a host of services enable them to do "one-stop shopping." Fourth, schools employ personnel who are trained to work with adolescents and are capable of delivering many of the services required by teenage parents (Kiselica & Pfaller, 1993; Lindsay & Rodine, 1989a).

In addition to these practical considerations, a long-standing philosophical tradition, as well as prior practice precedents, supports the idea that schools should help to address the social needs of children. Much of educational practice in the United States has been influenced by Dewey's philosophy of education, which emphasized instruction characterized by flexibility and responsiveness to individual student needs (Dewey, 1929; Schilpp, 1939). As evidence of this philosophy put into practice, Tyack's (1992) review indicated there is an extensive history of providing noneducational services to children in school settings. This tradition has been prompted and propelled over the years during periods of educational reform that had been spawned by changes in society. Several current educational theorists have reiterated and extended the concept of individualized instruction in calls for educational reform. For example, Darling-Hammond (1993) argued that school reform starts from the assumptions that students are not standardized and that teaching is not routine. Wagner (1993) proposed that schools "must find ways to connect the curriculum to adolescents' concerns, needs and individual interests . . . [and] adolescents need to feel part of a community in which they are known and cared for by responsible adults" (pp. 699-700). Hodgkinson (1993) warned that "we need to provide a seamless web of services, combining education, health care, housing, transportation and social welfare" (p. 623) to effectively help one third of our nation's students who are at risk.

Hodgkinson's (1993) forecast is an expression of the emerging philosophy of the welfare-educational system. According to Shapiro (1990), this philosophy is based on the principle of educational equity and the notion of the "whole child," which asserts that

> the ability to learn is inseparable from the satisfaction of an individual's physical and emotional needs. . . . Successful schooling is understood as necessarily linked to the provision of a much broader set of social services: adequate health care and access to preventive treatment; the availability of adequate food and nutritional resources; the opportunity to alleviate emotional and mental distress; and the provision of an adequate home and physical environment. (p. 143)

Although the development of school-based services is advocated, schools should not bear the burden alone. Rather, schools should serve as the operating base for multifaceted service programs, supported by multiple sources of funding and personnel from other institutions (see Chapter 3), thereby placing education within the broader structures of the welfare state. Although schools may play an important role as the lead institution in a service coalition, the major specific role of school personnel should be to provide for the educational and career needs of teenage parents and encourage agencies to set up shop in schools. Similarly, Murphy (1993) stated that schools must become more relevant to their communities by serving as more than just a place where children are educated. That is, schools should develop partnerships with social and health agencies, remain open for business 7 days a week, 12 months a year, and provide parents and children struggling to overcome the untold hardships of poverty a safe haven for health care, socializing, and recreation. Dryfoos (1994) advocated for the same type of school-community partnerships in her compelling argument in favor of full-service schools.

As schools consider their contributions to such partnerships, it should be remembered that school counselors are particularly well suited to provide educational and career counseling to teenage parents by the nature of their training, the career resources available to them in school guidance libraries, and their access to adolescents. School counselors also are trained to address the personal concerns of adolescents and develop referral services. Thus, because school counselors can play an integral part in responding to many of the needs of teenage parents, they are an obvious choice for participation in any pertinent service coalition, either as direct service providers or as consultants to other professionals (Kiselica & Pfaller, 1993).

How can educators and counselors help adolescent fathers fulfill their career potential while meeting their responsibilities as parents? Answering this question begins with an understanding that teenage parenthood can be the precipitant and/or the consequence of a career developmental crisis.

Teenage Parenthood:
A Career Developmental Crisis

Although several writers (e.g., Freeman, 1987; Hayes & Cryer, 1988; Montemayor, 1986; Robinson, 1988a) have recognized that teenage parenthood represents a *developmental identity crisis,* and although some (e.g., Freeman, 1987; Lindner, 1988; Polit, 1987; Robinson, 1988a) have argued that teenage parents need *vocational counseling and job training,* to date no one has conceptualized teenage parenthood as a *career developmental crisis.* In light of the compelling data suggesting that individuals tend to progress though life stages of career development (see Super, 1985) and recognizing that unplanned parenthood affects development, career counseling can be most effective with teenage fathers when it is approached from a culturally sensitive career developmental perspective.

In this section, Super's (1957) model of vocational development is described to provide the reader with a foundation for thinking about career development as a process that unfolds over time. It is hypothesized that unplanned adolescent parenthood can be the precipitant and the consequence of a career developmental crisis.

Super's Career Development Theory

Super (1957) suggested that career development progresses through five stages. The Growth Stage (birth to 14 years) is characterized by the development of one's self-concept. The self-concept may be redefined repeatedly as the individual moves through the remaining stages. During the Exploration Stage (15 to 24 years), the individual makes a tentative occupational choice (15 to 17 years), faces the transition from school to work (18 to 21 years), and experiences a period of trial (22 to 24 years) at one's first permanent role as worker or advanced trainee. In the Establishment Stage (25 to 44 years), the individual works on determining a permanent place in his or her field of choice. The task of developing security and seniority in one's career occurs during the Maintenance Stage (45 to 64 years) and is followed by the transition into and experience of retirement during the Decline Stage (65 years and older).

Although this developmental progression is common, Super (1985) acknowledged that some individuals never stop exploring, others move from one stage to the next without having successfully completed the requisite tasks of the prior stage, and many recycle through the stages in response to shifts in interests and values with age and experience. The ages and tasks deemed to be appropriate for particular stages also may vary according to the unique cultural experience of the client (see Cheatham, 1990a; Parham & Austin, 1994). These variations in career development are influenced by a variety of factors, such as socioeconomic level, values orientation, racial identity development, educational opportunity, and racism (Cheatham, 1990a; Herr & Niles, 1994; Parham & Austin, 1994), as well as major life events, such as unplanned parenthood (Kiselica & Murphy, 1994).

Unplanned Parenthood as a Precipitant and Consequence of a Career Developmental Crisis

It is common for adolescent males experiencing unplanned parenthood to report that the pregnancy interrupted their educational and career plans, thereby precipitating a career developmental crisis. With other adolescents, however, the unplanned pregnancy may be the a consequence of a preexisting career developmental crisis that can spark additional crises. Data from qualitative studies of teenage fathers indicate that many are poor, faced with limited opportunities, and raised in neighborhoods ravaged by crime (Achatz & MacAllum, 1994; Dash, 1989; Sullivan, 1985). These youth realistically may envision a life of poverty and a shortened life expectancy. Consequently, education may have little meaning to these youth and they may perceive career exploration to be an exercise in futility. Thus, a career developmental crisis exists prior to the pregnancy as these adolescents struggle to find some fulfillment and a sense of achievement in the context of limited life options. Although these youngsters consciously may have never expected or planned to become parents as teenagers, becoming a parent might represent a way to establish an adult identity. As Pittman (1986) stated, when disadvantaged teenagers cannot hope to find steady, full-time employment, or "even believe with any certainty that they will have survived the dangers of the streets to be alive at age 25 . . . the lure of parenthood stands unopposed" (p. 8). But parenthood can complicate the life of these teenagers further as they try to make additional career decisions in the face of the many responsibilities associated with paternity. Under these circumstances, adolescent fatherhood may be viewed as both the manifestation and the precipitant of career developmental crises.

In either case, the road to economic self-sufficiency for teenage fathers is arduous. Data from numerous studies examining the educational, vocational, and economic consequences of teenage parenthood indicate that for most teenage fathers, the Exploration Stage is disrupted, the transition from school to work is abrupt, and limited initial occupational options are viewed as permanent rather than temporary. For example, approximately one third of teenage fathers drop out of school (Children's Defense Fund, 1987a). According to Card and Wise (1978), the truncated schooling experiences of teenage fathers cause them to occupy lower-paying blue-collar jobs and enter the labor force earlier than their unmarried classmates. Because of their limited orientation to the world of work and in response to the many interpersonal stressors associated with premature parenthood, teenage parents lower their educational goals and vocational aspirations (Rus-Eft, Sprenger, & Beever, 1979). Not surprisingly, teenage fathers receive less education, earn lower salaries, and have less fulfilling work experiences than their nonparent peers over time (Buchanan & Robbins, 1990; Kerckhoff & Parrow, 1979; Lerman, 1985).

These findings suggest that teenage fathers are likely to be deprived from achieving tasks that Super, Starishevsky, Matlin, and Jordaan (1963) viewed as important during the Exploration Stage. That is, because teenage fathers typically drop out of school, they miss opportunities to learn how to use career resources, explore career information, develop career decision-making skills, plan for future occupations, and receive the requisite training for those occupations. Dropping out of school and/or demands to work or care for the baby diminish opportunities to participate with peers and adult role models though extracurricular activities. Because these latter experiences are so critical for the formation of the self-concept (see Super, 1983), adolescent fathers have difficulties clarifying their interests, abilities, needs, and values. Consequently, they have inadequate information about themselves, further hampering their career decision-making abilities. Lacking the prerequisite tools for effective career planning, it is not surprising that most teenage fathers experience vocational and educational frustration (see Elster & Hendricks, 1986; Elster & Panzarine, 1983b; Hendricks, 1988; Hendricks et al., 1981). A sense of hopelessness about the future often follows, leading many to experience what Super (1985) has described as premature career foreclosure.

Implications for Career Counseling

According to Gysbers (1988), viewing careers from a developmental perspective implies that career counseling must be responsive to the developmental long-term career needs of students, as well as to their more immediate career crisis needs. Based on this rationale, Kiselica, Stroud, et al. (1992) recommended that career and educational counseling consist of two phases. During the prenatal phase, counseling is crisis oriented and focused on helping the teenage father with immediate decisions related to school and work. During the postnatal phase, long-term educational and career planning occurs. Kiselica and Murphy (1994) provided specific ideas for how to integrate career development concepts into this two-phased counseling process. In the following section, the suggestions of Kiselica and Murphy (1994) are highlighted and extended.

Career Counseling During the Prenatal Phase

Super (1985) suggested that personal crises can destabilize career development in some individuals. According to Caplan (1961) and Parrad (1967), crisis situations demand that counselors take immediate steps to stabilize the situation for the client. Because teenage fathers are in a state of crisis once they learn about the unplanned pregnancy, they often respond with rash decisions, such as dropping out of school without weighing all of the alternatives and consequences associated with such an action. In light of this possibility, Kiselica, Stroud, et al. (1992) recommended that counselors can best assist young fathers during the prenatal phase by helping them with crisis-oriented decision making regarding school and work.

A major question to address during the prenatal period is whether or not the teenage father should drop out of school. In some school districts this dilemma is minimized by the provision of alternative schools or mainstreamed special educational programs for teenage parents. Typically, school-based programs provide infant care and a special school curriculum that allow the teenage parent to continue with an education and participate in work/study cooperative programs (Flood et al., 1985). Thus, the young father can earn money while attending school on a part-time basis, thereby increasing the likelihood that he will complete high school while supporting a family. Counselors arranging for alternative school placements are urged to support teenage fathers during the transition from the regular school to the alternative school setting.

When school districts lack alternative school options for teenage parents, the career counselor faces a more difficult challenge in preventing dropouts among this group. A critical first step in these instances is to help the youth make child care arrangements for the baby. According to the Children's Defense Fund (1987a), the provision of child care enables many teenage parents to continue with school, especially if it is coupled with other services, such as personal and vocational counseling.

Unfortunately, many teenage fathers will still decide to drop out of school. Counselors need to reach out immediately to young fathers who leave school and carefully investigate the reasons behind these decisions. In many cases, the young father had been losing interest in school prior to the pregnancy, either because of poor educational performance and/or a bleak outlook regarding the future, and the pregnancy provided him with a justification for leaving school. Reaching out to him, communicating a genuine concern for his hardships, and linking him up with special educational services might help to dissuade him from leaving school. If the youth resides in an area characterized by very limited economic opportunity, additional innovative strategies (see Chapter 11) designed to improve his life chances may be necessary to instill him with the belief that completing school is worthwhile.

In spite of these outreach measures, some teenage fathers will drop out because of continued academic difficulties and/or because of economic necessity. In these instances the counselor should be certain that the young parent has adequately explored all possible options by posing the following questions: Has the academically troubled student given special educational services a genuine try? Can the student remain in school while working during evenings and/or on weekends? How many hours must he work? Did he previously plan on attending college or technical school, and if so, what immediate changes in these plans are necessary (Kiselica, Stroud, et al., 1992)? Has he adequately examined the ability and willingness of his family and his partner's family to provide financial support (Kiselica & Murphy, 1994)?

Kiselica, Stroud, et al. (1992) advised that teenage fathers who opt to work, either on a part- or full-time basis, might need a "crash course" (p. 344) in job-seeking and job-keeping skills. Counselors also are advised to explore the teenage parent's attitudes toward work and his perception of job responsibilities. To develop the youth's job-seeking skills, counselors can use Galassi and Galassi's (1978) ideas on image management; Kerr, Claiborn, and Dixon's (1982) suggestions for teaching persuasion skills; and they can provide clients with instructions and simulations at writing resumes and job applications. *The Adolescent Parent Resource Guide* (Ohio State Department of Education, 1989), a comprehensive resource on the job-search process for teenage parents, contains sections on application, letter, and resume writing; interview skills; image management; and strategies for job success. To assist the young father to find job training, job placement, and educational assistance services, counselors can contact county employment offices for information about programs offered through the Job Corps and the Job Training Partnership Act (JTPA). Similar services typically are available through the local office of Goodwill Industries. To expand the job-keeping skills of teenage parents, counselors can emphasize the importance of good interpersonal relations and conduct pertinent training through Guerney's (1982) Relationship Enhancement, which is designed to enrich personal relationships and prevent problems that occur within them. These efforts will help teenage parents to develop realistic work expectations and find and maintain employment (Kiselica, Stroud, et al., 1992). Furthermore, assisting with concrete concerns, such as finding a job, is an excellent way to develop rapport and enhances the possibility that the teenage father will engage in the counseling process over the long term (Hendricks, 1988).

Sensitive counseling with school dropouts can unveil other reasons why young fathers leave school. In rare instances, an adolescent male is forced out of school by teachers and/or administrators who blatantly want to punish the boy for his role in an unplanned pregnancy. A more common response, fueled by a variety of conscious and unconscious reactions, is for school personnel to subtly discourage a young father from remaining in school. Both forms of treatment are prohibited by federal law under Title IX of the Education Amendments of 1972. This legislation bars public schools from discriminating on the basis of sex in the application of any rule concerning student pregnancy, parenthood, or marital status (U.S. Department of Education, 1991).

When counselors learn that young fathers have been coerced by school personnel to leave school, the appropriate intervention is to inform the boy of his legal rights and serve as an activist advocate on the boy's behalf. In upholding the youth's rights, both informal and formal steps should be considered, much of which applies to the work of school counselors and school psychologists.

Informal advocacy measures typically can rectify the situation before official steps are necessary. This work begins with an attempt to understand the motivations behind a colleague's behavior, which may reflect the influence of societal stereotypes and/or unconscious reactions. When biases are the factor involved, the belief that teenage fathers are exploitative youth can cause some school personnel to treat the young man with hostility, thereby giving him the implicit message that he is not welcome in school. In these instances, it can be helpful to approach a colleague to share information that might prompt him or her to think more complexly about teenage fathers. In other instances, discussions with a colleague might unveil unconscious forces at play. Mackey and Milloy (1974) have described a number of unconscious reactions of teachers and school personnel that may create a hostile climate for the teenage parent in school. For example, a teacher who has had trouble conceiving a child may unconsciously envy a teenager for his or her ability to produce one. Or, a male teacher could be very punitive with a boy who got a girl pregnant because of his recollections of and unconscious guilt about what he had done in his own adolescence. In these latter cases, the school counselor must sensitively explore the colleagues' hostility, point out these issues when they surface, and discuss how they affect reactions to the young parent.

When informal measures fail, it is recommended that the counselor report the violation to his or her immediate supervisor and be prepared to go over the supervisor's head if no immediate action is taken. In this scenario, counselors are advised to follow the chain of command, first reporting to the school administrator, and if that is unsuccessful, then contacting the local school board and the office of educational equity at the state department of education.

Dilemmas of this sort require courage on the part of the professional championing a teenage father's rights. He or she could be labeled a "troublemaker" for "making waves." This is a lonely and frightening position to be in, particularly if the person reporting the violation is a professional employed in the setting where the offense occurred. Therefore, the counselor is urged to find allies. Fellow professionals at the local level can be invaluable sources of moral support. Usually, officials at the state office of educational equity can provide assurance of protection from retaliation. The practice directorate of professional organizations, such as the American Counseling Association or the American Psychological Association, often can render expert guidance in such matters.

While seeking assistance for him- or herself, the counselor is reminded to support the teenage father. Affirm his desire to remain in school and keep reminding him of the importance of completing an education to compete in today's economy. Hook him up with teachers and peers who are sympathetic to his cause so that he does not feel isolated in his struggle. Inform his parents of his rights and empower them to demand from school officials that the appropriate action is taken.

Finally, some teenage fathers drop out of school without consulting or informing anyone about their decision. School programs that serve only those currently enrolled in school miss these potential clients. Identifying and assisting these youth to complete their educations and find meaningful employment require the use of the extensive outreach strategies discussed in Chapter 3, followed by the provision of the counseling interventions suggested in this chapter. Some of these youth may have experienced significant periods of unemployment and need help to overcome their frustration. Once again, the Job Corps, JTPA, and Goodwill Industries can assist these young men to find work through their various training and placement services. In addition, these offices often offer counseling groups to help discouraged workers rebuild their self-esteem and rekindle their motivation to look for work. Counselors also can write to the Center on Education and Training for Employment located at the College of Education at The Ohio State University. This office markets numerous publications on the subjects of the retraining and upgrading of skills for unskilled and underskilled workers. Besides using these resources, school personnel may wish to contact the coordinator of Adolescent Family Education for the Tucson, Arizona, school system (described in Lindsay & Rodine, 1989b) to learn about their outreach program for getting dropouts back into the educational system. Alternatively, school personnel can read about the strategies used by the staff in Public/Private Venture's Young Unwed Fathers Pilot Project (see Achatz & MacAllum, 1994) to enroll school dropouts in educational and job training programs.

Career Counseling During the Postnatal Stage

Crisis-oriented educational and career decisions typically represent a compromise between the teenage parent's preferred plans and the rapidly emerging responsibilities of parenthood. The purpose of this compromise is to help the youth weather the crisis period. Sometimes, teenage fathers lose sight of this fact, are lulled into a false sense of security by their initial salaries, and forsake their prior career aspirations (Kiselica, Stroud, et al., 1992). Others never develop career goals because of the hopelessness engendered in economically depressed communities. In either case, the teenage parent must be taught that career planning is a process, not an event (see Gysbers, 1988; Herr & Cramer, 1988). Premature career foreclosure must be prevented. Hence, it is imperative that teenage parents participate in long-term developmental career counseling.

Super (1983) recommended that developmental career counseling begin with a comprehensive assessment that measures the following: (a) the individual's abilities, as estimated by multiple aptitude batteries, such as the Differential Aptitude Test (Bennett, Seashore, & Wesman, 1972); (b) interests and values, as assessed by interest inventories, such as the Self-Directed Search (Holland, 1979); (c) commitment for work, as measured by the Salience Inventory (Nevill & Super, 1986); and (d) career maturity, as gauged by the Career Development Inventory (Super, Thompson, Lindeman, Jordaan, & Myers, 1981). Because space limitations preclude a detailed explanation of this assessment process, the reader is referred to several helpful references on the subject (e.g., Spokane, 1991; Super, 1983; Super, Osborne, Walsh, Brown, & Niles, 1992).

Super's (1983) approach to career assessment must be modified and extended according to the particular cultural background of the client to estimate adequately the client's readiness for career decision making and provide culturally salient information that the client can use in making such decisions. For example, the counselor is recommended to assess the influence of racial identity development on the values orientation of African American clients (Parham & Austin, 1994). This and other culturally sensitive adjustments in career assessment have been discussed at length by other scholars (Baly, 1989; Cheatham, 1990a; Herr & Niles, 1994; Parham & Austin, 1994) and are reviewed throughout Part II of this book.

After completing a developmental career assessment, career counselors can employ a number of useful resources that are specifically tailored to the needs of teenage parents and stimulate behaviors that are pertinent to the Exploration Stage of career development. For example, Garner (1989) has developed a career exploration curriculum for teenage parents titled *Workwise: A Career Awareness Course for Teen Parents*. This educational package includes units on occupations, developing a future and planful orientation to careers, coping strategies for the working parent, finding a job, and succeeding on the job. Whipple's (1987) *Career Orientation and Preparation for Teen Parents Curriculum*, which includes instructions for how to conduct a comprehensive career assessment, is similar to that suggested by Super (1983). Whipple's curriculum includes plans for field trips to work sites that correspond to students' career interests and numerous exercises designed to clarify interests and values, develop assertiveness and decision-making skills, enhance self-esteem, and expand occupational aspirations. *The Career Planning Workbook: From Astronaut to Zoologist—Career Survival Kit for Teen Education and Employment* (Lindner & Mellen-Sullivan, 1987) is similar in content to Whipple's curriculum. The *Adolescent Parent Resource Guide,* published by the Ohio State Department of Education (1989), contains sections on needs and values assessments, occupational choices, nontraditional jobs, career goals and decisions, as well as tips on job-seeking and job-keeping skills, financial planning, insurance, overcoming barriers to employment, and balancing family and work responsibilities. These special materials can be supplemented by the job-seeking and job-keeping resources mentioned earlier.

The career planning and exploration materials described above can be used to help all teenage fathers clarify their self-concept, become aware of occupational options and their associated training requirements, and develop effective decision-making skills. However, additional activities may be necessary to fully address the long-term career developmental counseling needs of specific cultural groups of teenage fathers. For example, according to Herr and Niles (1994) ethnic-minority clients may need to be taught skills to effectively cope with racism. In addition, individual and group career counseling with disadvantaged youth may be fruitless unless they are supported by policies designed to increase opportunities in economically depressed communities. These and other culture-specific career counseling considerations are addressed in more detail throughout Part II of this book.

The Current Status of Career Counseling With Teenage Parents

Understanding the developmental career counseling process provides a context for evaluating the current status of career counseling with teenage parents. On the whole, the pertinent literature reflects a narrow view of the subject: Career preparation is treated as an event through which the teenage parent is placed in a job. Numerous examples illustrate this perspective. In two of the most influential books on teenage fathers, *Adolescent Fatherhood* (Elster & Lamb, 1986) and *Teenage Fathers* (Robinson, 1988a), job-skills training is noted as being important, but no specific guidelines for conducting developmental career assessments and planning are offered. The same criticism holds for Pittman's (1986) discussion of vocational education with adolescent parents and for some descriptions of programs (e.g., Coyle-Williams & Wermuth, 1990; Orange County Public Schools, 1987) that were developed to address the educational and vocational needs of teenage parents.

A few articles do appear to approach career planning from a developmental process orientation. In discussing vocational education for teenage parents, Burge (1987) and Lindner (1988) emphasized the importance of assessing skills, interests, and needs; providing employability-skills training; and acquiring work experiences during school and job placement after school is completed. Polit (1987) described an employment training project for teenage mothers provided by the YWCA of Salem, Oregon. Initial training focuses on career exploration and the teaching of job readiness skills. Once students master these tasks, they are employed in several different work placements, which are combined with related classwork.

Although these latter examples indicate that a few model programs have incorporated a developmental flavor to career assessment and counseling with teenage parents, Polit (1987) concluded that these are the exception rather than the rule. Instead, it appears that vocational counseling, if provided at all, tends to focus on the crisis-oriented task of helping teenage parents to find a job. Longer-range career planning is largely forsaken. If practitioners and schools are to help teenage fathers achieve and maintain economic self-sufficiency and gratifying lifestyles, then they must conduct career counseling and planning from a developmental perspective.

Comprehensive School-Based
Service Programs

Educational and career counseling represent just some of the many needs of teenage fathers that schools may see fit to address. Although educators continue to debate whether or not schools should move beyond the mission of preparing students for work and higher education, many schools have developed comprehensive service programs for teenage parents. In this section, the characteristics of these programs are highlighted, issues involved in implementing school-based services effectively are discussed, and several exemplary programs are described.

Characteristics of School-Based Programs

In their review of the literature on school-based services for pregnant and parenting adolescents, Flood et al. (1985) reported that pertinent programs offer some combination of the following services: child care, contraceptive information and distribution, sexuality values clarification, parenting skills training, and case management/counseling and health services. The latter category includes medical, mental health, counseling advocacy, and liaison/referral activities.

The services available through school-based health clinics have changed over the past decade. Initially, health clinics focused almost exclusively on providing reproductive services, which included pregnancy counseling, prenatal care, testing and treatment of sexually transmitted diseases, pregnancy testing, and postpartum care. In recent years, however, school-based clinics have attempted to address a broader range of health issues. Phipps-Yonas (1980) argued that this transformation normalizes the use of the clinic for all students and avoids stigmatizing those who desire reproductive services. Consequently, many of the health-related services offered through school-based clinics now include the following: primary health care, physical examinations, laboratory tests, diagnosis and treatment of illness and minor injuries, immunizations, gynecological exams, birth control information and referral, pregnancy testing and counseling, referral for prenatal care, nutrition education, weight reduction programs, and counseling for substance abuse (Kirby & Waszak, 1992).

Issues for Schools

Parental Permission for Treatment and Confidentiality. Receiving parental permission is not a prerequisite to treating adolescents in some community health facilities, such as clinics operated by Planned Parenthood. However, before students can use school-based clinics, he or she must obtain signed parental authorization for all of the services potentially offered in the clinic. Although parental permission is required, the adolescents using the service must be assured of confidentiality regarding the specifics of their treatment and behavior (Flood et al., 1985). Thus, school-based case managers must develop procedures, on the one hand, for acquiring parental permission, and, on the other hand, for communicating to parents and other parties that no information regarding the adolescent's use of particular services will be divulged.

Case Management in Schools. Although many case management issues were discussed in Chapter 3, it is helpful to take a special look at how case coordination can be managed in school settings. Allen-Meares (1989) described the case management system used in a class called "Home and Family Education" (p. 194) an in-school, multifaceted service program for adolescent parents. This program used a team approach comprised of many different professionals who offered services related to their particular areas of expertise. The team was headed by a school social worker who coordinated team meetings and reported to the Assistant Superintendent of Special Education and the school principal. The team leader also worked with the administration to develop policies to define how the program fit into the mainstream of the educational system. Another team member, referred to by Allen-Meares (1989) as a "community resource coordinator" (p. 196), organized referrals to community services not available in the school. Thus, the team leader served as an administrative supervisor for the project while the community resource coordinator worked as the case manager, thereby fulfilling the service broker role described in Chapter 3.

Disciplinary Problems. A potential case management issue in schools is the problem of who responds to the disciplinary infractions of teenage parents. The difficult day-to-day stresses of being a parent as well as a student may contribute to poor attendance records by teenage parents. In addition, some student parents might take their frustrations out on fellow students or school personnel. In light of this possibility, Flood et al. (1985) recommended that program personnel develop policies for dealing with the disciplinary problems of teenage parents. These policies should state the conditions under which students are removed from service programs. However, these authors suggested no guidelines for defining the roles of team members as they relate to such policy. I recommend that the team leader be responsible for the reporting of attendance violations and other disciplinary activities and that the case manager be left to the business of counseling. A rationale for this arrangement can be found in S. B. Baker's (1992) discussion regarding discipline and the role of the school counselor:

> Discipline and counseling are antithetical. . . . If counselors engage in such negative interactions with students, no matter how deserving, it will be very difficult to also establish empathic, unconditional helping relationships with them. Students will then view going to the counselor's office as an aversive experience—one to be avoided if at all possible. (p. 281)

Mainstreaming Versus Special School Placement. Slavin and Madden (1989) reported that "pullout programs" (p. 4), that is, alternative schools designed to address the specific needs of at-risk kids, are one of the most widely used modes of service delivery for students with special needs. As an alternative to pullout programs, many schools employ "in-class models" (Slavin & Madden, 1989, p. 5), in which special education personnel work right in the classroom, or "mainstream services" (Ascher, 1985, p. 18), which consist of supportive programs offered in the regular school as supplemental services for at-risk students.

Ascher (1985) noted that there are pros and cons to both mainstream and separate programs for teenage parents. A separate program protects teenage parents from the embarrassment of peers and typically provides a range of services that can address the many needs of this population in one setting. However, pullout programs tend to offer a smaller range of courses, employ less qualified instructors, provide few, if any, extracurricular activities, isolate the students from his or her peers and are more expensive to operate than mainstreamed services. The advantages of mainstreaming are that it prepares a teenage parent to cope with the multiple roles of adolescent, student, and parent while allowing him or her to remain with friends and continue his or her regular course work. The disadvantages are that needed services often are not at hand and referrals are spotty (Ascher, 1985).

Given the pluses and minuses for both pullout and mainstream programs, in what direction should school personnel go in their attempts to serve teenage parents? Based on their review of the outcome literature on educational programs for at-risk children, Slavin and Madden (1989) concluded that specific qualities of programs, rather than the actual location of services, may be the most important variables in determining the effectiveness of at-risk efforts. That is, effective at-risk programs are comprehensive, intensive, and adaptive to the individual needs of each student. In addition to these characteristics, Card et al. (1992) noted that programs that employ skilled staff and integrate efforts with existing community services are more likely to enhance program effectiveness. Thus, it is suggested that school personnel choose settings that have the potential for incorporating these features into service programs for teenage parents.

Schools Have Ignored the Needs of Teenage Fathers. Ample evidence suggests that schools offering programs for teenage parents have ignored the needs of teenage fathers. For example, the majority of the school-based programs described in Flood et al. (1985) and Lindsay and Rodine (1989b) were focused on serving teenage mothers. In a systematic study of each school district in a midwestern state, Kiselica (1992) found that most districts were more likely to serve adolescent mothers than adolescent fathers. These data indicate that school systems are like other service settings in their tendency to discriminate against helping teenage fathers. Consequently, school personnel are challenged to reevaluate the manner in which they view and treat this population.

Model Programs

In spite of the widespread failure of schools to treat teenage parents equitably, a few progressive programs have taken an active role in helping young fathers. For example, the Booker T. Washington Alternative School, located in Terre Haute, Indiana, is an alternative school that helps both young mothers *and* fathers finish school. The school provides a child care center where young parents can take their children for $1 a day. Students attend school part of the day and may hold down outside jobs. The curriculum includes prenatal care and parenting skills as well as traditional high school subjects, such as English and math. Teachers and counselors pay close attention to the students' many needs and make referrals to outside agencies when necessary.

The New Futures School in Albuquerque, New Mexico is an example of collaborative school-based teamwork at its best. Working with professionals from the University of New Mexico Medical School and from other agencies and organizations, the school provides comprehensive health and social services. The school furnishes the space and the educational components, and the outside consultants render services according to their particular areas of expertise. For example, the university brings a prenatal care clinic to the New Futures School one day each week. The clinic team consists of an obstetrician, two nurse practitioners, a nutritionist, a family planning counselor, a laboratory technician, and a clerk. In addition, the school offers young parents pregnancy and family planning counseling; on-site child care; well-child health care; a Women, Infants, and Children Supplemental Nutrition (WIC) clinic; a health class; nutritional education; personal counseling; job training; and transportation.

Finally, the Teenage Parent Program (TAPP) is an exemplary program addressing the needs of both teenage mothers and fathers. Offered by the Jefferson County Public Schools of Kentucky, TAPP offers pregnant and parenting teenagers a full academic curriculum, on-site medical services, parenting classes that cover child development and medical information, health and nutrition training, breakfast and lunch programs, personal counseling, support groups for the entire family, and an on-site WIC office and child care services. TAPP has a national reputation for identifying and involving young fathers during the early stages of the pregnancy so as to prevent school dropout. The TAPP staff help student fathers to set long-term goals and stay in school while holding part-time jobs.

These programs can serve as models for schools committed to the goal of achieving equity in serving both teenage mothers and fathers. In addition, by following the example of these programs, schools can play a key part in a community-wide effort to help teenage fathers to fulfill their varied life roles as parents, students, workers, and providers.

PART II

Culture-Specific Considerations

The universal considerations discussed in Part I represent a general framework for counseling with teenage fathers in the United States. Although the subject matter reviewed in Part I can increase the counselor's awareness of issues that are common to teenage fathers, it lacks particular information about how to modify the counseling process and counseling interventions in a culturally sensitive manner with young fathers from this society's distinct cultural groups. Therefore, in Part II, culture-specific recommendations for counseling Anglo American, African American, and Hispanic American adolescent fathers are suggested. Although these chapters are organized according to each of the universal issues covered in Part I, the subheadings within the chapters vary to reflect the salient issues for each cultural group. Part II concludes with a discussion of several other cultural variables—social class, religiosity, and urban and rural environments.

As an introductory note to Part II, the reader is cautioned that the counseling strategies recommended for particular cultural groups must not be applied in a stereotypic manner. It should be noted further that there are large within-group differences for any cultural population of teenage fathers. Consequently, it is recommended that counselors use the suggestions contained in Part II to formulate tentative hypotheses about the potential cultural issues and problems faced by an individual father and then explore and test these hypotheses with that father. Proceeding in this manner, the counselor will discover the unique cultural perspective of each individual client.

8

Anglo American Teenage Fathers

Several scholars (e.g., Butts, 1989; Ladner & Gourdine, 1984; Scott-Jones, 1993; Williams, 1991) have criticized researchers and the mass media for a bias that shifts the focus of unwed adolescent sexual behavior, pregnancy, and parenthood almost exclusively to African American and Hispanic American teenagers and ignores the same problems among Anglo Americans. One consequence of this portrayal of the subject is that many professionals are unaware that the majority of teenage parents in the United States are Anglo Americans.

To achieve a thorough understanding of teenage parenthood in this country, the hidden problem of adolescent childbearing in the Anglo American community must be exposed and confronted. The purpose of this chapter is to raise awareness of adolescent sexual activity, pregnancy, and parenthood among Anglo Americans, convey the difficulties that Anglo American teenage fathers experience, and suggest culture-specific counseling interventions for this population. Because there sometimes is confusion about the meaning of the term *Anglo American,* it is necessary to define and clarify this term and highlight the value system characteristic of the Anglo culture in the United States. Therefore, this chapter begins with a profile of Anglo Americans that serves as a helpful background for understanding Anglo American teenage fathers.

A Profile of Anglo Americans

The term *Anglo American* has been defined in a variety of ways in the social sciences literature. For example, the term *Anglo American* and the acronym "WASP"—White Anglo Saxon Protestant—have been used to refer to Americans who are White, Protestant, and primarily of early British immigrant origins (see Simon, 1972). More commonly, the term *Anglo American* has been used broadly to refer to White Americans who have been in the United States a long time and have adopted the values and traditions of the Anglo culture that have come to dominate U.S. society (see Mead, 1971). The term *Anglo* also has been used by many writers (e.g., Black, Paz, & DeBlassie, 1991; Hendricks, 1988; Ruiz, 1981; Sue & Sue, 1990) to denote Caucasians in the United States who are not of Hispanic origin.

For the purposes of this book, this latter definition applies when Anglo American and Anglo are used. It is hypothesized that most non-Hispanic, Caucasian teenage fathers share, in large degree, the value system of the Anglo culture in the United States. A brief overview of this value system is presented in the next section. For a more thorough discussion of the subject, the reader can refer to Axelson (1993), Pedersen (1988), and Sue and Sue (1990).

The Anglo Value System

In their overview of the Anglo value system, Ponterotto and Casas (1991) concluded that several values pervade the majority culture in the United States. A synopsis of their overview is presented here.

Among Anglos, the individual is seen as the primary unit of the family or group, and independence and autonomy are highly valued. Competing and succeeding against others also are highly valued. Individual achievement and success are considered vital to one's self-esteem. Adherence to time schedules is important. Time is construed as linear ("Don't lose or waste time because it never returns"). Accepted standards for nonverbal and verbal behavior include the following: maintaining eye contact while speaking, a firm handshake, and verbal expressiveness. The ideal family unit is the nuclear family, consisting of two parents, one male and one female, and their children. Written arrangements in the form of contracts are respected. Linear analytic thinking, rather than intuitive and symbolic thinking, tends to dominate (Ponterotto & Casas, 1991). In addition to these values, Axelson (1993) observed that Anglos are strongly influenced by Judeo-Christian attitudes regarding sexuality and childbearing. Rigid moral codes prohibit out-of-wedlock childbearing.

Diversity Within the Anglo Culture

Ponterotto and Casas (1991) noted that not every Anglo possesses the value system described above. There are many cultural differences within the Anglo culture, as there are within other cultural groups in the United States (Ponterotto & Casas, 1991). Therefore, it is recommended that counselors use the overview provided above as a framework for understanding the prevailing value system among Anglos while remembering that great variation exists among Anglos in the extent to which they adhere to this value system. It should be noted that this variation is considered to be influenced, in large part, by the ethnicity of the client (see McGoldrick, 1982). Consequently, counselors are advised to explore the ethnic background of each Anglo American teenage father and the extent to which he and his family have acculturated to the dominant value system of the United States.

To prepare themselves for these endeavors, counselors may wish to consult Axelson's (1993) *Counseling and Development in a Multicultural Society.* Axelson (1993) described two major subgroups of Anglos in the United States, each adhering to overlapping yet different values systems. The first subgroup, the "Anglo Saxons," (Axelson, 1993, p. 72) consists of those Americans of English, Welsh, Scotch, Irish, and western European descent. The second subgroup, whom Axelson (1993) referred to as "White Ethnic Americans," (p. 85) comprises descendants of immigrants from southern and eastern European countries, including Austria, Hungary, Czechoslovakia, Greece, Italy, Sicily, Poland, Portugal, Spain, Russian, and Yugoslavia. Axelson's discussion aptly describes the historical experience of these groups in the United States and how the cultural values of the two groups are distinct.

To further appreciate the unique cultural background of particular Anglo American teenage fathers, it is recommended that counselors obtain *Ethnicity and Family Therapy,* by McGoldrick, Pearce, and Giordano (1982). This edited volume contains chapters on French Canadian, German, Greek, Irish, Italian, Jewish, Polish, Portuguese, Norwegian, and British families.

By reading these materials and remaining open to the uniqueness of particular clients, counselors can avoid forming inflexible cultural stereotypes about Anglo American teenage fathers.

Teenage Pregnancy and Parenthood
Among Anglo Americans

The largest increase in adolescent sexual activity over the past two decades has occurred among Anglo Americans. Between 1980 and 1988 the percentage of sexually active Anglo adolescent girls rose from 41% to 51% (National Center for Health Statistics, 1991). For every age group of adolescents, Anglo males are more likely than Anglo females to have had intercourse (Sonenstein, 1986). Once they become sexually active, Anglo adolescent females have sex more frequently and with more partners than do adolescent females from other cultural groups (Zabin & Hayward, 1993).

Despite the sharp increase in sexual activity among Anglo teenagers and a steady increase in the frequency of Anglo adolescent pregnancies between 1980 and 1988, the rate of teenage pregnancy in the population remained steady at about 11% during that 8-year time span (National Center for Health Statistics, 1991), possibly because of increased condom use among Anglos at first intercourse (see Ventura et al., 1992). However, although the Anglo adolescent pregnancy rate has remained stable, Anglos account for approximately two thirds of the teenage pregnancies and total births to women under the age of 20 in the United States (Henshaw, 1993). Furthermore, compared to teenagers in other countries, Anglo American teenagers have the highest pregnancy rate of any Western nation (Westoff, 1988) and the highest birth rate of all industrialized democratic nations (Jones et al., 1985).

Anglo American teenagers who become pregnant are less likely to be married than were pregnant adolescents in the past. In the 1950s, one third of first births to adolescents were conceived out of wedlock. In the 1980s, approximately two thirds of first births to Anglo adolescents were conceived premaritally (Scott-Jones, 1993).

Out-of-wedlock births to Anglo adolescents have skyrocketed over the past few decades. Since the mid-1950s, the percentage of out-of-wedlock births to Anglo American teenagers jumped almost 300%. Since 1980, the birth rate from unmarried Anglo women between age 15 to 19 has risen 33%, from 16.2 per thousand in 1980 to 21.5 per thousand in 1986 (U.S. Congress, 1989).

The growth in out-of-wedlock births among adolescents reflects a general trend toward single motherhood among Anglo women. The proportion of out-of-wedlock births among Anglo adult females increased from 4% in 1970 to 9% in 1982 (Moore, Simms, & Betsey, 1986). This trend, in combination with the increased acceptance of divorce among Anglos may, in part, account for the fact that the proportion of children in single-female-headed families more than doubled for Anglo Americans between 1960 and 1984, rising from 6.8% to 14.3% (see Children's Defense Fund, 1985).

Anglo single-parent families, especially those headed by adolescent mothers who have dropped out of school, are at risk for poverty. Among Anglo Americans, the poverty rates for married-couple families headed by a high school graduate under age 25, married-couple families headed by a dropout under age 25, single-mother families headed by a high school graduate under the age of 25, and single-mother families headed by a high school dropout under age 25 are 11.2%, 33.4%, 58.6%, and 84.6%, respectively (Children's Defense Fund, 1991a).

The relationship between poverty and unplanned adolescent childbearing among Anglo Americans does not appear to be bidirectional. That is, although premature adolescent parenthood places Anglo youth at risk for economic hardships, low family socioeconomic status has no effect on the chances that an Anglo adolescent female will become pregnant (Abrahamse, Morrison, & Waite, 1988). Rather, variables predictive of unwed adolescent pregnancy among Anglos include the following: low-tested academic ability, the absence of plans to attend college, problem behaviors in school (e.g., unexcused absences), a parent-child relationship characterized by poor communication and a lack of parent participation in the child's school program, the willingness of one's peers to consider childbearing out of wedlock, and one's own willingness to consider unwed childbearing. Among these variables, the talking/planning dimension of the parent-child relationship appears to be the strongest form of social control to prevent out-of-wedlock adolescent pregnancy among Anglo American girls (Abrahamse et al., 1988).

In summary, the sexual activity of Anglo American teenagers is increasing and, contrary to the notion that teenage pregnancy and parenthood are problems just for African Americans and Hispanic Americans, the typical adolescent parent in the United States is an Anglo whose child was conceived prior to marriage. In the words of June Dobbs Butts (1989), "The disturbance [teenage pregnancy] is growing steadily and stealthily . . . among whites . . . whose power heretofore has insured . . . privacy and protection from sensational news media coverage" (p. 146). Although unwed teenage pregnancy in the Anglo community appears to be a function of a complex social process involving the influence of several variables, a parent-child relationship devoid of a strong talking/planning dimension is a strong predictor of unplanned out-of-wedlock pregnancy among Anglo adolescent girls.

Anglo American Teenage Fathers

Marsiglio (1987) analyzed data from the National Longitudinal Survey of Labor Market Experience of Youth to determine estimates of the percentage of adolescent males who were responsible for a nonmarital conception as teenagers. His findings suggest that 3.4% of nondisadvantaged Anglos and 9.1% of poor Anglos who participated in the survey fathered a first child nonmaritally (Marsiglio, 1987). Combining the data for the two subgroups of Anglos indicates that nearly 5% of all Anglo males participating in the survey were responsible for an out-of-wedlock pregnancy while they were teenagers. Most of these males were 18 or 19 at the time their first child was born, but 6.2% of nondisadvantaged teenage fathers and 11.1% of poor teenage fathers were between 11 and 16 years old when their nonmaritally conceived child was born (Marsiglio, 1987).

Being responsible for an adolescent pregnancy appears to be a highly stressful life event for Anglo American males. Data from a longitudinal study of more than 1,600 Anglo males from the Houston area indicated that young men who were responsible for an adolescent pregnancy tended to be more psychologically distressed than males who did not have a girlfriend become pregnant during adolescence. Adolescent fathers who neither married nor cohabitated with the mother of the child were more distressed than those who did marry or cohabitate with the child's mother. Adverse psychological consequences for teenage fathers persisted into adulthood (Buchanan & Robbins, 1990).

Many of the particular difficulties of Anglo American teenage fathers are similar to those of teenage fathers from other cultural groups. These problems include the following: conflicts with their family of origin, lack of money, problems with the mother of the child and with members of her family, vocational-educational worries, concerns about the health of the mother and the infant, and anxiety about future parenthood (see Elster & Hendricks, 1986; Elster & Panzarine, 1983b; Hendricks, 1988).

Anglo American teenage fathers also may be like other cultural groups in their feelings for the mother and the child. For example, in one comparative study of African American, Anglo American, and Hispanic American teenage fathers, the majority of the fathers from each cultural group who perceived the relationship with the young mother to be one of love, both before and after the pregnancy, were unlikely to attempt to influence the expectant mother's decision regarding adoption or abortion and expressed an interest in their children's future (Hendricks, 1988).

In other ways, however, the experiences of Anglo American teenage fathers may be different from those of other cultural groups. Results from Hendricks's (1988) study indicated that Anglo American teenage fathers were less likely than African American adolescent fathers to complete 12 or more years of school and less likely than African American and Hispanic American teenage fathers to have their first coital experience with a girl before the age of 15; father a child before the age of 17; spend time with their friends after school, work, or in the evenings; and receive sex education from and share stories about sexual experiences with a friend. Anglo American young fathers were more likely than African American and Hispanic American teenage fathers to be raised in families with four children or less. Anglo

Americans were less likely than Hispanic American teenage fathers but were more likely than African American teenage fathers to grow up in homes with fathers present (Hendricks, 1988). Other data indicate that Anglo Americans are more likely than African American and Hispanic Americans to resolve an unplanned, out-of-wedlock adolescent pregnancy through abortion or marriage (see Alan Guttmacher Institute, 1981; Chilman, 1988; Furstenberg, 1976; Perez & Duany, 1992)

Another difference among these three cultural groups of adolescent fathers is that Anglo Americans report the highest levels of distress, followed by Hispanic American and then African American teenage fathers (Buchanan & Robbins, 1990), even though Anglo American adolescents enjoy a more positive status on most quality-of-life indicators than do African American and Hispanic American youth (see Children's Defense Fund, 1985). Several explanations for this difference are offered. The first pertains to the relative lack of educational and employment prospects for African American and Hispanic American males. As Buchanan and Robbins (1990) hypothesized, "Perhaps paternity serves as a marker of adult status, and this has psychological compensations in groups with less opportunity for conventional adult status transitions such as employment and educational attainment" (p. 422). A second explanation for the higher level of distress experienced by Anglo American teenage fathers pertains to their living arrangements after the child is born. Anglos are more likely than their African American and Hispanic American counterparts to marry their partners and live with their child (Marsiglio, 1987). Perhaps the responsibilities associated with marriage, the difficult adjustments experienced during the transition from the single life to marriage, and the stresses prompted by living with and raising a baby during one's teenage years heighten distress for Anglo adolescent fathers. A third and final conjecture is that the higher levels of distress among Anglos may be related to external pressure to marry (see Chilman, 1988; Furstenberg, 1976). Anglo fathers who violate this cultural expectation may experience considerable distress in reaction to the Anglocentric perception that they are living a culturally deviant lifestyle.

Implications for Counseling

Ironically, Anglo American teenage fathers, who are more likely than ethnic-minority youth to reap many of the benefits of our society, also are more likely than ethnic-minority youth to experience higher levels of distress associated with their role in an adolescent pregnancy. Yet because of the societal failure to confront the increased sexual activity and rise of unwed adolescent childbearing among Anglo American teenagers, the difficulties of Anglo American teenage fathers are likely to go unnoticed. Consequently, it is recommended that counselors employ macrolevel strategies to implore program developers and policymakers to carefully study adolescent parenthood in the Anglo American community and to develop appropriate services.

In addition to this macrolevel consideration, some microlevel considerations are warranted. First, because Anglo American teenage fathers are less likely than African American fathers to complete school (Hendricks, 1988; Marsiglio, 1986) and tend to be older than African American males at the time of first conception (Marsiglio, 1987), many Anglo fathers are unlikely to be identified through school-based outreach. Consequently, outreach extending beyond the school boundaries may be particularly important with Anglo American teenage fathers. Second, counselors working with Anglo American youth may encounter many young fathers wrestling with decision-making dilemmas regarding abortion and adoption because the use of these options is highest among Anglo American teenage girls (see Alan Guttmacher Institute, 1981; Perez & Duany, 1992). Third, because Anglo Americans are more likely than either African American (see Scott-Jones, Roland, & White, 1989) or Hispanic American (especially nontraditional Hispanic) adolescent fathers to marry (see Perez & Duany, 1992) as the means for resolving an out-of-wedlock pregnancy, marital counseling may be a critical component to service provision to young parents in the Anglo community.

Program Development Considerations

A variety of program development considerations, both micro- and macrolevel, are recommended for constructing services for Anglo American teenage fathers.

Microlevel Considerations

The potential for opposition to service programs from teenage fathers is likely in any cultural community. However, it is hypothesized that opposition will be strongest in Anglo communities for two reasons.

First, there are long-standing Anglo prohibitions against individuals engaging in premarital sexual relations. These restrictions are so well ingrained into the dominant, Anglo culture that the only legally sanctioned sexual act in the United States is private heterosexual intercourse between married adults (Welch, 1992). The avoidance of the teenage parent subject among Anglos may be a vestige of old Anglo taboos regarding sexuality. A mechanism for Anglos to avoid self-reproach is to deny that unwed teenage parenthood exists in the Anglo community, view adolescent childbearing as an ethnic-minority problem, and attack proposals for pertinent service programs as being unnecessary in Anglo communities. As evidence of this thinking, a service coordinator for a teenage parent program in New Haven, Connecticut, recently appeared on a nationally televised NBC news program, *A Closer Look,* to express her frustration with such avoidance of the issue. The coordinator shared her experience of repeatedly encountering a response among middle-class Anglos of, "This doesn't happen in *our* neighborhood." Furthermore, the coordinator decried these defensive responses and warned that the Anglo community had better wake up to its growing problems of unwed teenage pregnancy and parenthood.

A second reason for opposition to teenage parent service programs in Anglo communities is that Anglos are likely to believe that the proper way to handle the problem is to "legitimatize" the pregnancy through marriage. A concern associated with this belief is that the creation of service programs for pregnant and parenting teenagers would be unnecessary if more young men and women would do the "expected" and "responsible" thing by marrying. Furthermore, opponents argue that service provision discourages Anglo youth from marrying by placing some of the burdens for the caring of the mother and the child on the community.

Strategies for handling opposition to the provision of service programs, such as the gathering and distribution of data regarding teenage pregnancy and parenthood in an effort to educate concerned citizens about the problem in their communities, were suggested in Chapter 3. With Anglos, variations of these strategies may be necessary to counter the tendency of adults to deny the problem. For example, it may be necessary to enlist the media as an ally in alerting the community to the problem. Television broadcasts, such as the one described earlier, are powerful vehicles for informing the public that this problem cannot be ignored. Another successful strategy has involved locating courageous and conscientious reporters from local newspapers who have been willing to do accurate investigative reports that have stimulated action in Anglo communities.

In dealing with opposition, program developers can express their sensitivity to the Anglo cultural expectation that an out-of-wedlock conception should be "legitimatized" through marriage by emphasizing that one of the core services of a teenage parent program is ongoing marital counseling. By assuring adults that the service program has been designed to assist young parents who chose to marry, as well as parents who chose other pregnancy-resolution options, many objecting adults will grow more accepting of the idea.

A final microlevel consideration for program developers is that many Anglo families will want their children to marry quickly after the pregnancy is discovered to create the deception that the child was conceived after the marriage. These families often perceive that their children's participation in service programs for teenage parents "lets the secret out" about the out-of-wedlock conception. These perceptions, whether accurate or erroneous, are likely to cause embarrassment and shame for the family. Consequently, some families discourage their children from participating in teenage parent programs. Program developers should accentuate the confidential nature of service provision to prevent these reactions. In addition, by establishing service programs for teenage parents at family counseling centers that serve individuals from all age groups, young couples who are self-conscious about their position as teenage parents can maintain anonymity about their situation.

Macrolevel Considerations

Considering that nearly 60% of the teenage pregnancies in the United States occur among Anglos (U.S. Department of Education, 1991), awareness of the Anglo teenage parent problem must be extended beyond local communities to the national level. Congressmen and foundations need to be informed about teenage pregnancy and parenthood in the Anglo community and persuaded to support funding that will commission pertinent studies of the problem. It is recommended that scholars examining the subject of adolescent childbearing and parenthood widen their research agendas by supplementing their studies of ethnic-minority groups with investigations of Anglo American teenagers. These strategies may help to chip away at the stereotypic, societal image of teenage parenthood as an African American and Latino problem and improve our understanding of how to address adolescent pregnancy, childbearing, and fatherhood in the Anglo community. Most important, these efforts may prompt an increased delivery of services to adolescent Anglo parents whose hardships heretofore have been largely neglected.

Outreach and Rapport-Building Considerations

Anglo teenage fathers are likely to rely on themselves, their parents, siblings, or friends, but not a service agency, for help with a personal problem (Hendricks, 1988). No matter which source of support they might use, Anglo teenage boys tend to cope with the unexpected pregnancy by engaging in some direct action that produces some tangible result, rather than participating in activities designed to reduce emotional distress. For example, Panzarine and Elster (1983) studied the coping responses of 20 expectant Anglo teenage fathers. The investigators found that most of the young men involved themselves in some new or additional activity to improve their financial situation. Most of the fathers also prepared for their baby by engaging in such activities as buying clothes or fixing up rooms. Many sought information about pregnancy and parenthood by talking with others or observing and evaluating other parents. In addition, the fathers tended to fantasize about fatherhood and think about how they were raised.

These findings suggest that Anglo American teenage fathers are likely to be identified and assisted in counseling through the mediation of the fathers' parents or friends. Once the initial contact is made, focusing on practical concerns will enhance rapport. Furthermore, early contacts designed to provide the young men with information regarding their legal rights as a father and the legal rights of the child are likely to alter negative views of counseling settings. Anglo American teenage fathers are likely to discuss their fatherhood issues only after these action strategies have been pursued.

Generally, Anglos tend to be less suspicious and more comfortable utilizing counseling services than ethnic-minority clients. Anglo teenage fathers might be an exception to this predilection, however, because they are often the target of societal stereotypes about teenage fathers (see Chapter 2). Therefore, a nonjudgmental attitude and an advocacy stance are recommended to help Anglo teenage fathers to develop trust in the counselor.

Racial Identity Issues

Several scholars (Hardiman, 1982; Helms, 1984; Ponterotto, 1988) have proposed models of White racial identity development to explain the process Whites in American undergo in acknowledging their race and accepting the social implications of their racial group membership. These scholars suggested that the manner in which a White individual responds to ethnic-minority individuals varies according to the racial identity of that individual. Because Anglo American teenage fathers are White, it is important that counselors who are people of color understand White racial identity development before working with this population.

Hardiman (1982), Helms (1984), and Ponterotto (1988) have proposed separate yet overlapping models of White racial identity development. Sabnani, Ponterotto, and Borodovsky (1991) combined these three models to formulate a comprehensive model of White racial identity development consisting of five stages. Whites in the Pre-Exposure/Pre-Contact Stage lack an awareness of self as a racial being. Therefore, they have not explored their own racial identity, nor have they given thought to their roles as White people in an oppressive society. There is an unconscious identification with whiteness and an unquestioned acceptance of stereotypes about minority groups. During the Conflict Stage, there is an expansion of knowledge about racial matters, a process that is stimulated by interactions with members of minority groups or by information acquired elsewhere (e.g., through reading). This new information challenges individuals to acknowledge their whiteness and examine their own cultural values. The stage is characterized by a conflict between wanting to conform to White norms and wishing to uphold humanistic, nonracist values. In reaction to the Conflict Stage, the individual takes a strong pro-minority stance during the Pro-Minority/Antiracism Stage. Whites in this stage experience self-focused anger and guilt over their previous conformity to White socialization as well as anger directed toward the White culture in general. In response to charges of disloyalty from White peers and confrontations from minority group members who question the sincerity of a pro-minority stance, the White individual retreats from interracial contact during the Retreat Into White Culture Stage. Individuals in this stage find it easier and less complicated to overidentify with whiteness and interact with Whites than to engage in interactions between Whites and minority groups. Finally, during the Redefinition and Integration Stage, Whites acknowledge their responsibility for maintaining racism and identify with a White identity that is nonracist and healthy. Individuals in this stage see good and bad in their own group as they do in other groups (Sabnani et al., 1991).

In their review of the research examining the relationship between White racial identity development and racism, Ponterotto and Pedersen (1993) concluded that White persons in Stage 4, Retreat Into White Culture, are most likely to be negatively prejudiced toward racial/ethnic-minority individuals. In addition, individuals in the early stages of White racial identity development are also prone to racism and discomfort with ethnic-minority individuals. Individuals in the Pro-Minority/Antiracism and the Redefinition and Integration Stages appear least likely to be racist (see Ponterotto & Pedersen, 1993).

Extending these considerations to counseling with Anglo American teenage fathers, racial/ethnic-minority counselors are more likely to encounter racist responses and resistance from Anglos in the Pre-Exposure/Pre-Contact, Conflict, and Retreat Into White Culture Stages than Anglos in the other stages of White racial identity development. Therefore, racial/ethnic-minority counselors need to know how to assess White racial identity development to help them understand and respond to the behavior of Anglo American teenage fathers during the counseling process.

Although Helms and Carter (1990) have developed a White Racial Identity Attitude Scale, it is advisable to refrain from using such a formal instrument, because Hendricks's (1988) research suggested that the use of formal assessments, especially during the early stages of counseling, are likely to hinder the establishment of rapport with Anglo American teenage fathers. Instead, counselors can learn to informally assess for racial identity styles in everyday life by reading *A Training Manual for Diagnosing Racial Identity in Social Interactions* (Helms, 1990). By practicing the exercises in this book, counselors can learn how to recognize the racial identity style of an Anglo client during the initial counseling session.

Once the counselor has identified the White racial identity stage of the client, he or she will need to be prepared to respond to racial identity issues as they emerge in counseling. As long as they practice the outreach and rapport-building strategies mentioned earlier, racial/ethnic-minority counselors are likely to have little difficulty establishing and maintaining rapport with Anglo American teenage fathers who, at the start of counseling, are in the Pro-Minority/Antiracism and Redefinition and Integration Stages of White racial identity development. Pre-Exposure/Pre-Contact Stage clients are likely to be naive about racial issues. Consequently, they are likely to be unaware of their passive acceptance of White majority stereotypes about people of color and unknowingly express these toward the counselor. The counselor who is the target of this behavior will have to make a personal choice to either ignore or confront it. By choosing to ignore this behavior, the counselor will likely establish rapport with the client but also may pay the price of having to tolerate implicit racist and Eurocentric behavior. Confronting stereotypes may induce the client to enter the Conflict Stage, at which time the client gradually either may recognize or deny the racism of White society. Clients acknowledging racism could, after an extended period of time for self-reflection, enter a Pro-Minority/Antiracism Stage and express this behavior by strongly identifying with the counselor. With these clients, counseling will probably take a more productive turn. However, other clients may respond to the confusion, guilt, and anger inherent in the Conflict Stage by avoiding the racial/ethnic-minority counselor. It is recommended that the counselor help the client to recognize that his avoidance is an expression of this racial identity conflict. If the young father is unable to confront this issue, then a referral to a White counselor may be in order before the client drops out of counseling altogether. Referrals to White counselors also may be necessary for teenage fathers who are in the Retreat Into White

Culture Stage, because these youth are likely to express fear and anger toward a racial/ethnic-minority counselor by consistently avoiding counseling and/or relating to the counselor in a hostile manner.

Pregnancy Resolution

The majority of Anglo American teenage pregnancies are unplanned (Moore, 1992). Moreover, data reported by Hardy and Zabin (1991) indicated that most of the Anglo American teenage parents interviewed in their study reported that they had not discussed the possibility that pregnancy might occur. Thus, Anglo American teenage parents are like other cultural groups in that the pregnancy tends to be unintentional.

Abortion and Adoption

Although the abortion rate among Anglo women ages 15 to 19 declined about 7% between 1980 and 1987 (Henshaw, 1992), a higher proportion of Anglo American adolescents have abortions and place a child for adoption than do ethnic-minority adolescents. For example, data reviewed by Scott-Jones (1993) indicated that in 1985, 46% of married and unmarried 17- to 19-year-old pregnant Anglo adolescents had abortions, compared to 41% of pregnant African Americans from the same age group. Among all age groups of unmarried adolescent females, Anglos are more likely than ethnic minorities to resolve pregnancies by abortions (Henshaw, Kenney, Somberg, & Van Vort, 1989). Among all Anglo adolescent mothers, 19% place their children for formal adoption. By comparison, only 2% of African American teenage parents place their children for formal adoption (Burden & Klerman, 1984).

Economic factors have been proposed to account for the higher use of abortion by Anglo American teenage parents. Anglo teenagers are more likely to afford an abortion procedure due to the generally higher economic status of this population. By comparison, pregnant ethnic-minority clients, who are overrepresented among the poor, lack the finances to pay for an abortion. Although many of those same clients receive free medical services under Medicaid assistance, federal guidelines restrict funding for abortions under most circumstances (Moore et al., 1986), although these restrictions eventually may be eliminated by the Clinton administration.

Adoption is more frequently used by Anglos than by other cultural groups for two reasons. First, Anglos are likely to assume formal adoption service agencies will adequately meet the needs of the child, but ethnic-minority clients historically have been less trusting of agencies in this regard (Billingsley &

Giovannoni, 1970; Hill, 1977; see Chapter 8, this volume). Second, adoption services for White children have received substantially more financial support than adoption services for ethnic-minority children, thereby making the adoption of White babies easier (Reitz & Watson, 1992).

Like teenage fathers from other cultural groups, Anglo American teenage fathers perceive themselves to be unlikely to attempt to influence the young mother's decision on whether or not she should have an abortion or place the child for adoption (Hendricks, 1988). Case studies by Herzog (1984) indicated that Anglo teenage fathers can deeply regret not having been more involved in the decision-making process. Consider the anger, sadness, and confusion experienced by a boy named Joe, as described by Herzog (1984) in an account of his counseling experiences with a group of Anglo teenage fathers:

> Joe came to the group very shaken and reported that Liz . . . had not had an abortion after all. . . . Joe told us that he was very angry with Liz. She had deceived him. *Then he told us that he really hadn't had very much to do with her decision-making* [italics added] and certainly not with its implementation. Joe was clearly troubled. He developed a sleep disturbance and started to drink excessively. He asked if he could see me alone and then told me that he didn't know what he was feeling or what he should do. "There was really a kid inside Liz. What should I feel about that?" He thought he hated Liz. But he couldn't just shrug it off. That kid was his, whatever that meant. He felt that he should do something, but he didn't know what. Then Joe, who was in some ways the most "macho" member of the group, began to cry. He expressed a strong wish that I contact his parents. He particularly wanted his father to know, but he felt afraid of his reaction. At the next group meeting, Joe told about his meeting with me. He said that he felt "all screwed up about this father thing" and that he had decided to go into psychotherapy. (p. 68)

Although Anglo teenage fathers themselves tend to be uninvolved in the pregnancy-resolution process of their partners, expectant Anglo adolescent girls who are not considering marriage tend to rely on the input of their own mothers. Furthermore, the strength of the mother's influence on the option chosen by the girl appears to be strongest for those Anglos who abort and for those who choose to give birth but give the baby up for adoption. Maternal influence appears to be least for Anglo girls who keep the baby (see Rosen, 1980).

Implications for Counseling

As is the case with ethnic-minority teenage fathers, services for Anglo American teenage fathers should include abortion counseling. However, because Anglo Americans are much more likely than other cultural groups to use formal adoption services, it is advisable that counselors working with this population become well-versed in the adoption-related counseling procedures discussed in Chapter 4. No matter which pregnancy resolution option he favors, the father will need support in making his opinions known to his partner to prevent the type of shock and turmoil as that chronicled in the case example quoted earlier. In those situations in which the girl is leaning toward abortion or adoption, it is likely that her mother has been a major influence in the girl's decision to focus on these options. Therefore, efforts to help the father in communicating his preferences to his partner may have to include the involvement of the girl's mother.

Marriage and Single Parenthood

Traditionally, Anglo American teenage males who are responsible for a premarital conception are expected to marry their partner. As evidence of this cultural norm, Marsiglio (1987) found that Anglo American teenage fathers are more likely than their African American and Hispanic American counterparts to marry within 12 months of conception.

Although marriage is a common consequence among Anglo teenagers facing an unplanned pregnancy, in recent years a higher percentage of Anglo teenage mothers have chosen to remain single than in the past. In 1970, approximately 17% of the births to Anglos between the ages of 15 and 19 were to single mothers, but by 1982 the figure had risen to nearly 37% (Children's Defense Fund, 1985). Among Anglo teenage parents living in urban areas, the single-parent rate may be even higher. Hardy and Zabin (1991) reported that only 17 out of a sample of 56 Anglo American teenage fathers (approximately 30%) from the Baltimore area were either married to and/or living with the baby's mother. The Hardy and Zabin (1991) findings also suggested that, among Anglo males who are responsible for a teenage pregnancy, adolescent fathers are less likely than adult fathers to either marry and/or live with the baby's mother.

Although single parenthood is becoming more common among Anglo American teenagers, compared to other cultural groups Anglo Americans are more likely to view marriage as one of the most important goals in their lives and favor marriage at an earlier age (Moore et al., 1986). Furthermore, Anglo American teenage girls are more likely than their African American counterparts to perceive strong social condemnation of single childbearing and unfavorable reactions from peers and their male partners to a nonmarital conception (Moore et al., 1986). These findings suggest that expectant Anglo

American teenage parents are likely to experience considerable social pressure to marry and favor marriage as a means to resolve an premarital pregnancy.

Injunctions against out-of-wedlock childbirth may explain why pregnant Anglos are more likely than other cultural groups to marry (Furstenberg, 1976; Furstenberg & Crawford 1989; Moore et al., 1986). The stigma attached to nonmarital parenthood also might account, in part, for the finding that Anglo teenage fathers who neither marry nor live with their partners and children experience significantly more distress than do Anglo teenage fathers who marry or whose partners have an abortion (Buchanan & Robbins, 1990).

Two other factors also appear to account for the higher marriage rates among Anglo American teenage parents. First, the viability of marriage is greater for Anglos than for other cultural groups because Anglos generally receive more economic assistance from their families than the typical ethnic-minority teenager (Alan Guttmacher Institute, 1981). Second, because Anglo adolescent fathers tend to be older than adolescent fathers from other cultural groups, they also tend to have better earning ability, which places them in a better financial position to enter marriage (Furstenberg & Crawford, 1989).

Research findings indicate that the implications of marriage can be both positive and negative for Anglo adolescent parents. On the plus side, for Anglos marriage "legitimatizes" an out-of-wedlock pregnancy and can reduce the strong Anglo sense of social embarrassment associated with parenting a child out-of-wedlock. Also, marriage appears to enhance the economic future of the teenage mother. For example, single-female-headed Anglo families are four times more likely than families headed by a husband and wife to be poor (Children's Defense Fund, 1985). Approximately 59% of single-mother families headed by a high school graduate under the age of 25, and nearly 85% of single-mother families headed by a high school dropout under age 25 are poor. By comparison, only about 11% of married-couple families headed by a high school graduate under age 25 and 33% of married-couple families headed by a dropout under age 25 are poor (Children's Defense Fund, 1991a). For Anglos, marriage is not without some potential problems, however. Early childbearing may interfere with formal education far more among Anglos than among African American teenage parents (Marsiglio, 1986; Moore, Hofferth, Caldwell, & Waite, 1979). In addition, the responsibilities associated with early marriage may account for the high levels of stress reported by Anglo American teenage fathers. Furthermore, compared to marriages occurring between Anglos who are in their early 20s, Anglo marriages occurring during the teenage years are twice as likely to dissolve within 5 years (Children's Defense Fund, 1988b).

Implications for Counseling

Counselors must be aware of the tradeoffs associated with marriage versus single parenthood and review them with expectant Anglo teenage parents contemplating the marriage decision. In addition, Anglos who choose to marry may need extensive career and educational planning to prevent early career foreclosure, as well as supportive counseling to deal with the stresses of early marriage. Furthermore, Anglos who choose to remain single may require supportive individual and extensive family counseling to address potential feelings of shame associated with the status of being a young single parent.

Addressing Family Issues

Most of the research on family issues related to teenage pregnancy and parenthood has been focused on African American families. For example, although the classic longitudinal study of the burdens and benefits of adolescent parenthood on the family conducted by Furstenburg and his colleagues (Furstenberg, 1976, 1979, 1981; Furstenberg et al., 1987; Furstenberg & Crawford, 1989) included a small sample of Anglo American adolescent mothers, the major focus of the study was on inner-city African American teenage mothers and their partners. Although this and other research endeavors (e.g., Sullivan, 1985; Williams, 1991) have provided an understanding of patterns of family support and stress experienced by African Americans in response to teenage parenthood, little has been written about the same subject for Anglo Americans. Consequently, the issues discussed in this section are based on limited data and my clinical experience. Therefore, the reader is encouraged to use the counseling recommendations contained in this section tentatively until more comprehensive data on the subject are generated by scholars.

Notwithstanding this caution, it is recommended that counselors understand Anglo American family values before counseling Anglo teenage fathers and their families. In addition, counselors are advised to know how to recognize and respond to some common forms of dysfunctional parent-son interactions that might occur in Anglo American families during the process of family counseling. Finally, the strengths of Anglo families should be tapped in all efforts to engage the family in helping the young father.

Anglo American Family Values

Earlier in this chapter, some of the family values that are characteristic of the Anglo culture and their implications for counseling were highlighted. These and other family values are described here. Once again, however, the reader is cautioned to recognize the great variation that exists among those who have been defined as Anglos and supplement the perspectives contained here with those presented in the edited volume by McGoldrick et al. (1982) and by Axelson (1993).

Many of the values dominating contemporary society in the United States can be traced back to those espoused by Western Europeans who first settled in what is now known as North America. Those early settlers included the British, French, and Germans. Although there were some clear cultural differences among these and other European groups who later immigrated to the United States, they shared some common family values that have persisted over time, including the following: a dedication of duty to one's family, sensitivity regarding the open discussion of sexual matters, a tendency to count on oneself, the belief that family problems represent highly personal issues that should be resolved within the immediate family, and marriages oriented toward traditional gender roles and expectations (e.g., a man works at making a living while the woman works at raising children and making a successful family) (Langelier, 1982; McGill & Pearce, 1982; Winawer-Steiner & Wetzel, 1982).

Implications for Teenage Pregnancy and Parenthood and for Family Counseling. The value system of Anglo American families provides a framework for understanding how teenage pregnancy and parenthood is viewed by this cultural group. Anglos are likely to consider unplanned out-of-wedlock pregnancy as a violation of cultural norms. Because of the emphasis on individual responsibility, the burden of resolving the crisis will rest on the individual teenage father and might possibly involve the assistance of his parents. In light of the linear time orientation and the emphasis placed on individual achievement mentioned earlier in this chapter, he and his family are likely to view this unplanned event as a major impediment to his individual development and that a major portion of his life has been "lost." In response, he and his family may need to mourn this perception of lost time and personhood. In accordance with Anglo norms, the Anglo teenage father is likely to feel pressure to marry and form a nuclear family of his own and find employment so that he can serve as the provider for his partner and his child. His failure to fulfill these expectations, no matter what the reason, is likely to cause him considerable distress.

In spite of the fact that Anglo families use formal counseling services more frequently than do ethnic-minority families (see Atkinson, 1985; Cheung, 1991), Anglos prefer to work things out among themselves and consider themselves lacking in self-sufficiency when they are unable to do. Going to a professional to receive help is considered a sign of weakness, of being unable to help oneself. Consequently, Anglo Americans tend to view counseling as a shameful experience (see Langelier, 1982; McGill & Pearce, 1982; Winawer-Steiner & Wetzel, 1982).

Counselors can take several measures during the early stages of counseling to reduce the Anglo experience of shame evoked by participation in counseling. First, counselors can assure all family members of the confidential nature of the client-counselor relationship. Second, counselors can normalize the need for counseling by pointing out that it is common for an unplanned teenage pregnancy to throw many families into an acute crisis that requires professional assistance. Third, counselors can conceptualize counseling as a psychoeducational process that involves the teaching of skills to enhance development, rather than as a remedial process for "sick" people.

As an Anglo American teenage father enters counseling, he may be inclined to do so individually or he may be brought for counseling by his parents as they seek guidance for how to manage the crisis. A tendency to avoid involving extended family members occurs when family counseling is initiated. The young Anglo father and his parents are likely to be comfortable signing written contracts specifying agreements between the counselor and the client. There also may be an acceptance of the counselor's use of specific questioning and formal procedures that are used to explore and understand problems in counseling. Because of their conception of time, Anglo clients are likely to value arriving promptly for appointments and having set time limits for sessions (e.g., a 50-minute session once a week). They are likely to be comfortable at maintaining eye contact while speaking with the counselor and appreciate a firm handshake and verbal expressiveness.

Addressing Dysfunctional Parent-Child Interactions

Based on their study of a nationally representative sample of high school sophomore women, Abrahamse et al. (1988) concluded that a high-quality parent-child relationship appears to be the strongest source of social influence in preventing an unplanned out-of-wedlock pregnancy among Anglo American teenage girls. In the absence of such a relationship, Anglo adolescent girls appear to be at greater risk for becoming parents during their teenage years (Abrahamse et al., 1988). It is not known if the same holds for Anglo adolescent boys. However, based on the findings of Abrahamse et al.

(1988), it is reasonable to hypothesize that some sort of dysfunction or skill deficits in the family may have played a role in the adolescent male's premature entry into fatherhood.

In exploring this hypothesis, it is recommended that counselors avoid making premature conclusions about the quality of the parent-child relationship based on the parents' initial response to the pregnancy. Unplanned out-of-wedlock adolescent pregnancy tends to spark strong negative reactions among Anglo parents due to the strong Anglo cultural prohibitions against premarital childbearing (Moore & Peterson, 1989). As evidence of these reactions, Williams (cited in Moore et al., 1986) found that pregnant Anglo teenagers expected and received a more negative response from parents when they revealed their pregnancy than did pregnant African American teenagers who were also interviewed. According to Robinson (1988a), young fathers must bear similar reactions from their own parents and the parents of the pregnant girl. Because an early response of anger and rejection of the young father is not uncommon, even among Anglo mothers and fathers with a prior history of good parenting skills, this is not necessarily a sign of ongoing dysfunctional parent-child interactions. Data reported by Panzarine and Elster (1983) suggest that these negative reactions usually are followed by a rapid reappraisal of the crisis by the parents, resulting in a more supportive response by the young father's parents.

To ascertain the enduring quality of the parent-son relationship, the counselor can ask the boy to describe prior conflicts he has had with his parents and the manner in which those conflicts were addressed. In addition, the counselor can probe for information regarding the quality of the parent-son interactions over time. In general, warmth, the use of parental reasoning, consistent disciplining, marital harmony, and an authoritative style of parental control are qualities of effective parents (see Hetherington & Parke, 1979). Authoritative parents are not intrusive and permit their children considerable freedom within reasonable limits but are willing to impose restrictions in areas in which they have greater knowledge or insight (Baumrind, 1967). Parents who exhibit these qualities in their interactions with their children are likely to be accessible for counseling after they have had some time to recover from their initial shock regarding the pregnancy.

In general, ineffective parents are those whose long-term relationships with their sons have been characterized by parental hostility, the use of inconsistent disciplinary tactics and physical punishment in the absence of empathic reasoning, and an authoritarian style of parental control. In addition, ineffective parenting is associated with marital discord (see Hetherington & Parke, 1979). Authoritarian parents employ rigid and coercive means to control their children (Baumrind, 1967). Such parents are likely to be hostile and unpredictable during the pregnancy and after the birth of the child. Counselors may need to make repeated efforts to reach these parents and, to establish rapport, use the strategies suggested in Chapter 5 for working with dysfunctional families.

Although the parents of some Anglo teenage parents may be highly ineffective, my clinical impression is that the nature of the parent-child dysfunction among Anglo families is not usually severe. Instead, the problem commonly centers on the Anglo parents' discomfort with and consequent avoidance of discussing the subject of sex and contraceptives with their son, thereby missing critical opportunities to provide their son with important information for preventing unplanned pregnancies. With these families, a common positive consequence of the pregnancy, regardless of how it is resolved, is that the crisis will prompt Anglo parents to overcome their cultural prohibitions against discussing human sexuality with their son. A new era of openness to the subject emerges, with the parents taking a more active role in helping the son to answer his questions regarding sex and contraceptives and clarify his values regarding these topics and his plans for a family. Changes of this kind can play an integral role in preventing repeat unplanned pregnancies and indicate that Anglo parents can be a tremendous role in supporting their son.

Capitalizing on Family Strengths

Other evidence illustrates the supportive role that Anglo parents tend to play in response to the pregnancy. Hendricks's (1988) findings, which indicated Anglo teenage fathers typically turn to their families, particularly their mothers, for help with problems, support the notion that Anglo families do try to resolve their difficulties through negotiations occurring among immediate family members. In their study of the strategies employed by Anglo families to prepare expectant adolescent males for fatherhood, Panzarine and Elster (1983) observed that Anglo parents talk with their son about the fathering role to help him to clarify his responsibilities regarding child care and household tasks. In addition, Panzarine and Elster (1983) noted that father-son conversations about what being a father is like provides reassurance as the son makes the transition to fatherhood. Other data reported by the Alan Guttmacher Institute (1981) suggested that Anglo families tend to offer generous economic assistance to expectant teenagers when the family has the resources to do so. The provision of money is often intended to help young Anglo parents marry and establish their own independent households (Furstenberg, 1976).

The tendency of Anglo families to support teenage parents over the long-term is an expression of the cultural expectation to meet one's responsibilities toward one's children. Counselors can capitalize on this cultural norm by framing other therapeutic tasks as ways that the family members can "fulfill their duties" to one another. For example, there is a commonly held belief among Anglos that parents have a responsibility to play an active role in the education of their children. Counselors can use this value in prompting the adult parents to assist the teenage parents in learning child care skills, financial planning, and other important skills considered important to the raising of children and the management of a home. Furthermore, because Anglos tend to be a very task-oriented people, counselors are likely to be successful at assigning out-of-session therapeutic assignments to family members.

Addressing Issues With Peers

For Anglo American teenager girls, the attitudes of their school peers may have a strong and significant effect on her willingness to consider childbearing out of wedlock. Most of the pertinent research findings suggested that the peer groups of Anglo teenagers tend to view adolescent childbearing negatively and that the presence of such attitudes discourages early childbearing among Anglo teenage girls (e.g., Abrahamse et al., 1988; Williams, cited in Moore et al., 1986; Zelnick et al., 1981). However, other data from a national study conducted by Abrahamse et al. (1988) indicated that Anglo girls attending schools with a peer milieu for tolerating single adolescent childbearing are more likely to become pregnant as teenagers than girls attending schools with a peer milieu that is intolerant of single childbearing. Although similar studies employing representative studies of Anglo adolescent males have not been conducted, findings from one investigation of a small sample of Anglo teenage fathers reported by Elster and Panzarine (1983b) indicated that the friends of the young fathers had permissive attitudes regarding premarital sexual activity and pregnancy. The findings of these latter two studies suggest that peer attitudes favoring out-of-wedlock childbearing and parenthood may weaken mainstream Anglo cultural prohibitions against nonmarital conceptions and parenthood among some subcultural groups of Anglo American teenagers.

In light of this possibility, it is important for counselors to have a sense for the general degree of approval for risky sexual behavior and adolescent parenthood in particular populations of Anglo teenagers. Counselors may have to focus their efforts on teaching the young Anglo father skills for dealing with pressures to further engage in unsafe sexual behavior when the atmosphere is one that might encourage repeated paternity.

In addition to considering the potential role of the peer group in repeat adolescent pregnancies, it is recommended that counselors discuss with the young father how he might use his peers for support during his transition to fatherhood. For example, Panzarine and Elster's (1983) findings indicated that some expectant Anglo teenage fathers found comfort in talking with their friends about the fathering role. Counselors may need to directly advise some Anglo teenage fathers to employ this helpful coping strategy because these youth are likely to try and handle many of their stressors on their own, as is consistent with the Anglo cultural tradition of rugged individualism. Young Anglo men who are strongly influenced by the cultural message to "make it on one's own" could benefit from frank discussions about alternative perspectives to rugged individualism that would legitimatize their hidden desire to share their difficulties with someone else.

An Anglo teenage father also might shy away from seeking peer support because of anticipation that his peers might disapprove of him for his role in an adolescent pregnancy, an expectation that is realistic considering the negative view of teenage childbearing and parenthood commonly held by Anglo teenagers. In this case, it is recommended that the counselor seek out teenagers who might be supportive of a young man facing fatherhood and attempt to link these youth together. Also, encouraging the young father to join a teenage father support group will place him in contact with others who are likely to be empathic toward his experience.

Preparation for Fatherhood

There has been very little empirical research regarding the performance of Anglo American teenage fathers in fulfilling their duties as parents. The meager pertinent data that have been generated suggest that Anglo adolescent fathers vary in the manner in which they behave as fathers.

Hardy and Zabin (1991) conducted interviews with teenage mothers to investigate the paternal behaviors of 42 Anglo teenage fathers. Their findings indicated that the majority of the fathers had either daily or weekly contact with the mother and the child during the first 15 months after the child's birth. However, the frequency of contact declined slightly over this time period. A minority of the fathers were reported by the mothers to help too little in raising the child and provide too little financial support. Compared to a sample of African American teenage fathers who were also a focus of the Hardy and Zabin study, Anglo fathers were significantly less likely to help with child-rearing tasks but significantly more likely to provide financial support.

The findings of the Hardy and Zabin (1991) study should be interpreted with caution because of the sole reliance on the mothers' reports for information regarding the fathers. As was noted by Robinson (1988a), paternal interviews yield significantly different versions of child rearing from maternal ones.

Although the Hardy and Zabin study yielded some data regarding the frequency of contact with children and the type of support provided, a qualitative investigation by Gershenson (1983) produced information on how the characteristics of teenage fathers varied according to their level of involvement with their partners and their children. Gershenson (1983) interviewed 30 Anglo adolescent mothers regarding the performance of their partners in fulfilling their responsibilities as fathers. His findings indicated that most of the biological fathers could be categorized into three groups: (a) husbands, (b) former husbands or boyfriends who broke up with the mother during the prenatal period or shortly thereafter, and (c) former husbands or boyfriends who separated with the mother postnatally. Nine of the biological fathers were categorized as husbands. These males were reported by the mothers to demonstrate an ongoing commitment to both their spouse and their child. Although the mothers expressed some dissatisfaction in the marital relationship with the father, they tended to view the relationship as adequate in terms of the father's financial and emotional support of the child. These fathers appeared to be steadily employed and related to their children according to traditional male roles as fathers. Nine other fathers were described as belonging to the prenatal-separation group. The relationships between the mothers and these fathers appeared to have been very ambivalent. In response to the crisis of an unplanned pregnancy, both mothers and fathers from this group initiated the termination of their relationship. Fathers in this group tended to be steadily employed after the break-up but they demonstrated inconsistent contact and financial support of the child. Gershenson reported that the mothers desired little contact from these fathers, although they would have appreciated more financial support. The postnatal-separation group consisted of nine fathers who reportedly had either been married or had cohabitated with the mother of their child. These fathers were reported to experience long periods of unemployment, declining job status over time, and drug and alcohol abuse. In addition, these fathers were reported to be very controlling and physically abusive of their partners. The highly dysfunctional behavior of these fathers was reported to culminate in the mothers initiating separation and/or divorce. After the break-up, the fathers allegedly sought a reconciliation with the mother and yet demonstrated inconsistent contact and virtually no financial support of their children. Most of the mothers in this group doubted the father's sincere interest in parenthood and perceived the fathers postseparation visits as harassment.

Before the implications of Gershenson's (1983) findings are discussed, two methodological limitations of the study must be mentioned. First, as was the case with the Hardy and Zabin (1991) study, his method involved interviewing the mothers only. Robinson (1988a) criticized Gershenson for excluding interviews with the fathers and pointed out that paternal interviews might have yielded different versions of child rearing from the maternal reports. Second, Gershenson reported that the biological fathers ranged in age from 18 to 32 years at the time his interview was conducted. It is unclear from Gershenson's data how many of the biological fathers were actually teenage fathers at the time of the child's birth. Therefore, generalizations regarding Anglo teenage fathers that are based on this data must be tentative.

These cautions notwithstanding, Gershenson's (1983) findings are important because they indicate that there was no modal pattern of paternal behavior on the part of the Anglo biological fathers related to his study. The same is likely to be true of Anglo teenage fathers in general. However, Gershenson's results suggest some *possible* patterns of paternal responses by Anglo teenage fathers as a function of conditions that existed prior to the unplanned pregnancy. Anglo fathers who are committed to the relationship with the biological mother prior to the pregnancy are not only likely to marry, but also appear ready to devote themselves to the child and contribute positively to the psychological and economic well-being of the baby. A similar tendency was observed by Furstenberg (1976) and Furstenberg et al. (1987). Fathers who have ambivalent feelings about the mother prior to conception, however, seem to cope with the pain associated with an unplanned pregnancy by distancing themselves from both the mother and the child, thereby depriving the child of the potential benefits of the father-child relationship as well as important economic support. Fathers who display a high degree of preexisting psychopathology appear to rely on the mother in a dysfunctional way and become a disruptive force that may directly hinder the mother's adjustment to parenthood and indirectly harm the child. Although I have seen evidence of these patterns of behavior in my clinical work with teenage fathers, they have not been tied to particular points in the adolescent mother's pregnancy.

In light of these possible patterns, several considerations regarding preparation for fatherhood are warranted. Anglo fathers who have demonstrated commitment to the biological mother and child are likely to welcome the opportunity for parenting skills training. This training probably will enhance the young father's parenting skills and his relationship with his partner. For the other two types of fathers, however, prompt, confrontive interventions are in order.

Anglo fathers who are very ambivalent about the mother may need some preparatory counseling before parenting skills training is suggested. Unless these fathers are warned about their potential "flight" responses from a disturbing situation, they may disappear from counseling before fatherhood preparation is started. In discussing this issue, the counselor may have to walk a fine line between empathizing with a young expectant father's impulse to flee a difficult situation and confronting him to recognize the potential negative consequences for his child, his partner, and himself. This issue can become even more complicated when the biological mother and/or her family is giving the father a strong message to "get lost" and/or when his own family and peers may be encouraging his withdrawal from his paternal responsibilities. Again, the father needs to see the potential opportunities for enriching his and his child's life by his continued involvement. Getting this point across can be facilitated by employing the group psychoeducational strategies suggested in Chapter 6. Often in group settings, one or more Anglo fathers who are determined to remain active in their child's life will take on the role of empathizing with and confronting another father who is headed toward disengagement from his child and partner. Promoting such peer interactions on this issue tends to be more successful than counselor-led discussions of the subject.

Anglo fathers who fall into the group characterized by a high degree of preexisting psychopathology require extensive remedial psychotherapy before, during, and after training for fatherhood. When working with this population, counselors need to be prepared for the possibility of contacting a child protective services agency in those cases in which the father's behavior directly or indirectly harms the child. In most cases, however, the support of a dedicated counselor can prevent abusive behavior from occurring and pave the way for a potentially productive participation in fatherhood training.

Anglocentric View of Fatherhood and Masculinity

In the discussion regarding preparation for fatherhood in Chapter 6, it was suggested that teenage fathers need help in clarifying their attitudes regarding fatherhood and masculinity. In approaching this task with Anglo American teenage fathers, it is recommended that counselors develop an understanding of the Anglocentric view of fatherhood and masculinity.

Although there is great variation among Anglo males regarding their conceptions of fatherhood and masculinity, a prevailing and evolving ideal appears to exist among Anglos regarding the male role in the family. Prior to industrialization, the Anglo view held that fathers were primarily responsible for ensuring that their children grew up with an appropriate sense of values, acquired primarily from the study of religious materials (Lamb, 1987). Fathers were the ultimate authority figures in the home and strict disciplinarians of their children (Stearns, 1991). After the Industrial Revolution, the dominant motif became the father as the "breadwinner" for the family (Lamb, 1987), an emotionally distant figure who demonstrated his caring for his children by succeeding in work conducted outside the family (Seward, 1991). Because the demands of the industrial age took the father away from the home for increasing periods of time, shared leisure with children took on greater importance as a paternal vehicle for teaching skills and values (Stearns, 1991). Currently, the role of the father as a provider of nurturance and emotional support of his children has taken on increased importance (Lamb, 1987; Stearns, 1991). The modern Anglocentric ideal epitomizes the father as a kind, wise, and thoughtful figure who serves as an egalitarian head of the family and as a good friend or counselor to children, rather than as a distant breadwinner and strict disciplinarian (Mirande, 1991). Nevertheless, although breadwinner responsibilities have declined due to the increased intimate contact between fathers and children and the entry of mothers into the job market, traditional roles of Anglo fathers have not been fully replaced (Stearns, 1991). Values shifts among Anglo men may have resulted in an expanded definition of fathering, but the actual performance of caretaker and nurturing roles by fathers in intact families lags significantly behind that of mothers (see Pleck, 1985). Occupational roles still take precedence over the parental role in regard to men's prestige and power (Seward, 1991).

Based on these considerations, it appears that Anglo males who are caught in cultural changes regarding their roles as fathers are torn between the powerful forces of tradition that emphasize the breadwinner and disciplinarian roles, a competitive orientation to the world, and a veneer of invulnerability, on the one hand, and the emerging demands for nurturance and intimate involvement on the other. Consequently, Anglo teenage fathers probably are more likely to demonstrate male gender role conflicts than unacculturated Hispanic males, for example, who tend to favor a patriarchal tradition, or African American males, who have a long tradition of practicing egalitarian and flexible gender roles. Thus, while helping Anglo American teenage fathers to clarify their conceptions of paternity and masculinity, it is particularly important to be alert for these conflicts.

In responding to conflicts regarding paternal and masculine roles, it may help to suggest to Anglo teenage fathers that these tensions are understandable among males living in a society that is under a transition in values. Empathizing with a young father's confusion regarding his role as a father may reduce his associated anger and frustration that is sometimes directed toward the mother of his child. In addition, as a means of helping Anglo males view such conflicts as opportunities for creating greater bonds in the family, the counselor might share an observation noted by Seward (1991); that is, the father who can make the transition from being an aloof, distant authority figure to becoming an emotionally expressive and intimate one with his children is likely to provide a source of support for his family, serve as a diverse role model for his children, and, in the process, increase his own sense of well-being and morale.

Educational and Career Counseling

Early childbearing may interfere with formal education far more among Anglos than among African American teenage parents. Anglo school-age mothers are more likely to drop out of school because of a birth than are African American adolescent mothers (Moore & Waite, 1981). Approximately half of all Anglo teenage fathers fail to earn a high school diploma or a GED, compared to about a third of African American teenage fathers (Marsiglio, 1986). The drop-out rate may be even higher for Anglo adolescent fathers living in the inner city (see Hardy & Zabin, 1991).

The decision to leave school can have long-term, detrimental economic consequences. Anglos with less than 12 years of education have higher unemployment rates and earn lower salaries than those with a high school or postsecondary education (Children's Defense Fund, 1985). Anglo single-parent families, especially those headed by adolescent mothers who have dropped out of school, are at risk for poverty. Among Anglo Americans under the age of 25, the poverty rates for married-couple families headed by a high school graduate, married-couple families headed by a dropout, single-mother families headed by a high school graduate, and single-mother families headed by a high school dropout are 11.2%, 33.4%, 58.6%, and 84.6%, respectively (Children's Defense Fund, 1991a).

These data suggest that the completion of a high school education may improve the long-term economic status of Anglo adolescent parents, whether they are married or not. Therefore, Anglo teenage mothers and fathers can benefit from individualized educational planning that assists them in completing their educations while meeting their responsibilities as parents. In addition, data reported by Abrahamse et al. (1988) suggest that the development of college plans may inhibit unplanned pregnancies among Anglo adolescents. It was hypothesized by these researchers that the opportunities afforded by a college education may diminish the willingness of Anglos to engage in unprotected sex. Thus, the provision of continued educational planning may prevent repeat unplanned pregnancies among Anglo teenage parents.

The promotion of continued education may be difficult because of the tendency among Anglos to marry in response to the unplanned pregnancy. Although the percentage of Anglo teenage parents who marry has diminished in recent years, the pressure within this cultural group to marry remains strong. The expectation is that the young father should marry, quit school, and work to support his partner and child. It also is expected that the adolescent mother drop out of school, not only to care for the child, but to save the family embarrassment at having the pregnant girl "on display" in public places. As an added pressure to drop out, it remains commonplace in Anglo communities for school personnel to give expectant adolescent mothers an implicit message that they do not belong in school.

In light of the economic hardships and conflicts regarding school completion, it is not surprising that Anglo adolescent fathers report that they experience vocational-educational concerns. These concerns are present relatively early during the pregnancy and remain at a high level throughout the pregnancy and at least through the neonatal period (Elster & Panzarine, 1983b).

Although it can be helpful to advise expectant Anglo teenage parents and their families regarding their rights to a continued education and the pros and cons of dropping out of school, it also is recommended that school counselors work to educate Anglo teachers and administrators about this information. Thus, in addition to employing the strategies for countering opposition from the Anglo community, described earlier in this chapter, and the tactics for supporting educational decision making, discussed in Chapter 7, it may be necessary to conduct in-service workshops for school faculty and staff regarding the impact of adolescent parenthood on the adjustment of teenagers and their families and the benefits of continued education.

9

African American Teenage Fathers

To comprehend the complexity of the teenage parent phenomenon in the African American culture, mental health professionals must have an understanding of the historical experience of African Americans in this country. Highlights of this history are woven throughout this chapter to reveal how oppressive racist, economic, and political forces have fabricated destructive societal stereotypes about African American males, influenced the sexual behavior of African American youth, and eroded the traditional family structure in the African American community while prompting adaptive survival mechanisms by African American families. This chapter begins with brief profiles of African Americans and African American teenage fathers. In the remainder of this chapter, the salient issues of African American adolescent fathers are discussed and culturally sensitive interventions are recommended.

A Profile of African Americans

Numbering nearly 30 million people and representing more than 12% of the total U.S. population, African Americans constitute the nation's largest racial-ethnic minority group (U.S. Bureau of the Census, 1988). African Americans live and work throughout the entire United States (U.S. Bureau of the Census, 1988) and are represented by a diverse group of peoples, including the following: the descendants of Africans who were brought involuntarily to North America as slaves in the 1600s; Africans who recently immigrated to the United States; Spanish-speaking Blacks from Cuba, Puerto Rico, and Central and South America; and Blacks from the West Indies and Northern Europe (see Axelson, 1993; Ponterotto & Casas, 1991). The terms *Blacks, Black people, Black Americans, Afro-Americans,* and *African Americans* have been used interchangeably in the social sciences literature to describe this heterogeneous group of peoples.

Parham and Austin (1994) stated that the tremendous cultural diversity among African Americans must be recognized in counseling. Because psychological characteristics, such as racial identity attitudes, and cultural roots (e.g., African, West Indian) vary among African Americans and can affect the process of counseling, culture-specific hypotheses about this population must be tested with each African American client to avoid within-culture stereotyping. Similarly, Cheatham (1990b) argued that there is a need for a constant recognition of the many individual differences that exist within and between African American communities. Nevertheless, Cheatham (1990a, 1990b) added that it is equally important to understand the unique African American culture that has evolved in response to the historical experience of Blacks in America. This experience is highlighted in the following profile of African American teenage fathers.

A Profile of African American Teenage Fathers

In this section, stereotypes about African American teenage fathers are reviewed and more accurate information about adolescent sexuality, pregnancy, and parenthood among African Americans is presented. Special attention is devoted to the hardships of African American adolescents, particularly the difficulties encountered by African American males who become teenage fathers.

Stereotypes and Facts About Adolescent Sexuality, Pregnancy, and Parenthood Among African Americans

Ladner and Gourdine (1984), Butts (1989), and Battle (1988/1989) have criticized American society for the widely held misconception that teenage parenthood is solely a problem among African Americans. For example, Battle (1988/1989) objected to a 1987 CBS documentary on adolescent pregnancy, the *Moyers Report,* which projected adolescent pregnancy as the norm in the African American community. Such media depictions may represent the continuation of stereotypes regarding the sexuality of African Americans in general and African American males in particular. Wyatt (1982) suggested that these myths characterize African Americans as sexy, hypersexual, permissive people who have few morals about sexual promiscuity in or out of marriage, and depict African American males as superstuds with savage sexual appetites.

The notion that teenage pregnancy and parenthood are exclusive to African Americans also illustrates ignorance of the facts on the teenage pregnancy phenomenon in this country. It is necessary to separate fact from fiction and acquire an intricate understanding of the pervasive influence of political and socioeconomic forces on the sexuality of African American youth to develop an accurate profile of the African American teenage father.

In their review of the literature on the sexual activity of African American adolescents, Scott-Jones et al. (1989) concluded that African American adolescents become sexually active at an earlier age, are more sexually active, and are less likely to use contraceptives than are White adolescents. Between 1980 and 1988, the teenage pregnancy rate among African Americans increased nearly 9% (Henshaw, 1992). The teenage pregnancy rate among Blacks is approximately four times the rate for Whites, and the birth rate among Black adolescent females is approximately two times that of White teenagers (see Scott-Jones et al., 1990). In 1980, 48% of first births among Blacks occurred among women not yet 20; the majority of these occurred out of wedlock. By the time they turn 20, 41% of young Black women will already have at least one child (Moore et al., 1986). Thirteen percent of all Black adolescent girls are teenage mothers (Abrahamse et al., 1988).

Considering these data, one might easily conclude that teenage parenthood is principally "a Black problem." However, a review of other data graphically demonstrate, in the words of Butts (1989), that "teenage pregnancy is one fact of life which confronts all Americans whether urban or rural, rich or poor, White or Black, male or female" (p. 146). The fertility of White teenagers in the United States has been considerably higher than that in most other Western industrialized nations (Westoff, Cabot, & Foster, 1983). During the 1970s, there was a rapid increase in early sexual activity and pregnancy among Whites (Moore & Burt, 1982; Zelnick & Kantner, 1980). In the 1980s, approximately two thirds of first births to Anglo adolescents were conceived premaritally (Scott-Jones, 1993). In 1980, 25% of the first births to White women occurred to teenage girls, and approximately one third of these occurred out of wedlock (see Moore et al., 1986). The sharpest increases in out-of-wedlock childbearing have occurred among Whites.

Since 1980, the birth rate among unmarried White teenagers has risen 33% (U.S. Congress, 1989). Finally, Whites account for approximately two thirds of the total births to women under age 20 in the United States (see Moore et al., 1986). These facts confirm Butts's observation that teenage parenthood is not just a problem for African Americans.

Because teenage pregnancy and parenthood cut across ethnic and racial lines, why are they often conceived as a Black phenomenon? The answer is rooted within the historically different views of sexuality held by the Anglo and African American peoples and the Eurocentric interpretation of these differences promoted by the dominant Anglo culture in the United States. Blassingame (cited in Williams, 1990) reported that prenuptial sexual relations between Black men and women were common in the African heritage, "which had a view of sexual intercourse devoid of the negative and puritanical connotations given to it by Western European society" (Williams, 1990, p. 179). European missionaries who first traveled to Africa were shocked by this practice and viewed it as sinful. Later, Anglo Americans, influenced by an Euro-Christian perspective, continued to evaluate the sexual traditions of the slaves in the same manner. Over time, Anglo Americans grew to view African Americans as innately immoral in their sexuality (Wyatt, 1982). At the same time, to defend against shame in the White community, Whites developed a tradition of "hiding" out-of-wedlock children born to adolescents in their families (Butts, 1989). The current tendency for the media in this country to portray teenage parenthood as a Black phenomenon may represent a continuation of the Eurocentric tradition of misunderstanding and judging the African American experience while concealing parallel practices in the White community.

This is not to minimize the problem of teenage pregnancy in the African American community. Besides demonstrating that teenage parenthood is common among Whites, the facts also indicate that, as a proportion of all births, early and out-of-wedlock childbearing is more common among Blacks. In reaction to this reality, many scholars (e.g., Dash, 1989; Hendricks, 1981; Hendricks, Montgomery, & Fullilove, 1984; Hendricks & Solomon, 1987; Kunjufu, 1986; Madhubuti, 1990; A. Smith, 1988/1989; Staples & Johnson, 1992; Williams, 1991) have noted that teenage pregnancy and parenthood are critical issues for the African American community. These and other researchers have explained within a normative cultural context the high rate of early parenthood among African Americans.

Moore et al. (1986) conducted an extensive review of the literature to explore the factors underlying the higher rates of teenage pregnancy among African Americans. The authors concluded that many of the factors found independently to predict early childbearing—that is, inadequate information about human sexuality and contraception, poorly educated parents, school dropout, poor employment prospects, single-parent families—are found to be concentrated in those neighborhoods in which African American children are likely to be growing up. The authors also hypothesized that the aggregate influence of these separate factors may be greater than the simple sum of the separate effects, thereby placing African American youth at greater risk than other ethnic groups to become teenage parents. These findings suggest that teenage fatherhood for most African American, adolescent boys occurs within the context of many harsh realities. A further account of these hardships is provided to more clearly elucidate the challenges and problems faced by young African American males during the adolescent period of development.

Hardships of African American Adolescents

Like that of African American adolescents in general, the experience of Black teenage fathers is influenced by the tragic legacy of racism toward African Americans in the United States (see Franklin, 1982, 1989; Gibbs, 1984; Johnson, 1985; Leavy, 1983; Parham & McDavis, 1987; Poussaint, 1990; Ruiz, 1990; L. A. Smith, 1988, 1989). Over a century after the emancipation of Blacks from slavery, African Americans, as a whole, continue to be second-class citizens in this country by nature of their restricted educational and economic opportunities and their limited social mobility.

Statistics reported by the Children's Defense Fund (1985) provide a sobering account of the status of African American children in America. Compared to White children, Black children are *twice* as likely to die in the first year of life, be born prematurely, suffer low birthweight, have mothers who received late or no prenatal care, be born to a teenage or single-parent family, see a parent die, live in substandard housing, be suspended from school or suffer corporal punishment, be unemployed as teenagers, and live in institutions. Black children are *three* times as likely to be poor, have their mothers die in childbirth, live with a parent who has separated, live in a female-headed household, be placed in an educable mentally retarded class, be murdered between 5 and 9 years of age, be in foster care, and die of known child abuse. Black children are *four* times as likely to live with neither parent and be supervised by a child welfare agency, be murdered before 1 year of age or as a teenager, and be incarcerated between 15 and 19 years of age. Finally, Black children are *five* times as likely to be dependent on welfare and *12* times as likely to live with a parent who never married.

Other data reveal that the already alarming status of African American children has worsened in recent years. Compared to Black children in 1980, Black children in 1985 were "more likely to be born into poverty, lack early prenatal care, have an adolescent or single mother, have an unemployed parent, be unemployed themselves as teenagers and not go to college after high school graduation" (Children's Defense Fund, 1985, p. vii). In her analysis of the major social indicators, Gibbs (1984, 1988) concluded that African American youth were relatively worse off in the 1980s than they were in 1960 in rates of unemployment, delinquency, substance abuse, teenage pregnancy, and suicide. Significant subpopulations of African Americans, Gibbs has argued, are in danger of becoming permanently trapped in an impoverished underclass. Thus, the physical and psychological well-being of Blacks is not only poor compared to that of Whites, it also is "sliding backwards" (Children's Defense Fund, 1985, p. vi).

The historical restriction of opportunities and the bleak future of a substantial number of African American adolescents have been identified by several scholars (e.g., Abrahamse et al., 1988; Battle, 1988/1989; Butts, 1989; Scott-Jones et al., 1989; L. A. Smith, 1988, 1989; Sullivan, 1985) as playing a major role in the high teenage pregnancy rate among African American teenagers. Findings from studies of African American adolescent parenthood suggested that the vast majority of African American adolescent parents neither consciously planned their first sexual intercourse (Rogel, Zuehlke, Petersen, Tobin-Richards, & Shelton, 1980; Sullivan, 1985) nor intended to conceive a child (Moore, 1992; L. A. Smith, 1989; Sullivan, 1985; Williams, 1991; Zelnick & Kantner, 1980). However, as Abrahamse et al. (1988) and L. A. Smith (1988, 1989) have argued, many of these same youth may see less opportunity in their own futures and hence less to lose by becoming single parents. According to Gabriel and McAnarney (1983) and L. A. Smith (1988, 1989), because African American males perceive so many of the adult roles valued by American society as being closed to them, they may view parenthood as a way to achieve maturity and a sense of achievement. "Thus, although most Black male adolescents do not plan fatherhood, neither do they strenuously avoid it" (L. A. Smith, 1988, p. 270).

In light of the reduced life chances for African American youth, Gibbs (1984) and L. A. Smith (1988, 1989) have enjoined the helping professions to expand the focus of their efforts beyond the micro level of intervention by including macrolevel strategies for change. L. A. Smith (1988) wrote, "Service providers must become active politically to ensure that the high-risk status of young Black males, including fathers, becomes an issue on the national agenda" (p. 270).

Complications of Early Parenthood
for the African American Male

Although becoming a parent may represent an accomplishment for the adolescent raised in a world of limited opportunities, data demonstrate that parenthood nevertheless complicates the adjustment of the African American teenage father. Hendricks and his colleagues (Hendricks, 1981, 1988; Hendricks & Solomon, 1987) conducted a series of studies in which they interviewed an aggregate total of 167 African American unmarried adolescent fathers from Tulsa, Oklahoma; Chicago, Illinois; Columbus, Ohio; Washington, D.C.; and Albuquerque, New Mexico. The results of these studies indicate that African American males experience a range of problems associated with parenthood that are similar to those reported by Anglo American teenage fathers, including the following: conflicts with their families of origin and the unwed mother's family; difficulties understanding the young mother's emotions; hardships in completing school, getting a job, and fulfilling the financial responsibilities of fatherhood; a lack of knowledge about parenting skills and contraceptives; restricted freedom imposed by parenting duties; not being able to see his child as often as he would desire; and not wanting the young woman to have the baby.

Although African American teenage fathers are more likely than their Anglo American and Hispanic American counterparts to earn their high school diploma or a GED (Marsiglio, 1986), the results of three studies indicated that the educational achievement level of African American adolescent fathers was not as high as their nonfather classmates (Card & Wise, 1978; Hendricks et al., 1984; Marsiglio, 1986). The Card and Wise (1978) study also yielded findings that suggested a direct linear relationship between age at birth of first child and the level of education achieved by the fathers at 5 and 11 years past the expected date of high school graduation. At 11 years after high school, males who were adolescent fathers were overrepresented in blue-collar jobs and underrepresented in the white-collar professions. Thus, early fatherhood limited the number of years the fathers might otherwise have spent in school and, consequently, curtailed their occupational opportunities.

In addition to these hardships, the African American teenage father may encounter societal racism (L. A. Smith, 1988). Specifically, he could experience a host of racist reactions commonly and subtly communicated by White service providers to Black males in counseling, such as a priori assumptions that he is dangerous and an uncaring superstud because he is a Black male (see Wyatt, 1982).

Young African American fathers, especially those from the inner city, also might experience pejorative reactions from fellow African Americans, including service providers. L. A. Smith's (1989) described the reaction of an African American community toward a proposal to provide services for teenage fathers residing within the community. The community appeared divided in their attitudes toward adolescent fathers. Smith's impression was that although some community members regarded young fathers as an at-risk group in need of services, there was a lack of clear support for such services in the community. Many community members characterized adolescent fathers as "no good" (L. A. Smith, 1989, p. 217). Community members readily volunteered to act as mentors for adolescent mothers, but not for adolescent fathers. Other community members destroyed flyers used to recruit the target population. Disdain for adolescent fathers also was reported by some of the African American service providers who Smith interviewed. Like many of their White counterparts, these professionals harbored generalizations that adolescent fathers in the community were irresponsible individuals for whom outreach efforts would be a waste of time.

Finally, according to Goddard and Cavil (1989), the young African American father also may experience a dilemma about what values and cultural orientations to transmit to his children. Some African American teenagers grow up under the influence of two distinct and competing cultural perspectives. The traditional African culture stresses cooperation and the promotion of the collective good. Contemporary American culture accentuates competition and individualism. The onset of fatherhood may prompt a conflict for the young man as he attempts to decide which cultural value system to pass on to his children.

Implications for Counseling

Together, these findings on the problems experienced by African American adolescent fathers suggest that they require the full range of services described in Chapter 2. However, several other culture-specific interventions also are recommended. First, the African American teenage father might need to be taught strategies to cope with racism, such as those described in detail by Shade (1990). Second, counseling that is focused on his potential cultural value conflicts can help him to clarify his personal values. Third, culturally sensitive process skills are necessary to engage him in counseling. Fourth, White and Black service providers alike must examine their preconceived notions about the African American adolescent father. Fifth, mental health professionals can support policies designed to address the vulnerability of African American adolescents through political activism. Concrete suggestions for accomplishing each of these culture-specific recommendations are described throughout remainder of this chapter.

Program Development Considerations

In this section, the following issues related to program development in the African American community are addressed: (a) obtaining input from African American community leaders, (b) the roles of African American adult mentors and the African American church in the provision of services, and (c) responding to opposition by the African American community.

Obtaining Input of African American Community Leaders

Butts (1989) conducted telephone interviews with 10 of the nation's leading authorities on the status of service programs for African American teenage parents. Her findings indicated that more input from African Americans is needed throughout the development and management of pertinent service programs. Specifically, the respondents indicated that service programs for African American teenage parents typically have been developed by White-dominated institutions. The respondents claimed that such programs tended to be out of touch with the cultural experience of African Americans because they were designed without sufficient participation from the targeted communities during the program development phase. The respondents also criticized existing service programs for having too few African American administrators and clinicians. Based on these findings, Butts (1989) challenged White program developers who intend to serve Black clients to incorporate African American leadership into the planning, administration, and delivery of service programs.

Input from African Americans obtained during the program development phase typically results in the creation and delivery of services in a culturally relevant way. For example, the acclaimed *Simba Wachanga* (the Kiswahili name for young lions) program, described in Lindsay and Rodine (1989a), is a rite-of-passage program developed by African Americans for youth receiving services at the East End Neighborhood House in Cleveland, Ohio. The program is a culture-specific guidance system through which African American men serve as positive role models to their young males. The young men, who participate in the program 2 to 4 hours per week, are taught their African identity by older men, who are known as the Council of Elders. The Elders engage the "young lions" in African rituals designed to steer the boys to manhood. The boys also receive sex education and a wide range of training in life skills. The coordinator of the program is selected from a member of the Council of Elders.

Another program illustrating the development and implementation of services for African Americans by African Americans is the *Black Teenage Parenting and Early Childhood Education: Basic Curriculum Plan* (Nobles, Goddard, & Cavil, 1985), developed by the Institute for the Advanced Study of Black Family Life and Culture (see Goddard & Cavil, 1989). This six-module curriculum is designed to help African American teenage parents plan for their unique position of being Black, young, and a parent all at the same time. As such, it prepares teenagers for parenthood from a culturally consistent perspective (Goddard & Cavil, 1989).

Several other programs for teenage fathers developed by African Americans are described by Battle (1988/1989). These include the Comprehensive School Age Parenting Program at English High School in Boston, Massachusetts, and several projects initiated by the Chicago chapter of the African American fraternity Alpha Phi Alpha.

The Role of
African American Adult Mentors

Based on their work with inner-city African American teenage parents, Zabin, Hirsch, Smith, Streett, and Hardy (1986) concluded that this population can benefit from all of the services recommended in Chapter 3. Battle (1988/1989) added that such services particularly appeal to teenage fathers when they include staff members who are adult African American men who provide their time, energy, and attention to the younger males. The participation of adult male mentors who are African American is critical because men from other cultural groups may have difficulty empathizing with the historical experiences and the Africentric orientation of African American teenage boys. This issue is addressed at length later in this chapter in a discussion of fatherhood training with African American teenage fathers.

The African American
Church as a Lead Agency

Lee (1989) and L. A. Smith (1989) argued that service programs targeting African American adolescents are likely to be successful if they are offered in settings already trusted and used by the African American community. Because the African American church has a long tradition of functioning as a source of support for African Americans, it is considered by many scholars to be an ideal location for community-based programs (e.g., Anderson, Eaddy, & Williams, 1990; Lee, 1989; A. Smith, 1988/1989; Solomon, 1990). In terms of its help to African American males, historically the African American church has provided men with leadership experiences, been a center for the social and political activities of men, offered men job opportunities, and assisted troubled men to change their lifestyles from illicit street life to legal, productive, and stable ones (A. Smith, 1988/1989). Because of this legacy, the African American church would appear to be a logical choice as a service base for programs serving African American teenage fathers.

Other considerations suggest that the use of the African American church in this manner might present problems in engaging African American adolescent fathers for participation in service programs. For example, although the church has been a benefactor in many ways to African American men, it has failed to recruit large numbers of men as members (A. Smith, 1988/1989). A recent national study of religious life among African Americans by Taylor and Chatters (1991) suggested that males, especially younger males, are less likely than females to be actively involved in the church. Other data gathered by Hendricks suggested that African American unwed adolescent fathers are unlikely to be active church members (Hendricks, 1981, 1988) and unlikely to use the clergy as a source of help (Hendricks, 1988). Thus, in order for the church to become a viable center of services for African American teenage fathers, it must somehow attract young males in greater numbers.

Asante (1981) has voiced other controversial criticisms of the African American church that may have some bearing on the issue of helping adolescent fathers. Asante contended that the church has harmed African American male-female relationships in several ways. First, he charged that the African American church in the United States is out of touch with the African roots of its peoples. Therefore, it is not relevant to the African tradition of male-female relationships. Asante also criticized the church for defining a sexist role of males, making it easier for them to subjugate women. Finally, Asante alleged that the church preaches duty above love in regard to relationships, thereby teaching men and women to remain together long after the effective end of the relationship. In conclusion, Asante warned that the traditional church may do more harm than good to male-female relationships.

In an attempt to address such criticisms while proposing solutions to the apparent lack of interest of young African American males in the church, A. Smith (1988/1989) suggested a variety of roles that the African American church can take with respect to the issue of teenage fathers. First, the church can represent the African American community in service coalitions, thereby serving as a voice for the needs of the community. Second, the church can attract more young people to its congregation by engaging in open dialogues about sex and sexuality. Third, the church can become a strong base of support for teenage parents by offering such services as parenting training, family-life education, and so on. Fourth, the church can sponsor activities designed to enhance the self-esteem of boys and young men, such as rallying males in the community to channel their frustrations with the sociopolitical system through organized lobbying efforts. Finally, Smith recommended that the church should sponsor workshops and training designed to build positive African American male-female relationships. Smith argued that by taking these measures, the African American church can become more relevant to the lifestyles of adolescent fathers and it can promote healthy male-female relationships.

Program developers also might heed the suggestions by Solomon (1990) as potential considerations in developing church-based services for adolescent fathers in African American communities. For example, Solomon recommended that the church work in tandem with community agencies to develop service programs. The church should provide rooms at church sites that are identified by the agency's name on the door. This might ensure that the services will be perceived as community agency sponsored rather than church sponsored and therefore available to any member of the community rather than only to members of the particular church. Locating services at a church site would suggest the endorsement of the church and perhaps would be perceived as a less bureaucratic, less culturally alien program of services than those offered at agency settings.

Responding to Opposition
in the African American Community

L. A. Smith (1989) provided a detailed account of community objection to the development of a service program for African American teenage fathers. Although Smith eventually was able to implement her program, she encountered opposition from community members at every phase of the project. This reaction surprised Smith, for she expected the community to support the program in light of her extensive efforts to involve local leaders, institutions, and agencies in the project. In the past, such cooperative planning had resulted in community approval for programs helping young mothers. But the proposal for helping young fathers appeared to touch a nerve within the community. Smith concluded that the African American community in which she conducted her study reflected the negative attitudes of society toward Black adolescent fathers and warned that even culturally sensitive interventions for this population might be opposed because of the power of these stereotypes.

L. A. Smith (1989) offered several suggestions for other program developers confronted by community antagonism, including some of the counterstrategies described in Chapter 3, such as the use of the media to drum up community support and assurances that sexual education would not result in increased sexual activity. However, Smith added that program developers need to pledge to the community that the provision of services for young fathers will not jeopardize services for young mothers and their babies. Apparently, working class African Americans fear that the onset of new programs forecast that old ones are likely to be terminated.

Outreach With African American Teenage Fathers

Data from studies examining the help-seeking behavior of African American men (e.g., Gary, Leashore, Howard, & Buckner-Dowell, 1982) and teenage fathers (e.g., Hendricks, 1988; Hendricks et al., 1981; Hendricks & Solomon, 1987) indicate that African American males are likely to rely on themselves, a family member, or a friend and are unlikely to use an agency for help with a personal problem. African American teenage fathers, in particular, are likely to turn to their mothers for assistance (Hendricks, 1988; Hendricks et al., 1981; Hendricks & Solomon, 1987). African American males also will use the assistance of formal settings, such as hospitals, for help with their medical concerns (Gary et al., 1982; Hendricks, 1988).

These findings suggest that the mothers of teenage fathers and physicians could play a crucial role in identifying young African American fathers for counseling. Thus, in addition to employing the many outreach strategies mentioned in Chapter 3, it is recommended that outreach efforts be geared toward informing these mothers and physicians of pertinent programs. African American women can be reached through announcements made at church services or at service settings they are likely to use, such as ob-gyn clinics. Physicians of adolescent medicine at hospitals, clinics, and family medical practices can be offered in-service training about the features of existing programs, the skills necessary for talking to teenage boys about their sexuality and paternity, and the mechanisms for making referrals. For example, Dr. Robert Johnson, a physician and professor of adolescent medicine at the University of Medicine and Dentistry in New Jersey, teaches these subjects to medical students, psychology interns, and nurses who are likely to serve

African American teenage fathers residing in Newark, New Jersey. These educational efforts have raised a compassionate awareness among many professionals about the difficulties young African American fathers face and the strategies for helping them.

It is recommended that African American males who are identified as potential clients through the referral of a female friend or relative need to be approached by counselors in a particular, considerate manner. Boyd-Franklin (1989) advised mental health professionals to avoid using the female as a messenger, other than to ask the female to tell the male that the counselor will be calling. Then, the counselor should contact the male directly, inform him that the counselor learned about him through the female, spend considerable effort engaging the male with regard to his concerns, and set up an appointment for an individual meeting (Boyd-Franklin, 1989). In this manner, the early negotiations regarding the counseling process occur with the male himself and communicate to him a respect for his autonomy.

Once this meeting is determined, the counselor may have to carefully balance individual work with dyadic counseling, if the referring female is the male's partner, or in the case of family counseling, if the referring female is the male's mother. Hendricks's (1988) cautioned that dyadic counseling with African American teenage fathers should not occur during the initial session because of the potential tenuousness of the male-female relationship. Nevertheless, dyadic counseling may be necessary later on, after the counselor has established rapport with the adolescent father, to address issues between the couple and retain the partner as an ally in keeping the young father engaged in counseling. If the client is a minor and his mother is the referring female, the counselor may need her signed consent for the boy to be involved in counseling. Many mothers who take an interest in getting their sons to counseling will want to be a part of the counseling process. In these instances, it will be necessary to explain to the mother that some individual, confidential work with the son will be necessary but that the counselor will attempt to involve the mother as much as possible through family sessions. Through these measures, both the son's individuation and the mother's concern for her son will be acknowledged and affirmed.

Establishing and Maintaining Rapport

Numerous considerations enter into the rapport-building process with African American teenage fathers. Racial identity issues may affect the client's reactions to a counselor, ranging from acceptance to hostile tests of the counselor. White counselors, in particular, may be challenged by Black clients, as well as by fellow professionals. The physical environment of the counseling office, the attire of the counselor, and the language used by the counselor also can influence the establishment of rapport. Issues pertaining to client mistrust of the mental health system, countertransference, and theoretical orientation may need to be addressed. Finally, group interventions may enhance rapport.

Racial Identity Issues

According to Cheatham (1990b), counseling with African Americans may be affected by the racial identity development of the client. Cross's (1971, 1991) model of Black identity development, one of the most widely scrutinized models of its kind, is highlighted here to provide counselors with an understanding of the racial identity development of African American teenage fathers.

Cross (1971, 1991) proposed a model of Black identity development that focuses on *nigrescence,* the "process of becoming Black" (Cross, 1991, p. 157) in the United States. This model consists of five stages. Cross hypothesized that an individual moves from one stage to the next in a stepwise linear progression. An individual in the Pre-Encounter Stage may vary along a continuum from low salience (e.g., sees race as a hassle that has to be dealt with) to alienation from other Blacks. During the Encounter Stage, the individual experiences an event that causes the individual to begin the process of developing a more well-defined Black identity. In the Immersion-Emersion Stage, the individual idealizes Blackness, generally valuing and immersing him- or herself in Black experiences and denigrating anything associated with White culture. In the Internalization Stage, a new identity is incorporated. Hatred of Whites is replaced by a proactive Black pride. The individual is open to a bicultural or even a multicultural orientation. The final stage, Internalization-Commitment, characterized by a long-term commitment to activity in Black issues, results in identity resolution for the individual.

Parham (1989) extended Cross's model by proposing that racial identity development continues throughout the life span and that racial identity attitudes are subject to continuous change over time. Parham further argued that a person can start at one stage of awareness, continue through the process of racial identity development, and recycle through again in response to significant life events, such as new encounters with racism, which can cause racial identity confusion.

Black racial identity development may influence the counseling process and interventions used with African American teenage fathers. Clients in the Pre-Encounter Stage may be more open to working with a White counselor or a Black professional who identifies with the values of Anglos than with a Black counselor who has a strong Africentric orientation. Also, because Pre-Encounter teenage fathers may be alienated from finding support from fellow African Americans, parenthood for these fathers may be a very isolated experience; therefore, a particular emphasis may need to be placed on building a support network for the Pre-Encounter father. Young fathers in either the Encounter or the Immersion-Emersion Stage may be leery of working with and more likely to test a White counselor, highly emotional in their responses toward racial issues, and receptive to counseling that is embedded in an Africentric tradition, which is described later in this chapter. Finally, fathers in the Internalization or the Internalization-Commitment Stage may be accepting of either a White or Black counselor as well as a variety of Eurocentric and Africentric approaches to counseling.

An important issue regarding Black identity development with teenage fathers regards its assessment. Although counselors can formally determine the client's stage of Black identity development by administering the Black Racial Identity Attitude Scale (Helms & Parham, 1990), research by Hendricks and Solomon (1987) and Hendricks (1988) suggests that formal assessments conducted early on in counseling are likely to deter the establishment of rapport with African American teenage fathers and drive them away from counseling. Therefore, informal assessments are recommended. Furthermore, if Parham's (1989) proposition about recycling is correct, a client's current racial identity could change as a result of new life experiences. Thus, it is recommended that counselors make informal assessments of Black identity development throughout the counseling process and adjust the process and interventions used accordingly.

Another implication of Black racial identity development is that African American teenage fathers may need therapeutic assistance in resolving racial identity issues. For example, as Parham (1989) noted, some African American clients may need help to become "comfortable with the recognition that he or she is a worthwhile human being regardless of valuation and validation from Whites" (p. 217).

Challenges of the Counselor
by Clients and Fellow Professionals

Another implication of racial identity development is that counselors may be challenged by their clients. In this section, client tests of both White and Black counselors are discussed and appropriate counselor reactions are suggested. In the discussion regarding White counselors, the issue of challenges by other professionals also is addressed.

Client Tests of the White Counselor. White counselors often are tested by Black clients. Franklin (1982, 1989) noted that some streetwise, urban Black youth intentionally test the sincerity of White counselors by using scare tactics, such as relating antisocial exploits of indulgence in drugs, sex, alcohol, or delinquency. According to Franklin, the purpose of these maneuvers is to trick the counselor into making value judgments about the client and evaluate the counselor's knowledge and empathy for the sociocultural conditions of life for the African American adolescent. In addition to these tests of counselor sincerity and perspective taking, some youth in either the Encounter or the Immersion-Emersion Stage may have strong resentment of Whites that is directed toward the counselor.

In response to these challenges, it is imperative that the White counselor understand the many realities of African American adolescent boys described earlier and empathically communicate this understanding to the client by taking rapid, concrete action designed to help the client with his needs. In addition, the counselor must be careful not to act shocked by the very dramatic stories a youth might tell, judge the teenager for his behavior, and be scared off by hostility. Remembering that Black resentment toward Whites often is an understandable reaction to societal racism, the counselor should express his or her continued availability to help the youth with his many concerns. At the same time, the counselor must insist that he or she be treated with respect. Furthermore, although the goal of the counseling is to help the client with his problem, the counselor must be prepared to confront the client in a constructive manner when it is appropriate to do so, such as when a client gets nasty with the counselor or when the client reports having forsaken the use of a condom during sexual intercourse with a stranger. By behaving in this manner, the White counselor will convey to the client the implicit message, "We are going to treat each other as human beings worthy of mutual respect." When these measures are unsuccessful in establishing rapport, a referral to a Black counselor with an Africentric orientation may be necessary.

Challenges to White Counselors From Fellow Professionals. In addition to the tests posed by Black clients, White counselors may be challenged by fellow professionals about the appropriateness of Whites working with African Americans. These challenges reflect an ongoing controversy in the mental health literature pertaining to the question of whether or not a White counselor can serve the needs of a Black client adequately.

According to Cheatham (1990b), nearly two decades of research suggest that counselor skills and orientations, rather than specific ethnicity, appear to be the crucial factors in determining the quality of service delivered to

Black Americans. For example, Black clients who initially prefer a Black counselor might feel uncomfortable working with a White counselor during the early stages of counseling. However, the "effects of this preference may be transient and apparently can be disposed of effectively in an appropriate intervention" (Cheatham, 1990b, p. 383). Thus, White counselors can work successfully with Black clients provided they use culturally sensitive process and treatment skills. It also follows that Black counselors may be ineffective if the wrong approach is used.

What then are the qualities of effective counseling with African American adolescent fathers? Some of these attributes include dedication to extending services to young fathers, assertively advocating for teenage fathers, and relating to the client with caring, persistence, sincerity, patience, a sense of humor, and a nonjudgmental attitude. In addition, the counselor must communicate a sensitive understanding of the fathers' cultural background and be prepared to respond to several potential issues pertaining to African Americans in counseling, which are described in the sections following a discussion of client tests of the Black counselor.

Tests of the Black Counselor. In the preceding discussion of Black identity development, it was suggested that African Americans in the Pre-Encounter Stage may prefer a White counselor over a Black counselor who is strongly affiliated with African American culture. Thus, an African American teenage father who is assigned to an Africentric Black counselor may resent his not receiving services from a "good" professional and express hostility toward the counselor. In addition to being the target of this form of intraracial prejudice, the Black counselor may be perceived as an extension of the Black community that, as L. A. Smith's (1989) research has shown, often views teenage fathers with disdain.

For Black counselors beheld in these ways, the solution is the same as that encountered by the White counselor who is tested by Black youth; that is, it is important not to be discouraged easily, to empathize with the reasons for the client's hostility as well as act in a manner that commands respect, and to deliver an effective intervention as rapidly as possible.

The Physical Environment of the Counseling Office and the Attire of the Counselor

Solomon (1990) suggested that several features to the physical environment of the counseling office improve the attractiveness of the setting for African American clients from the inner city. She recommended placing desks at the periphery of the room, and the central area of the office should be furnished with sofas, chairs, and low tables with magazines. In this way, no interviews are held with the client facing the counselor separated by a desk.

Franklin (1982, 1989) discussed the importance of the physical appearance of the counselor in establishing rapport with African American adolescents. Franklin observed that African American adolescents, especially poor ones, tend to view clothes as materialistic symbols of achievement. Consequently, the youth who encounters a counselor dressed in a casual manner may view the informal clothing style as a contradiction of presumed professional status. That is, the very casually dressed counselor may not measure up to the youth's perception of how a professional should appear and the youth might conclude that the counselor must not be that important. Thus, to enhance rapport with the African American adolescent, Franklin recommended that counselors dress in a formal, professional manner.

The Language of the Counselor

Another issue discussed by Franklin (1982, 1989) is the consideration of language in establishing rapport with urban African American adolescents. Franklin argued that a counselor who can use the slang of African American youth unpretentiously might expedite rapport with this population. However, he warned that counselors who attempt to appear fluent in "street talk" but actually are not will lose credibility with some teenagers. Instead, he suggested that counselors who are unsophisticated in their knowledge of the vernacular of African American adolescents should acknowledge their ignorance of terms and encourage their clients to educate them about their meanings. Counselors also can learn about Black dialects through readings on the subject, such as Mitchell-Kernan's (1982) discussion of Black English.

Another issue pertaining to language in counseling is the resentment by African Americans of service providers who use their clients' first names. Cheatham (1991) noted that status issues, such as the manner in which people are greeted, are extremely important to ethnic-minority clients. Boyd-Franklin (1989) warned against calling African American clients by their first names without their permission to do so. Mitchell-Kernan (1982) and Boyd-Franklin (1989) reported that many African Americans consider this a presumptuous practice and find it offensive. Mitchell-Kernan (1982) explained that this indignation must be understood against the background of conventions that developed in the southern United States. According to these customs, Whites referred to Blacks by first names or kin titles, such as Uncle or Auntie, but were not afforded the respect of the title and last name. Therefore, to play it safe with African American clients, especially the parents of a Black teenage father, it is recommended that counselors use the titles "Mr." and "Mrs." during the early stages of counseling and use first names later in counseling, and only after the counselor has directly asked the clients for permission to do so.

African American Mistrust
of the Mental Health System

Sue, McKinney, Allen, and Hall (1974) and Smith (1981) have documented the discriminatory and culturally insensitive historical treatment of African Americans by the mental health system in the United States, such as providing inferior forms of therapeutic treatment to African American clients. These same authors have argued that African Americans justifiably are mistrustful of the mental health system because of this treatment. In addition to this reason for suspicion, African American teenage fathers fear that they will be judged by helping professionals for their position as unwed adolescent parents (Hendricks, 1988) or that helpers might report them to authority figures, such as child support enforcement officers (Kiselica, 1993). Thus, guarded, elusive, and hostile behavior on the part of the African American teenage father may be an understandable expression of his perception that the helping system is out to "get him."

In response to this behavior, counselors must neither misinterpret its meaning nor reciprocate resentment toward the client. Rather, the counselor should communicate to the client directly that he or she understands why the client might be mistrustful and assure the client of his or her sincerity in wanting to help. Then, the counselor should demonstrate this sincerity by rapidly addressing the client's most pressing concern.

Countertransference Issues

Jones (1985) noted that although any client can evoke countertransference issues in the counselor, it appears that African American clients elicit more complicated and frequent countertransference reactions. For example, as Smith (1981) suggested, the White counselor might avoid racial and cultural issues by referring the client to another counselor whereas the Black counselor might overidentify with the client's racial issues and overlook other concerns of the client. Jones (1985) argued that the counselor must develop a thorough self-understanding and cultural sensitivity prior to counseling with a Black client and maintain an acute self-awareness during the counseling process to prevent personal reactions from intruding in unhelpful ways.

Theoretical Orientation

Cheatham (1990b) has argued that counseling approaches focusing on client responsibility and introspection are ill suited for African American clients whose sociocultural experience is infused with themes of powerlessness. For example, beginning the counseling process with an African American teenage father by abruptly confronting his lack of sexual responsibility or by exploring his hidden motivations in becoming a father is likely to alienate the youth. Instead, Cheatham (1990b) recommended that paradigms emphasizing realistic, objective, and extrapsychic orientations are more appropriate. Similarly, Boyd-Franklin (1989) has argued in support of a multisystemic approach that calls for interventions with the individual, the family, the extended family, church and community networks, and the social services system.

Although addressing extrapsychic issues may be critical in the establishment and maintenance of rapport with the African American teenage father, this does not mean that African Americans are incapable of or disinterested in exploring their intrapsychic issues. On the contrary, clinical experience with numerous African American youth with troubled childhoods has taught me that many of these youngsters hunger to discuss and understand their unfortunate pasts and are able and willing to do so *once their more immediate, concrete, extrapsychic problems have been resolved.* That is, helping with extrapsychic concerns often engenders a client to believe that the counselor will handle intrapsychic issues sensitively. Thus, counselors should be prepared to follow their practical measures to help young African American fathers with insight-oriented counseling when it is appropriate to do so, such as conducting psychotherapy with the youth who aches to understand why he was abandoned by his own father. Similarly, L. A. Smith (1989) documented that African American teenage fathers have both extrapsychic and intrapsychic concerns and recommended that counselors strike a balance between meeting the emotional and socioeconomic needs of these clients.

The Potential Benefits of Group Approaches

Lee (1989) contended that group interaction is an important means of identity for African American youth. This practice is rooted in the African tradition of emphasizing communal relations, cooperation, and group cohesiveness. Therefore, he recommended that counselors can facilitate the counseling process greatly by using group interventions. Franklin (1989) also suggested the use of group activities with African American youth, particularly group psychoeducational approaches to counseling.

Pregnancy Resolution

As is this case with any cultural group of young men and women confronting an unintended pregnancy, African American adolescents and their families experience a broad range of reactions to the pregnancy. These responses contribute to a variety of measures to resolve the pregnancy.

Abortion

The abortion rate among African American adolescents has risen in recent years. Statistics reviewed by Moore et al. (1986) indicate that in 1972, the abortion rate was lower among Black teenagers than White, but by 1978, it was higher among Black teenagers. By 1980, Black women from all age groups accounted for approximately 30% of all abortions performed in the United States, with the rate among Black teenagers aged 15 to 19 being 1.7 times as high as the White rate for the same age group (Henshaw & O'Reilly, 1983). In 1985, the abortion rate among non-Whites aged 15 to 19 was 1.9 times that of White teenagers (Henshaw et al., 1989). Between 1984 and 1988, the abortion rate among non-White women aged 15 to 19 increased 13% (Henshaw, 1992).

According to Henshaw et al. (1989),

> the higher abortion rate of non-Whites is not due to a greater propensity to turn to abortion, however. Rather, their birthrate was 2.1 times greater than that of Whites in the same age-group. In fact, once pregnant, their likelihood of choosing abortion was slightly lower than that of Whites among women 15-17 (41 vs. 45) and slightly higher among those 18-19 (42 vs. 41). (p. 11)

In spite of the increased abortion rate, African American teenagers may have a great unmet desire for abortion due to the restriction on federal funding of abortion. According to Moore et al. (1986), because African Americans are more likely to be eligible for Medicaid, the funding restriction may have disproportionately reduced the incidence of abortion among this population. This consideration has served as the rationale for arguments in favor of restoring federal coverage of abortion under Medicaid, increasing the number of providers, establishing providers in counties without services, and providing abortions without parental consent or notification (see Alan Guttmacher Institute, 1981; Henshaw & O'Reilly, 1983). However, in light of the fact that abortion is already highly relied on by Black teenagers, Moore et al. (1986) suggested that efforts to reduce the incidence of early pregnancy, rather than strategies to increase the availability of abortion, should be a

policy priority of service programs serving the African American community. This recommendation may have particular merit for inner-city African
American communities in which competent education about human sexuality and contraception tend to be lacking (see Moore et al., 1986; Zelnick &
Shah, 1983) and in which adolescent males are unlikely to use effective
contraceptives and more likely to use unreliable forms of contraception, such
as withdrawal (see Scott-Jones et al., 1989).

Factors Associated With the Abortion Decision. Several factors are associated with the selection of the abortion option among expectant African
American teenagers. In a study of the pregnancy-resolution process of
African American, expectant adolescents conducted by Fischman (1977),
71% of those who chose abortion cited their age, the inability to support a
baby, or the interference of a baby with their education as reasons for their
decision and another 25% said that pressure from their family or boyfriend
had influenced them to have an abortion. Among those deciding against
abortion, 45% expressed a desire to have the child, one third cited their
feeling that abortion was taking a life, and 9% reported pressure from their
mother or boyfriend as reasons for giving birth to the child. Rosen (1980)
reported that African American adolescent mothers who terminated their
pregnancies tend to be strongly influenced by their mothers to choose
abortion as an option. In a study involving 94 African American females aged
13 to 17 who were unmarried and living in an urban area, Freeman and
Rickels (1993) also found that the decision to abort is greatly influenced by
the adolescents' mothers.

Less is known about the factors influencing the young African American
fathers' attitudes toward abortion. Johnson (quoted in Children's Defense
Fund, 1988a) observed that most expectant adolescent fathers treated in his
inner-city health clinic were African Americans who tended to fall into two
groups with regard to the abortion issue. One group, who was eager to agree
to an abortion and even to finance it, was more likely to be those planning
on attending college or some other form of higher education. The other
group, who was insistent on the continuation of pregnancy, worked and had
very limited educational aspirations. Whether or not males from either group
tended to have any influence on the pregnancy resolution of their partners
was unclear. However, data from studies of African American, adolescent
males who already are fathers suggest that, in spite of their opposition to
abortion, they are hesitant to influence an expectant mother's decision to
have an abortion, based on the belief that the abortion matter is a personal
decision (Hendricks, 1988; Sullivan, 1985). Consistent with this finding,
Freeman and Rickels (1993) found that the boyfriend's involvement in

deciding the pregnancy outcome was reported by African American teenage mothers to be quite limited.

In summary, the research suggests that most African American unwed adolescent males, whether they are personally for or against abortion, are unlikely to try to influence their partners' decision regarding this option. These youths may need help to anticipate the consequences of not sharing their views with their partners. For example, the young male who favors an abortion but says nothing about this opinion might regret his inaction when his partner opts to deliver and keep the baby. Or, a male who stays silent while his partner aborts a baby against his unstated wishes may later experience grief at having not campaigned for his child's birth.

Adoption

Almost all African American teenage mothers (approximately 98%) who bring their babies to term keep their babies (Burden & Klerman, 1984). Thus, formal adoption rarely is used by African Americans to resolve unplanned pregnancies. Two explanations are offered to account for this trend.

One reason for the low use of formal adoption services is that African Americans question the effectiveness of those services in adequately meeting the needs of African American children. According to Billingsley and Giovannoni (1970) and Hill (1977), historically the child welfare system has tended to place Black children in foster care homes and facilities rather than with blood relatives. These authors have argued that this practice violates the African American cultural pattern of relying on the support of the extended kinship network during times of crisis. Moreover, these authors charged that foster and adoption placements have been harmful to the developmental well-being of African American children. More recently, the National Black Child Development Institute (1989) conducted a 2½ year, five-city study on Black children who came into the foster care system in 1986 and concluded that the foster care system inadequately addresses the needs of Black children in spite of a decade of national efforts to reform the system.

Instead of using formal adoption services, which until recently has meant the complete severing of contact with the child, African Americans have a long tradition of practicing informal adoption, which, according to Boyd-Franklin (1989), is "a process whereby adult relatives or friends of the family 'took in' children and cared for them when their parents were unable to provide for their needs" (p. 52), such as in cases of teenage pregnancy. Sometimes, these forms of adoption are permanent, and in other instances, the child is taken in by immediate or extended family members until the biological parent is able to provide adequate care for the child

(Boyd-Franklin, 1989). Hill (1977) described informal adoption as an important mechanism for family survival that evolved during slavery and continues into present times. As evidence of the current widespread practice of informal adoption, data from the recent National Survey of Black Americans, in which 2,107 households were surveyed, indicated that 19% of the households with children contained minors who had been informally adopted (Hachett, Cochran, & Jackson, 1991).

A second reason for the low use of formal adoption by African Americans pertains to the role that money has played in the provision of adoption services. Reitz and Watson (1992) have pointed out that resources historically and inequitably have been funneled in the United States into private services for the adoption of healthy White children. On the other hand, public services for the adoption of minority children and those with special needs have been undersupported. Greater financial support to develop these services might increase their use by African Americans.

In light of these two issues pertaining to adoption, two interventions are called for. First, on the micro level, it is recommended that counselors encourage expectant African American adolescent teenage couples and their families who feel that they can not adequately care for a child to discuss the potential for informal adoption of the baby by relatives or friends. While exploring this option, counselors are advised to take safeguards to help the family prevent some problems that are associated with informal adoption. For example, according to Boyd-Franklin (1989), the family should carefully define the duration of the informal adoption to avoid confusion regarding the custody of the child later on. Also, the family should be wary of developing family secrets about who the child's biological parents are, for the child eventually may learn the identity of his or her parents and consequently perceive a violation of trust for having not been told the truth in the first place (Boyd-Franklin, 1989). Second, on the macro level, policy change strategies are needed to provide additional funding to improve the availability and quality of formal adoption services for African Americans.

Traditional and Common-Law Marriages

The proportion of births to African American teens that occur outside of traditional and common-law marriage is high. Eighty-four percent of the 351 African American teenage mothers studied by Furstenberg (1976) gave birth to their children out of wedlock, as did 98% of the 57 African American teenage mothers studied by Salguero (1984). In 1982, 87% of the births to African American teenagers were out of wedlock (Moore et al., 1982). Marsiglio's (1987) analysis of a 1984 national survey of youth indicated that African American teenage fathers tended not to marry or live with the mother of their nonmaritally conceived first child; only 15% of African American teenage fathers reported living with their first child. None of the 57 mothers in the Salguero (1984) study and only 3 of the 30 mothers in a study by Williams (1991) lived with their partners at the time of delivery. Only 8% of the 170 African American teenage fathers studied by Hardy and Zabin (1991) were either married to and/or lived with the baby's mother.

Even though African American teenage parents rarely resolve an unplanned pregnancy through marriage, data from several studies examining attitudes toward marriage and the family suggest that marriage is still a strong value among Black Americans regardless of the current rates in which this union is entered and dissolved (see Hatchett, 1991; Moore et al., 1986; Williams, 1990). Other findings suggest that the majority of African American teenage fathers report feeling genuine love for their partners, both during and after the pregnancy (Hendricks, 1981, 1988; Hendricks & Montgomery, 1983; Hendricks & Solomon, 1987). If it is true that African Americans value marriage and African American teenage fathers love their partners, why do so few African American teenage fathers marry the mother of their child? The proposed answers to this question are complex and varied.

One of the most frequently cited explanations for the low marriage rate is the economic marginality of African American teenage fathers. Their efforts to find work are likely to be frustrated, for the unemployment rate among African American males between the ages of 16 and 19 is 39% (see Malveaux, 1989). Thus, African American teenage fathers are likely to be either unemployed or earn insufficient income to support a family (Furstenberg, 1976; Hardy & Zabin, 1991; Salguero, 1984; Sullivan, 1985; Williams, 1991). Consequently, even though the young couple might prefer to marry, the teenage mother tends to live with her family, rely on their economic and emotional support, and delay marriage until the child's father or another male can prove his worth as an adequate provider (Furstenberg, 1976; Hardy & Zabin, 1991; Sullivan, 1985). Young mothers who delay marriage tend to be more successful at completing school and obtaining jobs than those who marry during the pregnancy or shortly after the birth of the child (Furstenberg & Crawford, 1989; Salguero, 1984). The economic hardships of African Americans may explain why the data from two national surveys, reviewed by Moore et al. (1986), suggest that the majority of African American adolescents between the ages of 11 and 16 express acceptance of early premarital childbearing even though these same youth express a desire to eventually marry.

Although joblessness and the lack of economic opportunities are important factors in the decisions of poor African American adolescent parents to
delay marriage, Williams's (1991) research suggests that other factors also
appear to play a role in these decisions. The majority of the 30 teenage
mothers in her study came from families in which their own mothers had
been teenage mothers, who, in most cases, never married. These girls were
raised in the absence of a father and were imbued with the belief that they
did not need a man to help them to bring up children. Some of the respondents' sisters and cousins were also teenage mothers. In light of these
powerful family influences, Williams concluded that many poor African
American adolescent girls are socialized to have out-of-wedlock children.
Williams also hypothesized that having children during the teenage years
and without marriage may be a variant lifestyle that is now institutionalized
among low-income African American single-parent households.

Related to this latter hypothesis are two historical analyses of the decline
of traditional marriages in African American families (see Ingrassia, 1993;
Williams, 1990). In brief, these authors have argued that the two-parent
stable household was the norm for African American families in the United
States until World War II. After the war, however, particularly since the
1970s, a series of economic dislocations have contributed toward the breakdown of the African American family. Unemployment and government
welfare policies have had an adverse effect on African American mating
patterns, particularly among the poor. The number of single-mother households has risen each subsequent decade. Many children, who were raised in
father-absent homes during the 70s and 80s, may have perceived this to be
an unpreferred but acceptable norm of behavior and repeated these patterns
once they reached the child-rearing years. Thus, although the single-parent
phenomenon in the African American community may have been caused, in
part, by economic forces a generation ago, it appears to be maintained by
both economic and socialization factors today.

Counselors who value marriage must keep these complex issues in mind
when working with African American teenage fathers, especially those who
are poor and from the inner city. Expectant African American adolescent
parents who decline to marry may be demonstrating an adaptive decision to
bleak economic circumstances and/or expressing a cultural norm of family
functioning, rather than displaying a lack of virtue.

Noncustodial Fatherhood

The statistics cited earlier on marriage among African American teenage
fathers indicate that most are in a noncustodial position as parents. As is the

case with any teenage father in this position in the United States, the African American teenage father must address issues of paternity, child support, and visitation.

One of the most striking features of noncustodial fatherhood in the African American community is that these issues tend to be negotiated in large part by folk rather than legal norms, although legal sanctions are often brought into play when folk negotiations break down. Sullivan (1985) observed that folk traditions dictate that the father experience genuine concern for his partner and her child and that he express this concern in the form of some type of concrete assistance to his partner and her family. If these steps are taken, then the paternity of the father will likely be recognized, even if he does not fulfill the legally defined responsibilities of a father, such as completing court-determined levels of child support (Sullivan, 1985). In addition, many teenage mothers will hide the identity of the father from child support authorities when the father abides by folk customs associated with paternity (Sullivan, 1985; Williams, 1991).

Data from several studies suggest that most African American teenage fathers meet these folk criteria, at least during the early stages of their children's lives. The vast majority of African American unwed adolescent fathers who have been studied have reported feeling love for their partners during and after the pregnancy and concern for their children's future (Hendricks, 1981, 1988; Hendricks & Solomon, 1987). Data from other studies suggest that most maintain an ongoing relationship with the mother and contribute their financial and emotional support to the mother and the baby (Sullivan, 1985; Vaz et al., 1983; Williams, 1991). Sullivan (1985) and Rivara et al. (1986) reported that the African American teenage fathers from their studies tended to support their partners and children in ways that might not be accounted for by official records of child support. Although most of the fathers from both studies had minimal economic resources to contribute to the support of their children, the majority of the fathers tended to compensate in a number of ways for what they could not contribute monetarily. For example, most fathers described playing with their children and assisting with such tasks as providing part-time child care, feeding their children, changing diapers, providing diapers and clothes, and taking their children on recreational outings. However, other data suggest that the frequency of contact between the couple and between the father and his child gradually declines over time (Hardy & Zabin, 1991; Rivara et al., 1986; Salguero, 1984). In these latter situations, if the father and his family also reduce concrete forms of support for the child, the recognition of his paternity and his right to visit may be jeopardized (Sullivan, 1985).

The consideration of these folk traditions raises two implications for counseling. First, counselors can help young fathers to maintain an ongoing relationship with their child by encouraging them to clarify with the mother and her family their expectations regarding child support. Second, at the macro level of intervention, counselors are urged to educate policymakers about the meaningful quality of nonfinancial support provided by African American teenage fathers and encourage these authorities to propose and implement policies that recognize these forms of support as substitutes for strictly financial criteria of child support.

Unmarried Custodial Fatherhood

During the negotiations between families about how to resolve the pregnancy, the mother and her family, due to their personal constraints for rearing the baby, may decide to "give" the child to the father and his family, provided they are willing to take on this responsibility. As is the case with other negotiations regarding pregnancy resolution in the African American community, especially in low-income urban neighborhoods, such arrangements typically are handled on an informal basis (Stack, 1974; Sullivan, 1985). A key issue for the counselor working in this situation is to help both families clearly define the terms of this arrangement so as to avoid custody disputes later on. Also, it is recommended that the counselor sensitively inquire about the motivations of the families in striking this settlement on an informal rather than a formal basis. If the families express a general mistrust of the system for addressing these matters, then the counselor should express his willingness to help the family navigate the legal system while tentatively suggesting to the family that future problems might be avoided if both families approach the court to formally award custody to the father and his family. With the support of a trusted counselor, some African American families are able to overcome their wariness of the legal system to resolve such matters. Other families, however, who continue to state their opposition to seeking a court settlement, may be expressing the need to hide a family secret from the court. For example, the mother may be addicted to drugs and her family may fear that any involvement with the courts may lead to the daughter's arrest. Counselors need to be attuned for these possibilities, respect a family's wishes, offer them help in resolving the "hidden" problem as well as the presenting problem, and try to get both families to clearly understand the agreement between them so as to prevent disputes later on in the child's life.

Addressing Issues With
the Extended Family and Peers

One of the greatest strengths of the African American family has been its ability to adapt, survive, and flourish in spite of centuries of institutionalized oppression and grave socioeconomic hardships. The accommodation of African American families to adolescent parents is an example of this adaptiveness. The variety of ways that African American families have positively responded to their children who have become teenage parents is chronicled in this section, as are the hardships associated with these adjustments. The difficulty that some African American parents have in supervising their children, the influence of socialization patterns, macrolevel interventions designed to strengthen African American families, strategies for engaging African American families in counseling, and the peer issues of African American teenage fathers are also discussed.

Patterns of Family Support

Traditionally, African American teenage parents have relied on the extended family to assist in the rearing of children born to teenage parents. Statistics on the living arrangements of African American teenage mothers indicate that 3% live only with their child. In the vast majority of cases, the mother lives within household units that include one or more other adults—typically the teenager's own mother, her siblings, or other family members (Abrahamse et al., 1988). Thus, although African American parents do not condone out-of-wedlock parenthood, most children born to teenage parents have been absorbed by African American families (Ladner & Gourdine, 1984).

Burton (1990), Stack (1974), and Sullivan (1985) documented that the raising of children born to African American teenage parents was usually accomplished within kin-based networks extending over frequently shifting household arrangements. Often, the arrangements included collaborative ventures by members of both the maternal and paternal families. The following example, reported by Sullivan (1985), illustrates the cooperative efforts of the families of a teenage father named Mike and his girlfriend:

> The complex child care arrangements were split almost equally between the two young parents' households. Her mother was home with her own 2-year-old and cared for her older daughter's baby during the morning. Then Mike came over between his morning and afternoon classes and took the baby back over to his house for the afternoon. His mother was at home all day and also his

older sister who was 19 and pregnant herself. When the mother of Mike's child got off work, she came over to his house, stayed there for dinner and part of the evening, then returned with the baby to her parents' home for the night. (p. 55)

Support of this kind can have tremendous benefits to the young parents and the child. The commitment of the family to the well-being of the adolescent parent enhances the probability that the youth will complete his or her education and become an independent adult (Salguero, 1984). In addition, the parenting skills of African American teenage parents can be positively influenced by knowledge of child rearing passed on by the teenagers' parents and grandparents (Stevens, 1984).

Some African American grandparents who assist teenage parents with the rearing of their children report that they profit in many ways from the experience. Through their interviews with elderly African American men and women, Burton and DeVries (1992) discovered that several of the grandparents, who had served a surrogate parenting role for the children of kin who were adolescent parents, experienced a sense of fulfillment in nurturing a legacy and having the opportunity to parent again. The grandparents also reported that caring for their grandchildren provided them with companionship, love, and a reason to live.

In light of the impressive support offered by African American families to their young parents, it is recommended that counselors tap the potential resources of the extended families in helping teenage fathers adjust to parenthood. However, it should be recognized that these requests for help may represent yet one more source of strain for some families who are already stressed by a host of problems.

Patterns of Strain

Even though African American families assist their adolescents in raising children, and even though this assistance can have many benefits for a variety of family members, the added responsibility of raising the child is a considerable burden for many families. The news of the pregnancy typically sends shock waves throughout the family (Sullivan, 1985; Williams, 1991). In low-income African American families, traditionally the maternal grandmother has been the family member most likely to assume the responsibility of caring for the child, at least until the mother has completed school and/or established an independent household (Furstenberg, 1976; Ladner & Gourdine, 1984; Williams, 1991). Recent data on the reactions of the current generation of African American grandmothers to their children's pregnancies suggest that many feel overwhelmed by the challenges of raising another generation of children, resent the role they are expected to play, and may be unwilling to provide the help needed by the adolescent parents (Burton & Bengston, 1985; Burton & DeVries, 1992; Ladner & Gourdine, 1984; Williams, 1991). Ladner and Gourdine (1984) suggested that this resentment is often found in women whose life situations are filled with difficult circumstances (e.g., poverty, poor housing, etc.) and that their child's premature parenthood represents "but another 'cross to bear' " (p. 23).

These troublesome circumstances require the many family counseling interventions described in Chapter 5. In addition, social policy measures designed to promote equal access to jobs and provide for adequate and affordable housing and improved health care for African American families are recommended.

Difficulties in Supervising Adolescents
for Low-Income, Inner-City African American Parents

One of the unfortunate experiences of life in the inner city for low-income African American parents is that they typically lack the resources to supervise their children when they are not in school. In his study of 11 teenage fathers from one urban community of African Americans, Sullivan (1985) reported that more than half of the households in the community were headed by only one parent. Many of these households included younger children who occupied most of the mother's time. When no young children were present, the mother usually worked. If both parents were present, both often worked low-wage jobs in an effort to survive. Most of these jobs required substantial commutes outside the neighborhood. As a result, teenagers were expected to care for themselves as much as possible. Williams (1991) reported similar problems regarding adult supervision among 30 African American families she studied from a different inner-city neighborhood, and Hare (1990) concluded that these problems are common among African American communities.

Abrahamse et al. (1988) examined the role of parental supervision as a factor in the social control of teenagers. Their analysis of this and other factors related to teenage pregnancy in African American communities yielded findings that suggested that the lack of parental supervision was a key factor in significantly increasing the probability that a African American adolescent girl would become pregnant.

These findings lend further support to the recommendations provided earlier that macrointervention strategies are necessary to strengthen African American families. In addition to those earlier recommendations, it seems apparent that African American families in the inner city need the assistance of highly structured programs that can provide quality supervision for adolescents while they are out of school. These include educational and job-training programs, recreational activities, and community service programs that help youth to invest their time and energies in activities that might prevent early sexual exploration and behavior.

The Influence of Socialization Forces

Besides the inability of families to adequately supervise inner-city youth, Hare (1990) and Williams (1991) argued that another factor that must be addressed is the role of some African American families in socializing their children to view single parenthood as an acceptable lifestyle. Bumpass (cited in Ingrassia, 1993) estimates that a African American child born today has only a one-in-five chance of growing up with two parents until the age of 16. The majority of these will live in single-mother households. In her ethnographic study of 30 African American teenage mothers and their families, Williams's (1991) reported that all of the girls' mothers overtly discouraged their daughters from becoming teenage parents. However, most of the mothers also had given their daughters implicit messages that early out-of-wedlock childbearing is an acceptable career by having been teenage mothers themselves and by having children by different fathers but never marrying. This lifestyle was reinforced by sisters, cousins, aunts, and peers who also served as role models of early childbearing. Research by Hendricks (1981, 1988) and Sullivan (1985) documented similar patterns of socialization among African American unwed adolescent fathers.

To offset transgenerational patterns of teenage parenthood in the African American community, several recommendations have been made by African American writers. Madhubuti (1990) has challenged African American men and women to recommit themselves to the institution of marriage with the goal of modeling two-parent living for their children. Williams (1990) has argued that achieving this goal will be difficult because of the low male-to-female ratio in the African American community. Consequently, he suggested that African American women consider marrying men from Africa or relocating to parts of the United States where the shortage of Black men is not as great. Williams (1990) also encouraged upwardly mobile African American women to consider establishing bonds with responsible and caring African American men whose socioeconomic status is lower than their own. Kunjufu (1986) has enjoined African American parents to systematically teach their children, especially their sons, from an early age about sexual responsibility. Finally, Parham and McDavis (1987) have urged African

American parents to provide more discipline and more nurturing activities for their sons.

Addressing Issues Related to Father Absence

Findings from several studies suggest that a large percentage of African American teenage fathers have been raised in father-absent homes. Thirty-five percent of the 20 adolescent fathers studied by Hendricks (1981) were from father-absent homes, as were 40% of the 40 teenage fathers interviewed by Hendricks (1988) in a later study. The majority of the 72 teenage fathers studied by Hardy and Zabin (1991) and 9 of the 11 young fathers described by Sullivan (1985) also were raised in father-absent homes.

In using the strategies discussed in Chapter 5 for addressing father-son wounds, counselors are reminded that the absence of the biological father in African American families is a complex phenomenon. Although it is likely that many boys hailing from such families may have long-standing feelings of abandonment, rejection, sadness, and anger toward their fathers, some others might not for a variety of reasons. As Madhubuti (1990) has observed, some single African American mothers are successful at raising sons who are not bitter and have positive self-esteem in spite of father absence. Boyd-Franklin (1989) suggested that many African American single-mother families are benefited by the presence and influence of male-extended family members, such as grandfathers and uncles, who serve as positive role models for young boys, thereby attenuating some of the effects of father absence. Finally, Sullivan (1985) documented that several of the adolescent males in his study had ongoing contact with their fathers who provided emotional and financial support to their sons, even though they did not live with the boys' mothers. These boys viewed their father-son relationship in a positive light.

Father Absence in the Mother's Home. Williams's (1991) research suggests that African American teenage mothers have significant issues with their fathers as well and that these issues may affect the manner in which they respond to the teenage father. For example, most of the 30 girls interviewed by Williams reported that their fathers did not play a central role in their lives. Williams suspected that the relationships that these girls had with their fathers set the stage for their attitudes toward the fathers of their own children and toward marriage, which was to assume that they could not count on a male and therefore did not need one. Thus, counselors who work with African American teenage mothers raised in father-absent homes are encouraged to help these girls examine the effects of their relationships with their own fathers on their judgments regarding the fathers of their children. Some girls, who presume that their partner will behave just as their absent father had, may need to be challenged to give the young father a chance to prove his commitment to parenthood.

Engaging African American Families in Counseling

Many of the outreach and rapport-building strategies pertaining to African American teenage fathers also apply to counseling that includes their families. In addition, Boyd-Franklin (1989) has proposed two other considerations in joining African American families in counseling. First, when African American family members arrive at counseling settings for a session, they often are accompanied by other individuals who are not members of the immediate family. Boyd-Franklin warned that it could be a mistake and an insult to the family to ignore these other individuals, for the family may view them as kin who should be involved in the counseling process, even if they are not blood relatives. Therefore, she recommended finding out who these people are and whether or not the family intends for them to participate in the counseling process. Second, Boyd-Franklin (1989) urged counselors to use the extended family throughout the counseling process because a traditional coping mechanism for African American families has been to rely on the kinship network during times of crisis. Thus, to strengthen one's allegiance with the family, it is important to assess which key members of the extended family have a special relationship with the teenage father and direct outreach efforts toward those loved ones as well.

Peer Relationship Issues

Among African American youth who become parents as teenagers there appears to be normative acceptance of beginning sexual relations and parenthood at an early age. On average, Black adolescents initiate intercourse at an earlier age than do Whites, and Blacks report having many more sexually experienced friends than do Whites (for a review, see Scott-Jones et al., 1989). More Blacks than Whites anticipate a positive response to pregnancy from peers (Moore et al., 1986). Black adolescents who attend schools in which there is a more tolerant view of unwed childbearing are more likely to become adolescent parents than youth who attend schools in which there is a less accepting attitude toward unwed childbearing (Abrahamse et al., 1988). Although data do not exist indicating that such tolerance causes teenage pregnancy, it can be assumed that tolerant attitudes do not discourage early childbearing (Moore et al., 1986).

Moore et al. (1986) concluded that such findings suggest that sex education that covers more than just reproductive physiology may be necessary to reduce the incidence of early pregnancy among African American teenagers who are poor and living in the inner city. Sex education and family life education programs with these African American youth may need to counter directly their perception that early and out-of-wedlock motherhood are relatively acceptable (Moore et al., 1986).

Approaching this subject with these youth is a delicate matter. Williams (1991) cautioned that the idea that marriage precedes childbearing is a norm that has lost most of its saliency for some African Americans from lower socioeconomic levels. Thus, attempts to teach this population to delay childbearing might be construed as the imposition of values on them. This represents an ethical dilemma for the conscientious counselor. On the one hand, because the counselor knows that early parenthood is likely to place African American youth at risk for a host of problems, it would seem appropriate to try to discourage early parenthood. On the other hand, some subcultural groups see single parenthood as an acceptable variant of family form. Is it right for the counselor to challenge this view?

The literature has not adequately dealt with this issue. However, the decision-making paradigm to counseling, described in Chapter 4, provides an answer to this ethical dilemma. Rather than imposing one's cultural value system on the client, it is imperative that the counselor present information regarding the likely outcomes associated with delayed versus early parenthood. If this information is shared within the context of sex and family-life education, then the client also will learn the necessary coping skills to prevent early parenthood. By proceeding in this manner, the counselor will avoid proselytizing for delayed parenthood while providing youth with accurate information and skills that might obviate their need to rely on their own limited experiences.

Preparation for Fatherhood

Systematic empirical research conducted by African American scholars (e.g., Connor, 1986; McAdoo, 1986, 1988) suggests that married African American fathers tend to have egalitarian relationships with their wives, firm expectations regarding their children's behavior, and a nurturant, warm, and loving relationship with their children. Thus, many potential role models in the African American community could teach young African American fathers about the important contributions of fathers to the emotional stability of the family. Several scholars (e.g., Battle, 1988/1989; Lee, 1989; Parham & McDavis, 1987) have suggested that counselors should organize psychoeducational groups that use African American role models to teach Black boys Africentric values regarding masculinity and fatherhood. Asante (1981), Parham and McDavis (1987), and Madhubuti (1990) argued that Africentric education would help Black males develop positive self-concepts and avoid destructive forms of behavior. In this section, the characteristics of a positive self-concept among African American males and some educational programs designed to foster them are reviewed. These ideas can be incorporated into the fatherhood training ideas discussed in Chapter 6.

Characteristics of
African American Male Role Models

Parker and Lord (1993) conducted a survey of male leaders in the African American community to identify the characteristics of healthy role models for young African American men. Their findings suggested that success models are (a) educated, (b) socially visible, (c) willing to volunteer their time to others, and (d) caring and committed to serving young African American men. Thus, African American males who have these qualities might be suitable role models for service programs geared toward African American teenage fathers.

What characteristics should role models attempt to imbue in African American boys? The answer may reside in research pertaining to the characteristics of psychologically healthy African Americans. Anderson et al. (1990) reviewed research examining factors that contribute to positive mental health among African Americans and concluded that mentally healthy Black people (a) are perceptive and adaptive to the environment; (b) are effective at problem solving and communication skills; (c) are nondefensive and open-minded, even though they may be vigilant toward a racist environment; (d) develop self-esteem based on comparisons to other Blacks rather than to Whites; (e) use family and the church as means of support for interpersonal and financial difficulties and formal resources (e.g., medical professionals) for health-related concerns; and (f) have a positive group identification. Based on these findings, it is recommended that program developers encourage role models to share illustrations of these positive coping strategies in their own lives. In addition, role models can teach young fathers Africentric values regarding masculinity and fatherhood.

Africentric Education

Vann and Kunjufu (1993) have criticized the educational system in the United States for teaching a deficit view of Black culture while ignoring the rich and vast legacy of the African peoples. They added that this focus has a negative impact on the psychological development of African American youth. The authors challenged educators to teach an Africentric, multicultural curriculum. Vann and Kunjufu (1993) emphasized these points by stating,

> If you have been taught your ancestors were illiterate, impoverished share-croppers, how would you feel about yourself? Because students internalize what they are taught, schools have a profound effect on the confidence and self-esteem of children. An Africentric, multicultural curriculum is a major step toward addressing these vital issues. (p. 491)

Consistent with these ideas, Asante (1981) asserted that an Africentric education can help Black males to improve their relationships with Black women, and Madhubuti (1990) proposed that Africentric education can promote responsible behavior among teenage fathers.

Nsamenang (1987) described masculinity and fatherhood from a West African perspective. According to this tradition, men have a deep-rooted sense of community that is built on the strong and extended kinship system. Children and family members are deeply valued. Pregnancy is such a source of joy and parents are the objects of such high regard that childlessness is considered the greatest of all personal tragedies. According to Nsamenang, this feeling is so strong that a West African couple would prefer to die in poverty and leave children than to die childless and rich.

In further describing the role of the father, Nsamenang (1987) stated that the father is the most esteemed member of the West African family and he is responsible to serve as the governing authority for his wife and children. Once a man becomes a father, he is expected to play a major role in decision making regarding his children. Though he may rarely show tenderness and nurturance to infants, which in the West African tradition is the mother's role, he does take a more guiding role with his children from the time they are toddlers through the remainder of the life span. In particular, he will raise his children to be respectful and obedient and his sons to emulate his role as father.

This portrait of the West African father suggests that one's child is to be cherished and that the father plays an ongoing, active role in his child's life. These and other Africentric values can be taught to African American teenage fathers through several curricula on the subject. For example, Wynn's (1992) *Empowering African American Males to Succeed* is a 10-step approach to teaching an understanding of the African culture to Black males. *Black Teenage Parenting and Early Childhood Education* (Nobles et al., 1985) is a six-module curriculum that prepares adolescents for parenthood from an African American cultural perspective. Lee's (1989) *Blackness: A State of Mind, A State of Being* is a six-session model that incorporates Africentric education into a self-enhancement program for Black adolescents. Counselors can consult Madhubuti's (1990) essay, "Never Without a Book: 200 Books All Black People Should Study" to locate supplements to these resources.

Educational and Career Counseling

Analyzing data acquired through the National Longitudinal Survey of Work Experience of Youth, a nationally representative study of youth between ages 14 and 22 who were interviewed in 1979 and again in 1983, Marsiglio (1986) found that African American teenage fathers had a higher probability of graduating from high school than did Anglo American and Hispanic American teenage fathers. Fifty-three percent of Anglo teenage fathers graduated in contrast to the 91% graduation rate of Anglo males who did not father a child as a teenager. The figures were 49% versus 75% for economically disadvantaged Anglos and 39% versus 72% for Hispanic males. However, 68% of Black teenage fathers graduated in comparison to 76% of nonfathers, indicating that the drop-out rate for Black teenage fathers was lower than that for the two other ethnic groups. Marsiglio (1986) suggested that the modest difference in graduation rates between Black teenage fathers and the other two groups might be related to the higher degree of social acceptability of early childbearing within the Black subculture.

Although the drop-out rate for African American teenage fathers is less than that of Anglo American and Hispanic American teenage fathers, African American teenage fathers are nevertheless more likely to drop out than are African American males who delay fatherhood until their 20s. Furthermore, when adolescent nonfather and father groups are lumped together, African American males are more likely to drop out than are Anglo American males (Marsiglio, 1986).

Why are so many African American youth uninspired to complete their high school educations? Several explanations have been offered. First, Franklin (1981, 1989) has argued that urban African American adolescents are likely to attend poor educational systems in which classroom time is often more consumed with maintaining order than with providing quality instruction. Under these conditions, the school environment provides few effective educational demands for students to take school seriously. Second, as was noted earlier, the Eurocentric orientation reflected in many school curriculums may be irrelevant to many African Americans and, consequently, might discourage their interest in education (Vann & Kunjufu, 1993). Third, the anticipated effects of racism might deter the educational aspirations of young African American males (Furstenburg et al., 1987; L. A. Smith, 1988). Fourth, poverty and the restricted work opportunities of African Americans might cause many to lower their occupational expectations and question the value of completing school (Baly, 1989). These reactions are understandable considering that Black children are three times more likely than White children to live in poverty (Children's Defense Fund, 1985) and the unemployment rate among Black adolescents has been twice the level of that for White youths for two decades (see Malveaux, 1989). Fifth, Dunn and Veltman (1989) hypothesized that a lack of academic preparation, underdeveloped interests, inadequate knowledge of career planning, and/or perceptions of opportunity might constrict the educational and career strivings of African American students.

Based on these considerations, several recommendations are offered. First, career counseling must be tailored to the particular needs of African Americans. Second, institutional interventions designed to make educational systems more meaningful for African American youth are needed. Third, public policy measures to combat discrimination and increase employment opportunities for African American males are necessary.

Africentric Career Counseling

Super's (1957, 1983) approach to developmental career counseling (see Chapter 7) can be modified to incorporate an Africentric orientation that is responsive to the culturally salient issues of African American teenage fathers. Factors that might influence the career development of African Americans need to be assessed. These include the following: the individual's perception of certain factors in the environment (e.g., one's view of the opportunity structure) and locus of control; the influence of significant others (Baly, 1989); the effects of racial identity attitudes on values, perceptions of opportunities, occupational stereotyping, career decision making, and workforce diversity (Parham & Austin, 1994); experiences of racism, disenfranchisement, economic hardship, and structural discrimination and their effects on the self-concept; and the preferred social order of the client and whether or not this factor is an enabling or disabling experience for the career development process. For example, a client with a strong Africentric social order will value affiliative experiences and cooperative relationships with others. This social order may cause the client to feel comfortable with careers that emphasize these values (an enabling experience), such as a career in the helping and teaching professions, but feel self-alienation (a disabling experience) in the competitive careers in the world of business (Cheatham, 1990a).

A career development program developed by D'Andrea and Daniels (1992) is a good example of an Africentric approach to helping African American youth. Implemented by a collaborative team of community residents, church leaders, public housing personnel, elected officials, human service professionals, and representatives from private industry, the program combined traditional counseling strategies with an Africentric cooperative group approach. Career development activities focused on addressing racial identity issues as they related to career concerns and on facilitating racial identity development. The participants, consisting of 40 inner-city African American 14 to 17 year olds, reported successful changes in their perceptions of work and of their place as African Americans in the work market.

Institutional Strategies for Improving
Educational Systems of African American Youth

Improving the educational systems of African American youth may prevent some boys who already are fathers from dropping out of school. In addition, data reported by Taylor, Kagay, and Leichenko (1986) indicate that schools that offer their students constructive learning opportunities and fulfilling extracurricular activities may help other African American youth to delay sexual activity, use contraceptives, and, consequently, prevent adolescent parenthood.

Several recommendations for making educational systems more meaningful for African American youth have been offered. Parham and McDavis (1987) and Lee (1989) urged schools to provide culturally relevant approaches to education for African American children. These authors argued that the infusion of Africentric educational programs (such as those described earlier in this chapter) into the overall curriculum is likely to reengage disenchanted African American teenagers in the learning process. These authors also contended that schools need to make the educational system more relevant to the parents of African American children. This task can be accomplished by having school counselors and administrative personnel establish liaisons between the African American community and the schools and develop formal programs designed to assist parents in communicating their academic expectations for their children (Lee, 1989; Parham & McDavis, 1987). Lee (1989) also urged counselors to teach parents about aspects of contemporary education, such as standardized testing and grading procedures so that parents can maximize their influence on adolescent academic development.

Creating educational programs that blend the goals of formal education and personal development represents another proposal for improving the educational experience of African Americans, particularly for youth who require both remedial education and assistance with interpersonal issues, which is often the case with teenage fathers. Franklin (1989) described the Street Academy of the Urban League as an exemplary institutional strategy for helping African American youth who have been alienated from formal education. The Street Academy strives to make the educational experience more personalized for African American teenagers by infusing personal and psychoeducational counseling into remedial education. For example, individualized educational programs are designed to address both deficits in academic skills, such as reading comprehension and mathematics, and psychosocial competencies, such as assertiveness, self-management, and problem solving.

In addition to these suggestions, L. A. Smith (1988), Lee (1989), and Hendricks (1992) challenged service providers to form cooperative educational programs between schools and the business sector to expand the experiences and opportunities available to African American adolescent males. Carrera (1992) proposed a similar idea by suggesting that institutions of higher education work with high schools to enhance the life chances of poor and alienated youth. As a model for such collaboration, Carrera (1992) developed a cooperative program between Hunter College of the City University of New York and the Children's Aid Society's Adolescent Sexuality and Pregnancy Prevention Program of the Harlem community of New York City. Designed to help adolescent girls and boys develop superordinate goals and delay childbearing, youth who complete the program with a positive recommendation from the program director are guaranteed admission as fully matriculated freshmen at Hunter College. This commitment serves as a concrete incentive to young people interested in furthering their education and affirms the fact that college is part of their future.

Public Policy Measures

To expand career opportunities for African American youth, numerous policy changes have been called for. Bowman (1991) called for the creation of new and progressive affirmative action programs to mitigate the widespread perceptions of work role marginality for African Americans and the unique life difficulties of African Americans entrapped in the underclass.

Bowman (1991) also favors a long-term industrial policy to address the differential impact that postindustrial displacement of unskilled jobs has on underprepared African American workers who increasingly drop out of the labor force because of job search discouragement. Malveaux (1989) supports increased federal provisions of financial aid for African American students, many of whom come from poor families, to increase their use of the higher educational system in the United States. This latter form of assistance may help to prevent unplanned pregnancies because the possibility of attaining a higher education is believed to inhibit early childbearing among African American adolescents (see Abrahamse et al., 1988).

10

Hispanic American Teenage Fathers

Less has been written about Hispanic American than African American and Anglo American teenage fathers in the social sciences literature. Nevertheless, the few scholars who have studied teenage pregnancy and parenthood in the Hispanic American community have provided some very clear recommendations for working with Latino teenage fathers. The most consistent urging from these scholars is that counselors working with the Hispanic American adolescent male must consider his degree of acculturation to the mainstream values and customs of U.S. society. Although other important characteristics of Hispanic American teenage fathers, such as the role of poverty in the lives of these youth, will be discussed, this chapter focuses heavily on acculturation level and the ways acculturation can influence nearly every facet of the teenage parent's experience. Specifically, the issues of how acculturation is likely to affect the young father's use of services, his response to the pregnancy, his perception of family and gender roles, and his and his parents' view of the educational system are discussed in this chapter.

A Profile of Hispanic Americans

The terms *Hispanic, Hispanic American,* and *Latino* are used interchangeably to describe a heterogeneous group of peoples who share a common

238

language, Spanish, and an origin in Spanish colonization (Nicholau & Ramos, 1990). The majority of Hispanics self-identify as Mexican Americans (62.6%), whereas approximately 11% are Puerto Rican, 5% Cuban, 14% Central and South American, and 8% other Hispanics (Perez & Duany, 1992).

The diversity of backgrounds and nationalities represented by the label *Hispanic* poses two problems for researchers trying to interpret data regarding the Hispanic population. First, the term *Hispanic* obscures differences among the cultural backgrounds of these assorted groups. Though sharing a common language, Hispanics show great variation in beliefs, values, and behavior (Brindis, 1992). Much of the literature regarding teenage pregnancy and parenthood among Hispanics, which is reviewed in this chapter, has failed to identify the specific cultural backgrounds of the subjects. Therefore, counselors are advised to modify the recommendations made here with their knowledge of the particular cultural backgrounds of the Hispanics they serve. Second, the cultural variables of race and ethnicity are often confused in data regarding the sexual activity, pregnancy, and childbearing of Hispanic adolescents. Hispanics are an ethnic group but are not a race of peoples. As Brindis (1991) noted, although there are differences in the preferred racial identification among the various subpopulations of Hispanics, in general about 95% of Hispanics who identify with a racial group identify themselves as White. In effect, this means that in any table giving racial and ethnic data, the numbers of White, Black, and Hispanic teens will add up to more than the total because some Hispanics are counted in both the Hispanic and White or Black columns. There is no simple way to correct for this double counting (Brindis, 1991). Thus, the reader is forewarned that some of the data cited in this chapter may not represent precise estimates of phenomena among Hispanic American adolescents.

Hispanics constitute the second-largest and fastest-growing minority group in the United States (Perez & Duany, 1992). With a mainland population of more than 22 million as of 1990 (Perez & Duany, 1992), Hispanics are expected to be the largest ethnic-minority group in the United States around the year 2020 (Nicholau & Ramos, 1990). Although Hispanics live in every part of the United States, more than half of all Hispanics live in California (34%) and Texas (19%), and about 85% live in these two states plus New York (10%), Florida (7%), Illinois (4%), New Jersey (3%), Arizona (3%), New Mexico (3%), and Colorado (2%) (Perez & Duany, 1992).

Hardships of Hispanic Americans

Perez and Duany (1992) reviewed a number of statistics and concluded that it is common for Hispanic Americans to struggle with a number of hardships. The majority of Hispanics (approximately 92%) live in urban areas and are disproportionally affected by the social and economic problems found in many cities. The unemployment rate among Hispanics is higher than that for the population in general. Hispanics who are active in the workforce are concentrated in low-wage jobs. One in four Hispanic families and one in three Hispanic children live below the poverty line. Puerto Rican children are the poorest of all poor children in the United States; more than half were poor in 1990. Hispanics enter school later, leave school earlier, and receive proportionately fewer high school diplomas and college degrees than other Americans. Mexican Americans have the lowest educational attainment of any of the five Hispanic subgroups. Thirty-two percent of Hispanic Americans, compared to 13% of Anglo Americans and 20% of African Americans, are uninsured. Compared to other Americans, Hispanics are more likely to contract certain diseases, receive less preventive care, and have less access to health education or health care. Finally, Hispanic Americans are more likely than Anglo Americans but less likely than African Americans to live in female-headed households. In 1990, 23% of Hispanic American families were maintained by a female with no husband present, compared to about 13% of Anglo American and approximately 44% of African American families (Perez & Duany, 1992).

In summary, the data regarding the status of Hispanic American adolescents suggest that, compared to Anglo American teenagers, Hispanic youth are more likely to be poor, less likely to complete school, more likely to be unemployed, and more likely to have low expectations for their future. In this context of limited opportunity, "Hispanic youth are vulnerable to engaging in risky behaviors like unprotected sex" (Perez & Duany, 1992, p. 7).

Adolescent Sexuality, Pregnancy, and Parenting in the Hispanic Community

The following statistics provide a picture of the sexual behavior of Hispanic teenagers. At every age, Hispanic American adolescent females are less likely than Anglo American and African American teenage girls to have had sexual intercourse. For example, compared to 74% of Anglo Americans and 78% of African Americans, 70% of Hispanic females ages 18 to 19 had sexual intercourse in 1988. Hispanic American males are more likely than their Anglo American counterparts and less likely that their African American counterparts to have had sexual intercourse by age 19. For instance, in 1988, 81% of Hispanic American young men, 76% of Anglo American young men, and 96% of Black young men had intercourse (Perez & Duany, 1992).

Hispanic American youth who are sexually active are infrequent and unskilled users of contraceptives. Among teenagers engaging in sexual intercourse, Hispanic American and African American young women are less likely to use contraception than their Anglo American counterparts. In 1988, almost half of Hispanic and Black adolescent females (46.1% and 45.9%, respectively)—compared to less than one third of White female teenagers (31%)—reported not using any contraceptive method at first intercourse (Perez & Duany, 1992). When contraceptive methods are used and are classified as effective or ineffective, more African American and Anglo American teenage males (60%) use effective methods of contraception than Hispanic American teenage males (50%). Similarly, among adolescent girls using contraceptives, about 70% of African American and Anglo American females use effective methods compared to 60% of their Hispanic counterparts (Mott, 1983).

The relatively high rate of sexual involvement of Hispanic males and the relatively low rate of effective contraceptive use by sexually active Hispanic teenagers help to explain the relatively high teenage pregnancy rate among Hispanics. According to Perez and Duany (1992), 16% of Hispanic American young women, compared to 10% of Anglo American and 19% of African American young women ages 15 to 19 were pregnant in 1985. Although only 9% of all adolescent females are Hispanic, about 17% of all teenage births are to young Hispanic women, indicating that Hispanics are overrepresented among teenage parents in the United States. In some states with large Hispanic populations, there is a high concentration of births to Hispanic teenage parents. For example, in California and New Mexico, about half of all births to teenagers in 1989 were to Hispanic adolescents (Perez & Duany, 1992).

Although the data regarding the number of Hispanic American teenage fathers are imprecise, the best available evidence suggests that Hispanic males, like Hispanic females, are overrepresented among the teenage parent population. For example, data from the National Center for Health Statistics (1983) indicated that among 18-year-olds, only .9% of Anglo American men had first births compared to 3.5% of Hispanic American men and 6.3% of African American men.

Complications of Early Parenthood
for the Unwed Hispanic American Male

Hendricks's (1988) conducted interviews with 56 unwed teenage fathers—including 31 Hispanic Americans, 14 African Americans, and 11 Anglo Americans—to determine the difficulties they experienced as adolescent parents. Compared to the other two ethnic groups, the Hispanic American fathers reported a wider range of problems. These problems included being told how to raise the child, responsibility of being a young father, meeting financial responsibilities, getting a job, health of the child, school, preparing for the child's future, setting goals for the future, and having a place to stay. These limited findings suggest that Hispanic American teenage fathers are likely to experience stresses involving the "self," another person, and other external factors.

Acculturation Issues

Acculturation is a process through which members of a subcultural group give up the cultural traits of the culture of origin and assume the traits of the dominant culture (Locke, 1992). Hispanic American youth vary in the degree to which they adhere to traditional Hispanic values and customs and the extent to which they have acculturated (deAnda & Becerra, 1989; Padilla, 1980; Szapocznik & Kurtines, 1980). According to Martinez (1989), less acculturated Hispanic youth adhere to traditional Hispanic values. Some key features of the traditional Hispanic value system and family organization are highlighted.

Traditional Hispanic Values. In brief, traditional Hispanics envision the family, or *la familia,* as a nuclear grouping consisting of a husband and wife and their children, but encompassing an extended family consisting of grandparents, aunts, uncles, and cousins (Martinez, 1989) as well as nonrelatives who are considered a part of the kinship network (Falicov, 1982). The nuclear family usually is large, consisting of the parents and four, five, or more children (Falicov, 1982). Couples are expected to marry young and have many children (Garcia-Preto, 1982). *La familia* is both patriarchal and mother centered. That is, fathers are the final authority figures in the home, the major if not the sole economic provider, the disciplinarian for and protector of the family, and the representative of the family in matters outside the home (Baca Zinn, cited in Mirande, 1988; Falicov, 1982). According to Baca Zinn (cited in Mirande, 1988; Falicov, 1982), mothers are highly valued family members who assume power behind the scenes and are responsible for the day-to-day functioning of the family. Mothers also typically provide child care and nurturance for the children (Falicov, 1982). Children are expected to have a dutiful respect for their parents (Mirande, 1988).

Attitudes toward sexuality among traditional Hispanics are greatly influenced by the doctrines of the Roman Catholic church (Martinez, 1979). Girls are forbidden to have sexual relations and childbearing outside of marriage

(Garcia-Preto, 1982; Martinez, 1989; Mirande, 1988). Females who violate this code of conduct bring *verguenza* (shame) to themselves and their families (Martinez, 1989; Mirande, 1988). A male who fathers a child out of wedlock also brings *verguenza* to himself and his family. The father is expected to acknowledge his paternity and meet his duties and responsibilities to his female partner, his child, and his partner's family (Zayas et al., 1987) to reduce such shame.

Acculturation and Teenage Parenthood. De Anda and Becerra (1989) suggested that acculturation is the key variable that influences Hispanic adolescents' attitudes, behavior, and knowledge about reproduction and contraception. Findings from their study of 82 Hispanic adolescent mothers indicated that daughters who were less acculturated were more compliant with parental traditional values systems and less likely to become pregnant before marriage than daughters who were more acculturated. Other findings reported by Abrahamse et al. (1988) suggested that the most powerful variable in deterring teenage pregnancy among Hispanic adolescent girls is traditional religiosity. Thus, it appears that adherence to traditional values acts as a strong deterrent to premarital sexual behavior for Hispanic adolescent girls.

Acculturation level also appears to be related to how the Hispanic teenager responds to the pregnancy. Traditional Hispanic girls who are pregnant are unlikely to resort to an abortion. Expectant Hispanic adolescent parents who are traditional in their values appear to be more likely to marry or live together to resolve the pregnancy than their nontraditional counterparts (de Anda & Becerra, 1989; Salguero, 1984).

Implications for Counseling

Service providers are advised to adapt their programs to the particular cultural traditions and historical experiences of specific Hispanic cultural groups. It is beyond the scope of this book to discuss all of these cultural variations, but the reader is encouraged to consult several resources that provide cultural background information on the many Hispanic subgroups (e.g., Alvarez, 1973; Bernal, 1982; Cordasco, 1973; Duran & Bernard, 1973; Fagan, Brody, & O'Leary, 1968; Falicov, 1982; Fitzpatrick, 1987; Garcia-Preto, 1982; Inclan, 1985; Lopez & Petras, 1974; Meier & Rivera, 1981; Mirande, 1985; Montijo, 1985; Rodriguez, 1989; Rogg & Cooney, 1980; Rubinstein, 1976; Ruiz & Padilla, 1977; Szapocznik & Kurtines, 1980; Szapocznik, Scopetta, Arnalde, & Kurtines, 1978; Thomas, 1977). In addition to these considerations, acculturation issues must be attended to throughout the counseling process. Finally, macrolevel interventions are needed to improve the life status and opportunities of Hispanic youth. Suggestions for achieving these latter two recommendations are contained throughout this chapter.

Program Development
and Outreach Considerations

Knowledge of several national organizations dedicated to serving Hispanic Americans, issues related to program development with Hispanic teenagers and their families, and several successful projects that have been conducted in the Hispanic community can be helpful to practitioners interested in developing culturally sensitive services for Hispanic American teenage fathers.

National Hispanic Organizations

Program developers working in Hispanic communities may wish to consult with two organizations dedicated to the study and service of Hispanics in the United States—the National Council of La Raza (NCLR) and the National Coalition of Hispanic Health and Human Services Organizations (COSSMHO). The addresses and phone numbers for these organizations are presented in Appendix 10.1, and brief descriptions of each are provided below.

National Council of La Raza (NCLR). NCLR exists to improve life opportunities for all Hispanic Americans through applied research, policy analysis, and advocacy. NCLR provides technical assistance and capacity-building support to Hispanic community-based organizations and public information activities designed to inform Hispanic communities and the broader American public about Hispanic status, needs, and concerns (Perez & Duany, 1992).

NCLR is of particular interest to counselors working with teenage fathers because it attempts to address teenage pregnancy, parenthood, and related issues in the Hispanic community through its participation in pertinent programs. For example, in February 1991, NCLR initiated the Teen Pregnancy Prevention Replication Project, which was designed to document and replicate the development of community-based pregnancy and parenting programs specifically aimed at Hispanic youth (Perez & Duany, 1992). Because of its participation in this and other programs, NCLR staff can advise program developers on issues of resource development, program operation, and management or governance that are associated with the administration of parenting programs for Hispanic teenagers.

National Coalition of Hispanic Health and Human Services Organizations (COSSMHO). COSSMHO is another national organization that conducts research and advocates for Hispanic health and social service needs. Because COSSMHO also develops and administers national demonstration projects related to Hispanic children, families, and youth (Perez & Duany, 1992), it can provide valuable resources to program developers targeting adolescents and teenage parents in the Hispanic community.

Program Development Issues

The following program development issues pertaining to teenage pregnancy in the Hispanic community have been gleaned from Perez and Duany (1992). First, program developers are recommended to determine if existing adolescent parenting programs exist and, if so, to evaluate whether or not those programs address the needs of Hispanic teenage parents. Second, resistance in the Hispanic community toward services for teenage parents can be minimized by promoting these programs as a part of broader agency efforts to champion the positive development of economically disadvantaged Hispanic teenagers. Presented in this way, adolescent parenting projects are likely to be viewed as a way of enhancing parenting and employment skills to improve the life chances of the young Latino family. Third, pertinent programs can include community-based organizations that already serve Hispanic youth and their families because Hispanic youth and parents feel more comfortable in community agencies that reach out to their families as a whole.

Several of the program development suggestions offered by Perez and Duany (1992) pertain to the staff employed at teenage parenting programs. Program administrators are advised to hire staff fluent in Spanish to eliminate language barriers for Hispanic youth and their parents, especially Hispanics who are recent immigrants to the United States. It can be especially helpful to employ staff who live in or are intimately connected with the neighborhood they serve so that local youth know that staff are accessible. In addition, programs are recommended to employ culturally sensitive, nonjudgmental staff who are responsive to Latino subgroup differences. In particular, staff should be able to recognize and sensitively respond to cultural values regarding gender roles.

This latter point is illuminated by considering Salguero's (1984) discussion of acculturation issues among teenage parents who adhere to traditional

Hispanic values regarding gender roles. Salguero found that a community of traditional Hispanics served by the Teenage Pregnancy and Parenting Program (TAPPP) of New Haven, Connecticut, were isolated from the greater community due to their lack of assimilation into the mainstream. Salguero reported that it was important to engage this community by teaching TAPPP staff to be sensitive to the cultural value conflicts of traditional Hispanic teenagers. For example, traditional Hispanics adhere to traditional gender roles of men and women, such as the belief that a woman should remain at home, rather than working or attending school, once the child is born. Meanwhile, the father seeks employment and becomes the economic provider for the family. This value may clash with the demands of the opportunity structure in the United States and the necessary qualifications for taking advantage of this structure. That is, the route out of poverty often demands a two-salary income commanded by both fathers and mothers who are well educated and therefore qualified for higher-paying jobs. Thus, to improve the status of one's family, the teenage mother may need to continue her education, a challenge that could pose a value conflict for her, her family, and her partner. Salguero recommended that program developers teach their staff to avoid attempting forced acculturation of such clients. Rather, the staff should be taught to empathize with these conflicts and offer traditional Hispanic youth and their families decision-making counseling as they attempt to redefine their values or fashion compromises between traditional and mainstream values.

Finally, the role of the Catholic church may also be important in programmatic efforts to address Hispanic adolescent pregnancy and parenting. Martinez (1979) hypothesized that it seems probable that Hispanics are more influenced by the doctrines of the Roman Catholic church than are other U.S. Catholics. Based on this consideration, in a subsequent article Martinez (1989) implied that the Catholic church could play a vital role in the revitalization of Latinos in the United States by its participation in pertinent programs.

Exemplary Programs

Several programs have been acclaimed for their efforts to sensitively serve Hispanic teenage parents. Three community-based organizations featured by Perez and Duany (1992) are *Centro de la Comunidad Unida Decisiones Para Jovenes* (United Community Center's Decisions for Youth) of Milwaukee, Wisconsin; *Chicanos Por La Causa, Via de Amistad* (Chicanos for the Cause, Pathway to Friendship) of Phoenix, Arizona; and the Guadalupe Center's Westside Teenage Pregnancy Program of Kansas City, Missouri. Although the *Decisiones Para Jovenes* program is principally a teenage pregnancy, primary prevention project, it features components designed to manage the needs of pregnant teenagers. Other noteworthy programs are Holy Family Services of Weslaco, Texas, and the New Futures School of Albuquerque, New Mexico, both of which were described by Lindsay and Rodine (1989b). All five of these programs employ bilingual staff who reach out and provide special services to the Hispanic community. For example, *Via de Amistad* provides a baby-sitting service that is staffed by Hispanic women from the community who participate in the Foster Grandparents program; the services offered through the Westside Teenage Pregnancy Program were designed to consider ethnic differences in nutrition, education, parenting, and family dynamics.

Outreach and Rapport-Building Considerations

Hispanics are less likely than Anglos to use professional counseling services (De La Cancela & Guzman, 1991; Rogler, Malgady, & Rodriquez, 1989). Rogler et al. (1989) described two theories that have been proposed to account for this tendency.

The *alternative resource theory* proposes that the underuse of services by Hispanics is due to a reliance on informal rather than formal resources, such as the extended family, neighbors, friends, the *compadrazgo* or coparent system, and indigenous healers. For example, traditionally in Hispanic families godparents or "coparents" assist the biological parents in ensuring the welfare and religious education of the children. In times of crisis, the godparents might be asked to assume serious obligations toward their godchildren, such as taking them into their homes whenever necessary. Spiritual healers also might be called on during troubled times to use a variety of prayers, potions, and herbs to influence the spiritual world to effect positive actions for the family.

The *barrier theory* focuses on cultural and institutional barriers that discourage Hispanics from using the mental health system. Cultural barriers are the incongruities between Hispanic and mainstream values and customs. For example, individual counseling is incompatible with the Hispanic family orientation to problem solving. Institutional barriers are structural characteristics of the mental health system, such as prejudice and discrimination, leveled at Hispanics. Barrier theory predicts that when cultural and institutional obstacles diminish over time, use rates increase.

Rogler et al. (1989) reported that there is empirical support for both theories. They recommended that for formal counseling to be effective, mental health professionals must use the informal support systems of Hispanics and reduce barriers between Hispanics and the mental health system. This consideration is woven into the following discussion regarding outreach and rapport building with Hispanic Americans.

Outreach Strategies. The identification and recruitment of Hispanic American teenage fathers begins with an understanding of the support networks of these youth and their female partners. Research by Hendricks (1988) suggests that Hispanic American teenage fathers tend to come from intact families with five or more children. They tend to rely on their families for help and feel particularly close to their mothers. Similarly, research by deAnda and Becerra (1989) suggested that Hispanic American teenage mothers consider their families, especially their mothers, to be important sources of support and influence. These findings may explain, in part, why Hispanic youth prefer community agencies that reach out to their families as a whole (Perez & Duany, 1992). Because of this preference, outreach strategies designed to engage young Hispanic fathers are recommended to include outreach to the fathers' families.

Sensitivity to language barrier problems is required in all efforts to inform Hispanic families about teenage father parenting programs. Many Hispanic Americans have difficulty understanding and speaking the English language. Therefore, in communities with a large Hispanic population it is recommended that all printed advertisements regarding adolescent father programs be written in both English and Spanish. Public service announcements spoken in Spanish on Latino radio stations also are recommended.

Many other measures are necessary for reaching out to Hispanic families in a culturally sensitive manner. Nicholau and Ramos (1990) identified numerous recruitment techniques found to be effective by the coordinators of 42 school/parent partnerships who participated in the Hispanic Policy Development Project, a program designed to strike down some of the barriers between Hispanic parents and schools. Although these strategies were developed for involving parents in their children's educational experiences, they also may be useful to counselors seeking parent participation in teenage parenting programs. A warm, personal meeting with the parents, in their primary language, at their homes or at the school was the strategy deemed most effective by 98% of the coordinators. In some cases, two or three personal contacts were necessary. As a prerequisite to these encounters, it also was important to understand the status of the targeted families by answering the following questions: Are they single parents, welfare parents, working mothers, intact families, large families, immigrant families, or native-born families? Do they speak English? Who are the primary caretakers of the children—the mothers, the fathers, or the grandparents? Are the neighborhoods dangerous? Do they live near or far from the school or service center? Is transportation available? Do the fathers permit the mother to go out alone? Are there places or institutions in the neighborhoods where the families gather or feel comfortable? Do many families appear troubled? According to Nicholau and Ramos (1990), the projects that took the time to answer these questions succeeded.

Other successful outreach strategies included the following: employing staff who were sensitive to Hispanic cultural issues and concerned about Hispanic families; following up home visits with friendly phone calls and invitations to activities at the schools; posting principals or teachers outside the school in the mornings and in the afternoons to personally greet parents who drop off and pick up their children; helping parents to develop parent-to-parent support networks; designing parent-school activities to be fun and informal, especially by planing the first event outside the school at some location that clearly was the parents' turf (e.g., one particular group of school personnel served parents dinner at a local McDonalds); making sure that activities avoided rigid agendas and addressed some need or concern of the parents (e.g., in one community, school personnel responded to the parents' worries about AIDS in the community by providing information on AIDS prevention); conducting small group interaction activities to provide in-depth and specific skill development; and recognizing parents for their efforts in newsletters (Nicholau & Ramos, 1990).

In addition to these family-oriented outreach strategies, other tactics can be employed to target the adolescent males themselves. For example, Perez and Duany (1992) reported that the *Decisiones Para Jovenes* program had difficulty involving teenage fathers when it offered a male-only sexual education component. However, when this curriculum was offered with job readiness training and job placement, the component was filled to capacity. Hispanic adolescent fathers also might be attracted to programs that offer legal advice. Hendricks (1988) found that only 1 out of 31 Hispanic teenage fathers reported that he was willing to turn to a social service agency for help with a problem. However, the majority of those same fathers claimed they might seek out a human service agency if it provided information regarding their legal rights as a father and the legal rights of the child.

Rapport-Building Strategies. Practitioners can consider several suggestions for enhancing rapport with Hispanic male adolescents. Several of these pertain to the characteristics of the counselor. Padilla and Salgado de Snyder (1985) concluded that dominant Spanish-speaking clients are more positive about their counseling experience when the counselor is bilingual or when trained bilingual interpreters are available. However, although bilingualism may be helpful, it may not be sufficient to ensure positive client attitude and therapeutic gain (Padilla & Salgado de Snyder, 1985). Atkinson, Poston, Furlong, and Mercado (1989) found that prospective clients preferred counselors to be older and of the same sex, with more education, similar attitudes, and a similar personality, rather than those who were merely ethnically similar.

Other rapport-building considerations pertain to skills used throughout the counseling process. During the first session, disclosure of the counselor's background may increase rapport, regardless of ethnic differences (Franco & Levine, 1980), as might the sharing of information about the nature and process of counseling (Padilla & Salgado de Snyder, 1985). During initial sessions, it is advantageous to greet the client as soon as he arrives, even if it requires a brief interruption of an ongoing conversation (Black et al., 1991). Small talk at the beginning of the session may help to ease tension for the Hispanic male (Ruiz & Padilla, 1977).

Ruiz (1981) discussed the importance of assessing the Hispanic client's acculturation prior to counseling and the basing of treatment on an objective assessment of the degree of acculturation that the client manifests. For example, although some Hispanics may be very traditional, others are bicultural, and still others are sufficiently assimilated to be considered an Anglo. Ruiz (1981) provided case vignettes to show that the "most Hispanic" client is unlikely to benefit from retrospective, insight-oriented counseling but instead needs concrete help with realistic problems confronting them in their everyday lives. With the "most Anglo" client, however, most models of counseling can be used.

Applying Ruiz's (1981) recommendations to counseling with Hispanic teenage fathers, it is suggested that action-oriented, problem-solving approaches are appropriate for traditional Hispanic males throughout the course of counseling. With acculturated young fathers, although problem-solving approaches are necessary during the crisis stage of counseling (e.g., helping the youth and his partner to resolve the pregnancy), other approaches to counseling (e.g., object relations counseling to address long-standing parent-child wounds) may be called for. Although these proposals are consistent with Ruiz's (1981) recommendations, Hendricks's (1988) research on Hispanic teenage fathers, which indicated that they are turned off by formal questionnaires, suggests that formal assessments of acculturation probably should be avoided. Instead, the counselor can estimate the boy's acculturation level by discussing his values system to determine how consistent or deviant it is from that of traditional Hispanics.

Finally, much has been written about rapport building with Hispanic families. This topic is covered in the section "Addressing Issues With the Extended Family."

Pregnancy Resolution

According to several sources, the manner in which an unplanned pregnancy is resolved among expectant Hispanic teenagers appears to be greatly influenced by acculturation level. Martinez (cited in Children's Defense Fund, 1988a) observed that highly acculturated Hispanic males tend to respond to the pregnancy differently than do traditional Hispanic males. For example, Martinez reported that traditional males are more likely than their nontraditional counterparts to acknowledge paternity and to either marry or cohabitate with their partner in their own independent household or in the home of a relative. Similarly, in his study of young Hispanic fathers, most of whom were Puerto Rican, Sullivan (1984) concluded that traditional Hispanic males who impregnate a girl out of wedlock receive family and community pressure to get a job, start contributing money immediately, and participate in the new family of which he is the head.

Acculturation level may explain the comparatively low abortion rates among pregnant Hispanic adolescents. Hispanic American teenage women have lower rates of abortion than Anglo American and African American pregnant teenagers. Compared to 41% of Anglo Americans and 38% of African American teenage pregnancies, 31% of the pregnancies to Hispanic adolescents ended in abortion in 1985 (Perez & Duany, 1992). Salguero (1984) suggested that the lower rate of abortion among pregnant Hispanic adolescent women reflects a negative attitude toward abortion. This attitude, he argued, is based on the Hispanic conception of motherhood and womanhood. Although expectant teenage parents may be ambivalent about the pregnancy, abortion is not considered an option for adolescents from traditional Hispanic families. Instead, a pregnant adolescent is expected to give birth to the child and make an effort to leave home and live with her mate as an expression of her independence and her commitment to motherhood (Salguero, 1984). In support of these claims, Salguero (1984) reported data indicating that of 30 pregnant Hispanic adolescents participating in the TAPPP program for a particular year, only one voluntarily aborted. Furthermore, of the 29 girls who gave birth to children, 39% lived with her partner during the pregnancy and 55% lived with her partner 3 months after delivery. By comparison, none of the African American teenage mothers in the TAPPP program lived with their partners either during the pregnancy or three months after delivery.

Another possible explanation for the lower abortion rates among Hispanics is that Hispanic males are likely to oppose a partner's decision to have an abortion. Buchanan and Robbins (1990) found that Hispanic adolescent males whose partners terminated a pregnancy experienced more distress than males who became fathers. Although Hendricks's (1988) findings suggest that a Hispanic boy perceives himself to be unlikely to attempt to influence the expectant mother's decision to have an abortion, it is possible that the expectant adolescent's decision is influenced by her sensing that an abortion would greatly upset her partner.

Marriage rates also may be influenced by acculturation level. In a study of 82 Hispanic teenage mothers, with 43 of the mothers classified as nontraditional and 39 as traditional Hispanics, deAnda and Becerra (1989) reported that approximately 67% of traditional but only 44% of the nontraditional Hispanic mothers were married and lived with their boyfriends. The influence of traditional Hispanic values may also explain why approximately two thirds of all Hispanic teenage fathers live with their children (see Marsiglio, 1986) and why Hispanics in general tend to marry at an earlier age than do other cultural groups. For example, as of 1982, 25% of Hispanic females and 12% of Hispanic males had married before the age of 20. Sixteen percent of Anglo females and 6% of White males had married. Four percent of African American females and 1% of African American males had married before the age of 20 (Moore et al., 1986). In spite of the tendency of Hispanic teenagers to marry at an earlier age, however, the majority (59%) of births to Hispanic adolescents were out of wedlock in 1988.

Regardless of the path that is taken to resolve the pregnancy, it appears that Hispanic males are likely to influence the decision of the expectant female and support her during the pregnancy-resolution process. In a study of 36 pregnant Hispanic adolescent girls, Berger et al. (1991) found that nearly all of the expectant mothers considered their own opinion to be the most important factor in the decision. However, 62% of the girls who chose to deliver the baby and 57% of the girls who opted for abortion reported that the father of the baby was the second most influential person during the pregnancy resolution process. Berger et al. (1991) also found that 90% of the delivery and 86% of the terminate groups thought the father of the baby would be the person most supportive of their decision. Other findings by de Anda and Becerra (1989) suggest that traditional Hispanic teenage mothers are more likely than nontraditional mothers to be supported and influenced by their partners during the prenatal period.

Next to the girl herself and her partner, the girl's mother was perceived by the expectant adolescents to be most influential of the girl's decision in the Berger et al. (1991) study. The mother also was seen by the girls as being the second most supportive person after the father of the baby (Berger et al., 1991).

Less is known about sources of help for the expectant Hispanic teenage father during the pregnancy-resolution period. However, Hendricks's (1988) findings suggest that, in general, Hispanic adolescent fathers rely on their families and friends for help with a problem and that they feel closer to their mothers than any other family member.

Implications for Counseling

During the pregnancy-resolution phase of counseling, it is recommended that counselors pay particular attention to the influence of acculturation level. Counseling strategies may vary with traditional and nontraditional Hispanic youth. In either case, however, the mother of the pregnant adolescent could be a key figure in the girl's decision making (Berger et al., 1991) and a source of support to her daughter during the prenatal period (Berger et al., 1991; de Anda & Becerra, 1989), although the mother of the expectant father might be his most likely source of help. Therefore, with both traditional and nontraditional expectant teenage parents, the counselor is advised to explore the client's feelings about involving either his or his partner's mother during the pregnancy-resolution process.

Pregnancy-Resolution Counseling With Traditional Hispanic Adolescents. The previous literature review indicates that traditional Hispanic teenagers and their families are likely to experience considerable shame when a pregnancy occurs out of wedlock. For these clients, a premarital pregnancy represents a violation of a cultural norm. In their attempt to manage the crisis, they may rely on traditional Hispanic values as their guide to resolving the pregnancy. That is, the expectant mother is likely to give birth to the child and keep her baby, the couple is expected to acknowledge their responsibilities as parents, and they are likely to experience family pressure to either marry or cohabitate. Furthermore, both parents may be pressured to drop out of school to take on the traditional gender roles of parents: the father to serve as the economic provider by working, the mother to act as the primary caregiver for the baby.

As the counselor attempts to help the traditional Hispanic clients resolve the pregnancy, it is recommended that he or she explore the hypothesis that abortion may be a forbidden option. It is also reasonable to assume that an expectant mother's decision to have an abortion will cause significant distress for a traditional Hispanic male. In these latter cases, the expectant father should be encouraged to express his feelings to his partner before the abortion is performed, and if the abortion is completed, he may need supportive counseling to address the emotional difficulties this causes him.

In addition to these considerations, it is prudent to assess for feelings of shame among all family members. These feelings must be acknowledged and then strategies can be used to convert a sense of dishonor into more positive feelings. For example, a child is a deep source of pride to Hispanic families. By tapping the affections of the grandparents of the new baby, humiliation can give way to joy. One way that the counselor can help the young parents to convert the shame reactions of the grandparents into a sense of pride is to strongly encourage the teenage parents to demonstrate responsible parenting, a move that is likely to meet with approval of the grandparents.

After supporting the traditional values of the family, the counselor can sensitively educate the families about the potential costs of school dropout. Hispanic teenage parents who leave school to fulfill traditional parenting roles are likely to forsake opportunities that might have been afforded by continued education. Efforts should be made to see if the family can strike a compromise between traditional gender role expectations and the necessity of completing an education. For example, the teenage mother might enroll in a school-based teenage parenting program in which she can fulfill her responsibilities as caregiver while continuing her education. In addition, perhaps the family can assist the teenage mother while the teenage father completes his education through GED classes and then receives advanced training in night courses. Throughout the process of discussing these topics, counselors are advised to explore with clients the consequences of modifying traditional gender role expectations, for such a move could result in alienation from the family and community.

Pregnancy-Resolution Counseling With Nontraditional Hispanic Adolescents. Research findings suggest that as Hispanic adolescents become more acculturated, they are less likely to be influenced by their parents and more likely to respond to the pregnancy in nontraditional ways. For example, highly acculturated Hispanic teenage mothers are less likely to marry than are their traditional counterparts (deAnda & Becerra, 1989) and nontraditional males are less likely to acknowledge paternity (Martinez, cited in Children's Defense Fund, 1988a). Thus, counselors may be free to discuss a wider range of alternatives for resolving the pregnancy with the nontraditional Hispanic client than is the case with a traditional one. This implies that the decision-making counseling may be more complex and demands that the counselor challenge the client to carefully consider the ramifications of accepting options that might represent a violation of subcultural norms.

Another consideration regarding the pregnancy resolution process for nontraditional couples is that the expectant father may have less influence over his partner's decision than is the case among traditional couples. Therefore, the counselor may need to use the strategies described in Chapter 4 for helping males who are excluded from decision making regarding the pregnancy.

Addressing Issues
With the Extended Family

In an effort to address issues between the Hispanic teenage father and his family, counselors are advised to use their knowledge of the traditional values and family organization of Hispanics, described earlier, throughout the counselor process. This section suggests counseling skills designed to eliminate cultural barriers between the counselor and Hispanic families.

Establishing Rapport
With Hispanic Families

During the initial encounter with the family, especially the teenage father's parents, it is recommended that the counselor address the family in a polite and formal manner and express his or her warmth for the family (Falicov, 1982; Garcia-Preto, 1982). The early phase of the first session should focus on conveying an interest in each family member present, rather than focusing on procedures, such as acquiring precise background information on the family (Falicov, 1982; Garcia-Preto, 1982). Falicov (1982) suggested that these strategies are culturally consistent with the Hispanic notion of *personalismo,* which was described by Bernal (1982) as an orientation toward people over concepts and ideas. In moving toward a discussion of the unplanned pregnancy, address the reactions of the adult father first, then the reactions of the mother, then those of other adults, and finally those of older and younger children. Falicov (1982) and Garcia-Preto (1982) suggested that this approach shows respect for the traditional age/sex hierarchies of Hispanic families. At the end of the first session, the counselor should send the family home with a task that is not too elaborate and phrased as something the family might try should the opportunity arise (e.g., ask the adult father and the adolescent father to discuss their views on masculinity and fatherhood). According to Falicov (1982), such tentative directives are consonant with the Hispanic values of serendipity and spontaneity in interpersonal relationships.

The first discussion of the unplanned pregnancy is likely to evoke a range of emotional reactions, including surprise, anger, joy, and excitement. For example, Montanez (quoted in Martinez, 1989) chronicled the reactions of Hispanic grandmothers to out-of-wedlock teenage pregnancies:

> The really interesting sight is that of grandmothers walking arm in arm with their teenage granddaughters who are obviously pregnant. It's easy to tell that she is proud that she will be a great-grandmother soon. At the same

time it is clear that she is confused and somewhat bewildered at the new morals and the new configurations that her family is taking in the United States. Yes, she was pregnant when she was a teenager, but she was married first. (p. 164)

Reactions such as these illustrate that unwed teenage parenthood can precipitate cultural value conflicts for Hispanic families. Recognizing that this event often represents a crisis for the Hispanic family, the counselor must respect and empathize with negative emotions and quickly move to take concrete action, such as linking the family up with appropriate services (e.g., job training and placement for the young father). These actions will establish trust with the family.

An additional strategy for strengthening trust is to broaden the focus of counseling beyond the issue of the pregnancy to a consideration of how the counselor can help the family with stressful external life events, such as poor housing, unemployment, and so on, and with issues related to immigration experiences. Discussing these latter issues may open up considerable family pain associated with the hardship of leaving one's native land and dear relatives. By remaining sensitive to these issues throughout counseling, the counselor will communicate concern for the needs of the entire family and help them through the crisis of the unplanned pregnancy. After the crisis phase has passed, counselors can help Hispanic adults to consider and plan for traditional initiation rites or *fiestas,* such as the baptism of the child, as a means of refocusing their energies in a more positive light.

Engaging Adult Hispanic Fathers

A special topic of engagement with Hispanics pertains to the role of the adult father in family counseling. Falicov (1982) and Garcia-Preto (1982) acknowledged that Hispanic men are less likely than Hispanic women to participate in counseling due to the male tendency to refrain from asking for help with personal problems. Hispanic men can be recruited for counseling, however, if practitioners know how to reach out to them in a culturally sensitive manner. Falicov (1982) warned that helpers can be unfavorably influenced by negative stereotypes about *machismo.* For example, there is a tendency to view Hispanic men solely as tough and proud individuals who are unlikely to admit when they want assistance. Counselors who view Hispanic men in this simplistic way are likely to have difficulties engaging them in counseling. Falicov suggested that counselors counter this bias by using the positive cultural meanings of *machismo,* such as loyalty, fairness, responsibility, and family centrality as a bridge in engaging Hispanic fathers.

For example, to engage the father of an Hispanic adolescent male, the counselor might visit the father in his home, express his or her willingness to help the father's family during the crisis of the unplanned pregnancy, and convey his or her need for the father's help.

Ongoing Process Skills

Throughout the remainder of the first and subsequent sessions, other strategies also will facilitate rapport with Hispanic fathers in particular and Hispanic clients in general. The counselor is advised to avoid direct confrontation or demands for great self-disclosure, which are patterns of communication normally reserved for intimate relationships. The use of analogies, proverbs, and popular songs is consistent with Hispanic means of conveying ideas and opinions (Falicov, 1982).

Because Hispanic families tend to rely on informal networks for support (Rogler et al., 1989), counselors are encouraged to explore with the family the possibility of using this network during counseling. Falicov (1982) recommends considering a wide range of informal helpers, including relatives, friends, the *compadrazgo* or coparent system, priests, and family physicians.

Although the use of the immediate and extended families and other members of the support network is preferred, it is recommended that the counselor conduct some individual sessions with the adolescent father to discuss issues that he might not bring up with his parents present. For example, several researchers have documented that younger Hispanics and second-generation Hispanics acculturate at a faster rate than do older and first-generation Hispanics (Padilla, 1980; Szapocznik & Kurtines, 1980). These intergenerational differences in acculturation can cause cultural value conflicts between Hispanic children and their parents. Szapocznik, Scopetta, and King (1978) hypothesized that the greater the disparity in acculturation between Hispanic family members, the greater the family tensions and stresses. The acculturated teenage father may privately disagree with his parents' traditional values, such as the belief that he should legitimatize the pregnancy by immediately marrying his pregnant partner. If the young man has plans for carrying out such a nontraditional belief, he runs the risk of seriously challenging his parents' authority, insulting their value system, and experiencing rejection from his family. Individual counseling can help the youth to anticipate the consequences of his plan before he finalizes his decision. Individual counseling also can provide the adolescent with an opportunity to rehearse how he can discuss difficult issues with his parents, no matter what the content of those issues.

Addressing Issues With Peers

Hendricks (1988) found that 52% of the 31 Hispanic teenage fathers he interviewed reported receiving sex education from a friend. Forty-five percent reported that they shared knowledge of their sexual activities with a friend and that they were likely to go to a friend for help with a personal problem. These findings suggested that the friends of the fathers might have influenced the father's sexual behavior and his use or nonuse of contraceptives and that the friends may have been the first people the fathers confided in when learning about the pregnancy.

In light of these possibilities, it is recommended that counselors establish an ongoing relationship with Hispanic youth groups to tap their capacity for altering risk-taking behavior among Hispanic males, identifying teenagers who have been involved in an unplanned pregnancy, and offering support to teenage parents. This issue of identifying young fathers may be particularly important with traditional Hispanic adolescent boys, who are unlikely to turn to formal counselors for help, because their peers might serve as a bridge to engagement in counseling.

Preparation for Fatherhood

Four culture-specific counseling recommendations pertaining to group approaches to fatherhood training with Hispanic adolescent males are suggested. First, the counselor can use culturally relevant resources and ideas for conducting group counseling. Second, counselors should understand how fatherhood is viewed in the Hispanic culture and convey this understanding during discussions of views of masculinity and fatherhood with Hispanic males. Third, variations in child-rearing practices should be respected and particular skill deficits should be addressed during parenting skills training. Fourth, sensitivity to traditional Hispanic values and the needs of Hispanic youth and their families is required during sex and family-life education.

Culturally Relevant Guidelines
for Conducting Group Counseling

Ho (1992) posed several considerations for group counseling with Hispanic adolescents that are relevant for the current discussion. Ho noted that Hispanic American children are taught not to interrupt or push to make a point, avoid admitting a failure and personal problems, and refrain from confrontation. By comparison, Anglo American youth tend to be verbose, articulate, and aggressive during group interactions. In light of these cultural differences in verbal interaction, Ho warned that Hispanic adolescents participating in culturally heterogeneous groupings may experience confusion in knowing how to respond. In addition, Ho recommended that whenever possible, Hispanics adolescent should be grouped together, arguing that their commonality in subculture and language facilitates group rapport and progress.

Other recommendations by Ho (1992), pertaining to the ongoing group process with Hispanic adolescents, can be considered in addition to those described in Chapter 6. Warmth and respect on the part of the counselor will convey to the adolescents the notion of *personalismo.* Hispanic youth are likely to be accepting of a counselor who conveys this quality. In addition, they are apt to respect a counselor who formally takes a clear leadership role throughout the group process. Finally, Hispanic teenagers tend to respond positively to short-term, interactive groups that address concrete needs.

Counselors attempting to apply the fatherhood preparation modules described in Chapter 6 with Hispanic males are reminded that traditional Hispanic youth are discouraged from discussing topics related to sexuality (Brindis, 1992; Ho, 1992). For this reason, small groups consisting of five or six males may be necessary to draw out males who are hesitant to share their opinions on sexuality (Brindis, 1992). Counselors might also employ a culturally relevant film, *What Can a Guy Do?* (Serious Business Company, n.d.), to facilitate discussions of the Hispanic males' reaction to fatherhood and their sexual behavior and responsibilities. This film depicts three couples—African American, Anglo American, and Hispanic American—from the time each discovers the possibility of pregnancy through their experiences in coping with this difficult situation. Interspersed are presentations of a cross-section of high school students who respond to the questions, "How did you learn about birth control?" and "Whose responsibility is birth control?" Angel Martinez role-models an understanding adult in a family planning agency for this film, which strives to help male adolescents overcome personal and social barriers to getting information about birth control.

Discussing Views of
Masculinity and Fatherhood

Counselors who are culturally different from Hispanic teenage fathers must avoid imposing their cultural views of masculinity and fatherhood on their clients. Furthermore, they are encouraged to understand how male roles are defined within the Hispanic culture.

There appears to be wide variation among Hispanics in their perceptions of the gender and family roles of men. For example, Mirande (1988, 1991) observed two general models of Chicano fathers that are espoused by scholars of Chicano family life. According to the *traditional model* (Mirande, 1988, p. 94), the father is the ultimate authority figure who avoids intimacy with other family members to maintain their respect. His primary responsibilities are to provide for his family, act as a strict disciplinarian of his children, and represent the family in activities with the outside world. His wife, submissive to his wishes, is responsible for the daily needs of the children, including their needs for warmth and affection. In the *emergent model* (Mirande, 1988, p. 97), the Chicano family is more egalitarian and the power of the male is less absolute than was previously believed. According to this more recent model, fathers are seen as involved with their children in less authoritarian and more nurturant ways.

Studies of teenage pregnancy and parenthood suggest that both types of fathers, and many variations in between the two extremes, are represented among the Hispanic teenage father population. One investigator (Salguero, 1984) reporting on the relationships between Hispanic teenager fathers and their partners found that the fathers *did* tend to act in traditional ways in how they related to the mothers of their children. That is, they expected their partners to abide by their wishes, which included dropping out of school to care for the baby and tolerating exaggerated forms of *machismo* behaviors, such as demonstrations of fearlessness and episodes of excessive drinking. Other Hispanic teenage fathers, however, have been found to have very warm feelings for the young mother and her child (see Hendricks, 1988) and partake in the nontraditional role of assisting with the child care of the baby (see de Anda & Becerra, 1989).

While conducting fatherhood preparation groups, counselors should be sensitive to the many views of masculinity and fatherhood among Hispanic teenage fathers. Counselors can use disparate conceptions of maleness and the role of fathers to promote responsible parenting behavior. For example, though the traditional male may avoid emotional and physical expressions of affection toward his partner and child, he still may have a strong sense of duty as a provider. Counselors can tap his sense of family devotion by asking the group members to discuss instrumental ways that the young father can help his family, such as giving gifts to his partner and child, or working on projects, such as preparing the baby's bedroom. With the nontraditional father, counselors can focus not only on these instrumental possibilities, but also ask the father to describe to the group how he sees himself as being the gentle protector, provider, and nurturer of his children and family.

By encouraging both traditional and nontraditional males to describe their prototypical conceptions of how to assume responsibility for one's masculine behavior, the counselor may help the young fathers to expand their repertoire of masculine behaviors. However, these discussions might also unveil value conflicts between members who have different rates of acculturation. When these difficulties emerge, the counselor should encourage the participants to show tolerance for their different roles and expectations regarding fatherhood and masculinity.

Hispanic Teenage Fathers and Parenting-Skills Training

Two major issues are associated with parenting skills training with Hispanic teenage fathers. First, counselors should be able to recognize and respect culture-specific parenting practices of Hispanic Americans. Second, large numbers of Hispanic teenage fathers may be unschooled in the parenting skills necessary to promote the academic competence of their children.

Culture-Specific Parenting Practices. Falicov (1982) warned counselors that Hispanics may differ from other Americans in specific child-rearing customs. For example, a 5-year-old child sitting on his mother's lap or a 3-year-old child drinking out of her bottle, although not in line with Anglo norms, are consistent with Hispanic ideals that stress nurturance as opposed to autonomy.

Counselors are reminded to remain sensitive to these variations during parenting skills training with Hispanic teenage fathers. One resource counselors can use to achieve this goal is a parenting skills curriculum developed by COSSMHO. This manual, titled *Strengthening Families: A Curriculum for Hispanic Parents* (COSSMHO, n.d.) focuses on strengthening the parenting skills of Hispanics within a context of Hispanic cultural and social transition.

Teaching Parents to Promote Their Children's Academic Competence. Nicholau and Ramos (1990) argued that an essential topic for parenting skills training with most low-income Hispanic parents is the subject of teaching their children basic academic skills. These authors concluded that a variety of factors (e.g., poverty, undereducation, language barriers, and a parochial experience of the world) limit the Hispanic parents' development of specific practices (e.g., talking and reading to children and encouraging their curiosity) that lay the academic skills foundation. Because these practices begin in the home, the parents must be informed about the value of out-of-school activities designed to stimulate their children intellectually. Nicholau and Ramos (1990) provided professionals with numerous suggestions for how parents can engage their children in constructive learning activities, such as reading, writing and drawing for fun; taking trips to museums, zoos, and libraries; watching educational television; and pursuing hobbies and other intellectually enriching ideas.

Because Hispanic teenage fathers tend to be low academic achievers themselves (see Marsiglio, 1986) and hail from families with limited educational experiences (see Perez & Duany, 1992), it is unlikely that they will be sophisticated in methods for promoting the academic competence of their own children. Therefore, it is recommended that counselors use the many pertinent suggestions contained in Nicholau and Ramos (1990).

Sex and Family-Life Education

As was mentioned previously, Hispanic adolescent males tend to either refrain from contraceptive use or they use ineffective means of contraception, such as withdrawal (see Mott, 1983; Sonenstein, 1986). Hispanic teenage fathers who have participated in an unplanned out-of-wedlock pregnancy are evidence of such practices. These young men can benefit from sex and family-life education designed to prevent additional unplanned pregnancies. However, many of these same young fathers may hail from families who are highly influenced by the doctrines of the Roman Catholic church and, consequently, are opposed to educational programs on contraceptive use. Furthermore, many traditional Hispanic American families may view sexual education as the purview of family rather than educators and practitioners. Therefore, it is recommended that counselors discuss and clarify the values of the young fathers and his family before proceeding with training in contraceptive use. Nevertheless, clients opposed to contraceptive education might be receptive to family-life education that can deter further risky sexual behavior by helping the youth to recognize the many responsibilities associated with parenthood.

Numerous resources are available in Spanish for teaching sex and family-life education to Hispanic teenagers. The Center for Population Options in Washington, D.C., publishes curricula concerning reproductive health and family planning options, such as the Spanish version of Hunter-Geboy's (n.d.) booklet *Como Planear Mi Vida*. Sunburst Publishing provides a toll-free number (see Appendix 10.1) for ordering its many videos, brochures, and books that cover such topics as AIDS and sex education. The film *Men and Contraception: A Shared Responsibility* (Planned Parenthood Association of Metropolitan Washington, D.C., n.d.), which is available in Spanish, presents ways men can be more involved with all methods of contraception.

No Time Soon (ODN Productions, n.d.) is another film that is useful for stimulating discussions regarding sexuality with Hispanic males. The video focuses on two teen males, one Black and one Hispanic, who speak frankly about their own experiences and perceptions regarding sex, birth control, relationships, school, and what they do to avoid becoming teenage fathers.

Besides using educational materials that incorporate culturally relevant issues for Hispanics, Brindis (1992) urged counselors to lobby state boards of education and state and federal policymakers to develop culturally relevant family-life education programs on a state and national scale. Moran and Corley (1991) provided a persuasive argument for why such measures are necessary. In their study of the sources of sexual information and sexual attitudes and behaviors of Hispanic American adolescent males, Moran and Corley (1991) found that Hispanic males report being more likely to learn sex education from friends and from experimentation than from sex education classes. Yet the authors also learned that the preferred source of sexuality information among Hispanic adolescent males is additional formal sex education. Furthermore, the authors reported that formal sex education has a positive association with the use of condoms by Hispanic adolescents. Moran and Corley (1991) concluded that policies in support of providing sex education in the schools are needed to make sex education available to greater numbers of Hispanic youth who need them. Moran and Corley (1991) also hypothesized that the increased provision of sex education will be particularly helpful to the young Hispanic American male from traditional households, who, out of respect for his elders, does not ask questions related to sexuality.

Educational and Career Counseling

Dropping out of school, particularly among teenage parents, is a problem throughout the Hispanic American community. Statistics reported by Wetzel (1989) indicate that drop-out rates among Hispanic Americans remain higher than among other groups. In 1987, Hispanics represented 18% of all drop-outs, and the percentage of Hispanic American dropouts was almost double that of African Americans—34% compared to 18% (Wetzel, 1989). An estimated 59% of Hispanic dropouts leave school before completing 10th grade (Nicholau & Ramos, 1990). Compared to African American and Anglo American youth, data show that Hispanic pregnant teenagers are more likely to drop out of high school and less likely to re-enroll to obtain their diplomas. About one quarter of young Hispanic mothers who had children during their teenage years had completed high school by their mid-20s, compared with more than half of Anglo American and two thirds of African American teenagers interviewed in 1982 (Children's Defense Fund, 1991b). Only 39%

of Hispanic American teenage fathers graduate from high school, compared to 72% of Hispanic nonfathers (Marsiglio, 1986).

Several factors appear to influence the high drop-out rate among Hispanic Americans, including family socioeconomic background, English language ability, and whether or not the individual was born in the United States (Ford Foundation, 1984). In addition to these factors, the traditional Hispanic view that the mother should provide child care in the home and the father should work to support his partner and child contributes to the decisions of Hispanic teenage parents to drop out of school (Salguero, 1984). Several counseling strategies are recommended to counter these many forces.

Involving Parents in the Educational System

Counselors are advised to work with school personnel to educate Hispanic parents about the importance of school to further economic opportunities for their children who are adolescent parents (Liontos, 1992). Many Hispanic parents also need to be appraised of alternative education programs for pregnant and parenting teenagers.

Counselors need to understand that many barriers between the Hispanic community and school personnel can interfere with attempts to communicate this information to Hispanic parents. The interaction between poor Hispanic parents and the schools their children attend tends to be strained, in large part because of misconceptions held by both teachers and Hispanic parents. According to Nicholau and Ramos (1990), teachers often view Hispanic parents as not fitting in because the parents don't speak English or as not caring about their children's education because the parents don't participate in parent-school activities. Hispanic parents commonly perceive teachers as intimidating and cold authority figures whom they should not approach with questions. Consequently, both parties feel that the other does not care (Nicholau & Ramos, 1990).

As a first step of an intervention designed to counter these misconceptions, Nicholau and Ramos (1990) recommended that schools provide in-service programs that educate school personnel about cultural factors influencing the parent's approach to the school system. Most Hispanic parents want their children to succeed in school. However, the parents behave in a manner consistent with the way they were expected to behave in the countries in which they or their parents were born. In Spanish-speaking countries, the role of parents and the role of school in relation to education are sharply delineated. Parents have a duty to instill respect and proper behavior in their children, but it is the school's job to instill knowledge. Parents in these countries also view the educational system as a bureaucracy governed by educated professionals they have no right to question. These cultural influences make Hispanic parents appear disinterested in their children's educational progress, but this is not the case (Nicholau & Ramos, 1990).

Although this knowledge can remove some of the cultural barriers preventing school officials from engaging Hispanic parents in the educational planning for the teenage father, other measures may be necessary to induce parents to feel comfortable with the educational system. Many of these were mentioned earlier in the description of the recruitment techniques found to be effective by the coordinators of 42 school/parent partnerships who participated in the Hispanic Policy Development Project. In addition to these, Nicholau and Ramos (1990) reported other activities that may help to keep Hispanic parents involved with school systems. Here are some examples that are appropriate with Hispanic parents whose children are adolescents:

Community projects, such as painting murals, planting gardens, or mounting a drive against neighborhood drug dealers. Such activities build spirit and a sense of community, they allow parents to make direct and visible contributions, and they do not place the parents in the position of being judged.

Tutoring and homework centers, where students receive assistance with homework, and parents attend workshops and parenting classes. Informal workshops are conducted initially on the issues the parents identified, and later on subjects that the schools felt were priorities.

Specific strategies recommended by Nicholau and Ramos (1990) may help to engage the fathers of Hispanic teenage fathers to their sons' school environments, such as overseeing sporting events, painting a classroom or a mural, or moving furniture. Fathers prefer working on such projects with other fathers in the evenings and on weekends.

Counselors and school personnel who make these varied efforts to reach out and engage the parents of Hispanic teenage fathers will enhance their chances of teaching the parents about the U.S. system of education. Moreover, because of the supportive involvement of their parents, the young fathers are likely to improve their attitudes toward school, their participation in class, and their study habits (see Nicholau & Ramos, 1990).

Make the Educational System
More Relevant to Hispanic Children

Brindis (1992) recommended that schools develop educational programs that reflect and respond to the community surrounding the school. For example, schools should hire bilingual teachers and classroom aides and develop parent volunteer programs. In addition, schools can extend teacher training opportunities to include multicultural issues that affect classroom teaching and curriculum development (Brindis, 1992). These may help some young fathers to feel less alien in the school environment.

Macrolevel Educational Interventions

Because young Hispanic males tend to be locked out from the educational opportunity structure in this country, mental health professionals may need to join the fight to alter state and federal policies that have a bearing in the educational system in the United States. For example, Haycock and Duany (1991) argued that because schools put less of everything into the education of Latino students, more money needs to be directed toward school systems with high populations of Hispanic students. Brindis (1992) called for the development and expansion of programs that provide access to postsecondary education by guaranteeing payment for college costs, public service programs to repay loans, extending loan deferment periods, and linking repayment to postcollege income.

Consulting With National Hispanic Organizations Dedicated to Preventing School Dropout

The retention strategies mentioned thus far, along with those discussed in Chapter 7, represent just some of the many ways counselors can work to prevent Hispanic teenage fathers from dropping out from school. Counselors who want to learn of more pertinent retention ideas can refer to Appendix 10.1 for the address and phone number of ASPIRA Association, which sponsors the Hispanic Community Mobilization for Dropout Prevention program. Appendix 10.1 also contains information for contacting the Hispanic Policy Development Project. Both organizations focus on creating community awareness and providing practical information to Hispanic parents to help them be more effective participants in their children's education. The national offices of each provide technical assistance, training, and materials to promote the development of school/parent partnerships in children's education.

Address Culturally Salient Career Issues

Hispanic Americans struggle with a variety of salient career issues. Well-paying, unskilled jobs are rapidly disappearing, and today's entry-level jobs offer lower salaries and require higher skills (Liontos, 1992). Hispanic males from lower socioeconomic levels lack sufficient employment and volunteer opportunities, role models, and employment training opportunities (Perez & Duany, 1992). They also may experience discrimination in the workplace.

In recognition of the employment barriers they face, Hispanic youth tend to have low career expectations (Arbona, 1990), even though their career aspirations are as high or higher than those of Anglos (Arbona, 1990; Arbona & Novy, 1991). Limited career opportunities may cause many students to become discouraged about school and their future job outlook, thereby negatively affecting motivation and self-esteem.

These considerations must be factored into the career assessment and counseling activities described in Chapter 7. In addition, according to Kiselica, Changizi, Cureton, and Gridley (1995), special career services are needed to liberate low-income Hispanic students from the trap of permanent poverty.

Work Attitudes and Values. The parents and guardians of many Hispanic students are uninformed about the realities of the workforce and unaware that their own cultural values may not be congruent with the work ethic in our society. Many children, therefore, are not learning the attitudes and values at home that are necessary to be successful in the workforce in the United States today (S. B. Baker, 1992; Lee, 1989). Consequently, it is necessary that school counselors and social workers help some Hispanic American teenage fathers develop attitudes and behavioral skills that will lead to success in the U.S. job market. In addition, they may need assertiveness skills training to locate and compete for jobs and counter possible discrimination in the workforce (S. B. Baker, 1992).

Role Models. Exposing Hispanic American teenage fathers to a diverse group of role models from the Hispanic community might foster their curiosity about occupations, stimulate information-seeking behaviors, and prevent premature career foreclosure. According to Herr and Niles (1994) and Lee (1989), numerous activities such as field trips to work sites, work simulation activities, minicourses, hands-on workshops, career nights, and mentoring programs can effectively involve role models in the lives of ethnic-minority youth.

Career Placement and Testing Skills. The parents of Hispanic youth may be uninformed about how to teach their children to seek jobs and prepare for standardized tests (S. B. Baker, 1992; Lee, 1989). Therefore, Hispanic teenage fathers may need special training in learning skills for career placement and preparing for and taking career placement tests. Some useful placement skills include the following: interviewing strategies and preparation, how to complete job and/or college applications, producing resumes and cover letters, and preparation for placement tests. For interview preparation, counselors can help students "learn to project expertness, trustworthiness, and attractiveness" (S. B. Baker, 1992, p. 151). Preparation for placement tests includes test wiseness, test coaching, and how to deal with test anxiety (S. B. Baker, 1992).

Reducing Employment Barriers in the World of Work. To reduce the employment obstacles faced by Hispanic adolescents, Brindis (1992) recommended that counselors work to develop community partnerships between businesses, churches, community-based organizations, and parents that focus on improving the employment of Hispanic adolescents. Martinez (1989) added that counselors must support policy measures that provide employers with incentives to hire Hispanic youth.

APPENDIX 10.1
Consulting Organizations for Developing
Service Programs for Hispanics

National Council of La Raza (NCLR)

810 First Street, NE
Suite 300
Washington, D.C. 20002
(202) 289-1380
(202) 289-8173 fax

National Coalition of Hispanic Health
and Human Services Organizations (COSSMHO)

1501 16th Street, NW
Washington, D.C. 20036-1401
(202) 387-5000
(202) 797-4353 fax

Spanish Publications Available
From Sunburst Publishing

Sunburst Publishing provides a toll-free number (1-800-431-1934) for ordering its many videos, brochures, and books produced in Spanish that cover such topics as AIDS and sex education.

Consulting Organizations for Preventing
School Dropout Among Hispanics

Hispanic Community Mobilization for Dropout Prevention

ASPIRA Association, Inc.
1112 16th Street NW
Washington, D.C. 20036
(202) 835-3600

Hispanic Policy Development Project

250 Park Avenue South
Suite 500A
New York, NY 10003
(212) 529-9323

11

Social Class, Religiosity,
and Urban and Rural Environments

Besides ethnicity and race, three other cultural variables associated with
teenage fatherhood have been discussed in the social sciences literature, in
descending order of coverage: social class, religiosity, and urban and rural
environments. To assist counselors to think more broadly about cultural
influences on teenage fathers, each of these variables is reviewed here.

Social Class

According to Tischler (1990), the term *social class* is defined as "a
category of people who share similar opportunities, similar economic and
vocational positions, similar lifestyles, and similar attitudes and behavior.
Class boundaries are maintained by limitations on social interaction, inter-
marriage, and mobility into that class" (p. 221). Social class includes other
variables, such as occupational prestige, educational level, and income level
(Erickson & Gecas, 1991).

Social class has a significant influence on people's lives. In the words of
Erickson and Gecas (1991),

One's standing in the social class hierarchy affects where and how one lives; how long one lives; one's educational and occupational circumstances, and those of one's children; and a multitude of other life conditions. Because of the association of social class with differences in power, privilege, resources, and life conditions, we can expect social class to have a pervasive influence on family relations as well. (p. 114)

Social class is an important variable affecting the route to teenage pregnancy and parenthood, how an unplanned adolescent pregnancy is resolved, and the adjustment to parenthood, including conceptions of fatherhood and the behaviors of fathers.

Social Class and the Route
to Teenage Pregnancy and Parenthood

Adolescent parents are disproportionately represented among the poor (Children's Defense Fund, 1986b; Hofferth, 1987a). Teenage girls from families living below the poverty level are three and a half times more likely to be teenage mothers than teenage girls whose families live above the poverty level and five times as likely to be teenage mothers as are teenage girls whose families live on incomes more than 300% above the poverty line (Children's Defense Fund, 1986b).

Poverty interacts with a cluster of social, psychological, and familial factors to make poor adolescents particularly vulnerable to life stresses, including those associated with early parenthood (Chilman, 1988). As socioeconomic status decreases, rates of sexual activity and early pregnancy and parenthood rise (Hogan & Kitagawa, 1985; Moore et al., 1986). Teenagers from lower socioeconomic levels engage in premarital sexual activity at an early age (Chilman, 1983), and their sexual activity is highly conducive to repeated teenage pregnancy and parenthood (Group for the Advancement of Psychiatry, 1986). Economically disadvantaged males are more likely than advantaged males to father a child as an adolescent (Marsiglio, 1987). The influence of socioeconomic level is so powerful that it mediates many of the observed differences in adolescent pregnancy rates between different cultural groups. For example, although the adolescent pregnancy rate among African Americans is higher than that among Anglo Americans, no differences between the adolescent pregnancy rates of these two ethnic groups are found when the effects of income and basic skills are controlled for (Children's Defense Fund, 1986b). Thus, the factors leading to teenage pregnancy are much more likely to affect children who live in disadvantaged environments.

These effects may operate through a perceived lack of options and desirable alternatives for the future (Miller & Moore, 1990; L. A. Smith, 1988). That is, poor teenagers may perceive less incentive to avoid early childbearing because of limited future opportunities (Moore & Burt, 1982; L. A. Smith, 1988). In addition, adolescent males who live in poverty may view fatherhood as a normative cultural experience that gives them some means of identity and role clarification (Robinson, 1988a; L. A. Smith, 1988).

Statistics regarding the relationship between socioeconomic level and quality-of-life indicators support the contention that poor adolescents have limited life opportunities. One child in five in the United States is born into poverty (Kiesler, 1993). They tend to live in stressful, dangerous, and unhealthy surroundings. Children raised in such environments are much more likely than economically advantaged children to abuse drugs, witness and be the victim of violence, and experience academic difficulties (Dryfoos, 1990).

Poverty significantly diminishes the chances that a teenager will complete high school or attend college. Among 18- to 21-year-olds in the United States, only 49.8% of the poor completed high school, compared to 77.3% of those living above the poverty line, and only 27.3% of poor high school graduates complete one or more years of college, compared to 37.7% of the nonpoor high school graduates (see Children's Defense Fund, 1985).

Economically underprivileged adolescents have limited opportunities in the marketplace, in part due to the educational disadvantages described above, but also because of structural discrimination and unemployment in economically depressed areas. New jobs opening up in the economy disproportionately are service positions, and employees are often paid too little to rise above the poverty level. Many jobs taken by the poor do not include benefits, and the availability of benefits is decreasing (Kiesler, 1993). Thus, underprivileged males are unlikely to earn sufficient salaries and benefits to support a family. In the face of these dismal realities, unwed parenthood may be perceived as one of the few available life options that can provide some disadvantaged teenagers with a sense of purpose and identity in their lives.

Welfare Availability: An Incentive for Adolescent Childbearing? Many critics of the welfare system have charged that the existence of AFDC acts as an incentive for early childbearing. Although this is a popularly held explanation for teenage pregnancy in the United States, there is little empirical support for this theory. Although early childbearers are more likely to be in households receiving AFDC (see Hofferth, 1987a), welfare availability does not appear to be associated with adolescent sexual activity or pregnancy (see Children's Defense Fund, 1986b; Hofferth, 1987b). Nor do the levels of welfare benefits appear to be related to adolescent childbearing; welfare benefit levels have been falling in recent years, but the rates of unwed pregnancy have risen (Ellwood & Summers, 1986). However, welfare availability may be associated with whether or not a pregnant girl decides to abort, marry, or bear an out-of-wedlock child and with whom she chooses to live (see Hofferth, 1987b). These effects were explained by Moore and Burt (1982):

> Although it seems unlikely that the meager benefits available to welfare mothers would actually induce a young woman to become pregnant, it is possible that the availability of welfare support encourages a teenager, once she is pregnant, to bear a child when she might otherwise have obtained an abortion. Welfare may also make it possible for a woman to avoid marrying the father of her child if she has doubts about his stability or earning ability. A teenager may see any amount of money as a source of independence, since it enables her to set up her own household free of parental control and supervision. In addition, the availability of welfare may be a deciding factor in whether an unwed mother keeps her child or gives the child up for adoption. (pp. 109-110)

A common myth associated with the welfare-as-an-incentive-for-teenage-pregnancy hypothesis is that welfare recipients adhere to a set of values that is distinct from and inferior to middle-class values. That is, welfare-dependent individuals lack a work ethic, accept AFDC due to an inherent laziness, and would rather have children and "live off the government" than work for a living. The findings from studies conducted by Chrissinger (1980) and Glass (1982) pose a challenge to these assumptions. Chrissinger (1980) examined the factors affecting employment of welfare mothers and found that in those cases in which recipients refused to work, they based their decision not on an attitude toward work in general but on the type of work available. The job they were most likely to refuse was the low-paid, low-status job of maid. In addition, Chrissinger's results indicated that the need to care for young children affected a mother's decision to work. Chrissinger (1980) concluded that "only economic factors appear to significantly affect the welfare mother's decision regarding work" (p. 52). Similar findings were reported by Glass (1982) in her study of employed and unemployed welfare recipients. Glass concluded that *it is not personal characteristics but structural factors in the workplace* that determine the choices AFDC recipients make about work. Glass noted that welfare recipients generally faced limited employment markets with jobs characterized by low wages, few if any benefits, and no provision for absence due to reasons such as illness in the family. Glass argued that welfare recipients generally may end up far worse economically and physically if they forfeit their AFDC benefits.

In light of such findings, Orcut, Nakamura, and Nakamura (quoted in Wodarski & Lockhart, 1987) stated,

> We are too ready to assume that the poor bring on their misery by their inadequacies and misguided behavior. No doubt sometimes they do, but how has it happened that almost all poverty research focuses on the conditions, needs and behavior of the poor? Isn't it at least possible that some of the causes of poverty have something to do with the way our entire system functions? (p. 51)

Another stereotype associated with the welfare availability hypothesis is that the male partners of teenage mothers lack a work ethic, that they therefore do not work and cannot support their families, and that if these young fathers were forced to pay more in child support, the number of young mothers on welfare would be reduced greatly. Although it is true that many economically disadvantaged adolescent fathers may accept their partner's use of welfare services, research from several studies suggest that these fathers tend to have a very strong desire to work but have difficulty finding sustained employment (e.g., Achatz & MacAllum, 1994; Barth et al., 1988; Hendricks, 1988; Klinman, Sander, Rosen, Longo, & Martinez, 1985; Sander & Rosen, 1987). Furthermore, destitute teenage fathers tend to provide some financial assistance or support to their partners in a variety of nonfinancial ways, such as helping with child care, providing clothes, and so on (Achatz & MacAllum, 1994; Danzinger, 1987; L. A. Smith, 1989; Sullivan, 1985, 1988; Williams, 1991). Nevertheless, the major "intervention" used to reduce the number of adolescent mothers on the welfare rolls during the Reagan-Bush era was to enforce child support payments of noncustodial fathers. Yet several social policy authorities have cautioned that such measures are unlikely to remove adolescent custodial parents from AFDC (e.g., Children's Defense Fund, 1986b; Danziger, 1987), and a recent analysis of these enforcement procedures have demonstrated that they are thus far unsuccessful (see Glass, 1990). Thus, public policy has taken an ineffective approach to dealing with impoverished teenage fathers, punishing them for the economic problems of their partners, rather than recognizing that these fathers, too, are victims of the savage inequalities of our society.

Social Class, Pregnancy Resolution Options, and the Adjustment to Parenthood

It has been proposed that social class affects the pregnancy resolution process and the adjustment to parenthood. Specifically, social class is related to abortion use, welfare dependency, living arrangements, marriage, marital stability of teenage parents, and conceptions of fatherhood and paternal behavior.

Socioeconomic Level and Abortion Use

Single middle-class women are more likely than single lower-class women to have an abortion (Chilman, 1979, 1988). The lack of financial resources to defray abortion costs prevents many poor adolescents from having an abortion. According to Chilman (1988),

> This lack of resources has become especially important since the so-called Hyde Amendment was passed by Congress in 1976 and upheld by the Supreme Court in 1979. This amendment prevents the use of federal funds for meeting the costs of abortion for low-income women unless their lives are endangered by the pregnancy. (p. 27)

According to Rubin (1988), although abortion remains a controversial issue, freedom of choice for pregnancy resolution is supported by most of the adult population in the United States. This freedom is not present for those who lack the funds to pay for an abortion if they choose to end the pregnancy (Rubin, 1988).

Social Class and Welfare Dependency

The poorest population groups are those in which early out-of-wedlock childbearing rates are the highest (Vera Institute of Justice, 1990). A premarital first birth among early childbearers increases the probability of going on welfare for those not enrolled and reduces the probability that those already enrolled will exit welfare (see Hofferth, 1987a). Approximately one third of teenage mothers ages 16 to 19 receive welfare (Danziger, 1986). Sixty percent of all single mothers are unemployed or on welfare at some time after becoming a single parent (see Hanson, 1985). Approximately 70% of the total number of AFDC recipients under age 30 began motherhood as teenagers (Moore & Burt, 1982). Thus, "Teenage pregnancy and early childbearing are problems primarily because they grow out of and reinforce poverty" (Vera Institute of Justice, 1990, p. 2).

Single adolescent mothers tend to exhibit the following characteristics that present obstacles to their securing employment that can extricate them from the welfare roles: larger number of children; younger children at home; health problems; and deficits in education, job skills, and work experience

(Sanger, 1979). In light of these considerations, it is not surprising that disadvantaged teenage mothers are at great risk for long-term poverty (see Klerman, 1991) and that, among welfare recipients, young never-married women are the group at greatest risk for long-term reliance on welfare (Children's Defense Fund, 1986b). Also, it is understandable that under-privileged teenage fathers can do little to move their partners away from AFDC, considering the financial liabilities of these fathers (Achatz & MacAllum, 1994; Children's Defense Fund, 1986b; Furstenberg, 1976; Hardy & Zabin, 1991; L. A. Smith, 1989; Sullivan, 1985, 1989; Williams, 1991).

Social Class, the Living Arrangements of Teenage Fathers, Welfare, and Marriage

There appears to be a relationship between social class and the living arrangements of teenage fathers. For example, according to findings obtained by Marsiglio (1987) analyzing data from the National Longitudinal Survey of Labor Market Experience of Youth, among Whites, 77% of economically "nondisadvantaged" (p. 240) adolescent fathers but only 58% of economically "disadvantaged" (p. 240) adolescent fathers lived with their first child. Although Marsiglio offered no explanation for these findings, it is proposed here that poor males are less likely to live with their child because of limited resources and the effects of welfare policies.

Because poverty limits career opportunities, poor males are likely to fill the bottom of the occupational hierarchy and lack the financial resources to support a family. Consequently, a destitute teenage father may be forced to rely on the mother's family and/or welfare for support, two options that typically preclude his considering marriage or cohabitating with his partner and child (Chilman, 1988; Furstenberg, 1976).

Historically, policies regarding AFDC discouraged the involvement of fathers in family life. Until recently, in most states, a family's support payments were reduced, or even eliminated, if a male lived in the household, whether or not he was employed. Also, Medicaid coverage of prenatal care and childbirth would have to be given up in the event of marriage, unless the father qualified as unemployed in a state with unemployed father coverage. Consequently, although many impoverished teenage parents may want to marry, they may remain single to avoid jeopardizing AFDC benefits, including Medicaid. Thus, welfare policies have not only deterred marriage (Moore & Burt, 1982) and paternal participation in the family (Erickson & Gecas, 1991), but they have helped to socialize generations of poor children to view father absence from the home as a acceptable model of family functioning.

Thus, even though some states have changed AFDC policies to support a father's presence in the family without jeopardizing the family's social service benefits, some destitute young mothers and fathers do not consider marriage or cohabitation because they accept single parenthood as a normative lifestyle within their culture.

Socioeconomic Level and Marital Stability

Economic resources appear to be strongly linked to marital stability. A recent U.S. Bureau of the Census report indicated that poor parents are nearly twice as likely to break up as those with money. One out of seven married couples below the poverty line splits up, compared to one out of 13 couples with higher incomes (see Bovee, 1993).

In his analysis and discussion of failed marriages experienced by adolescent mothers, Furstenberg (1976) documented that economic difficulties were high on the list of reasons offered by teenage mothers about why their marriages had failed. More than one out of every four adolescent mothers from a failed marriage attributed the failure to her husband's inability to support his family. The probability for a broken marriage was higher for women married to males with a lower-earning status than for those mothers married to mates with a higher-earning status; among the lower-status males, the probability of separation within 2 years of the wedding date was .45, while it was only .19 for the men who were classified as higher status. Furstenberg reported that the marriages of higher-status mothers also tended to be more stable, that individuals of higher status tended to marry one another, and that marital cohesion was more strongly related to the economic success of the male than to that of the female, although their economic well-being as whole contributed to conjugal stability.

In his interpretation of these findings, Furstenberg (1976) noted that most of the males in his study were in a weak economic position prior to the conception of the child. He hypothesized that an ill-timed marriage may have further limited their prospects for economic advancement by compelling them to terminate school and enter the labor force under less than favorable circumstances. He suggested that the lower-class male may have been seen as a poor investment by his spouse, and that over time personal differences tend to be evaluated with less tolerance when economic resources are low. He argued that there is simply less reason to maintain a problematic relationship when an adolescent female is not dependent on the male for support. He concluded that the most important link in the chain between an unplanned adolescent pregnancy and later marital failure is the weak economic position of the male who fathers a child out of wedlock.

A failed marriage can plunge an underprivileged family into worse economic straits. According to Clifford Johnson, the family support director for the Children's Defense Fund (cited in Bovee, 1993), a marital split sends a poor family spiraling further into poverty as the father's departure slashes income from the family. As one poverty-stricken young father explained to me after a divorce from his wife,

> It's like you can't do yourself or your family any good when you're poor and divorced. You now got two houses to support instead of one, and the money you had to begin with barely made ends meet when you were together. Both my ex and me are worse off than we were before, even though I send them as much as I can. If it weren't for me living with my parents again, I'd be out on the street. And my ex and my kid had to return to the welfare home she was in before we got married.

Social Class and Conceptions of Fatherhood and Paternal Behavior

Although it is reasonable to assume that social class could affect the paternal attitudes and behaviors of teenage fathers, pertinent empirical research has been focused on adult and not adolescent fathers. Therefore, this discussion of social class and teenage fathers is based on research conducted on adult men.

In their review of the research literature on social class and fatherhood, Erickson and Gecas (1991) concluded that there is no simple causal relationship between the two variables among adult males. Nevertheless, there do appear to be class-related differences in conceptions of fatherhood and paternal behavior. The following suggested class differences were gleaned from Griswold (1993).

Compared to fathers from the lower class, upper-class fathers historically have been more likely to read literature related to child rearing, listen to radio talk shows on child care, attend child study groups and parent-teacher association meetings, read or tell stories to their children, use reasoning to deal with misbehaviors, be emotionally expressive and affectionate with their children, and are less likely to resort to spanking as a disciplinary tactic. Working-class family life is centered around inculcating respectability and obedience in their children and internalizing proper standards of conduct. For the middle class, the goal was to raise a child who acted according to the dictates of his or her own principles. For the working class, the goal was to produce a child who obeyed parental demands.

Class differences in paternal behavior have been attributed to the disparate opportunities and life circumstances of fathers from the different classes.

Upper-class fathers have been afforded more educational and leisure opportunities that would support behaviors such as studying child development and child rearing and reading to children. Lower-class fathers are denied these opportunities and, moreover, are employed in settings that require them to exhibit obedience and constraint. These fathers may want their children to conform to external authority because the parents themselves are willing to accord respect to authority in return for job security and respectability. Upper-class fathers, on the other hand, can take for granted high income, stability, and respectability. Consequently, their emphasis with their children is on teaching self-direction and interpersonal relations.

Implications for Counseling and Public Policy

Disadvantaged teenage fathers are not going to make it as fathers or as productive members of society unless sweeping changes are made in public policy that affects family relations. This section contains implications for counseling and numerous recommendations for reforms in public policy, and it concludes with a special note about teenage fathers from the upper class.

Implications for Counseling

It is critical that counselors working with disadvantaged teenage fathers understand the cultural forces at work in the onset of an unplanned pregnancy, the manner in which the pregnancy is resolved, and the living arrangements of young adolescent parents who choose to keep the baby. It must be recognized that restricted life circumstances may heighten the acceptance of adolescent parenthood as a vehicle toward identity formation for many poor adolescents; that noncustodial single fatherhood may be a function of economic necessity, rather than the expression of a preferred lifestyle, or of long-standing welfare policies that have helped to socialize many or our nation's young people to view single motherhood and absentee fatherhood as an accepted and normal form of family functioning; and finally, that attitudes toward fatherhood and paternal behaviors of the poor represent adaptive adjustments for survival in the context of limited opportunities.

These complex issues must be understood prior to the initiation of counseling. In addition, counselors from the middle and upper classes, in particular, may need to explore their values regarding premarital sex, pregnancy resolution, family form, and child rearing to determine if they might conflict with the values of some disadvantaged young fathers.

Once a counselor has endeavored to comprehend the complex hardships of the disadvantaged teenage father, he or she can communicate this understanding through dedicated efforts to help this client overcome life obstacles. Among impoverished adolescent males, the prevention of teenage pregnancies, the prevention of repeat adolescent pregnancies, and effective service to young men who already are fathers require innovative socioeconomic and educational efforts (Dryfoos, 1994; Group for the Advancement of Psychiatry, 1986), such as the creation of full-service schools, described in Chapter 7, which offer not only quality education but also support services, including health, mental health, family services, recreation, and culture (Dryfoos, 1994).

Because many poor adolescent males may have dropped out of school, full-service community-based programs also may be necessary in some communities. For example, the Children's Aid Society's Adolescent Sexuality and Pregnancy Prevention Program is a holistic, long-term community center-based, multidimensional program for adolescents in the Harlem community of New York. This program has been implemented at three community center sites, and it operates every afternoon and evening during the week and at two of the three sites on weekends. The components of the program include family-life and sex education, academic assessment and help with homework, job clubs and career awareness, mental health services, and self-esteem enhancement through the performing arts. In addition, all program participants—both adolescents and their parents—are guaranteed admission as fully matriculated freshmen at Hunter College of the City University of New York on completion of high school or its equivalent and the recommendation of the program director. Financial aid for college expenses also is available. The features of college admission and financial aid for college provide participants and their families with superordinate goals that may help to offset the lure of teenage fatherhood. An evaluation of the program conducted after 3 years of operation indicated that 59% of the nearly 400 program participants were males. Participants were found to have generated significantly lower pregnancy rates than community adolescents who were not in the program (Carrera, 1992).

Counselors employed in either school- or community-based programs for the needy should remember two important points. First, economically disadvantaged teenage fathers are likely to be engaged in repeat unplanned pregnancies. Therefore, while employing family planning as part of services to prepare adolescent fathers for parenthood (see Chapter 6), it should be emphasized that a second unplanned child increases economic stress and the possibility that the young man's partner will be forced to join the welfare rolls or to remain dependent on welfare if she is already receiving it. Second, educational programs developed for underprivileged teenage fathers should be flexible to allow the fathers to work at their own pace as they juggle the demands of their parenting responsibilities, part-time work, and their studies.

Implications for Public Policy

To better the lives of underprivileged teenage parents and their children, several public policy reforms are suggested. These proposals are intended to effect the following: father involvement in the family, education and job training, reforms in child support enforcement policies, comprehensive case management, and increased benefits and cash assistance.

Promoting Father Involvement in the Family. Currently, welfare policies discourage father involvement and marriage among the poor. Changes in the welfare system are needed to provide young fathers with incentives to fully engage in family life, rather than drive fathers away from their families. In the words of Erickson and Gecas (1991),

> Changes in public policy are needed so that poor fathers who are unemployed or do not earn enough to support their families will not have to choose between leaving their home so their family is eligible for AFDC, or remaining with their family, thereby making them ineligible. . . . Gender-neutral policies are required which provide benefits to any parent who needs to stay home with his/her child. Such a program would allow the most employable person to seek work without jeopardizing the family's social service benefits. (p. 130)

Education and Job Training. Welfare programs could provide both parents with incentives and support services to complete their educations. Moore and Burt (1982) recommended the development of publicly supported job training, apprenticeship, supported work, job readiness, and job search programs for teenage parents. The job training segment of such programs should be focused on occupations that pay significantly above minimum wage, so that earned income is greater than welfare and its associated benefits (Moore & Burt, 1982). Job-training programs for young fathers that have this focus would bolster young mothers' chances of economic self-sufficiency, both by encouraging marriage and increasing child support (Children's Defense Fund, 1986b). For these programs to be of particular benefit to teenage parents, the age for eligibility in many job training programs will have to be lowered. In addition, continuing Medicaid for a year after employment is secured may be necessary to ease the transition from welfare to self-support (Moore & Burt, 1982).

Of course, educational and job training programs will be useless unless teenage parents have access to affordable child care. Most welfare mothers (Mott, 1979) and teenage mothers (Children's Defense Fund, 1987a) cite inadequate child care as the primary barrier to their continued education and their entry into the labor market. Consequently, Moore and Burt (1982) and

Burke (cited in Butts, 1989) recommended that program developers experiment with supplementing welfare support to teenage mothers with child care, on the condition that recipients complete school and/or job training. Child care services could be provided free of charge or made available on a sliding scale (Moore & Burt, 1982). Alternatively, programs could develop training to enable welfare mothers to become in-home day care providers to increase the availability of child care and enhance welfare recipients' sources of nonwelfare income (Moore & Burt, 1982). Moore and Burt (1982) argued that this strategy should pay off in the long run, with fewer additional babies, more education, and more salable skills. The provision of child care services also would lessen the economic burdens of teenage fathers by reducing expenses that they may be required to provide to their partners.

The Children's Defense Fund (1986b) recommended several key elements to work-related programs designed to meet the needs of teenage parents on AFDC. These include the following:

- Individualized assessments to identify barriers to employment
- A range of education, training, and other supportive services to meet diverse needs and a case management system to ensure that teens benefit from the services
- Voluntary participation and choice in the selection of program activities
- Appropriate transitional child care and health care coverage to protect the health and well-being of the children while the parents make the transition to work and self-sufficiency
- Continued follow-up after teens are placed in jobs to ensure that obstacles to employment are eliminated (p. 16)

The Children's Defense Fund emphasized that because most pertinent programs have focused on adolescent mothers dependent on welfare, they have ignored the pressing employment needs of young fathers. The Children's Defense Fund (1986b) warned that a continuation of this practice "may produce perverse results, exacerbating the disincentives to family formation already posed by high rates of joblessness among young men and by the absence in half the states of income support for unemployed two-parent families" (p. 17).

Some states have already developed innovative welfare programs designed to promote education and job training for young women while providing child care services. For example, the Learning, Earning, and Parenting Program (LEAP), a nontraditional welfare program offered in Ohio, pays teenage parents to stay in school. Those who miss no more than 2 school days a month (without a valid excuse) get an extra $62 in their monthly welfare check. Those who do not get docked $62. The bonuses and sanctions can play an important role in a welfare family's income, because a mother with one child typically receives $274 a month. In addition to bonuses, adolescents in the LEAP program also get transportation assistance, child care, and case managers who monitor their students and encourage them to stay in school. A recent evaluation of the program indicated that 61.3% of teenagers already in school continued to attend classes when they were eligible for the LEAP program, but only 51.1% of those in school but not eligible for LEAP persisted with their educations. The gap was even wider for teenagers who had already dropped out. With LEAP, 46.8% came back to school at some point during the year. Without it, only 33.4% resumed their educations (Belsie, 1993).

Government-sponsored programs for young men that are similar to the LEAP program are needed, as are programs for providing teenage fathers with incentives to complete school and remain active with their children. Two innovative service projects for young fathers could be used as models for the development of new programs that promote education and family involvement. The On Track Program, sponsored by the Child Support Enforcement Division of the Marion County Prosecutor's Office of Marion County, Indiana, provides young fathers with financial incentives to participate in their children's lives and in child-rearing classes. Public/Private Venture's Young Unwed Fathers Pilot Project (Achatz & MacAllum, 1994) is designed to promote the earnings and earning potentials of young men, their parenting skills, and their involvement with their children.

Reforms in Child Support Enforcement Policies. Noncustodial adolescent fathers who clearly have the capacity to financially support their child should be required to do so. However, although enforced support payments from teenage fathers may be likely to move some families off welfare temporarily, assistance to many impoverished young fathers to increase their earning capacity through continued schooling or job training might be a wiser investment (Achatz & MacAllum, 1994; Children's Defense Fund, 1986b). Furthermore, instead of chasing after the poor to support the poor, enforcement programs should provide young fathers with reduced support payment requirements in exchange for involvement with one's family, as is the case in the On Track Program. The Children's Defense Fund (1986b) recommended that fathers in school or training programs who have no earned income perhaps be allowed to supplement a token cash contribution with in-kind support, such as clothing, diapers, or baby-sitting, for as long as they are enrolled in the special program and enhancing their future economic stability. This approach is being used with some of the fathers participating in a special program operated in New York City by the YWCA and the Vocational Foundation, Inc., and is funded by the city's human resources administration (Children's Defense Fund, 1986b).

Comprehensive Case Management. One aspect of the LEAP program is that it represents a more holistic approach to welfare service than is traditionally the case. According to the Children's Defense Fund (1986b), programs such as the these, which offer comprehensive case management, are necessary to improve the lives of low-income teenage parents. Moore and Burt (1982) agreed, suggesting that such a transformation in welfare services is necessary to stem the tide of teenage pregnancy and parenthood among the poor. Moore and Burt recommended using welfare offices as sites to offer low-cost services to potential and current teenage parents, such as preventive services to welfare recipients, including prevention of first births, by working with welfare families who have teenage children. They also recommended that welfare programs could help to prevent subsequent births by providing services directly to teenage mothers who receive welfare. Prevention could also be enhanced by extending these same services to the male partners of teenage mothers.

Moore and Burt (1982) recommended a host of other ideas to holistically serve teenage parents. Signs offering adoption counseling and referral might encourage expectant teenage parents who did not perceive adoption as an option. Educational material on children that is in the waiting room and/or is enclosed monthly along with welfare checks could be tried. Designating one or more caseworkers as teenage parent specialists could also facilitate service delivery as well as group discussions, field trips, and information sharing.

The idea of comprehensive case management for pregnant and parenting teenagers was adopted in California in 1985 through the initiation of the California Adolescent Family Life Program. Funded by the California state government, this program employs case managers who assist pregnant adolescents and teenage mothers in securing a wide range of educational, employment, health, and psychosocial services. In a recent evaluation of the program, Rounds, Weil, and Thiel (1992) reported that preliminary data indicate that the case managers generally have been successful in linking clients to the majority of their needed services.

Although government-sponsored comprehensive case management services for teenage fathers are rare, the results of the Maine Young Fathers Project (Brown, 1990) for fathers ages 15 to 25 demonstrate that comprehensive case management holds considerable promise for enhancing the lives of socioeconomically deprived teenage fathers. In brief, the case managers from the Maine project helped their clients, most of whom had low-income backgrounds, to increase their use of a variety of services to effect positive educational, work, and family experiences. Brown (1990) concluded that several key features to the successful case management strategies were used in the Maine Young Fathers Project. A Goal Attainment Scaling System, used to assess client needs, develop case plans, and monitor client progress, was considered to be "the backbone of the case management service system" (Brown, 1990, p. 86). Linkage agreements were another essential feature because they ensured that the fathers could access services through referrals made by the case managers. Public policies to promote the implementation of similar comprehensive case management strategies are needed.

Increased Benefits and Cash Assistance. Four other policy changes discussed in the literature call for increased benefits and cash assistance to destitute teenage parents. First, Edelin (cited in Butts, 1989) argued in favor of Medicaid funding for abortions so that poor women will no longer be locked out from considering abortion as an option. Second, Butts (1989) criticized the federal policy maintaining a standard, nationwide cut-off point for establishing that a family's income is at or below the poverty level. This practice ignores regional differences in the relative cost of living. Butts (1989) recommended that adjustments should be made for the relative cost of living (Butts, 1989). Third, because AFDC benefits in most states are so low that they fail to provide even a minimum level of subsistence, cash assistance to young families must be increased. Fourth, many full-time workers with two children earn an income equal to only 75% of the poverty level. Therefore, supplemental assistance should be available to young employed parents who can be considered among our nation's "working poor" (Children's Defense Fund, 1986b).

Securing Funding and Effecting Changes in Public Policy. Developing full-service programs that prevent unplanned teenage parenthood and serve existing teenage parents is an expensive proposition, whether they are school- or community-based. Dryfoos (1994) reported that school-based health and social service programs cost between $100,000 and $300,000 a year depending on the size of the school and the comprehensiveness of the program. Obviously, such programs require significant and multiple sources of funding. However, most practitioners encounter a range of difficulties associated with identifying potential sources of funding, meeting the varying eligibility requirements for funding, and remaining fully accountable to funding sources for expenditures. These obstacles discourage many would-be program developers from getting their ideas off the ground.

Overcoming these impediments demands that program developers have expertise about funding resources. The reader is referred to Chapter 3 for pertinent recommendations regarding this issue.

In addition to understanding and using sources of funding, counselors hoping to make a difference in the lives of disadvantaged teenage fathers must be willing to become activists for policy change. Although it is beyond the scope of this book to review political activist strategies, the reader is referred to Dryfoos (1994) for her extensive recommendations for political action at the local, state, and federal level to improve the life circumstances of our nation's economically underprivileged youth.

Teenage Fathers From the Upper Class

Teenage fathers come from all socioeconomic strata. Yet very little attention has been devoted to the study of teenage fathers from the upper class. The scarce literature on this population suggests that upper-class fathers, compared to lower-class fathers, receive greater amounts of economic assistance from their families (Alan Guttmacher Institute, 1981) and are more likely to marry (Furstenberg, 1976), live with their child (Marsiglio, 1987), and experience marital stability (Furstenberg, 1976). Clearly, more research is needed to identify and describe the paternity issues and experiences of upper-class teenage fathers.

One disturbing implication of the lack of research on upper-class teenage fathers is that professionals may view this population, by virtue of their higher status in society, as not requiring the assistance of counseling. Although it is true that young fathers from the upper classes may be spared many of the life hardships endured by fathers from the lower classes, advantaged teenage fathers are similar to their less advantaged counterparts in that both may experience emotional difficulties associated with resolving the unplanned pregnancy and negotiating the transition to parenthood during one's teenage years. In addition, upper-class teenage fathers are probably more prone to experiencing social condemnation for their role in an unplanned pregnancy. Furthermore, clinical experience suggests that adolescent boys from well-to-do communities tend to have very high career aspirations and expectations and well-defined plans for attending college. A premarital pregnancy triggers a career developmental crisis for these youth and a dilemma for the family. In sum, the pregnancy is the precipitant of significant emotional turmoil.

Because advantaged teenage fathers are less likely than their disadvantaged counterparts to experience financial difficulties, less emphasis may be needed in the way of responding to practical needs. Consequently, more energy can be placed on preparing the young man for fatherhood, addressing the impact of the pregnancy on the family, providing the young father with emotional support, teaching tactics for responding to and coping with social condemnation, and adjusting educational and career plans to accommodate for the demands of fatherhood.

Religiosity

Because religious institutions traditionally set standards for appropriate sexual conduct and for resolving unplanned pregnancies, it is reasonable to assume that religiosity might influence the sexual behavior of adolescents. Limited support for these hypotheses has been generated by correlational research on the subject. Among adolescents, low religiosity is associated with earlier initiation of sexual activity for both sexes (see Chilman, 1983). Adolescent girls who express a religious affiliation are less likely to become single parents than unaffiliated adolescent girls (Abrahamse et al., 1988). Rates of single parenthood are lowest for adolescent girls who describe themselves as being "very religious" (Abrahamse et al., 1988).

Other research findings have indicated that religiosity may affect the decision making of adolescents responsible for a premarital conception. Compared to adolescent males with nonfundamentalist religious beliefs, fundamentalist teenage boys are less likely to favor abortion as a means to resolve a pregnancy (Marsiglio & Shehan, 1993). Results of Marsiglio's (1987) analysis of a national survey of youth demonstrated that among teenage fathers who had been responsible for a nonmaritally conceived child, those who had been raised according to the teachings of the Catholic church were significantly more likely than non-Catholic fathers to live with their children and marry their partners.

Abrahamse et al. (1988) suggested that religiosity may affect single childbearing rates in ways that differ from one individual to another. For some young people, religious commitment may delay the initiation of sex or reduce the prevalence of premarital intercourse. For others, it may discourage the use of effective methods of contraception. For still others, it proscribes abortion as a means of resolving a premarital pregnancy. In other instances, religiosity may simply prohibit childbearing outside of marriage (Abrahamse et al., 1988).

Consistent with these suggestions, Marciano (1991) argued that the relationship between religious values and abortion is complex and not straightforward. It is reasonable to assume that strong religious orthodoxies (e.g., Roman Catholic, Mormon) would inhibit the use of abortion. Research findings have indicated that there is a negative association between religiosity and the probability of abortion among those experiencing a premarital pregnancy (e.g., Moore & Caldwell, 1977). High religiosity also is associated with more negative attitudes toward abortion (Marsiglio & Shehan, 1993; Moore & Burt, 1982). Yet, Marciano noted, very high numbers of Catholic and Mormon women seek and have abortions. Furthermore, she commented that despite the strong emphasis on chastity in each of those faiths, premarital sex and unwanted pregnancy obviously occur in noticeable numbers.

> What religion may "cause," therefore, is not necessarily a reduced likelihood of abortion. Rather, the abortion findings speak more of how certain orthodoxies inhibit contraceptive preparedness, and less about how religious belief influences the decision taken in unwanted or unplanned pregnancy. (Marciano, 1991, p. 140)

Thus, it cannot be assumed that religious affiliations necessarily guide the decisions of youth involved in an out-of-wedlock pregnancy. In addition, it should not be surmised that a teenage father who expresses affiliation with a particular religion adheres to the values of that religion (e.g., if Catholic, then he is opposed to abortion). There is no way to know, simply by identifying a father's faith group, which values he accepts, which he practices, and which he ignores. Furthermore, "the outcomes of religious beliefs for fatherhood may be less a matter of a denomination's action upon a man, than the man's consent to the denomination's teachings" (Marciano, 1991, p. 145).

Even if an adolescent father has a clear religious orientation, he may not necessarily rely on his religious convictions during the emotionally charged crisis of an unplanned out-of-wedlock pregnancy. Although the young man typically may make decisions based, in part, on his religious beliefs, customs, and values, during the crisis of an unplanned pregnancy he and his partner may be ruled by emotion and temporarily forsake their religious convictions, only to regret this course of action later.

These considerations demand that counselors investigate the religious background and degree of spiritual conviction of the teenage father, identify and evaluate church-based services that he might use, and use the religious faith of the client as a source of strength and religious resources as tools in counseling. In addition, counselors must mediate religious value conflicts between teenage parents, address religious-based reactions to participation to abortion, and recognize how some religious beliefs could be a source of danger. Each of these subjects are discussed in turn.

Exploring Religiosity

If a young man expresses an affiliation with a particular religion, then it will be necessary to explore the extent to which he abides by its teachings. When religion is central to a young man's life, the counselor should discuss with him the religious implication of every major decision regarding the resolution of the pregnancy and the rearing of his child. Even if he as an individual is not very religious, the counselor should inquire about the religious values of his and his partner's family. Specifically, the father should be asked, "What role should the religious convictions of your family and that of your partner's families play in your decision making?" Ignoring this question could result in the father making a decision that clashes with the values of either family involved and could set the stage for a major conflict that might have been avoided.

Identifying Church-Based Services

Another reason for exploring the religious affiliations of the young father and his partner is to determine if his or her church may be a source of support to either parent at some point during the prenatal of postnatal period. Ministers can offer spiritual guidance to a young confused couple struggling with an unplanned pregnancy. Some churches sponsor Mentor Mother or Mentor Father programs through which older parents offer guidance on pregnancy and parenthood for young expectant parents. Other churches provide quality child care services to their members either free of charge or at below-market rates. A common practice of churches is to have food, clothing, and diaper drives for young families in need. Many ministers are trained to counsel their members on relationship problems or can refer young couples with relationship issues to competent counseling professionals in the community who have established a good working relationship with the church.

Besides these church-based services, sex education for youth is becoming more commonplace in churches and church-affiliated schools. Scales (1981) described several church-based sex education programs. The Roman Catholic church has developed a curriculum titled *The Benziger Family Life Program,* which is used for Grades 1 through 8, and features an accompanying parent's guide. The United Methodist Church is involved in training ministers and lay leaders in running sex education discussions. The United Church of Christ publishes periodicals addressing the subjects of sexuality and teenage pregnancy and has conducted the Neighbors in Need project, in which funds were granted to local organizations attempting to combat unplanned teenage pregnancy. The Synagogue Council of America, an umbrella organization that coordinates several groups of Jewish congregations, sponsors the publication and distribution of educational materials on love, sex, and marriage from a Jewish point of view. The Unitarian Universalist church has produced a multimedia presentation titled *About Your Sexuality,* a sex education program designed for use with junior and senior high school-age youth and their parents (Scales, 1981).

Evaluating Church-Based Services

As a broker of services for teenage parents, counselors are challenged to learn about the range of church-affiliated services for teenage parents. In addition, counselors must develop a sense of the quality of these services and their potential impact on the young parents who use them.

Teenagers responsible for out-of-wedlock pregnancies experience varied reactions from church congregations and ministers. Clinical experience suggests that church communities typically are sources of acceptance, support, and comfort that offer highly competent services to teenage parents. For example, in one parish, a compassionate priest helped two warring families to negotiate their differences for the sake of the adolescent parents, provided the young father with a lead on a job, recruited caring parish members to assist the couple in raising the child, and arranged for tutoring services so that both parents could continue their studies. In addition, the priest placed both parents in charge of responsibilities in the church to help them feel like an active, contributing presence in the parish community. In other cases, however, adolescent parents and their families have been viewed as sinners and treated with scorn and rejection, or they have been inadvertently harmed by ministers practicing services beyond their official competencies. For example, one young couple decided to seek spiritual guidance from their minister in resolving a premarital pregnancy. The minister's response was to call the couple up to the alter during a Sunday service and ask the congregation to pray that the couple be healed from their "sexual addiction." Subsequent to this service, the couple and their families were shunned by the majority of the church community. This treatment caused the couple considerable heartache because this church had been central to their spiritual and social lives. In another instance, a young man went to his pastor for counseling because he was depressed and suicidal about his girlfriend's pregnancy and her parents' refusal to allow him to see her. Instead of referring the expectant father to a competent professional helper, the pastor counseled the boy over a 3-week period, during which he dismissed the client's depression as "utter nonsense" and scolded the boy for not being a stronger person.

These case vignettes demonstrate the potential harm or good that can result from the reactions of clergy and church communities to unwed teenagers dealing with unplanned pregnancy and parenthood. Mental health professionals must have a feel for how various churches are likely to respond to childbearing teenage men and women, share this information with teenage parents so that they can anticipate how they might be treated, and discuss with their clients the extent to which they want to involve the church in their pregnancy and parenthood experience.

Using Faith as a Source of Strength

When discussions about religiosity and church-based services reveal that the young father has strong religious convictions, his faith can be used as a source of strength in counseling. A strong faith can help a young man make sense of the pain that is often associated with adolescent parenthood. Therefore, counselors may wish to provide religious explanations for hardship to a young man who is high in religiosity. Moreover, because many religions, such as Judaism, Mormonism, Roman Catholicism, and Islam, accord power to fathers as the heads of their families (Marciano, 1991), the religious teenage father can reestablish order and direction in his life after the throes of the crisis pregnancy by taking his valued position as the head of his new family.

Religious Resources on Counseling

Many counselors prefer to leave the actual process of spiritual counseling with teenage parents to a priest or minister. However, other counselors, who have strong religious convictions and qualifications for providing spiritual guidance, may wish to conduct spiritual counseling with teenage parents during the crisis pregnancy.

Several resources can assist counselors who are motivated and qualified to address spiritual matters with teenage parents. Parrott's (1993) article on counseling adolescents from a Christian perspective is a recommended first reading for the novice on the subject. Worthington's (1987) book, *Counseling for Unplanned Pregnancy and Infertility,* contains in-depth coverage of a Christian approach to crisis counseling for unplanned pregnancies. Books by Mannion (1986) and Crawford and Mannion (1989) include strategies for promoting psychospiritual healing among individuals whose lives have been affected by abortion. Chapin's (1991) moving work, *Within the Shadow,* is an inspirational resource counselors can consult for a biblical look at suffering and the process of grieving, which might be of help to religiously oriented young fathers who have experienced emotional hardships during either the pregnancy-resolution period or the transition to fatherhood.

Addressing Religious Value Conflicts

The process of evaluating the religiosity of teenage parents permits the counselor to assess the compatibility of values held by the young expectant parents. When the parents agree on the same religion and use the teachings of that faith in guiding their decision making, their relationship will likely be free of value conflicts. In addition, as has been demonstrated through research conducted by Hoge, Petrillo, and Smith (1982), when young parents agree on religion and have a good relationship with their children, the transmission of values to their children is enhanced. Thus, the common values of a couple can provide direction during the crisis pregnancy and help the parents give their children clear messages about the values they want their child to adopt. The couple that disagrees about values, however, is likely to experience conflicts pertaining to such issues as abortion. Furthermore, if the parents disagree on which values they want to teach their children, the children may be uncertain of their values and they may internalize their parents' hostility.

Shapiro (1987) offered the following advice to couples from different religious backgrounds who disagree about what values and traditions to pass on to the child:

> The most important thing to discuss is how strong your feelings are about religious practices. In my clinical practice, I saw a Jewish man married to a Protestant woman, and they were having difficulty over his strong desire to have any male child circumcised. She felt that the practice was brutal, unnecessary, and a form of mutilation. It was only when he revealed that he could not identify with a son who was different from himself that she was able to listen to the emotional importance of the circumcision for her husband. (p. 262)

Contributing to value conflicts during the pregnancy resolution period are the differential socialization histories of males and females in our society. According to Marciano (1991), males have been socialized to reject external authority when it contradicts their personal goals or desires. Consequently, some males may be more likely than their partners to forsake traditional religious considerations and be intolerant of a partner who cannot do the same. In these situations, the role of the counselor, once again, is to try to help the young father recognize how central traditional religious values may be to the mother's identity and self-esteem.

Whether or not a teenage father follows the teachings of a particular religion, the young man should be made aware of the critical role fathers play in shaping the values of their children, particularly their daughters (see Whitbeck & Gecas, 1988). Even when they are not conscious that they are doing so, fathers socialize their children to adhere to certain values deemed important by the father. Given the potential influence he may have on his child's value system, the young father needs to clarify and evaluate his own values and consider which values he intends to teach his child.

Addressing Reactions to Abortion

The participation in an adolescent mother's decision to have an abortion can prompt intense psychic conflict for a highly religious male. A father who is affiliated with a religion, such as Catholicism, that counsels against or condemns premarital sex and abortion, but who nevertheless supports his partner in having an abortion, may need to feel some type of meaningful punishment as a means of penitence for his actions. It is believed that the religious young man views such penance as atonement for having committed a sin (Marciano, 1991). For example, one adolescent male had accompanied his girlfriend to an abortion clinic, paid for the procedure, and never told his or his partner's parents. Because the young man was a member of a fundamentalist Protestant church and a family that opposed premarital sex and abortion, he felt considerable guilt over his actions. He made reparations for his "sins" by deciding to be more respectful of his parents' rules regarding curfews that he previously had opposed and ignored and by volunteering at a shelter for homeless families. In his mind, he had made amends through these measures and, consequently, felt better about himself afterward. Similar coping mechanisms were observed by Shostak (1979) in his study of men who had accompanied their partners to abortion clinics. Based on such findings, Marciano (1991) suggested that a "penitential" approach may help some young men participating in an abortion to cope with their feelings of having violated religious doctrines.

Potential Problems of Religious Beliefs

Marciano (1991) noted that there are dangers of abuse of power when a father uses religious grounds to justify authoritarian rule as the leader of the family. Such fathers need to be reminded that rigid, abrasive rule of the family can undermine its health, that authority must be guided by love and not become a compensation for low self-esteem and other inadequacies.

Another pertinent issue discussed by Marciano (1991) is that religion may "justify" a refusal by a father or other family member to participate in family therapy, on the grounds that religion has provided the "answer" and none other is needed. "No religion, however, is tolerant of the absence of charity toward strangers, let alone loved ones, and a therapeutic reply to religious resistance could use religious beliefs themselves as a starting point for counterbalancing religion-based resistance to help" (Marciano, 1991, pp. 156-157).

Urban and Rural Environments

Living environments are classified as either urban or rural. According to Tischler (1990), an urban environment is "an area that contains a central city and the continuously built-up and closely settled surrounding territory that together have a population of 50,000 or more" (p. 562). By comparison, a rural environment is a less densely populated area consisting of small towns interspersed among farmlands and wilderness regions.

Urban and rural environments differentially influence how fatherhood is defined and how parents raise their children. Typically, researchers interested in studying teenage fathers have turned to the inner cities because of the prospect of finding large concentrations of young fathers. Consequently, teenage fatherhood in rural areas is a largely unexplored subject. Nevertheless, teenage pregnancy and parenthood do occur in rural America, posing challenges to young expectant parents that are similar to, and yet distinct from, those of adolescent parents in urban areas. These cultural variations are reviewed, beginning with a discussion of the urban teenage father experience. In considering both environments, counselors must move beyond common stereotypes regarding urban and rural living. As will be demonstrated, there is a tendency to simplistically view inner-city environments as hopeless, valueless wastelands and rural environments as ideal, carefree oases.

Urban Teenage Fatherhood

Much of the literature on teenage fathers has been focused on describing the pitiful conditions of urban environments and how those conditions play a contributory role in the path to unplanned fatherhood for adolescent males. This literature has served the significant function of raising awareness among helping professionals and policymakers about the hardships of urban living for teenage boys and, subsequently, of prompting the development of inner-city outreach programs designed to prevent unplanned fatherhood and assist adolescent males who already are fathers.

Although the value of this literature should not be overlooked, it is necessary to note that there are many positive aspects to the urban communities in which adolescent fathers reside. Understanding these desirable features can direct counselors to identify and use existing strengths in inner-city neighborhoods. Accordingly, this section begins with a balanced discussion of urban environments by highlighting both the advantages and disadvantages of urban living.

Advantages and Disadvantages of Urban Life

DeFrain, LeMasters, and Schroff (1991) argued that although the city "has been portrayed as depraved center of evil" (p. 169), there are many positive aspects of urban environments. People residing in cities live in relatively close proximity with families of diverse racial, social, ethnic, and religious backgrounds. Multicultural interactions can facilitate a relatively more tolerant atmosphere for cultural differences. Cities also tend to have a broader range of services and activities available in a very circumscribed geographical area than is the case in rural areas. Therefore, urban dwellers tend to have access to services when they need them (DeFrain et al., 1991).

In 1991, I chronicled how inner-city youth and families in Newark, New Jersey, adopted to urban life in a way that enriched even the depressing aspects of the city environment. I described how children, through imagination and creativity, conceived of and used rubble-strewn lots as playgrounds where they frolicked with companions. I also observed how churches represented oases of hope and community in seemingly decaying communities. Finally, I marveled at the diversity and richness of foods, music, mannerisms, customs, and dances that were representative of the different cultural populations who inhabited the many neighborhoods of Newark (Kiselica, 1991).

Sullivan (1989) commented on some of the affirmative qualities of three Brooklyn, New York neighborhoods—one primarily Anglo American, the second predominantly African American, and the third largely Hispanic American—in which a high number of adolescent fathers resided. Characteristics common to all three neighborhoods included a strong desire of the fathers to find formal employment, emotional and financial support from parents and extended family members, and a community belief that it is honorable for a man to support his partner and child.

These considerations indicate that cities are complex environments in which many uplifting experiences occur; nevertheless, the many problems endemic to urban environments should not be ignored. Urban children are likely to be exposed to a culturally diverse population of people and, therefore, a wide range of values that could cause them to question the values of their parents (DeFrain et al., 1991). Urban youth also may be subject to greater peer influences regarding values formation than is the case with youth in rural areas (DeFrain et al., 1991; Freeman, 1989). The readily accessible forms of media available in urban areas may challenge family values further (DeFrain et al., 1991; Freeman, 1989). These challenges to the value system of the family may threaten some parents and could contribute to value conflicts between generations within families.

When values conflicts regarding sexual expression occur between urban parents and their children, the parents may feel overwhelmed as to how to prevent a child from participating in a teenage pregnancy. One traditional preventive measure is for the parents to carefully scrutinize the free time of their children. However, because many inner-city parents work long hours, have long commutes, or care for younger children, these parents typically are unable to provide the kind of direct supervision that wards off unplanned pregnancies. Although many of these parents may hope to resolve this dilemma by expecting the schools to provide their children with skills for dealing with pressures to engage in premarital sex, it appears that most sexually active inner-city youth are likely to report poor use of contraception (Vera Institute of Justice, 1990).

Other salient problems for a substantial number of city-dwelling youth include underemployment and unemployment. Relatively well-paying, blue-collar jobs that once sustained inner-city communities are disappearing. The effects of this economic erosion is that more and more urban adolescent fathers have significant periods of unemployment and irregular employment (Sullivan, 1989). In their study of adolescent fathers in Baltimore, Hardy and Zabin (1991) reported that the majority of these fathers suffered serious degrees of socioeconomic disadvantage, with little hope of major improvement unless substantial job training and placement efforts were to become available to them. "This social disadvantage seemed in most instances to have been an antecedent and concomitant rather than a direct consequence of premature parenthood" (Hardy & Zabin, 1991, p. 111). These economic disadvantages made it difficult for most of the fathers to establish stable families and financially support their children. The same was true for most of the urban-dwelling fathers studied by Achatz and MacAllum (1994), Brown (1990), and Sullivan (1989).

Alarming numbers of city youth fill their idle hours by "hanging out" in the streets, often turning to illegal drug use as a way to pass the time (Freeman, 1989; Sullivan, 1989). Many of the urban fathers studied by Sullivan (1989) and Achatz and MacAllum (1994) were involved in exploratory economic crimes, such as selling marijuana. The blocked access to employment for some of these youth led to more sustained and prevalent involvement in intensive criminal activities and periods of probation and incarceration.

Freeman (1989) discussed the interaction of peer group values and depressed economic circumstances in the route to unplanned adolescent fatherhood. Freeman reported that counselors working with inner-city youth are noting greater peer-generated pressures to engage in unprotected sex. She hypothesized that parenthood is a means for some urban males to express their "maturity" in an environment that lacks many of the other socially accepted vehicles to adulthood status, such as finding a job. The poor who live in central city ghettos are subject to the range of stressful problems characteristic of urban decay, including crowding, violence, alcohol and drugs, and homelessness. Consider, for example, this teenage father's account of his inner-city neighborhood that he shared during a counseling session:

> Man it's crazy out there! People be runnin' the streets and sellin' dope at all hours of the night, strapped with guns and ready to tear somebody up over nothin'. Some jokers'll drive right up to your house and shoot the place up just because they think you *mightta'* dissed [disrespected] 'em about somethin'.

Such conditions may place added pressures on adolescent males to find some way to "get ahead" in life. Fatherhood may represent one way that a young man can exert control in a highly unpredictable environment.

Implications for Counseling

Because so many of the young fathers in urban areas are from lower socioeconomic levels, the pertinent counseling considerations described earlier in this chapter apply to inner-city youth. Additional recommendations are offered here. These include the following: challenging ethnocentric interpretations of inner-city life, designing programs to serve culturally diverse populations, intervening with peer groups, and addressing intergenerational values conflicts.

Challenging Ethnocentric Interpretations of Inner-City Life. Life in the city may need to be viewed more complexly by some counselors in order for them to consider working in inner-city regions. Because some counselors hold the simplistic, stereotypic belief that urban zones are nothing more than desolate, ruthless environments, they avoid considering working in the city, choosing instead to counsel in the relative comfort of suburban areas. Many other counselors, who are employed in metropolitan regions, still miss out on enjoying the beautiful qualities remaining in those locales because they view neighborhoods near their work sites from the culturally encapsulated perspective of the middle class. Such counselors may need to broader this perspective to more fully appreciate the existing positive features of inner-city environs. This issue is illustrated by my (Kiselica, 1991) description of how a multicultural internship experience helped me to confront my ethnocentric interpretations of Newark, New Jersey:

> My new experiential understanding of my clients served as a dramatic contrast to the images I had carried with me since childhood. Each day as I commuted in and out of the city, my old unidimensional pictures of the environment yielded to new multidimensional perceptions. Scenes of the city, once only heart-rending, were now also heartening to me. . . . Although I continued to be repelled by the decay of the city and I still observed the troubles of its residents, I was also enlivened by the diversity and vitality of its people and their cultures.
>
> As I reflect on this reappraisal process, I now realize that my internship experiences were causing me to challenge my own unique view of the world. My initial view of the city had been influenced by my perspective as a middle-class White—as an outsider and a passerby who previously had a very limited perspective of life in the inner city. . . . I had been culturally encapsulated, limited in my perceptions by my middle-class interpretations of what I had seen. By challenging my ethnocentrism, I had taken a critical step in growing as a multicultural counselor. (p. 129)

Designing Programs to Serve Culturally Diverse Populations. Because there tends to be great cultural diversity in urban environments, inner-city fatherhood programs may need to be responsive to heterogeneous groups of teenage fathers. For example, it may be necessary to recruit culturally diverse adult male mentors for fatherhood training courses. Also, because there may be many instances in which the mental health professional finds his or her cultural background to be very different from that of the teenage father, a thorough understanding of the culture-specific recommendations suggested throughout Part II of this book is paramount.

Intervening With Peer Groups. To prevent repeat unplanned pregnancies, both urban teenage fathers and the peers with whom they associate need structured programs to fill their free time with purposeful activities that serve as alternatives to high-risk sexual encounters. According to Dryfoos (1994), one remedy is the provision of optional year-round public school programs. Such programs will not only give inner-city youth alternatives to "hanging out in the streets," but they also will accord some peace of mind to overworked parents who are unable to furnish personal supervision of their children. Counselors can lobby school boards and educational personnel to make the paradigmatic changes that are necessary to more adequately meet the multifarious needs of youth residing in our nation's cities.

Besides providing meaningful activities to adolescent males, Freeman (1989) argued that efforts to change the sexuality of young urban men must target the macho, sexually irresponsible image of men that is portrayed through the media messages that bombard urban youth. Although Freeman offered no specific antidotes for this particular problem, it is suggested here that destructive images portrayed in the media might be countered through the good will of positive adult male role models who talk with young fathers about their views on sexuality and personal values.

Addressing Intergenerational Values Conflicts. Teenage fathers in urban areas are likely to have intercultural contact that could prompt the questioning of family values. Therefore, counselors working with these fathers need to be skilled in negotiating intergenerational values conflicts. Counselors must be clear of their own values before mediating the values conflicts of others. Otherwise, the potential exists that counselors will not recognize values clashes when they occur and may inadvertently take sides and impose their own values on culturally different clients during family counseling sessions. For example, an elderly Hispanic couple from a culturally diverse neighborhood in Trenton, New Jersey, brought their youngest son in for counseling because he was against marrying his girlfriend who was pregnant with his child. The counselor, a traditional Anglo American female, sided with the parents, viewed the young man as an emerging delinquent, and began employing highly confrontive counseling designed to "help the boy to recognize and accept his responsibility." Unfortunately, in interpreting the struggle this youth had with his parents, the counselor had failed to consider the cultural context of the inner-city neighborhood in which the boy was raised. His parents were natives of Puerto Rico who held the traditional Hispanic view that an unplanned out-of-wedlock pregnancy should be resolved through marriage. However, the son grew up observing many other younger and destitute Hispanic and African American couples who were comfortable with single-parent arrangements. As a result, he saw no problem in fathering an out-of-wedlock child because "nearly everybody else around me does it nowadays." When the counselor was encouraged by her supervisor to conceive the boy's attitude from this contextual perspective, she was able to shift her counseling focus away from "rehabilitating a deviant" to helping the family resolve their intergenerational values conflict. Without taking sides, the counselor helped both parties to understand the other's perspective and gradually helped them achieve a compromise on the matter; the boy did not marry his girlfriend but he agreed to religiously provide financial support to her and maintain an ongoing relationship with his child.

Rural Teenage Fatherhood

According to DeFrain et al. (1991), Americans have an idyllic vision of life in the country, especially farm life. However, although rural environments have many positive features, the hardships of rural living can be highly stressful. Rural fatherhood must be understood in the context of the complexity of rural life. This includes appreciating the advantages and disadvantages of life in rural areas and the economic and social crises of rural America.

Advantages and Disadvantages of Rural Life

There are many advantages to country living. In rural settings, limited life experiences may help to maintain the distinct values of the family. Because rural families reside in culturally isolated enclaves, they are less likely than urban children to be influenced by the values of different cultures. Also, compared to urban youth, rural adolescents are exposed to a smaller peer group. Consequently, in rural areas, parents may exert greater influence than adolescent peer groups on the formation of values. Another asset of rural living is that the chores required of farm children provide structure for children's free time and instill children with a strong work ethic and a sense of self-sufficiency. Finally, familiarity with one's neighbors provides a sense of community and belonging (DeFrain et al., 1991).

Other characteristics of rural environments are less desirable. Because rural children live in isolated racial, social, ethnic, and religious enclaves, they may be less prepared to deal successfully with the wide variety of people represented in our multicultural society. Combined with fundamentalist thinking, the cultural encapsulation of rural life can breed intolerance of the culturally different. The physical isolation of rural environments often means that there are fewer recreational activities and social services, and the distance between existing services is often so great that rural inhabitants have difficulties accessing services. Rural farm families also experience less time for leisure due to the numerous responsibilities associated with the maintenance of a farm. Many farm mothers and fathers must work second part-time jobs to supplement the unstable and usually insufficient wages provided by the farm income. Consequently, their children may lack adult supervision and sufficient contact with their parents (DeFrain et al., 1991).

The lack of adult supervision can provide adolescents with ample opportunities to experiment with and engage in sexual relations. For example, several rural teenagers have confessed to me that they have "done it" in the barn or in the woods while their parents were at work.

Even when rural parents think that they are aware of their children's whereabouts, it is easy for sexually curious adolescents to deceive their parents and find private places for sexual encounters. For example, one young father told me about a ruse he and his girlfriend had concocted to fool their respective parents about their plans for a date one night. The couple had told their parents that they were going to the movies. Instead of driving to the theater, however, they drove to a remote cornfield, where they parked in the darkness and began "to make out." "One thing led to another" and the couple's first child was conceived that night in the car.

In small communities like the one in which this incident occurred, personal problems, such as an unplanned adolescent pregnancy, can quickly and easily become everyone else's business. Thus, the close-knit atmosphere of the small town can become intrusively disturbing during times of private crisis.

Economic and Social Crises of Rural America

The family farm is a dying way of life in this country. Since 1930, the percentage of the total United States population living on a farm declined from 25% to less than 3%. This dramatic reduction in the farm population was due to a series of economic catastrophes in the agricultural sector that forced many rural families off their farms and has left most remaining farm families in serious financial difficulty (DeFrain et al., 1991).

The exodus from farm life has tragic consequences for families who know no other form of existence. Many rural families mourn the loss of a sacred way of being, their special attachments to the land, crops, and animals, and their deeply valued self-sufficiency. This sentiment is captured in a statement made by a man who lost his farm due to involuntary foreclosure:

My family went back four generations on this piece of land. Farming wasn't a job; it was a way of life. I couldn't go to the auction. I couldn't see it all being taken. I feel like such a failure. (Hughey, Heppner, Johnston, & Rakes, 1989, p. 475)

Because formal education historically has not been highly valued by farm families— engaging in physical labor and managing animals is deemed more important than textbook learning or handling people—they typically are ill prepared to deal with the transition to other careers and ways of life. In effect, families forced to leave the farm can be considered "rural refugees" (DeFrain et al., 1991, p. 177) whose lives are often fraught with anger and despair.

Those families who have managed to survive on the farm tend to live with an impending sense of doom. Their surrounding towns are shrinking as supporting businesses fold, schools consolidate, and hospitals and other vital service centers find it necessary to close their doors or cut back on services. As parents devote more of their physical and psychological energy to economic survival, the emotional needs of the family can be put on the back burner (DeFrain et al., 1991).

Many of the emotional difficulties of farm families are also experienced by nonfarming families and communities in rural areas. One third of the nation's students live in rural communities (Liontos, 1992). Although it is true that some rural communities are thriving, many struggle to survive in the face of the economic and social hardships described above (Helge, 1990).

Implications for Counseling

Culturally sensitive counseling considerations with rural teenage fathers pertain to outreach efforts, the counseling process, the pregnancy resolution phase, and marital counseling.

Outreach Considerations. Teenage pregnancy and parenthood can represent a significant added stressor to families endeavoring to cope with the crises of rural America. Yet because rural Americans tend to be self-reliant and independent, they are unlikely to turn to counselors for assistance during times of crisis (DeFrain et al., 1991; Hughey et al., 1989). Thus, particular forms of outreach are necessary to engage rural families in counseling. For example, because rural Americans have a strong work ethic but face widespread economic difficulties, some rural teenage fathers are likely to be engaged in counseling through programs that have a career counseling emphasis. Others may be engaged by capitalizing on the rural value that "neighbors help their neighbors" and the tendency of rural community members to listen to their peers. Thus, teenage parenting programs in rural areas can employ community members to conduct outreach to families of teenage parents. Another potentially effective outreach strategy is to offer teenage parenting programs through the Cooperative Extension Service. Due to its long tradition of providing counseling, education, mediation, and farm crisis workshops to farm families, the Cooperative Extension Service is likely to be trusted and accepted by rural families as a place where adolescent parents can receive help.

Extending services to rural families in sparsely populated areas presents particular difficulties due to the low tax bases for funding services and the great expanses of land that exist between central service areas. Developers of adolescent parenting programs in such areas can borrow strategies from professionals in the rural mental health fields to reach isolated populations, such as the opening of part-time satellite offices in churches or schools throughout geographically large counties and using airplanes to shuttle staff to and from those satellite sites. Obviously, the provision of these services depends on adequate funding, so program developers will have to become well acquainted with the grant procurement procedures reviewed in Chapter 3. Brown (1990) reported that formal linkage agreements between service agencies facilitated the use of services by young fathers living in remote regions of Maine.

In addition to these formal measures, program developers might try piecing together the necessary services for teenage parenting programs by forging informal cooperative ventures between school districts. For example, school counselors throughout the massive region of Aroostook County, Maine have an unofficial policy of combining resources among school districts to more adequately serve students from different school districts. One illustration is a multischool approach to providing a comprehensive career awareness night. One school may serve as the host site for the event. Two other schools from remote distances from the site school may provide buses that pick up and drop off students from a number of school districts. Still other schools may take on the responsibility for calling and making arrangements with guest speakers. By cooperating in this manner, schools can minimize expenses and provide the type of quality service that might not be possible when one school attempts to offer the service on its own. Liontos (1992) recommended that the entire community—social agencies, businesses, civic and volunteer organizations, police, churches, and the justice system—all combine their resources in a similar manner to overcome the problems of scarce resources and isolation in rural areas.

Counseling Process Issues. Before counseling is initiated, careful consideration must be given to the prospect of cross-cultural, counselor/client dyads. Because highly isolated areas may breed inflexible cultural encapsulation, many clients are likely to be in the first stage of racial identity development, regardless of the client's race. As was mentioned in the earlier chapters of Part II of this book, clients in the first stage of racial identity development may harbor biases against working with the culturally different. Therefore, it would appear that a counselor who is culturally similar to the client may be more effective in establishing rapport and using culturally preferred counseling interventions. This possibility must be assessed carefully with each client on an individual basis.

Once rural families begin the counseling process, several strategies are recommended to establish rapport, keep the family engaged in counseling, and respond to the holistic needs of the family. Parents of a teenage father may interpret their son's participation in a premarital unplanned pregnancy as yet another sign that an endearing way of life, characterized by traditional family values, is falling by the wayside. With such parents, during the pregnancy resolution phase of counseling the counselor can effectively join the family by recognizing and sensitively responding to this cultural issue. Specifically, the parents of the teenage father may need supportive counseling to address their economic worries and their fears regarding the changes in rural life. In addition, the parents might benefit from counseling strategies explicitly designed to assist farm families in career transitions, such as the Career Options for Missouri Farm Families developed by Hughey et al. (1989). By using these strategies to address the entire needs of the family, the counselor is likely to develop a strong and lasting rapport with the family.

Teenage fathers from rural areas are likely to find it difficult to communicate their difficulties because they tend to be socialized to be silent about their pain. The counselor may need to be tolerant of a young man who speaks with a halting style and appears hesitant to talk about his feelings. Active rather than passive counseling is called for. Particular attention may need to be directed toward the young man's experience of "living in a fishbowl"— that is, that most, if not all of his entire small community knows about his fatherhood.

Pregnancy Resolution Considerations. During the pregnancy resolution phase, rural teenage parents are likely to oppose abortion due to the highly conservative values that tend to dominate rural environments. Instead, the young, expectant father generally favors the traditional route to resolving the pregnancy: a quickly arranged marriage to his partner. Encouraging the young couple to slow the decision-making process long enough to carefully consider the pros and cons of their options may be vital in preventing some hastily formed, dysfunctional marriages.

Another pregnancy-resolution consideration pertains to difficulties associated with arranging abortions in rural areas. Clinical experience suggests that many adolescents who live in small-town rural America opting for an abortion consider this a private matter and are concerned that their experience be handled in a confidential matter. Although such sensitivity is also common among many adolescents in urban areas, it is easier for urban dwellers to protect their privacy through the anonymity afforded by heavily populated areas with a high concentration of abortion clinics. In tiny rural towns, it is difficult to conceal one's intentions about having an abortion— the word simply has a way of leaking out. I have known teenage couples to drive 2½ hours from their hometowns to obtain an abortion and then drive back the same day, all in an effort to ensure that no one discovers their secret. But many other youth who are concerned about this issue cannot use this strategy to preserve their anonymity because they have no means of transporting themselves to such far-away places. In other instances, privacy is not of great concern to the expectant couple but availability of abortion services is the problem. Because abortion clinics in rural environments tend to be scattered over great distances, transportation to clinics is once again an obstacle.

To circumvent these problems, carefully crafted linkage agreements enabling case managers to refer rural teenagers for abortion are needed. Also, the issue of patient confidentiality and a clinic staff's ability to honor it must be ongoing topics of in-service training.

Marital Counseling. Once married, adolescent parents in rural areas prefer to adhere to traditional gender roles characterized by the husband earning an income and the wife providing child care. The young father who accepts his parenting responsibilities typically finds it necessary to work two or more jobs to support his family because the range of employment opportunities tend to be limited and characterized by low pay. In many cases, rural teenage fathers may work "under the table" for local farmers, putting in long hours while earning an hourly rate that is below the minimum wage. Time spent at work can limit his ability to share intimate moments with his family and opportunities to engage in recreational activities. Furthermore, the self-esteem of the rural male may be so intricately tied to his ability to work that he may have trouble slowing down and learning how to relax and relate to his partner and children through leisurely activities. Meanwhile, his wife is likely to remain in the marriage, even if the couple experiences marital tensions, because of the influence of the traditional belief that "you make a marriage work no matter what it takes" and because her ability to leave a bad marriage is hampered by the limited career options available for women in rural areas. Neither is inclined to seek marital counseling because of the attitude that a person with problems "pulls himself (or herself) up by the bootstraps."

These difficulties highlight the importance of making marriage and family counseling readily available. Repeated outreach may be necessary to engage the couple in counseling. Rural fathers who do agree to participate in marital counseling may exhibit ongoing somatic symptoms. Consequently, marital counseling initially may need to be focused on alleviating the father's "pain." Over time, the counselor can gradually shift to the deeper issues at hand, especially if an active, problem-solving approach is taken. In addition, the issue of self-sufficiency may need to be directly challenged. Most people in rural areas are generous individuals who are willing to volunteer to help others. The young couple may need to be reminded of this fact and often can be convinced to accept assistance from family and friends by pointing out that, by doing so, they will help would-be volunteers feel better about themselves. Sometimes the simplest and yet most effective intervention is to arrange for caring adults to baby-sit for free from time to time so that the couple can have some unstructured quality time together.

PART III

12

Summary and Case Studies

The purpose of this chapter is to assist the reader in applying a multicultural approach to counseling with teenage fathers. This chapter begins with a review of the major points made thus far in this book. The key concepts of multiculturalism as a generic approach to counseling are reiterated. The application of the generic multicultural model with teenage fathers is described. Some of the similarities and differences among teenage fathers from diverse cultural backgrounds are highlighted to illustrate the permutations in counseling that are called for in helping these populations. This chapter concludes with a description of several actual case studies of multicultural counseling with teenage fathers.

As a preliminary note, the reader is advised that the material contained in this chapter represents an integration of the wealth of information presented in the earlier chapters of this book. It is assumed that the reader has read these earlier chapters first in order to have a thorough grasp of the multicultural perspective to counseling and appreciate the complex cultural contexts in which teenage fatherhood occurs.

This chapter is intended to enhance the reader's understanding of this earlier subject matter.

Overview of the
Generic Model of Multiculturalism

According to the generic model of multicultural counseling, it is assumed that both universal issues (those that cut across cultures) and culture-specific considerations (those that are unique to particular cultural groups) can affect human behavior and the counseling process. Effective counseling, therefore, relies on an understanding of and an attending to both the similarities and cultural differences between any counselor and client. The generic model is based on a broad definition of culture that includes demographic variables (e.g., age and gender), status variables (e.g., socioeconomic status), and affiliations (formal and informal), as well as ethnographic variables such as nationality, ethnicity, language, and religion. An implication of the model is that all counseling is multicultural (Pedersen, 1990, 1991b).

Multicultural Counseling
With Teenage Fathers

When applying the generic model of multiculturalism with teenage fathers, it is suggested to consider several universal issues. First, counselors must clarify their attitudes regarding premarital adolescent pregnancies and their feelings about teenage fathers. To accomplish this task, counselors need to acquire accurate information about teenage fathers. Second, practitioners interested in offering a comprehensive service program for adolescent fathers must understand the tasks of program development, identify and recruit teenage fathers for the program, and establish and maintain rapport with this population. Third, the teenage father who is counseled during the pregnancy-resolution phase will need assistance with his decision-making counseling, including a review of the options of abortion, adoption, marriage, noncustodial single fatherhood, and custodial single fatherhood and the legal issues associated with those options. Fourth, the unplanned pregnancy occurs within the contexts of two existing family systems and the young father's peer network. Addressing issues pertaining to the family and peers of both the young father and his partner are crucial. Fifth, the teenage father can benefit from counseling designed to help him prepare for the important responsibilities of being a parent. Sixth, because an unplanned pregnancy can affect the educational and career plans of the teenage father, educational and career counseling are warranted.

Each of these universal issues is played out in unique cultural contexts. Several culture-specific variables and the manner in which they influence how the pregnancy is resolved and how fatherhood is experienced have been discussed in the literature. These variables include the ethnicity of the young father (Anglo American, African American, and Hispanic American), his socioeconomic status, his religiosity, and his living environment (rural vs. urban).

Similarities and Differences
Among Teenage Fathers
From Diverse Cultural Backgrounds

A comparison of the experiences of teenage fathers from diverse cultural backgrounds indicates that there are many commonalities as well as potential differences. Similarities and differences between cultural groups are discussed according to each of the universal considerations mentioned earlier.

Differences among groups are offered as hypotheses for the counselor to explore with actual clients, rather than as within-group stereotypes. The examples provided are illustrative rather than exhaustive. Again, it is assumed that the reader has completed the first 11 chapters of this book before reading this section.

Clarifying Attitudes About Teenage Fathers

Similarities. Regardless of a young father's cultural background, the counselor must clarify his or her attitudes regarding unplanned adolescent pregnancy and teenage fatherhood. Rigid stereotypes about teenage fathers must be confronted and altered in light of accurate information regarding the characteristics of teenage fathers, the hardships they face, and the variations in how they respond to an unplanned pregnancy and how they fulfill their responsibilities as parents.

Differences. Counselors who have the potential to work with Anglo American, African American, Hispanic American, rich or poor, highly religious or nonreligious, and urban or rural teenage fathers must identify and examine ethnocentric biases they might hold about any of these specific populations. For example, Anglo American counselors working with African American teenage fathers are advised to divest themselves of Eurocentric images of the Black male as a hypersexual and hyperaggressive human being. Understanding the normative cultural context of particular groups can counter culturally encapsulated thinking.

Program Development and Recruitment

Similarities. All teenage fathers can benefit from comprehensive service programs. In addition, it appears that the provision of job training skills, career counseling, and legal advice is likely to entice most teenage fathers to participate in service programs for young fathers.

Differences. In Anglo American communities, program developers may have to work particularly hard at overcoming the tendency of community members to deny that teenage pregnancy is a problem. Strong Anglo American prohibitions against out-of-wedlock childbearing may result in greater pressure for young couples to marry. Consequently, programs accentuating marital counseling services may be more acceptable to an Anglo American community.

In African American and Hispanic American communities, program developers must be sure that community leaders from each of these ethnic groups are included in the development and implementation of programs to ensure the programs are responsive to the community's unique needs. For African Americans, the Black church may be seen as a trusted focal point for services, whereas the Catholic church may be a major force in Hispanic American communities. Program advertisements in both English and Spanish are necessary in Hispanic American communities.

Because poverty interacts with other variables to place impoverished adolescents at high risk for unplanned parenthood, poor neighborhoods may need to be a priority for the allocation of funds to support adolescent pregnancy prevention and service programs. In addition, to enhance the chances of attracting poor teenage fathers to service programs, it is recommended that programs delivered in poor neighborhoods contain components designed to improve the life opportunities of participants.

In populations characterized by a high degree of religiosity, the provision of abortion counseling services could alienate the community. Personal safety may be a salient issue for adolescents seeking services in dangerous urban environments, but adolescents from rural areas may need special assistance in overcoming transportation problems associated with accessing services scattered across vast geographic areas. In addition, due to its long history of serving rural families, the Cooperative Extension Service might take a lead role in rural service coalitions for teenage fathers.

Establishing and Maintaining Rapport

Similarities. Due to a fear of being judged, most teenage fathers are leery of helping professionals. Understanding societal stereotypes about teenage fathers, working as a nonjudgmental advocate for young fathers, assisting with a young man's most immediate concern (usually of a practical nature) and communicating empathy, care, and support appear to facilitate rapport with the majority of adolescent fathers. In addition, most teenage fathers are likely to trust counselors who are comfortable with the traditional relational style of males, which is action rather than feeling oriented.

Differences. Anglo teenage fathers and young fathers from higher socioeconomic levels and with strong religiosity are most likely to require support in managing strong family and social condemnation for their role in an out-of-wedlock pregnancy.

African American teenage fathers are victimized by both general societal stereotypes about teenage fathers *and* societal myths about the Black male. These unfair generalizations heighten suspiciousness of would-be helpers, especially if the helper is Anglo American. Suspiciousness of the mental health system is complicated for African American and Hispanic American youth by the historical maltreatment of these populations by helping professions. Recognizing and discussing these issues in a reassuring manner can facilitate rapport.

Knowledge of Black English and appropriate use of titles is important with African American males, and fluency in Spanish and the conveyance of *personalismo* can enhance rapport with Hispanic Americans.

Responding to the immediate practical needs of impoverished youth, even if these needs are not related to the pregnancy, should be foremost on the counselor's agenda. Inner-city youth, in particular, might test the counselor regarding his or her understanding of and sensitivity toward urban problems. Also, some young fathers from a lower socioeconomic level may wonder if contact with counselors could result in problems with child support enforcement officials. Assuring the young father of the confidentiality of services could allay such fears.

Rural teenage fathers might appear hesitant in counseling, conflicted between a desire to be helped and the cultural value of self-sufficiency. Active, directive counseling can help these fathers feel more comfortable. In highly isolated areas, the potential for ethnocentric thinking on the part of the client might be high and could pose problems between counselors and clients from different races.

Issues of racial identity development could affect all counselor/client dyads. Therefore, counselors are advised to understand the racial identity development models for both Whites and Blacks, identify their clients' stages of racial identity development, and know how to handle issues of racial identity development in counseling.

**Pregnancy Resolution
and Legal Considerations**

Similarities. Decision-making counseling is required with all teenage fathers deliberating the outcome of the unplanned pregnancy and the relationship with the partner and child. Young fathers wrestling with these dilemmas
need accurate information regarding the pros and cons associated with each
pregnancy-resolution option, including facts pertaining to the possible legal
ramifications of each potential decision.

Differences. The options available to teenage fathers from higher socioeconomic strata, who tend to be Anglo American, typically are greater than those
available to impoverished youth. For example, affluent males are more likely
to afford abortion or marriage if they pursue either option, but these options
may not be economically feasible for the poor. Although a minority of
unplanned adolescent pregnancies are resolved by the use of adoption, Anglo
Americans are much more likely than African American and Hispanic Americans to place their children for adoption. African Americans, in particular,
are likely to rely on informal adoption by extended family and nonblood
relatives than on formal adoption. Abortion is likely to be considered an
unacceptable option by highly religious and traditional Hispanic males and
their families. Anglo American and traditional Hispanic American males are
likely to experience family pressure to marry as a means of resolving an
unplanned out-of-wedlock pregnancy.

Addressing Issues With Families and Peers

Similarities. Because families and peers can influence the probability that a
young man will become a father prematurely and his responses to the
pregnancy and parenthood, it is recommended that counselors attempt to
engage family members and peers in the counseling process. Counseling that
addresses both the pregnancy-related issues and ongoing conflicts are likely
to produce positive results.

Differences. Reasons for being uncomfortable with counseling vary among
ethnic groups. Because Anglo Americans and rural Americans tend to value
self-sufficiency and individualism, they may see themselves as weak if they
participate in counseling. When Anglos do engage in counseling, they
usually prefer to limit participation to immediate family members. African
Americans and Hispanic Americans tend to have a mistrust of the mental

health system. Overcoming these respective reasons for discomfort are crucial for the development of a therapeutic family counseling process.

African Americans and Hispanic Americans tend to rely on extended family members to resolve family problems. Therefore, this support network may need to be included in the counseling process with these two ethnic groups to effect a positive intervention. With African Americans, the participation of "nonblood relatives" in counseling may be vital because they are considered a part of the extended family system. The inclusion of the coparent system with some Hispanic American families may be warranted.

Poor families and inner-city families may appear hesitant about counseling due to a fear that counselors will not appreciate their many difficulties. In addition, the necessity of coping with a host of difficulties may curtail their availability and energy for counseling. Addressing the multisystemic needs of such families may foster trust and participation in counseling.

With highly religious families, counseling offered through the referral and with the blessing of a trusted minister can improve the counselor's credibility. Counseling services based in a church setting are likely to be perceived as safe and approachable. Tapping the religious family's spiritual approaches to healing can enhance the utility of interventions that are used.

Preparation for Fatherhood

Similarities. All expectant adolescent fathers need to clarify their attitudes regarding masculinity and fatherhood and learn effective parenting skills and sexually responsible behavior. Addressing father-son wounds may be particularly important in preparing the adolescent male to accept his responsibilities as a father.

Differences. Counselors need to know Anglo, African, and Hispanic perspectives on the father's role to provide culturally sensitive parenting skills training with Anglo American, African American, and Hispanic American teenage fathers. The use of culturally indigenous role models from each of these three ethnic groups is likely to enhance training. Views on masculinity and paternal behavior also are shaped by rural, urban, and class-related norms for behavior. A contextual understanding of these cultural influences enhances efforts to assist young men during the transition to fatherhood. For example, sensitivity regarding the influence of poverty, restricted life opportunities, and welfare policies on the family structure of teenage fathers from lower socioeconomic levels will be important in appreciating their approach to fatherhood and family life. Highly religious fathers, particular those who are devout Roman Catholics, may not be amenable to sexual responsibility training that focuses on contraceptive use, but traditional Hispanic American families may view sexual education to be the purview of family rather than educators and practitioners.

Educational and Career Counseling

Similarities. Across cultural groups, young men who father children during their teenage years are more likely than their nonfather peers to drop out of school. Young fathers who are enrolled in school and contemplating their educational and career plans need information regarding the pros and cons of dropping out of school, as well as advice regarding their rights to a public school education. Those who have dropped out of school already require extensive outreach designed to assist them to complete the type of education/training that will make them competitive in the job market and a self-sufficient supporter of their families. Both enrolled teenage fathers and dropouts need to understand that career development is a developmental process, not a one-time event. Finally, schools are logical sites for comprehensive service programs for teenage parents.

Differences. Among teenage fathers, African Americans are more likely than Anglo Americans and Hispanic Americans, respectively, to graduate from high school or earn a GED. Although crisis counseling to prevent school dropout and re-enrollment strategies are required with all three populations, these services may need to be a high priority in Anglo American and Hispanic American communities. Super's developmental-stage model of career development may be most appropriate with middle- to upper-class Anglo Americans, but may need to be modified to understand the career patterns and realities of African American, Hispanic American, and disadvantaged Anglo American populations. For example, the role of racism, disenfranchisement, economic hardship, structural discrimination, and Black racial identity development should be considered in assessing the career development of African Americans. The infusion of Africentric education into existing school curricula make the educational experience more meaningful for African American males. African American, Hispanic American, and disadvantaged Anglo American youth may benefit from outreach strategies designed to reconnect their alienated parents to the educational system. Teenage fathers who are members of farm families experiencing economic hardships may need specialized career counseling to assist them with the transition from an agrarian-based to a nonagrarian-based income. Policy measures to improve the quality of education and the safety of educational environments are needed for inner-city school systems.

Case Studies

The generic multicultural model provides the professional with a framework for formulating a rich array of culturally sensitive hypotheses to explore with the teenage father. This process is illustrated in each of the following case studies in which I served as either the counselor, the supervisor, or the consultant. All of the names, and, in some cases, the identifying details, have been changed to protect the confidentiality of the clients, supervisees, and consultees involved.

Although young fathers from each of the three ethnic groups discussed in this book are the subjects of the following case studies, their idiosyncratic concerns, issues, and behaviors are not suggested to be representative of their respective ethnic groups. Rather, these cases are provided to demonstrate for the reader how to use the generic multicultural model in generating and testing culturally sensitive hypotheses with members of particular cultural groups.

Another feature of these clinical vignettes is that the stage of counseling and the cultural variables at work vary from case study to case study. In the case of David T, the pregnancy-resolution phase of counseling is emphasized, as are the cultural variables of an Anglo American background, upper socioeconomic status, high religiosity, and a rural environment. The postnatal phase of counseling and the cultural variables of an African American background, low socioeconomic status, high religiosity, and a rural environment are accentuated in the case of Maurice W. Last, both the pre- and postnatal counseling process and the cultural variables of an Hispanic American background, a low socioeconomic status, strong religiosity, and an urban environment are brought to life in the case of Carlos R.

An additional aspect of each of the following case studies is that the counseling process is described in detail to provide the reader with an appreciation for the intricate and delicate work that is required in helping young fathers. Rather than reporting ideal clinical scenarios in which every intervention is completely successful, both successful *and* unsuccessful strategies are shared to realistically spotlight the thorny problems often associated with counseling adolescents involved in unplanned out-of-wedlock pregnancies.

The Case of David T

David T was a 16-year-old Anglo American male, an only child from an upper-middle-class rural community. David was referred for counseling by his mother after she became concerned about a radical change in David's behavior. Previously, David had been a highly energetic and happy boy, whose only significant prior adjustment difficulty was dealing with a learning disability and associated academic troubles. Over the past 3 weeks, he had appeared sullen, was snappy, and had spent significantly greater amounts of time either away from home or in his bedroom talking on the phone. Whenever Mrs. T had asked David to explain his sudden change in mood and behavior, he responded by telling his mother to mind her own business. Thus, she was not sure what was bothering him, although she suspected that "it may have something to do with his girlfriend, Nancy, since I think it's her that he's been spending so much time with on the phone."

During the first phone contact with Mrs. T, she expressed her hesitancy in turning to a counselor for help by stating, "The way I was raised, we believe in taking care of ourselves." In clarifying this matter with Mrs. T, the counselor discovered that Mrs. T was the daughter of a prominent farmer in the area. The counselor hypothesized that Mrs. T might be expressing a conflict associated with the value of self-sufficiency, so he expressed his empathy with the mother's discomfort in using a professional and assured her that he would keep her concerns in the strictest confidence. He also inquired as to what had prompted Mrs. T to seek help in spite of her reservations. She responded that she felt she couldn't turn to her family for assistance because they already viewed her as "an embarrassment" because she "was divorced from her husband and a single mother." Moreover, she reported receiving little support from her ex-husband, who allegedly had sporadic contact with David since the divorce, which occurred when David was 10 years old. She felt alone and confused, "almost in a crisis," because of David's recent behavior and decided that she needed someone on whom she could rely.

On this last note, the counselor sensed that Mrs. T had rushed her response and didn't want to be pressed for any more information. Privately the counselor wondered if there was an event in Mrs. T's past that might prove significant in understanding her reaction to David's recent behavior. Also, he suspected that Mrs. T probably came from a very traditional Anglocentric family who was intolerant of variant family forms. He noted that he should explore these hypotheses further in future counseling sessions.

During the early stages of counseling, Mrs. T agreed that her son could meet with the counselor alone to discuss what might be disturbing him. Furthermore, although she would participate in family counseling with David later, both she and the counselor agreed that the information disclosed during David's individual sessions should remain confidential.

When the counselor first met with David in the outpatient wing of a community mental health center, he explained to David the agreement that had been reached between the counselor and Mrs. T regarding confidentiality. The counselor also informed David that he would be asked to participate in family counseling sessions later in the course of treatment.

Initially, David appeared hesitant to talk, especially in the counselor's office. The counselor surmised that David might feel uncomfortable with face-to-face, highly intimate self-disclosure, so he invited David to go for a walk to a nearby store where the two might buy a snack. As they strolled down the street together, the counselor noticed that David repeatedly kicked a stone, so the counselor also kicked a stone while asking David about his interests and hobbies. Rapport between the two gradually improved, especially after they ate some french fries and drank soda together while discussing David's and the counselor's favorite rock-and-roll groups and football teams.

During the walk back to the counselor's office, David revealed that he was worried about what his mother might think about him and then blurted out that his 15-year-old girlfriend, Nancy, had missed her period. This was followed by a long, rambling monologue through which David disclosed significant issues surrounding his own birth, his parent's marriage, and his relationship with Nancy and her family.

David was pretty certain that he was conceived out of wedlock, although the circumstances of his birth were never openly discussed by anyone in his immediate or extended family. Nevertheless, he had long suspected that he was "a bastard child" because he perceived that he always had been treated "differently" by his relatives. David sensed that his parents had never been compatible, even when he was a young boy. It seemed that his parents had either always argued or tried to avoid one another. When they finally divorced, he was relieved at first, hopeful that it might result in his having a better relationship with both parents. But when his father "pretty much disappeared from the scene," David began to feel that he had been "cheated by life."

David found great comfort, or so he thought, in his relationship with Nancy. The two had started dating when he was in the ninth grade, she in the eighth. Within 3 months, they were having sexual intercourse and he felt that she was all that mattered in life to him. Only once during the many times that they had intercourse did David use a condom, "and even then I wasn't sure if I was using the thing right anyway." At first, he worried that Nancy might become pregnant, but "after nothing happened the first few times, I figured it couldn't happen to us unless we did it every day."

In recent months, his "love" for Nancy abated, although they still dated and occasionally had unprotected sex. He reported feeling "all closed in" and "interested in some other girls my age." In addition, Nancy's parents allegedly always treated him with disdain, "like I came from the wrong side of the tracks or something." He couldn't see himself staying with Nancy much longer, considering how uncomfortable he was with her parents. Shortly after he began contemplating a break-up with Nancy, she worriedly alerted him that she had missed her period. This is why he had been so angry and preoccupied lately.

After listening quietly to David's long self-disclosure, the counselor expressed his empathy for the shock and confusion David was experiencing. The counselor then described to David his approach to counseling, and, in three sessions held over the next 10 days, followed through with counseling designed to help David through the crisis.

The counselor learned from David that he did not want to inform his mother what was going on until Nancy could take a pregnancy test. After a home pregnancy test produced positive results, the counselor informed David about a nearby Planned Parenthood clinic where Nancy could receive a free medical examination regarding her pregnancy status. A visit was arranged, and the results indicated that Nancy was 9 weeks pregnant.

David was stunned by this news, and he required considerable supportive counseling. Decision-making counseling was initiated, involving a careful consideration of the pros and cons associated with abortion, adoption, marriage, single noncustodial parenthood, and single custodial parenthood. This counseling assisted David in clarifying that he was opposed to abortion and adoption, stating that his parents "could have killed me or given me away but they chose not to." He respected this decision on their part, stating that he believed it was "one of the few things I am grateful to them for in his life." David was also sure that he did not want to marry Nancy—at least not now. However, he reported that Nancy wanted him to marry her so that they could raise the baby "like a proper family should."

At this point, the counselor encouraged David to consider including his mother, his father, Nancy, and her family in the counseling process. David agreed that he was open to working with all of these parties in counseling, but he wanted to involve his mother first. In addition to this issue, the counselor expressed concern that neither David nor Nancy had discussed the pregnancy with their parents. He urged David to support Nancy during the stressful task of informing her parents about the pregnancy. The counselor assured David that he would support David in telling his mother.

In a fourth counseling session, the disclosure of the pregnancy to Mrs. T provoked a strong emotional response. Mrs. T sobbed periodically throughout the session, stating that she had always wanted what was best for her son but felt that he had "placed a hex on himself for life." With supportive direction, the counselor helped David to ask his mother about his own birth, prompting Mrs. T to cry all the more. Yet as she described the circumstances surrounding his birth, both David and Mrs. T appeared to experience catharsis and a new form of bonding brought about by the final unveiling of a long-held family secret.

With a mixture of grief and relief, Mrs. T told David that he *had* been conceived out of wedlock. She reported that she had been a junior in high school, his father a senior, when the pregnancy occurred. By the time they realized that Mrs. T was pregnant, she "was already beginning to show." When the adolescents informed their parents, both families responded with outrage and ordered the young couple to be married, even though they had dated for only about 3 months prior to the pregnancy. A "shotgun" wedding was arranged, and everyone in attendance pretended to not know the couple's private circumstances, in spite of the fact that rumors about Mrs. T possibly being pregnant were spread throughout their small hometown. Mentioning this last point, Mrs. T looked downward to hide the expression of hurt and shame on her face.

After a brief pause, she continued. Her and her husband's parents quietly pooled their resources to pay for the down payment on a modest house, into which Mr. and Mrs. T moved after their marriage. Although the couple continued to receive financial support from their respective parents, all was not well. They both felt like outcasts from both their families and the community, even though most of the people in their lives treated them with a superficial cordiality. In addition, the two began to fight, and, over time, they grew so distant that it seemed they "were simply roommates rather than husband and wife." After 10 years of the hostility, the Ts divorced.

Mrs. T now turned her attention to David, stating that she always felt that she had been an "inadequate mother" to him. Nevertheless, with great feeling, she told her son that she always had loved him, always had wanted what was best for him, and now was devastated because she feared that he would have to face what she had endured for so many years.

After the counselor expressed empathy for Mrs. T's feelings and thanked her for her courage in opening up to David, he then prompted David to respond. David stated how sorry he felt for all that his mom had been through, and, in a very timely and healing gesture, assured her that he had always appreciated her in spite of their family difficulties. Then, haltingly, he apologized for letting her down by "getting Nancy pregnant." But he quickly followed this statement by asserting bitterly that he didn't think he could rush off and marry Nancy "the way you and Dad did."

Throughout the remainder of this and a subsequent session, David and his mother agreed that David should not marry Nancy, at least not in the immediate future, due to his strong ambivalent feelings toward her. Mrs. T and David also planned for arranging a meeting between them, Nancy, and her parents to discuss the resolution of the pregnancy. In addition, they decided to inform David's father about the crisis and to invite him to join David initially in an individual counseling session, and, if possible, in subsequent family sessions.

Over the next several weeks, the counselor's energies were devoted to juggling significant problems that emerged in response to these plans, beginning with a withdrawal from the situation by Mr. T. He was virtually nonresponsive to the news of the pregnancy and he refused to participate in the counseling, in spite of heartfelt requests by both Mrs. T and David that he join them in this endeavor. The counselor also employed numerous tactics to engage Mr. T, including phone calls, letter writing, and personal visits. He also received permission from David and his mother to contact one of Mr. T's brothers, because it was thought that he might have a positive influence on Mr. T. Unfortunately, all of these tactics were to no avail.

Because David was crushed and bitter over his father's retreat from the crisis, the counselor developed a multifaceted, long-term approach to healing David's father-son wounds. Through individual counseling, he helped David to mourn his prior disappointments regarding his relationship with his father and understand that his father's retreat from the issue could represent an attempt by Mr. T to protect himself from his own painful memories that might have been triggered by David's own situation. Individual counseling was supplemented by family sessions, through which the counselor recruited the support of David's mother and the support of one of her adult male cousins who always had sympathy for Mrs. T's situation and a fondness for David. David also was referred for adjunctive group counseling offered at a Planned Parenthood center. Through this program, David received group fatherhood training with other teenage fathers, and he was hooked up with a mentor father from the community, a successful lawyer who once had been a teenage father himself. These various forms of male support seemed especially vital to David's gradual recovery from his feelings stemming from paternal abandonment. In addition, they inspired him to vow that he would try to be a better father to his child than his own father had been to him.

Concurrent with these issues, the counselor assisted David and Mrs. T in responding to conflicts between them and Nancy's family. Nancy's parents were devout Baptists who believed that marriage was the only acceptable way to resolve the pregnancy. They accused David of being just like his mother, viewing him to be another "loser from a loser family" who had manipulated and exploited their daughter. His hesitation in marrying Nancy was seen by them as further evidence that he was not worthy to be the father of their grandchild. He was given an ultimatum: Marry Nancy or forgo contact with her and his child. He was warned to make up his mind quickly, for Nancy's parents wanted to settle this matter immediately.

The reaction of Nancy's family prompted a reconsideration of David's preference regarding the resolution of the pregnancy. Initially, he wanted to give in to the demands to marry, out of fear that access to his child would be blocked forever. However, the counselor informed David that he had certain legal rights regarding paternity, and he referred David and his mother to the organization Parents' and Children's Equality, where they were provided with detailed information regarding those rights and advice on how to petition the court to establish paternity and child visitations. Fortified by this information, David and his mother remained adamant about his not rushing into a marriage.

Realizing that the tension between the Ts and Nancy's family might escalate now that the Ts were certain David would not marry Nancy in haste, the counselor pursued a strategy to de-escalate the situation. He encouraged David and his mother to balance their desire to confront Nancy's family with an attempt to appreciate the cultural/religious perspective of Nancy's parents. He also asked them to imagine the anxiety Nancy's parents must be experiencing during this crisis. In particular, he suggested that her parents might suffer stinging social embarrassment among their well-off Anglo friends if it were revealed publicly that Nancy had conceived and given birth to a child out of wedlock.

This strategy was successful in altering Mrs. T's attitude toward Nancy's parents. With support from the counselor, she steadfastly initiated contacts with Nancy's mother, expressing her recognition of the mother's concerns. Several times, Mrs. T "swallowed her pride," refusing to respond with resentment when Nancy's mother made disparaging remarks about Mrs. T and her son, all the while appealing to the women's potential concern for what might happen to Nancy if she were completely forbidden from seeing David again. The counselor also attempted to make headway with Nancy's parents through phone conversations. Although Nancy's parents still refused to allow David to have contact with Nancy, it seemed that the tone of their reactions to David and Mrs. T were softening.

During this standoff between the two families, 2 months passed, and David's anxiety over not seeing Nancy intensified. On one rare night when Nancy's parents left her at home with her grandmother, she called David on the phone, suggesting that he sneak into the house to see her. He did so, only to be discovered there by Nancy's father when they returned home. Nancy's father berated David, the two engaged in an argument, and Nancy's father threw him off the front porch onto the lawn, warning him to never see his daughter again.

After this incident, David and his mother decided to take the necessary legal steps to establish his paternity, a process that demanded the counselor to be extra supportive of David. After his child, a beautiful son, was born, his paternity was legally recognized by the courts and conditions of formal visitation and child support were arranged. Although tensions between the two families remained high, Nancy's parents were eventually impressed by David's continued interest in the well-being of Nancy and his son. Furthermore, they recognized the harmful impact of their behavior on Nancy, who grew more and more depressed the longer she went without seeing David. Gradually, they permitted David to spend more time with Nancy and the baby, and, in time, they developed an amicable relationship with him.

As for the educational progress of both adolescents, Nancy remained in school through March of her sophomore year. After her baby was born a month later, she completed her courses for the academic year through a home studies program with the assistance of a private tutor who was paid by her parents. At the end of the summer, she returned to school, dropping the baby off each day at an infant child care center operated by her church. These services were financed by the mutual financial support of Nancy's parents, Mrs. T, and David.

David's educational progress was less smooth. Because he experienced long-standing frustrations with school due to his learning disability, he already was eager to drop out, and he initially argued that the pregnancy was a justification to leave school immediately. However, he eventually opted to remain in school for two reasons. First, the counselor informed David and his mother about the economic hardships of teenage fathers who leave school, information that caused him to question the wisdom of leaving school. Second, other teenage fathers, participants in the program at Planned Parenthood who had dropped out of school, related their regrets about quitting school and their difficulties in the workforce. They urged David to find a way to remain in school, and so he did.

David accepted an invitation from his counselor to participate in career counseling. The counselor conducted career assessments that indicated that

David might find satisfaction and success in a field in which he used his mechanical abilities. After David explored information on pertinent careers, he expressed an interest in auto body repair and talked with school personnel about what relevant training he could receive at the high school level. He opted to enroll in an auto body repair class while working part-time in the evenings and on weekends in a gas station to earn money to help support Nancy and his son. The counselor developed a long-term career counseling plan in which a timetable for teaching David additional career-seeking and career-keeping skills was charted.

David's interest in a career in auto body repair became an issue in family counseling after Mrs. T expressed her disapproval of this plan of action. She stated that she wanted "something more for David out of life" than working in an auto repair shop. As mother and son discussed this issue, it became clear that Mrs. T was responding to a subcultural norm that only certain occupations were acceptable within her social circle of well-to-do friends. This disclosure prompted David to vent years of pent-up anger he had felt toward his mother because of what he perceived to be her unrealistic expectations of him. It seemed that Mrs. T had never fully understood the limitations that his learning disability had placed on his academic performance. Furthermore, it appeared that she had hoped that she could win genuine acceptance in her community if her son entered a prestigious career. The counselor intervened by offering Mrs. T some bibliotherapy material on leaning disabilities, information that convinced her to reconsider her expectations regarding David. The counselor also gently confronted Mrs. T to examine the role of the hurtful, emotional blackballing by her community since her experience as a teenage parent in shaping her aspirations for David. Subsequently, she supported David's career plan, and, consequently, his resentment toward her dissipated. Nevertheless, Mrs. T continued to struggle with her own fears about potential pejorative reactions by her friends and family to her son's career. To assist her to resolve this particular issue, the counselor empathized with Mrs. T's feelings and helped her to develop some rational-emotive coping statements.

Over time, David experienced great joy in the moments he shared with his son. Relating to his own child eased the pain he felt regarding his father and seemed to make his other hardships tolerable. Periodically, he and Nancy had conflicts between them and with their respective parents regarding role boundaries in the management of the baby. The counselor helped them to negotiate these issues.

David also had difficulty continuing in the young fathers group and seeing any of his male friends because of the many demands on his time.

Attending the young fathers group became particularly problematic because it was held about 45 minutes from David's hometown.

The issue of lost time from peers was difficult to resolve, for there truly
was little time for David to socialize with peers, either in informal or
therapeutic settings. The counselor arranged for several young fathers to
coordinate family picnic days attended by them and their children. However, the fathers discovered that it was difficult for them to enjoy one
another with several young children to care for at one time. Consequently,
only two such outings were held before the idea fizzled. A couple of older
men who were employees of the gas station where David worked took him
out to eat from time to time, and although David appreciated their company,
he still missed the camaraderie of "his buddies." After responsibilities
repeatedly interfered with David's spending time with his friends, the
counselor worked on helping David to shift his expectations regarding
these contacts by focusing on the quality rather than the quantity of their
time together. Nevertheless, he still missed his friends. Finally, because the
young fathers group was held so far from David's house, the counselor
arranged with the group program coordinator that David be allowed to
participate on an irregular basis as David's schedule permitted. As a result
of this arrangement, David used the group as a periodic means for support
and education, rather than as an ongoing source of friendship.

Through his remaining visits to Planned Parenthood, he learned proper
use of contraceptives and committed himself to practicing safe sex. At
termination from counseling, he had a new steady girlfriend and had not
been involved in another unplanned pregnancy. In their last session together, the counselor handed David a card with words of encouragement
and an expression of the counselor's fulfillment in working with David and
his family. In return, David thanked the counselor for the difference he had
made in his life and gave the counselor a memento of their work together,
something that David had created during his spare time in the auto body
class: a welded metal stick figure holding what appeared to be a baby.

Case Analysis. David's experiences illustrate the universal challenges as
well as the joys involved in assisting a teenage father during both the prenatal
and postnatal period of counseling. Counseling process skills conducive to
the relational styles of boys were used in this case. David's case also depicts
the complex case management challenges encountered by counselors who
work with young fathers, such as juggling many problems at the same time,
using the referral network, conducting family and individual counseling, and
addressing unresolved multigenerational family issues while problem solving about the current demands placed on the family and conflicts between

the families of the teenage mother and father. This case is typical of counseling with young fathers in that there is rarely an ideal solution to all of the problems that emerge, even with the assistance of a supportive, dedicated counselor. In addition, this case portrays the conflicts of a young man who is an adolescent at the same time that he is attempting to master the transition to fatherhood.

Several culture-specific issues were also evident. First, throughout the counseling process, the counselor had to address the many ramifications of the social stigma associated with unwed adolescent parenthood in Anglo and upper socioeconomic environments. Second, sensitivity toward the self-sufficiency philosophy of rural Anglo families helped the counselor to establish rapport. Third, the strong religious convictions of Nancy's family strongly influenced the pregnancy resolution process and the counselor attended to this cultural variable. Fourth, the ample resources of these economically privileged families truly facilitated the ability of the adolescent parents to continue with their education. Fifth, characteristics of rural living complicated the counseling process. The counselor had to help David and Mrs. T to cope with the visibility regarding and reactivity to their crisis in a small rural town. Mrs. T needed additional assistance in overcoming "the scarlet letter" that had been placed on her by her community for having been an adolescent parent herself. Also, the distance David had to travel to participate in a teenage fathers program posed logistical problems that were never resolved to complete satisfaction.

The Case of Maurice W

Maurice W was a 19-year-old African American male who was the older of two children from a single-parent household headed by Maurice's mother, Mrs. W. Maurice lived with his mother, his maternal grandmother, his 17-year-old sister, and an assortment of relatives who inhabited the home from time to time. The family resided in a tight-knit, poor African American neighborhood located on the outskirts of a small, predominantly Anglo American town situated in a very isolated rural region. Maurice was the noncustodial father of a 1-year-old girl he had fathered by his former girlfriend, Melissa, an 18-year-old Anglo American who resided in a middle-class Anglo section of their town.

Maurice was identified as a potential client for counseling after details of his many hardships were conveyed to a counselor by Melissa, who herself had recently started counseling to address difficulties associated with her adjustment as an adolescent mother. Through his contact with Melissa, the counselor learned that Melissa and Maurice had dated for about a year prior to the pregnancy, much to the dismay of Melissa's parents, who were enraged that she would have a relationship with a Black male. After several clandestine rendezvous, Melissa became pregnant. Her parents were incensed when they heard about the pregnancy and tried to force her to have an abortion. When she refused, they threw her out of the house and she dropped out of school. They subsequently rejected any attempts by Melissa to contact them.

Until the baby was born, Melissa lived in the apartment with an older girlfriend while working part-time in a local department store. After the birth of her child, she applied for and was awarded welfare, Medicaid benefits, and subsidized housing. After moving into her own apartment, she enrolled in the Teenage Mothers Program offered through the school district. This program provided free on-site child care, parenting skills training, nutritional counseling, and a cooperative education arrangement through which she attended academic classes in the morning and worked as a beautician trainee in the afternoons. After sensing the heartache Melissa experienced in reaction to her parents' rejection, a perceptive and caring nurse employed by the Teenage Mothers Program was successful in convincing Melissa to participate in personal counseling.

Throughout her period of transition to parenthood, Melissa maintained an ongoing relationship with Maurice. Initially, the two had talked about getting married. However, neither one of them thought that they could afford to live together in their own dwelling. Although Maurice worked full-time as a delivery boy in the service center of a local automobile dealership, he had no benefits and his meager wages virtually precluded his renting an apartment and supporting a family. The couple also had considered moving in with Mrs. W, but her house already was overcrowded by the changing composition of relatives who relied on her hospitality during periods of financial hardship. In addition to these economic considerations, Maurice had been raised in a single-parent home and had several friends and relatives who were single parents and so was not uncomfortable with the role of a noncustodial father living apart from his child. Melissa and Maurice decided that their best alternative was for Melissa to apply for government assistance and for her to move into one of the two "welfare projects" located in their town.

After Melissa had settled into her apartment, Maurice visited her and their daughter regularly. He was careful not to spend too much time at Melissa's apartment, fearing that his presence there might result in her forfeiting some or all of her welfare benefits. Thus, much of their time together was enjoyed at Mrs. W's house, who welcomed their presence, especially opportunities to "spoil" her granddaughter.

During the first 6 months of the baby's life, Maurice had tried as best he could to offer financial assistance to Melissa. He divided his paychecks into thirds, giving a third to his mother, a third to Melissa, and keeping a third for himself. Sometimes out of his own share of the earnings, he would buy toys and disposable diapers for the baby.

This pattern of support ended, however, when Maurice was laid off from his job. For the next 6 months he could not secure employment. Although he continued to have contact with Melissa and their daughter, he became more frustrated with his inability to find work. Melissa could sympathize with Maurice's frustration, but she couldn't understand the intense anger he began to demonstrate. He grew hostile toward her, spent less time with her and the baby, and began hanging out and drinking with several friends, whom Melissa described as "lowlifes." Melissa also suspected that Maurice might be seeing another girl, and she was filled with jealousy and felt abandoned. She asked the counselor if he might be willing and able to help Maurice.

The counselor responded that he would be glad to help, but that the manner in which he proceeded would be determined by Maurice's response to an invitation to participate in counseling. If Maurice was agreeable to couple's counseling, then the counselor would see both Melissa and Maurice. However, if Maurice preferred his own counselor, then the counselor would use the services of another professional, one of the counselor's supervisees, who would attempt to work with Maurice. Melissa agreed to this plan, so the counselor suggested that she contact Maurice and invite him to come in for a session.

Although Maurice told Melissa that he was interested in working with her on their relationship in counseling, he did not join her for each of the next two sessions. With Melissa's permission, the counselor attempted to call Maurice. Each time he called, Mrs. W answered the phone and reported that Maurice was not home. Although the counselor left messages for Maurice, his phone calls were never returned.

The counselor hypothesized that Maurice's behavior indicated that he either did not want to work on his relationship with Melissa, or that Maurice, as an African American male, might be reluctant to see an Anglo counselor who worked in a small private practice located in a White neighborhood. The counselor decided to investigate these hypotheses by paying a visit to Maurice's home. He first called Mrs. W, asking her permission to stop by her home to introduce himself and explain about his interest in Maurice. Mrs. W was receptive to this initiative, and when the counselor stopped by her house, she warmly invited him into her home. The counselor explained to Mrs. W that his calling on Maurice had been prompted by Melissa's desire to have him join her in counseling. The counselor emphasized that he wanted to help Maurice in any way that he could. The counselor added that, even though he was a stranger to Mrs. W and her family, he would be glad to help them with any difficulties they might have. The counselor also stated that he was dedicated to helping all young people and he provided Mrs. W with the name of an African American minister in the community who would serve as a reference for the counselor. Before he left, the counselor and Mrs. W talked a bit about her interests, which were centered on activities associated with her church. He thanked Mrs. W for her time, and asked her to have Maurice give him a call.

Several weeks passed and there was still no word from Maurice. One day, however, the counselor received a frantic phone call from Mrs. W. She explained that there had been some kind of altercation in her neighborhood between several young men, including Maurice, and the police. Maurice was in jail. Would the counselor help? The counselor promised Mrs. W that he would stop by the jail on his way home from work to arrange for a visit with Maurice.

Before he could make these arrangements, however, the counselor was surprised to discover later that afternoon two African American men seated in the waiting room of the private practice in which he worked. One was Maurice, the other was the minister from Mrs. W's church who had posted bail for Maurice, and, on Mrs. W's request, had transported Maurice to the counselor's office. The minister greeted the counselor, stated that he understood that Maurice might like to talk with the counselor alone, and reported that he would be back in an hour to pick up Maurice.

Although the counselor had another appointment scheduled for this time, he asked his receptionist to inform his next client that he would be running late and that he apologized for this inconvenience. He then met privately with Maurice in his office for about 20 minutes.

The counselor introduced himself to Maurice, stated that he was happy to meet him, and repeated much of what he had said previously to Mrs. W. The entire time he spoke, Maurice watched the counselor carefully. The counselor then stated that he imagined Maurice might be upset about what had happened earlier today, and then asked Maurice if he cared to talk about his encounter with the police. Willingly, Maurice volunteered that a friend riding a motor scooter had been stopped by the police in their neighborhood. As several neighbors watched, the police "got rough with him for no reason at all. When we went to help him out, the next thing we knew, cops were all around us, and we were being hauled off to jail." Maurice felt the police had been in the wrong throughout their handling of the incident and was pretty sure that the charges against him would be dropped. As a result of a strong community reaction to the incident, the charges against Maurice and several males from his neighborhood were dismissed, although the boy on the motor scooter was convicted of disorderly conduct and simple assault on a police officer.

After processing this experience with Maurice, the counselor acknowledged to Maurice that he had learned quite a bit about him through Melissa's disclosures in counseling. Speaking softly, Maurice responded that he knew this and that he was grateful for the way the counselor had helped Melissa. After a brief pause, he added that he had planned to come and see the counselor for some time but because things had been going so poorly for him lately, he had had doubts that counseling could help. On this note, Maurice looked down to the ground and was silent.

The counselor informed Maurice that anything they discussed would be held in the strictest confidence and he assured Maurice that he had nothing to do with the welfare or child support enforcement offices. The counselor then asked Maurice if he was interested in giving counseling a try, and, if so, what might he like to work on first. Maurice responded, "Yes, I'd like to get my life together." The counselor then asked Maurice if he would prefer his own counselor or participate in counseling with Melissa. Maurice replied that he was interested in both individual and couples counseling but that he would like to work with this counselor rather than somebody else.

Sensing that he had established a good initial rapport with Maurice, the counselor expressed his enthusiastic interest in working with Maurice and then described to Maurice how the counseling would proceed. He stated that they could alternate individual and couple sessions. He forewarned Maurice that he might want his permission to include Maurice's mother and other family members at some time in the future. Finally, he reviewed with Maurice the issues that they might discuss alone, including his difficulties in finding a job, the possible contributory role of racism in how he has been behaving lately, his feelings regarding fatherhood, and the advantages and disadvantages of his association with his current circle of friends who abused alcohol and drugs. As the counselor mentioned these subjects, Maurice's attention was riveted on the counselor. The counselor ended the session by asking Maurice if he was open to reviewing these topics. Although Maurice simply replied, "They're OK," he had a hopeful expression on his face and appeared eager for the counseling to begin.

Over the next year, the counselor met with Maurice in both individual and couples counseling. Because the counselor hypothesized that many of Maurice's personal issues were affecting his relationship with Melissa, individual counseling was emphasized for several months, even though a few sessions were held with Melissa.

Because a priority of the individual counseling was on helping Maurice to get a job, ongoing career counseling was implemented. The counselor referred Maurice to a career assessment, training, and placement program, which was sponsored by the Joint Training Partnership Act and offered at the nearby county employment training service. Because Maurice had no car, transportation to the service became an issue. The counselor worked out a schedule of drivers to take Maurice to and from the center. The team of drivers included the minister and several adult members of Mrs. W's church, extended family members, and the counselor himself.

Although the professionals at the employment service conducted their assessment and training, the counselor helped Maurice to identify and address issues that negatively affected his career self-efficacy, including the interacting influences of Maurice's father, friends, and racism. Although Maurice never lived with his father, the two had a positive relationship and a bond that still existed even though Maurice's father now lived in another state. In spite of his fondness for his father, however, Maurice was always somewhat disappointed that his father rarely worked and had provided little toward the financial support of his family. Maurice understood that many of his father's career difficulties were the result of institutional racism that blocked his father from employment in fields that were open only to Anglos. Having seen his father victimized by discrimination, Maurice feared that his own efforts to succeed would be met with the same treatment, especially considering the entrenched racism in his area of the country. He was further discouraged by the attitudes of many of his peers who had "given up on life at an early age and turned to drugs and the streets to make a living." Maurice had already found confirmation of his fears by the hostile treatment he received from Anglos during his recent job search and the condescending manner in which he was regarded by Anglos working at his prior employment site. His recent withdrawal from Melissa and his child and his association with delinquent peers were a sign that he was on the verge of giving up.

To counter these effects, the counselor employed several strategies. First, the counselor empathized with Maurice's anger over the historical treatment of African Americans and pointed out to Maurice how he might have internalized societal hatred. Second, the counselor shared with Maurice readings on Africentrism and essays by African American writers, such as Madhubuti, to provide him with an alternative perspective on his heritage and his situation. Third, the counselor arranged for Maurice to meet with an African American male graduate student in counseling who had several heart-to-heart talks with Maurice about the realities of racism and some self-enhancing strategies for dealing with it. Fourth, the counselor contacted an affirmative action officer at a nearby university who was willing to inform Maurice about current affirmative action policies and how Maurice could rely on the Equal Opportunity Commission to address any complaints he had regarding unfair treatment in the workplace.

These strategies were effective in gradually mitigating Maurice's anger and eliminating his self-defeating behaviors. Having been armed with skills to deal with racism, he felt more hopeful about the job training, and he pursued studies to be a medical technician.

Subsequently, Maurice was able to concentrate on his relationship with Melissa and their child. Although he became more responsive to her needs and he spent more time with his daughter, the counseling helped the couple to realize that they had significant incompatibility problems, which had contributed toward the downturn in their relationship. Eventually, they both decided to date other people, even though they wanted to remain friends and have cordial interactions with their child.

During his work with Maurice and Melissa in couple's counseling, the counselor had a few opportunities to witness Maurice and Melissa in interactions with their baby. Through these observations the counselor recognized that Maurice could benefit from information on how to manage a young child. He discussed the idea of Maurice enrolling in a child development course offered in the afternoons through a social service agency. Maurice was opposed to the suggestion of attending formal classes, although he was receptive to the idea of improving his child care skills. He was amenable to the next recommendation by the counselor that he borrow some child development videos, view them at home, and then discuss the subject matter with the counselor in his office. After following through with this plan, Maurice became more adept at handling his daughter.

Although these positive developments encouraged Maurice, other events pertaining to his friends and family slowed his progress from time to time. For example, some of Maurice's friends interpreted his positive changes in behavior as attempts "to become a honky." These remarks hurt Maurice, and he occasionally hung out with the wrong crowd and blew off counseling sessions in an effort to win their acceptance. After Maurice missed two consecutive sessions, the counselor tracked him down with the assistance of Mrs. W, who was instrumental in persuading Maurice to resume counseling.

To help Maurice cope with the reactions of his peers, the counselor explained in layman's terms the stages of Black Racial Identity Development, which assisted Maurice in understanding his friends' behavior. The counselor once again welcomed the assistance and generosity of his graduate student, who shared with Maurice similar reactions that he had encountered when he visited his hometown during breaks from his studies. His advice gave Maurice confidence that he could survive as a bicultural individual.

Another issue pertaining to Maurice's peers were their attitudes regarding contraceptive use. By this time, Maurice had a new steady girlfriend, with whom he was sexually active. Based on exploits described by some of his friends, Maurice felt pressured not to use "a baggie" (i.e., a condom). Through counseling, Maurice was taught strategies for dealing with this pressure. Eventually, he decided to use condoms regularly but to hide the details of his sexual life from his friends.

Other measures were necessary to help Maurice weather a tragedy in his family. During the course of counseling, Maurice's grandmother died in an automobile accident, a loss that sent Mrs. W into a reactive depression. Her ability to manage her family was hampered during this period, and boundary issues exploded between Maurice, his sister, and an aunt and her children, who had moved in with Mrs. W for a brief period. The counselor attended the service for the grandmother, and, subsequently, paid a visit to Mrs. W to see how she was faring. Because of these contacts, Mrs. W was receptive to bringing her family for counseling when their problems emerged.

Through family counseling, Mrs. W was able to express to her relatives that her mother's loss made it too difficult for her to care for so many people in her home at the present time. Brainstorming sessions with the family led to the identification of kin in another state who were willing to take in the aunt and her children until Mrs. W got back on her feet.

After this change occurred, Mrs. W found more energy to mourn the loss of her mother through counseling with her minister and Maurice's counselor. As the mood in the home returned to normal, Maurice's performance in his training improved, and the counseling sessions became spaced out over longer periods of time.

During this phasing-out period, Maurice and the counselor had a rather spontaneous and touching session, during which Maurice thanked the counselor for all of his help. Maurice confessed that part of the reason he had avoided the counselor many months earlier was that he had been called "some pretty nasty things" by a few adults when Melissa became pregnant, especially Melissa's parents. He had figured that this counselor would treat him the same way. Furthermore, Maurice reported that he had thought, "There's no way I gonna' tell this White man anything about myself " but that, as a result of their first encounter, he decided that the counselor was "all right." The counselor responded by thanking Maurice for the feedback and the compliment. The counselor also described how wonderful it had been for him to get to know Maurice and his family. On this last note, Maurice pulled out a present from a paper bag he had carried into the counselor's office and he handed the present to the counselor. Wrapped in aluminum foil with a card attached, the gift was a loaf of cinnamon-raisin bread that had been baked by Mrs. W. In the card, she had expressed her gratitude for the counselor's assistance with her family, with a concluding comment, "God bless you." This was truly a special moment that the counselor has always cherished. He responded to these acts of kindness by bringing thank you cards to both Maurice and Mrs. W at their home and expressing the joy he had received in sharing in their experiences.

When he last contacted his counselor, Maurice was well on his way to becoming a medical technician and was having regular, enjoyable contacts with his daughter. As for Melissa, she graduated from the Teenage Mothers Program, had secured a job as a beautician, and was dating a new boyfriend, a college student who expressed a fondness for Melissa's daughter. Unfortunately, her parents still would have nothing to do with her, and, from time to time, she met with the counselor to mourn the fact that her child still had no interactions with her maternal grandparents.

Case Analysis. Maurice's case is similar to David's in that they both dramatize the intensely difficult and yet rewarding experiences awaiting counselors who work with teenage fathers. Instead of prejudging Maurice for his reduced contact with his child and partner, the counselor endeavored to understand the complex factors that might account for his behavior and worked persistently to achieve a solution. Complicated case management strategies were required to help Maurice negotiate the often conflicting roles of adolescent and father. As is the case with most teenage fathers, he needed special assistance to address multigenerational family issues and conflicts with peers, find gainful employment, and prevent a second unplanned pregnancy. It was necessary to address the needs of the significant others in his world, including the mother of his child and the members of his immediate family, to successfully help him.

Several culturally sensitive features of the counseling conducted in this case study warrant closer examination. First, the counselor recognized that racial mistrust could be an impediment to engaging Maurice and his family in counseling. Therefore, he used the following strategies to help this African American family overcome their mistrust of the mental health system and a White counselor: conducting repeated and varied outreach tactics, including phone calls, home visits, extending oneself in nontraditional ways (e.g., driving Maurice to and from the job training center); being flexible with his schedule during the initial crisis; and expressing an ongoing, genuine concern for the well-being of the family. Second, the counselor addressed the contribution of racism in the historical experience of this family and in Maurice's self-defeating behaviors and poor career self-efficacy. Third, culturally relevant interventions were employed, including the use of the Black church, positive African American male role models, and the extended kinship network for support, as well as educational materials regarding an Africentric perspective. Fourth, issues of Black racial identity development were examined. Fifth, variant forms of family functioning were accepted as adaptations to the conditions of lower socioeconomic status. Sensitivity toward the fears of an indigent couple trying to cope with the welfare system were demonstrated.

The Case of Carlos R

Carlos R was 17 years old and the oldest of six children from an intact Puerto Rican family. Mr. R, Carlos's father, worked full-time as an unskilled laborer in a meat-packing plant and part-time as a dishwasher in a local diner. Mrs. R, Carlos's mother, served as the primary caregiver for the children and managed the affairs of the home during the many long hours that Mr. R worked. Their children included four boys and two girls who ranged in age from 2 to 17 years.

The Rs lived in a three-bedroom apartment located in a crowded, inner-city community, consisting primarily of Hispanic and African American families. Most of the families residing in Carlos's neighborhood were poor and the area was plagued by many of the problems confronting our nation's inner cities, including a high rate of illegal drug trafficking, substandard housing, and gang violence. Although Mr. R's earnings from his two jobs were so low that he could barely provide for his wife and children, he nevertheless dreamed of saving enough money to buy a house in the suburbs where he believed his family would have a better chance in life. As he worked toward this goal, he and his family struggled to survive, finding hope and affiliation through their neighborhood Roman Catholic church and their extended kin, many of whom lived in the same community. Within this context, Carlos became a teenage father.

Carlos was recruited for counseling by a high school guidance counselor who had heard through his informal contacts with several students in Carlos's school that Carlos's 17-year-old girlfriend, Claudia, was pregnant. Because the counselor had a good rapport with most of the students Carlos's age, Carlos was not surprised when the counselor approached him regarding the rumor that Claudia was pregnant.

Carlos was glad to have an impartial adult to confide in regarding this crisis, and he readily talked about his pregnancy. He and Claudia had been dating since they were freshmen in high school but had engaged in sexual intercourse for the first time only recently. Although he had known that condoms could prevent a pregnancy, Carlos reported that he had not used any because their sexual relations were spontaneous and unexpected.

When he learned that Claudia was pregnant, Carlos had mixed feelings. On the one hand, he was excited about the prospect of their having a child and decided immediately that they should marry. On the other hand, he understood that this event would send shock waves throughout family. His parents had urged him to complete school, for they both had been high school dropouts who regretted not having more formal education. Carlos was doubtful that he could complete school now, and he feared that his parents would be bitterly disappointed in him, even though he was certain that they would want him to marry Claudia. Carlos also realized that the pregnancy would bring great shame to his family. As the eldest of six children, his parents expected him to set a positive example for his younger brothers and sisters. Clearly, he concluded, he had let his parents down in this regard.

As worried as he was about his own parents' reaction, he was even more concerned about facing Claudia's parents. They were a very traditional Mexican American couple with strong ties to the Roman Catholic church. They taught their daughter that an honorable young lady should remain a virgin until she was married. They had often criticized adolescent mothers in their neighborhoods for shaming their families. The news of their own daughter's out-of-wedlock pregnancy would be a bitter pill to swallow. What's more, they had treated Carlos like a son since the day he started dating Claudia. He felt that he had greatly disappointed them and that they would be ashamed of him.

The counselor surmised that Carlos appeared to have his mind set on marrying Claudia. Nevertheless, the counselor conducted decision-making counseling to be sure that Carlos had not rushed his decision without carefully considering the implications of each of the pregnancy-resolution options. Carlos asked Claudia to join him in counseling as the two further considered their situation. Because this process confirmed the clarity of their desire to marry, the focus of counseling was switched to addressing the forecasted reactions of Carlos's and Claudia's families.

The couple decided that they would tell their parents together, Carlos's parents first, Claudia's parents second, in the privacy of their respective homes. The counselor encouraged the couple to inform their parents that he would be available to help them with their reaction to the pregnancy.

As predicted, breaking the news to their parents was very difficult. Carlos's parents were stunned by the news. Although they supported the couple's plans to marry, they felt great shame. Carlos's father took the news especially hard and wondered out loud why he had worked so hard to give his son a chance in life when his son would go ahead and make such a terrible mistake. As for Claudia's parents, they too felt ashamed and agreed with the idea of marriage.

Although the parents quickly contacted each other to discuss arrangements they could make with the church for a wedding, all four adults were badly shaken and discouraged by the crisis. Mr. and Mrs. R turned to their own parents for guidance and support. Although both sets of grandparents were deeply saddened by the news, their overall reactions were of great comfort to the Rs. Carlos's paternal grandparents offered to take the young couple in after they were married until they could afford a place of their own. Mrs. R's parents promised to assist in any way possible.

Coping for Claudia's parents was more difficult because their extended family, including both sets of grandparents, lived in Mexico. They already felt cut off from their family due to the great geographic distance between them, and this latest crisis heightened their sense of isolation.

Claudia's father decided to contact the counselor for advice even though the father's English was poor. When the counselor spoke with the father over the phone, he hypothesized that the school environment might be an awkward setting to discuss so delicate a matter with this immigrant man. He offered to meet the father either at the father's home or in some other potentially comfortable setting, perhaps at the rectory of the local Catholic church. The father thanked the counselor for these offers but stated he could stop by the counselor's office after work because the school was located just a couple of blocks from the father's place of employment, a machine shop were he worked as a drill press operator.

The two met in school late one afternoon to discuss the father's dilemma about how to help his daughter in this difficult situation. Because the counselor did not speak Spanish, he had made arrangements for an interpreter to join him at the meeting in case one was needed to communicate with Claudia's father. When Claudia's father appeared for the session, the counselor warmly shook the father's hand, apologized for not knowing Spanish, and asked the father if he desired that an interpreter be present. Claudia's father responded that the interpreter might be helpful, and then he proceeded to discuss what was on his mind regarding Claudia.

Through the interpreter, he explained that it is "our way" for the woman to remain at home to care for the child while the husband works to support his family. He anticipated that Claudia would follow in this tradition. Yet he recognized that it was increasingly difficult for a couple to make it in the world today unless both parents worked. Claudia had intended on completing training as a secretary. Now she couldn't complete this training because a baby was on the way. He felt so frustrated and wasn't sure what he could do to help her.

The counselor recognized that Claudia's father was experiencing a cultural values conflict. With probing, he clarified that the father was torn between the desire to support his daughter in fulfilling a traditional role as mother and the recognition that some alternative plan might be more beneficial for his daughter in the long run. The counselor sensed that Claudia's father was searching for information regarding ways that Claudia could complete her schooling. Very tentatively, the counselor told the father about a teenage mother's program that would provide child care for Claudia's baby while she continued her studies. The counselor added that he understood the use of this program would represent a radical departure from the Hispanic tradition that the father had described. Thus, the counselor recommended that Claudia's father discuss the issue further with Carlos, his parents, Claudia, and Claudia's mother to air their opinions about such a plan.

Subsequent to this session, Claudia's father again contacted the counselor to provide him with feedback regarding the meeting that had been held by the two families. Collectively, they concurred that it would be best for the young couple's future if Claudia could complete school while Carlos worked to support the family. However, they were opposed to "strangers" caring for the baby, preferring instead that Mrs. R care for the child in her home while Claudia attended school. Once Claudia completed school, she would take over the rearing of her child until the child was in school herself, at which time Claudia would seek employment as a secretary.

The counselor was pleased by the news that the two families had taken so many steps to manage this crisis together. Still, he was worried that the proposed plan contained no provisions for Carlos to complete his education. So he asked Claudia's father if the counselor might be allowed to join one more joint family meeting to share some tentative suggestions he had about Carlos's education and career. When the families agreed to this idea, the counselor asked them to consider the pros and cons of modifying their plans in ways that might maximize Carlos's career development. A frank discussion regarding the limited opportunities facing Carlos without the benefits of additional education followed. The family decided that Carlos should work now to fulfill his obligations as the "head of his family." Once his child was old enough to return to school, Carlos would resume his education under the guidance of the school counselor. The parents of the young couple were particularly enthused about this plan when the school counselor told them about a special outreach program for ethnic-minority students offered by the admissions office of a premiere state college. The counselor promised to monitor the progress of the couple over the years and arrange for them to receive information about this program at the appropriate time so that both of them could consider it as a means to further their educations.

By the conclusion of this meeting, all family members involved were satisfied that the crisis had been managed satisfactorily. However, two other long-term issues remained to be addressed: the young parent's readiness as caregivers and the possibility that another unplanned pregnancy could complicate the previously mentioned educational and career plans of the couple. Based on his interactions with both families, the counselor was confident that the couple would receive loving guidance from their families on how to nurture a baby. He complemented this assistance by suggesting to both Carlos and Claudia that they enroll in a free childbirth and child development course offered on Saturdays by a local hospital. Concurrent with this training, the counselor had several individual sessions with Carlos to discuss his readiness for fatherhood. Through these meetings, the counselor learned that Carlos and his father had several reassuring conversations about the role of the father and that Carlos was looking forward to having a child. The counselor also discovered that Carlos had anticipated the implications of having a second unplanned child and that he was contemplating using contraceptives after marriage. The counselor asked Carlos to consider carefully his Catholic upbringing and the church's opposition to contraceptive use. Carlos stated that although he considered himself to be a practicing Catholic, he disagreed with this particular doctrine of the church and had decided that he would use contraceptives until he and Claudia were ready to have their second baby. In light of Carlos's decision, the counselor referred him to a health educator who provided him with accurate information about birth control.

By the time of the baby's birth, most of the shame associated with the pregnancy gave way to widespread joy over a new addition to the family, a husky little boy. All of the aforementioned plans proceeded as they had been arranged, except that Carlos had repeated difficulties in the workplace. Although Carlos had dropped out of school, the counselor maintained contact with Carlos and learned that Carlos lost his first job in a local factory after just 6 weeks of employment. The counselor provided Carlos with emotional support and job-seeking skills training until Carlos was able to secure a position 4 months later working on the loading dock of a bread company. Because his unemployment stressed the family's ability to support the young couple, the counselor linked them with a variety of services that provided free baby formula and diapers.

One night while working the evening shift on the loading dock, Carlos was mugged by several youth who stole Carlos's wallet and broke his nose. At the time, Carlos had made the mistake of having $130 in his wallet. Losing this money was a temporary yet sizable financial setback for his family, because they survived from paycheck to paycheck. The counselor contacted a priest from Carlos parish and informed him of this incident. The priest responded by sending Carlos a food basket from the church's food drive for the poor. The counselor also contacted Mrs. R, who was caring for the baby and her own children at the time, and asked her if she might be interested in some free clothing for the children. When she answered affirmatively, the counselor asked for donations from his friends and neighbors and gave them to Mrs. R for her family. The items not used by Mrs. R were in turn passed on to the her parish priest to be distributed to other needy families.

In addition to these strategies, the counselor spent considerable time discussing with Carlos safety survival tactics in the inner city. For example, he advised Carlos not to carry any more cash than was absolutely necessary in his wallet. In addition, he suggested that Carlos always keep a $20 bill inside his shoe so that he would have cash on hand if his wallet was stolen again. Furthermore, he urged Carlos to leave work with groups of employees so that he might reduce the possibility of being attacked. Last, the counselor encouraged Carlos to approach the management at his work site about taking additional security measures for their employees. This latter suggestion resulted in the locking of the shipping yard gate at all times that trucks were not passing through them.

The bond that had been established between the counselor and both families grew stronger over time after the baby's birth. The counselor was invited to the baby's christening, truly an expression of the families' respect for and gratitude toward the counselor. He honored the families by attending the service and by accepting their invitation to join them for a celebratory meal served afterward at the home of Claudia's parents.

Three years after the birth the baby, Claudia graduated from high school and took over the daily care responsibilities of her son. The couple continued to live with Carlos's paternal grandparents while he prepared to take the GED examination. The couple were determined that Carlos would go on to college once their son was in school and hoped that he would earn a degree in computer systems management.

Case Analysis. Carlos's case vividly portrays that unplanned teenage preg-nancies can create high drama for two existing extended families. His case also demonstrates the complicated decision making and ongoing counseling required to help teenage fathers satisfactorily resolve their educational and career dilemmas in a manner that best serves their child and family. The counselor's visibility of and contacts with the student body enabled him to successfully reach out and establish rapport with Carlos.

Many culture-specific considerations were highlighted by Carlos's situ-ation. Rapport was facilitated by a very warm, caring, and personal approach that is appreciated by Hispanic American families. Perhaps this was most evident in the counselor's participation in the christening celebration. Had he turned down the families' invitation to join them in this event, he might have insulted them and damaged the respect he had earned previously. The counselor communicated his sensitivity regarding potential language barri-ers by employing an interpreter. Careful handling of the cultural value conflicts experienced by several members of these two Hispanic American families helped them to achieve plans of action with which they were comfortable. The counselor recognized the importance of the teachings of the Catholic church in the decision-making process and he used the church as a natural support mechanism. He also respected and encouraged the families' reliance on their extended families for assistance. Appreciation for the difficult socioeconomic condition of the families was demonstrated by the brokering of services to help the family with their financial hardships. Finally, the counselor attended to the realities of urban living by reviewing safety survival strategies.

Conclusion

In this chapter, the process of multicultural counseling with teenage fathers was illustrated through the presentation and analysis of three actual case studies. In the next chapter on implications for training and research, the role of the practitioner as a collaborative researcher is discussed.

PART IV

13

Implications for
Training and Research

Educators can play a critical, indirect role in addressing the needs of adolescent fathers by offering appropriate training experiences and conducting research that advances our understanding of the perspectives of teenage fathers, how they become parents prematurely, their special adjustment difficulties, and how to effectively help them. This chapter contains suggestions for preparing helpers-in-training to serve teenage fathers. Also, prior research on teenage fathers is critiqued and suggestions for future research are offered. Recommendations for integrating research and practice are provided and ethical principles pertaining to research with adolescents and multicultural research are reviewed.

Training Recommendations

Teenage fathers come from a variety of cultural backgrounds and they experience a wide range of adjustment difficulties posing complicated case management challenges. In order for mental health professionals to be competent in serving teenage fathers, it is recommended that they complete several training objectives, beginning with extensive training in multicultural counseling. In addition, they need to develop the knowledge base and skills for working with teenage parents, clarify their attitudes about this population and the culturally different, and participate in supervised internship programs providing students with opportunities to directly counsel young fathers.

Training in Multicultural Counseling

Because teenage fatherhood is a phenomenon that cuts across socioeconomic, racial, ethnic, and geographic lines, it is imperative that youth service professionals obtain extensive training in multicultural counseling. This training will help practitioners to understand the diverse cultural contexts in which teenage pregnancy and parenthood occur and develop skills to make culturally appropriate interventions. As Pedersen (1988) and Sue, Akutsu, and Higashi (1985) noted, when competency in multicultural counseling is achieved, cultural barriers to counseling are likely to be diminished and the effectiveness of cross-cultural counseling is likely to be enhanced.

Developing the Knowledge Base
and Skills for Counseling Teenage Parents

Training would-be helpers to counsel adolescent fathers should include coverage of the subjects of both teenage fathers *and* teenage mothers, because an adequate understanding of adolescent pregnancy and parenthood must include a recognition that two partners are involved in an unplanned conception, how the pregnancy is resolved, and, if the child is carried to term and delivered successfully, how he or she is parented. With this knowledge base, counselors will be able to serve the entire new family system that results from the pregnancy, thereby enhancing the development of the young father, mother, and baby. Pertinent instruction can be offered in graduate/professional schools and through continuing education programs in counseling, psychology, social work, nursing, medicine, divinity, home economics, vocational education, and other related fields.

Educators can prepare their trainees to be competent service providers by infusing the topic of teenage parenthood into relevant courses and by teaching necessary helping skills. Sections of courses on adolescent development could be devoted to the subjects of the adjustment difficulties and opportunities for growth that are associated with teenage pregnancy and parenthood. Similarly, sections of courses on multicultural counseling could be focused on cultural variations of adolescent childbearing and fatherhood. In classes on primary prevention and consultation, trainees can be taught skills for helping to prevent unplanned pregnancies among adolescents. Because many schools are beginning to offer school-based services for teenage parents (see Flood et al., 1985), school counselors are likely to work with this population. Therefore, it is recommended that courses pertinent to school counseling include a review of the subject of teenage parenthood. Trainees will need to learn outreach strategies, because teenage fathers often have difficulty in identifying and getting to services (see Brindis et al., 1987; Hendricks, 1988; Robinson, 1988a). Because so much of the work with teenage parents requires assisting them with critical decisions (e.g., Should I drop out of school? Should I marry? Should I keep the child or consider abortion or adoption?), helpers can benefit from training in decision-making counseling. Outreach and decision-making strategies could be taught in courses on the techniques of counseling. Courses on family and career counseling are appropriate venues for teaching counselors skills for addressing the family and educational/career conflicts that are often associated with the crisis of an unplanned, adolescent pregnancy (see Children's Defense Fund, 1987a; Kiselica & Murphy, 1994; Robinson, 1988a). These same skills also might be covered in psychology or sociology courses regarding particular cultural groups (e.g., a course on African American studies). It is realistic to expect that no one counselor can respond to all of the needs of teenage parents. Therefore, trainees will need to be taught referral and consultation skills and how to work collaboratively with other helping professionals (Kiselica & Pfaller, 1993). Finally, because research is critical for the advancement of our knowledge about teenage fathers, training in a wide range of the methods of research, including experimental, qualitative, ethnographic, and single-study research procedures, is recommended.

As an alternative to covering discrete aspects of the subject of adolescent pregnancy and parenthood in a variety of courses, specialized courses and workshops on the topic can be offered. Another option is to provide in-depth coverage of the subject in a section of a course on adolescent counseling.

Dryfoos (1994) recommended that training include cross-disciplinary instruction involving schools of education, psychology, public health, nursing, and social work. This approach will prepare youth service workers who are competent at offering the type of comprehensive services that are deemed necessary for helping teenage parents.

Clarifying Attitudes About Teenage Parents and the Culturally Different

Whether pertinent training is offered throughout an entire curriculum or through specialized courses, it is essential that trainees clarify their attitudes about teenage parents and the culturally different and then divest themselves of stereotypes about these populations. As Egan (1990) noted, counselors are similar to all people in their tendency to evaluate others according to societal prejudices. Egan (1990) suggested that counselors safeguard against this tendency by suspending judgment of clients in an effort to understand their clients' experiences and point of view. Counselors whose judgments of teenage parents and the culturally different interfere with the counselor-client relationship have a responsibility to refer their clients to an appropriate colleague (see Kiselica & Pfaller, 1993).

Educators can assist students with the task of clarifying their attitudes regarding teenage parents and the culturally different by employing some pertinent exercises from the literature on developing multicultural awareness. For example, Weeks, Pedersen, and Brislin (1986) cite several activities that are designed to clarify trainee feelings with regards to the prospect of working with a new client population. Instructional manuals by Dillard (1983), Parker (1988), and McGrath and Axelson (1993) contain other exercises with a similar purpose. Particular attention should be directed at helping trainees to identify their stage of racial identity development and how it might affect their interactions with the culturally different, a goal that can be achieved by using Helms's (1990) *A Training Manual for Diagnosing Racial Identity in Social Interactions.*

After students have clarified their attitudes about teenage parents and the culturally different, counselor educators should instruct them about ethical responsibility vis-à-vis counseling teenage parents. Again, any professional whose biases about teenage parents or culturally different clients would inhibit the development of a therapeutic relationship should refer such clients to another counselor.

Internships and Teenage Parent Service Programs

Several writers (e.g., S. B. Baker, 1992; Baker & Shaw, 1987; Sprinthall, 1984) argued that trainees traditionally have been schooled in the practice of one-on-one remedial counseling and suggested that training should be expanded to include outreach and preventive counseling with large groups of clients. Students who are provided with the opportunity to practice these latter forms of counseling typically respond with enthusiasm, commitment, and a sense of fulfillment (Sprinthall, 1984).

Preparing students to assist teenage parents is an excellent mechanism for providing trainees with these types of experiences. By working collaboratively with counselor educators and other trainers of mental health professionals to establish school-based internship experiences with teenage parents, practitioners can play an important role in preparing more counselors who will assist the teenage parents of the future. The efforts of educators to groom trainees for this role will be limited unless clinicians are willing to provide field supervision to interested trainees. Such service will enhance the training experience of students by providing them with opportunities to conduct outreach (i.e., identifying and recruiting teenage parents) and preventive group counseling (e.g., group counseling to prevent teenage parents from dropping out of school and parenting skills training to teach them how to care for their children). The additional people power supplied by enthusiastic interns will enable seasoned professionals to increase the number of teenage parents that can be served.

Creative, dedicated planning and interprofessional collaboration may be required to expand the service mission of some internship sites that are focused on serving only teenage mothers. Some professionals employed in teenage mother programs may be interested in extending services to teenage fathers but lack the resources to do so. The addition of interns might allow these programs to include young fathers, because many interns work for free or are paid lower wages than full-time employees. Program coordinators might contract with educators to have interns placed at the site every semester so that a young fathers program can be offered on a continuing basis.

Extra efforts to develop internships at sites serving populations that historically have been neglected would provide a tremendous service to our society. In addition, such opportunities may be extremely rewarding for the participating interns. For example, I described my experiences working in a multicultural internship with underserved populations as immensely valuable:

> My cross-cultural internship offered me unique opportunities to develop my professional skills while partaking in profoundly fulfilling experiences. These experiences introduced me to a new culture, taught me about the workings of family and societal systems, and challenged me to become an effective service provider. In the process, I confronted my fears and cultural biases, clarified many of my values, and discovered new facets to my identity. Also, I developed new counseling skills that subsequently have been very helpful in my work with both culturally similar and culturally different clients. By experiencing the beauty of other cultures, by witnessing people with dignity and determination in the face of life's worst difficulties, and by realizing how very much I could contribute to the healthy psychological development of fellow human beings, I had participated in one of our profession's most enriching endeavors. (Kiselica, 1991, p. 129)

A Critique of Research on Teenage Fathers
and Suggestions for Future Research

Prior research on teenage fathers has been critiqued in several reviews of the literature on teenage pregnancy and parenthood. These reviews abound with recommendations for future research on adolescent fathers. In this section, the conclusions and recommendations from this literature are integrated with my updated research critiques and suggestions, and they are organized according to reviews of the basic research on teenage fathers and the outcome research evaluating the efficacy teenage father service programs. This section also contains an original review of the research on societal attitudes about teenage fathers.

Reviews of the Basic Research on Teenage Fathers

Robinson and Barret (1982), Parke and Neville (1987), and Robinson (1988a) identified several deficiencies in much of the basic research on teenage fathers. First, teenage fatherhood has received little empirical attention because of the historical neglect of the role of fathers in the family and parenting literature. Robinson (1988a) cited numerous examples from the literature to support this contention. For example, a 1980 special issue of the *American Journal of Orthopsychiatry* dealt with teenage pregnancy. Only one out of seven of those articles addressed adolescent fatherhood. Second, generalizations about teenage fathers were based on several inferential sources of information, including interviews of adolescent mothers regarding their male partners, teenage fathers subsumed within a larger population of older unmarried fathers, antecedent studies conducted on teenagers before they become fathers, and adolescent males who are not necessarily teenage fathers. A third, related problem is that only 21 studies from 1973 to 1987 included exclusive samples of teenage fathers, and most of these included small samples, were highly descriptive in nature, and did not include comparison groups. The fourth problem is that some of the direct studies of teenage fathers suffered from unrepresentative sampling restricted to young fathers from clinical populations.

I recently conducted a review of the basic research literature published since 1988 and discovered that many of the criticisms raised by Robinson and Barret (1982), Parke and Neville (1987), and Robinson (1988a) still apply today. Several findings support this conclusion. First, the subject of teenage fatherhood *still* receives sparse coverage in the basic research literature. Dozens of basic research studies published since 1988 pertained to adolescent mothers in the United States but only a handful of studies (e.g.,

Anderson, 1990; Buchanan & Robbins, 1990; Heath & McHenry, 1993) were focused on American males who had fathered children during their teenage years. Second, although a few studies (e.g., Achatz & MacAllum, 1994; Christmon, 1990a, 1990b; Fernandez, Ruch-Ross, & Montague, 1993; McGovern, 1990) included samples of teenage fathers, these subjects were subsumed within a larger population of older fathers, making it difficult to determine which of the reported findings and recommendations apply to the teenage males. Third, even though there is a burgeoning literature on fatherhood, the particular subject of teenage fatherhood is largely neglected. For example, in a 1993 special edition of the *Journal of Family Issues,* which was devoted to contemporary scholarship on fatherhood, none of the seven articles from this issue were focused on teenage fatherhood, and the subject was virtually ignored throughout the entire issue.

These recent findings indicate that many of the recommendations made in the 1980s regarding future basic research on teenage fathers have, for the most part, been unheeded. Therefore, they remain valid for the 1990s and are worth repeating here. For example, in an effort to improve on the methodological shortcomings of prior basic research on teenage fathers, Robinson (1988a) recommended numerous suggestions for future scholarship on the subject. These included the following: increase the sheer quantity of direct research on teenage fathers; conduct collaborative research projects with helping professionals in the field to increase access to teenage fathers; use representative samples of teenage fathers; ensure that studies of both teenage fathers and older fathers contain separate analyses and conclusions for each group to avoid questionable generalizations about younger fathers; investigate for variations among teenage fathers according to demographic variables, such as socioeconomic status and race; describe teenage fathers with positive nomenclature, rather than negative terminology, such as "putative fathers" and "precocious fathers"; employ research designs that contain comparison groups, such as teenage fathers, adolescent nonfathers, older adult fathers, married teenage fathers, and unmarried teenage fathers; conduct longitudinal studies to chronicle the attitudinal and behavioral continuities and changes in the fathering and family life of teenage fathers over time; and use a multimethod approach to data collection, including self-reports and interview techniques, behavioral observations measures, and ecological and interactional assessments.

A variety of other recommendations for future research pertain to multicultural considerations. Ooms (1981) called for more research focused on teenage sex and pregnancy as they occur in families of different socioeconomic levels, racial, ethnic, and religious backgrounds and rural versus urban environments. Ooms (1981) also urged researchers to make more careful assessments of the ways in which the organization and delivery of services may conflict with the cultural values, attitudes, and practices of clients. Kiselica and Pfaller (1993) made similar recommendations and suggested that efforts to investigate such cultural issues will be enhanced by employing a broader range of research methods, including qualitative and ethnographic strategies.

A ripe topic for inquiry is the relationship between limited life opportunities, adolescent pregnancy and parenthood, and other factors that mediate this relationship. Specifically, as suggested by Moore and Burt (1982), future research should address how teenagers view their social and economic career opportunities and how those views affect their decisions about their sexual behavior, contraception, and parenthood.

According to Parke and Neville (1987), other research could magnify our understanding of the adolescent father's role in the pregnancy resolution process by addressing the following questions: What percentage of pregnant teenagers involve their partner in their decision making? What are the characteristics of those young couples who choose abortion, adoption, single parenthood, or marriage as a means to resolve the unplanned pregnancy?

Issues pertaining to the families of teenage fathers warrant further investigation. Ooms (1981) recommended that research is needed to determine the ways in which families and other informal support systems (e.g., peers, the church) provide assistance to teenage parents and their children. Furthermore, Ooms argued that parents of teenagers need to be asked their views regarding their children's needs, the needs of the family as a whole, and the service needs of their children.

Regarding fatherhood issues, we know little about the variables that distinguish young men who support their partner and child from those who do not. We know even less about how the developmental status (social, cognitive, emotional, and physical) of the teenage father affects the quality of his interactions with his child (see Parke & Neville, 1987). Also, according to Lamb and Elster (1986) and Parke and Neville (1987), there are meager data on the adolescent males' knowledge of child development, the actual parental behavior of adolescent fathers, and the effects of that behavior on their offspring. Future research is needed to address these shortcomings.

Research on the prevention of repeat unplanned adolescent pregnancies has been focused almost exclusively on adolescent mothers (see Hofferth, 1987b). More information is needed to identify effective strategies that may prevent teenage fathers from becoming fathers again. For example, the course on preparation for fatherhood, which was described in Chapter 6 of this book and suggested as a program for preventing additional unplanned pregnancies, needs to be evaluated.

Finally, Marsiglio (1986) proposed an agenda of research focused on the educational attainment of adolescent fathers. In brief, Marsiglio suggested that researchers should attempt to achieve the following: (a) specify more fully the conditions under which fathering a child retards a young male's schooling and explain what factors enhance a young father's chances of fulfilling his educational plans and (b) clarify the role of the teenage father's partner and his family in his education and career.

Reviews of Outcome Research

Numerous scholars have noted that there is a lack of research evaluating the efficacy of teenage father counseling programs (Ascher, 1985; Kiselica & Pfaller, 1993; Kiselica, Stroud, et al., 1992; McGee, 1982; Robinson, 1988a; Smollar & Ooms, 1987). According to McGee (1982) and Robinson (1988a), outcome data are limited because most service providers cite anecdotal reports (e.g., testimonials from program participants and staff's observations of changes in clients' lives) as evidence of service effectiveness. Empirical outcome research is lacking. Kiselica and Pfaller (1993) suggested that this gap in research might be attributable, in part, to the fact most extant service programs target young mothers and exclude young fathers. Consequently, the majority of the few outcome studies of teenage *parenting* programs are actually evaluations of teenage *mother* programs (see Hofferth, 1987b).

A current review of the literature that I conducted supports these observations and hypotheses. Much of the recent outcome literature regarding service programs for teenage parents is limited to teenage mother programs (e.g., Cullen, 1988; DeLatte, Orgeron, & Preis, 1985; McAfee & Geesey, 1984; Polit, 1989). Moreover, some of the articles on service programs for adolescent fathers contain only anecdotal evidence for program effectiveness and a pejorative language is used to describe young fathers (e.g., Watson & Kelly, 1989).

Evaluations of a handful of service programs for young fathers have been reported in the literature. These included the following: Public/Private Venture's Young Unwed Fathers Pilot Project (Achatz & MacAllum, 1994), conducted with 155 fathers at six sites located throughout the United States; the Maine Young Fathers Project (Brown, 1990), a statewide service program that assisted 53 clients in Maine; the Maximizing a Life Experience (MALE) Group (Huey, 1987) administered to eight students enrolled in a suburban high school; and the Teen Father Collaboration (Klinman et al., 1985), a nationwide demonstration project that served 395 adolescent fathers at eight different settings. Separate outcome data were reported in a study conducted by investigators evaluating the Teenage Pregnancy and Parenting Project

(TAPP) in San Francisco, which was one of the program sites for the Teen Father Collaboration. The TAPP study involved 121 fathers. Typically, a range of services were offered through these programs, including parenting and job skills training, educational planning, supportive counseling, life skills training, and legal advice regarding such matters as child support and establishing paternity. The ages of the young fathers served varied from program to program. In three of these projects (Achatz & MacAllum, 1994; Barth et al., 1988; Brown, 1990), teenage fathers and adult fathers were studied, whereas the other studies were focused on teenage males only.

A variety of encouraging outcomes were reported in these studies. In all of the programs, the majority of the participants expressed favorable attitudes toward the treatment. Other outcomes included the following:

- Positive gains among program participants in terms of school and GED enrollment rates (Achatz & MacAllum, 1994; Barth et al., 1988; Huey, 1987; Klinman et al., 1985)
- Employment rates (Achatz & MacAllum, 1994; Barth et al., 1988; Brown, 1990; Huey, 1987; Klinman et al., 1985)
- Wages and benefits earned (Achatz & MacAllum, 1994)
- Knowledge regarding child support laws, legal rights, and responsibilities (Achatz & MacAllum, 1994; Huey, 1987)
- Birth control and pregnancy resolution options (Huey, 1987)

Barth et al. (1988) reported that fathers participating in the TAPP program demonstrated greater involvement in the prenatal care of their infants than did a control group of adolescent fathers. Also, the infants of the TAPP fathers had higher birthweights than the infants of the control fathers. Brown (1990) reported a variety of other positive results from her ambitious project with adolescent fathers in Maine, including the following: increased use of resources for food, clothing, and transportation; more frequent use of wellness/sick care services for both the father and his child; heightened participation in parenting skills training; more responsible use of birth control; increased frequency of interactions between the father and his child; more fathers establishing paternity; greater use of a support system; improved interpersonal relationships; increased utilization of public aid; greater implementation of plans to manage financial affairs; and increased paternal financial support of the child. Additional favorable findings were reported by Achatz & MacAllum (1994) in their summary regarding the large-scale Public/Private Venture's Young Unwed Fathers Pilot Project: use of job-readiness training and a fatherhood preparation curriculum; increased declaration of paternity and child support payments; and positive changes in attitudes toward the child support system.

Although the results of these five studies are promising, in each study the investigators failed to employ control group comparison designs. Thus, the significance of these findings is unclear. As was noted by Moore and Burt (1982), when control groups are excluded from outcome studies,

> It is possible that successful programs do some "creaming"—that is, the most motivated and able teens among the program's potential clients actually participate in the program. Without controlled research, we cannot know whether client characteristics, program services, or some combination of the two, are actually responsible for producing good effects. (p. 155)

In addition to these methodological limitations, some unfortunate outcomes were reported in the study by Achatz and MacAllum (1994). These included diminished contact between the fathers and their children over time, increased discord between the fathers and their partners, and limited use and completion of classroom vocational and on-the-job training.

Brown (1990) also noted some disappointing results, including an overall decline from pretest to posttest in efforts to achieve educational goals and disconcerting pretest to posttest rises in the frequency of repeat unplanned pregnancies, family violence, and failure on the part of a young father to acknowledge a substance abuse problem. It should be noted, however, that these latter findings may have been a function of imprecise reporting by the young fathers at the time of the baseline assessment. In her interpretation of these particular findings, Brown (1990) hypothesized that her baseline assessment may not have been as accurate as her posttest assessment. The baseline data had been collected shortly after the participants had entered the program. At that time, some case managers may have neither earned the trust nor had a thorough background knowledge of their clients. Consequently, some fathers may have presented a rosier picture at pretest than what had actually existed. Over time, however, the fathers may have felt more comfortable in disclosing information regarding such sensitive issues as violence in the home, thereby providing a more accurate report of their situation at posttest. If this were true, then the effects are that the pretest to posttest changes would appear worse than they actually were.

In summary, the bulk of the outcome research has been focused on evaluating the efficacy of female-oriented services and the handful of outcome studies pertaining to services for teenage fathers have been hampered by methodological limitations and problems of interpretation. In response to these shortcomings, Furstenberg et al. (1989) and Kiselica and Pfaller (1993) called for more outcome research to assess the clinical utility of service programs for teenage fathers. In addition, Kiselica and Pfaller (1993) suggested that outcome research will be enhanced by the employment of randomized pretest-posttest, control group comparison designs to assess more clearly the effectiveness of interventions with young fathers.

Although these suggestions are legitimate, significant logistical problems commonly encountered in research with teenage fathers make it difficult for investigators to conduct randomized pretest-posttest, control group comparison designs. Obtaining random, representative samples of teenage fathers is difficult because of the many problems involved in identifying adolescent fathers (see Chapter 2, this volume; Children's Defense Fund, 1988a). Furthermore, according to Kiselica (1993), due to the wariness of young fathers toward service providers, it is unlikely that most researchers will be able to recruit a large enough sample of teenage fathers at any one point in time—even among teenage fathers who volunteer to participate in studies —to randomly assign them to two or more different treatment conditions. Instead, what typically happens in the development of service programs for young fathers is that a few young men will "check out" an agency and, after they feel comfortable with a setting and are convinced that the staff will help them effectively, the fathers gradually spread the word to other young men who eventually get involved with the agency too. But participation of these youth over time tends to be inconsistent. Although some adolescent fathers attend structured programs regularly, others participate irregularly, drifting in to an agency at critical times when they may need help, drifting out when they are preoccupied with other concerns that, in their minds, take priority over what is offered in the service program. Although this tendency may be a nuisance to researchers because it poses threats to the internal validity of an experimental outcome study, veteran practitioners argue that effective recruitment demands flexibility regarding such issues as attendance. For example, in Indianapolis, Barber and Munn (1993) developed the Brotherhood Program to enhance the adjustment of inner-city adolescent males, many of whom are teenage fathers. When Munn started this outreach project, initially only a handful of males responded and their participation was inconsistent. However, as the reputation of the program filtered throughout the community, the number of participants has grown to the point that now more than 30 males participate at varying times throughout the year. A similar pattern was noted by Brown (1990) in her report regarding the Maine Young Fathers Project, by Achatz and MacAllum (1994) in their summary of the Public/Private Venture's Young Unwed Fathers Pilot Project, and by the staff administering the Teen Father Program at J. P. McCaskey High School in Lancater, Pennsylvania (see Cohen, 1993). Achatz and MacAllum (1994),

Brown (1990), and Munn (personal communication, September 21, 1994) believe that flexibility is a crucial characteristic to successful program development with young fathers. This opinion also was expressed to Hendricks (1988) by a variety of practitioners who had participated in a study assessing the practitioners' opinions regarding effective outreach strategies with teenage fathers.

The issues raised above underscore the complicated difficulties social scientists face in conducting outcome research in the field and may explain why the outcome studies cited earlier (i.e., Achatz & MacAllum, 1994; Barth et al., 1988; Brown, 1990; Huey, 1987; Klinman et al., 1985) were largely descriptive in nature. In recognition of the roadblocks hindering experimental outcome research, several scholars have concluded that traditional experimental designs and associated measurement procedures are appropriate for analog research strategies but are ill suited for field research involving clinical populations (e.g., Barlow, Hayes, & Nelson, 1984; Kazdin, 1982). Similarly, Ooms (1981) argued that researchers studying teenage parents and their families can no longer rely solely on standard research methodology (e.g., elaborate controlled experimental designs) that was developed for laboratory research. Instead, Ooms recommended the increased use of qualitative methods of research.

It appears then that qualitative and quasi-experimental methods may be more appropriate from a logistical standpoint for outcome research with teenage fathers than are experimental designs, but the former are subject to threats to internal validity. Thus, there are clear tradeoffs in the type of research methodology used. What, then, should the researcher do?

From a practical point of view, many researchers may have to rely on quasi-experimental designs, qualitative research, and single-case research designs to evaluate program effectiveness with teenage fathers. Although it is beyond the scope of this book to describe these approaches to research, interested readers can consult texts by Ponterotto and Casas (1991) and Heppner et al. (1992) for introductory discussions of the use of these methods in outcome research. Cook and Campbell's (1979) text is considered a classic on the subject of conducting quasi-experimental studies and analysis for field settings. A variety of other resources provide thorough coverage of the subjects of qualitative research (e.g., Bodgan & Biklen, 1992; Dey, 1993; Marshall & Rossman, 1989; Meloy, 1994; Neimeyer & Resnikoff, 1982; Strauss & Corbin, 1990) and single-case designs (e.g., Kazdin, 1982; Kratochwill & Levin, 1992; Yin, 1989).

Although it is likely that investigators will continue using nonexperimental methods to evaluate interventions used with teenage fathers, the goal of conducting group comparison studies should not be abandoned. Several investigators have demonstrated that experimental outcome research with troubled adolescents in field settings *can* be accomplished (e.g., Feindler, Marriott, & Iwata, 1984; Kiselica, Baker, Thomas, & Reedy, 1994; Reynolds & Coats, 1986). Although it is very difficult to complete research of this kind successfully, careful planning and professional collaboration can make group comparison outcome research with teenage fathers possible, an issue that is discussed in more detail later in this chapter. In addition, the prospects for conducting experimental outcome research with this population appear improved in light of recent developments in the field. For example, a handful of school districts in the United States have developed parenting programs that all teenage parents—mothers and fathers—are required to attend. Progressive programs such as these are potential gold mines for researchers interested in conducting comparison group studies with teenage fathers. My clinical experience suggests that school counselors and social workers employed in such programs are eager to help adolescent fathers and assess the impact of different approaches to helping them. The support and cooperation of these professionals might make it possible for researchers to design and implement experimental studies evaluating the effects of different treatment conditions on the adjustment of adolescent fathers. The results of such research will complement the findings obtained from qualitative and quasi-experimental investigations and fine-tune our efforts to assist this population effectively. Readers interested in learning the methods of experimental outcome research are referred to Heppner et al. (1992) and Kazdin (1992).

Review of Research on
Societal Stereotypes About Teenage Fathers

McGee (1982) suggested that many school districts do not provide services to pregnant and parenting teenagers because school personnel do not believe that adolescent parenthood should be a concern of the schools. Allen-Meares (1984) and Robinson (1988a) subsequently hypothesized that opposition to serving teenage parents might represent the expression of societal biases that call for punitive actions against teenage parents. In addition, Allen-Meares (1984) and Robinson (1988a) argued that inaccurate and harmful stereotypes about teenage fathers are manifested in service programs that offer support to teenage mothers while neglecting the needs of teenage fathers.

According to Kiselica and Pfaller (1993), these charges raise two important questions: Do counselors harbor negative attitudes toward teenage fathers? Is there a bias against serving teenage fathers?

Do Counselors Harbor Negative Attitudes Toward Teenage Fathers?

Although much has been written about societal stereotypes regarding teenage fathers, such as Robinson's (1988a) suggestion that there are five societal myths about adolescent fathers (see Chapter 2), only five empirical studies of the subject have been conducted. St. Pierre (1980) investigated the relationship among vocational educators' attitudes toward adolescent parents, their degree of open-mindedness, and their knowledge of the problem of adolescent parenthood. In addition, these variables were examined by sex of vocational educators as well as by sex of adolescent parents. St. Pierre developed the Adolescent Parents Attitude Scale (APAS), a self-report measure, to assess attitudes regarding teenage parents. The APAS consists of 25 items and two subscales, one measuring attitudes toward pregnant adolescents, the other assessing attitudes regarding adolescent expectant fathers. The study was conducted with a representative sample of vocational educators employed in Pennsylvania. The findings indicated a significant relationship between both male and female vocational educators' degree of open-mindedness and attitudes toward male and female adolescent parents. The same was found for the relationship between their knowledge and attitudes. The higher their degree of open-mindedness, the more positive were their attitudes toward both adolescent parents. Those with a higher knowledge of the problem of adolescent parenthood had a more positive attitude toward both male and female adolescent parents. Both male and female vocational educators had equal attitudes toward male and female adolescent parents, and those attitudes were generally positive toward both sexes of adolescent parents. Finally, even though male and female vocational educators who were more open-minded had more positive attitudes and those who had greater knowledge of the problem had more positive attitudes, female vocational educators had significantly greater knowledge of the problem and more positive attitudes than their male cohorts.

In a related study, Cunningham and Burge (1983) employed the APAS to assess the attitudes of school counselors and vocational educators regarding teenage parents and reported findings consistent with those of St. Pierre (1980). The authors found that a representative sample of secondary counselors and vocational directors employed in Virginia generally held positive attitudes toward both teenage mothers and teenage fathers. In addition, similar attitudes were held toward teenage mothers and fathers.

The findings of these two studies suggest that vocational educators and school counselors are similar in their attitudes toward teenage parents, that those attitudes generally are positive, and that similar attitudes are held toward teenage mothers and fathers. In addition, attitudes toward teenage parents may be mediated by other variables, such as open-mindedness.

Although these findings are encouraging regarding the attitudes of professionals toward teenage fathers, they also are hampered by two methodological problems. First, the samples of professionals surveyed were limited geographically to Pennsylvania by St. Pierre (1980) and to Virginia by Cunningham and Burge (1983). Additional research employing representative national samples of professionals are needed to provide a more conclusive picture of how teenage parents are viewed. A second and more substantial problem is that the psychometric soundness of the APAS, the measure employed in both studies, is questionable. Although the reliability of the overall scale is 0.862 and the pregnant adolescent subscale is 0.828, the adolescent expectant father subscale reliability is 0.615. The latter reliability is below the minimum reliability of .70 suggested for measures used for purposes of basic research (see Kaplan & Saccuzzo, 1989). Consequently, scores obtained on the adolescent expectant father subscale may be prone to measurement error, thereby making the meaning of subscale scores unclear. Perhaps a more serious psychometric flaw of the APAS is that no studies of the validity of the instrument have been conducted. Thus, it is not certain if the APAS actually measures attitudes regarding teenage parents.

Another self-report measure, the Questionnaire on Fathers (QOF), was developed by Barth (cited in Brown, 1990) to assess perspectives on and knowledge about services to teenage fathers. Brown (1990) used this instrument to conclude that the case managers and supervisors participating in the Maine Young Fathers Project held positive and realistic attitudes about working with adolescent fathers. Unfortunately, Brown (1990) reported no psychometric data on this measure, and an extensive review of the literature failed to identify any published studies in which the psychometric properties of the QOF were assessed. Thus, the reliability and validity of the QOF for the purposes of assessing attitudes about teenage fathers are unknown.

Two other empirical studies of attitudes about teenage parents have been conducted. Rotzien (1992) developed the Attitudes Toward Teenage Parents Scale (ATTPS), which consists of two subscales, the Attitudes Toward Teenage Mothers Scale (ATTMS) and the Attitudes Toward Teenage Fathers Scale (ATTFS). Because the reliability of all three scales were low (reliability coefficients for the ATTPS, ATTMS, and ATTFS were .58, .45, and .52, respectively), Miller, Rotzien, Kiselica, Clark, and Erkis (1995) conducted a follow-up study designed to improve the psychometric properties of the measure. Preliminary results suggest that the ATTPS, ATTMS, and ATTFS now meet psychometric standards for reliability.

Miller et al. (1995) are in the process of conducting a factor analysis of the ATTPS to assess its construct validity. These authors hope to construct a psychometrically sound measure that researchers can use to study attitudes regarding teenage parents held by the following different populations: teenage parents themselves, other adolescents, professionals who work with teenage parents, and other adults. Through such research, variations in attitudes among different populations will be documented. Findings of such research will inform program developers, service providers, and policymakers about groups who are likely to reject or support teenage fathers and service programs for young fathers.

In addition to this research, it is recommended that future investigations explore the potential role of other variables, such as open-mindedness, in mediating attitudes toward teenage fathers. St. Pierre (1980) found that male and female vocational educators who were more open-minded had more positive attitudes toward teenage parents. Cunningham and Burge (1983) found a significant relationship between vocational educators' attitudes toward adolescent parents and attitudes toward sex roles such that the more nontraditional the respondents' attitudes toward sex roles the more accepting they were toward teenage parents. Cunningham and Burge argued that this finding is similar to St. Pierre's (1980) report of a positive relationship between the degree of open-mindedness and attitudes toward teenage parents, because acceptance of the changes in sex roles could be viewed as an indicator of open-mindedness.

Cognitively complexity is another variable that may be related to stereotypic thinking about teenage fathers. Bieri (1955) formulated the notion of cognitive complexity and defined it as a measure of an individual's capacity to examine and process information in a multidimensional fashion before coming to a conclusion. Bieri et al. (1966) hypothesized that people who are more cognitively complex are more capable than others of seeing multiple perspectives. Consequently, more cognitively complex individuals are less likely to form biases in judgments (Bieri et al., 1966). Based on these considerations, Pedersen (1988) suggested that cognitive complexity is a desirable characteristic of counselors involved in multicultural counseling and research, endeavors that require individuals to entertain in an unbiased manner a variety of cultural perspectives at the same time.

According to Gard (1993), there appears to be strong initial support in the literature suggesting that clinical judgments are affected by the level of cognitive complexity of counselors. Watson (1976) found that highly conceptually complex counselors used greater amounts of client information to form hypotheses than less conceptually complex counselors. Holloway and Wolleat (1980) reported that counseling students who were highly conceptually complex sought and used significantly more client characteristics to understand a client and form hypotheses compared to their less conceptually complex peers. Spengler and Strohmer (1994) found that biased counselors were less cognitively complex than their nonbiased colleagues.

Based on prior research on the role of cognitive complexity in counselor judgments, it is reasonable to hypothesize that cognitively complexity is another variable that may be related to stereotypic thinking about teenage fathers by counselors, although this relationship has yet to be explored by investigators. Furthermore, cognitive complexity may be especially important in counseling teenage fathers from a variety of cultural backgrounds. It is recommended that future research be directed at examining these conjectures.

Is There a Bias Against Serving Teenage Fathers?

Considerable evidence suggests that there is a bias against serving teenage fathers. Qualitative data reported in several national reports evaluating the status of services for teenage parents indicated that most pertinent federal, state, and local service programs have focused on the needs of teenage mothers while only a few programs have provided limited services to teenage fathers (e.g., Children's Defense Fund, 1986a; Smollar & Ooms, 1987; U.S. Congress, 1986). Quantitative studies conducted by Kiselica (1992) and Kiselica and Sturmer (1993b, 1995) yielded similar results, suggesting that this trend occurs in both agency and school settings that offer services to teenage parents, including outreach programs specifically targeting teenage parents. A qualitative investigation of adolescent service programs by L. A. Smith (1989) revealed that a number of employees of agencies located in an unnamed city in North Carolina were hostile to the idea of working with young fathers whom they blamed for the problems of adolescent mothers.

The latter finding by L. A. Smith (1989) suggests that there may be a relationship between the attitudes of professional helpers toward teenage parents and the provision of services. Empirical research evaluating this hypothesis is needed.

In addition, investigators are urged to develop and evaluate methods for changing stereotypic thinking and biases about teenage fathers by helping professionals.

Finally, Brown (personal communication, January 17, 1995) hypothesized that funding bodies might be opposed to awarding grants to administrators applying for money to support the development of young father programs. Thus, the intentions of professionals genuinely interested in helping teenage fathers may be thwarted by a bias against this population at the funding level. This conjecture warrants investigation.

Integrating Research and Practice

An ongoing controversy in the mental health literature concerns the apparent lack of interplay between research and practice. A brief summary of this issue is necessary as a means of introducing some potential solutions to the shortcomings of research on teenage fathers.

The Research-Practice Gap

Both researchers and clinicians have been criticized for a gap between clinical research and counseling practice. Researchers have been reproached for their lack of contact with actual clients and for employing research strategies that are incapable of addressing the complexity of clinical phenomena. A consequence of these limitations is that the findings of research often are of limited value to most practitioners. Therefore, most practitioners are not avid readers of research publications and, as a result, are not influenced by most research findings (see Barlow et al., 1984; Fishman, 1981; Levy, 1981). It also has been lamented that many service providers lack the methodological skills to conduct sophisticated research (see McGee, 1982; Strupp, 1981). The results of numerous studies, reviewed in Haynes, Lemsky, and Sexton-Radek (1987), indicate that very few clinicians do engage in research. Thus, practitioners contribute to the void between research and practice through their failure to conduct research in their counseling practices.

A Proposed Solution
for the Practice-Research Gap

A wide range of solutions for this nagging problem have been proposed (see Claiborn, 1987; Gelso, 1993; Haynes et al., 1987; Hoshmand & Polkinghorne, 1992; Howard, 1986; Kanfer, 1990; Kiselica & Pfaller, 1993; Pfeiffer, Burd, & Wright, 1992; Stricker, 1992). It is beyond the scope of this book to provide a thorough analysis of these recommendations. However, one common recommendation—that academicians and practitioners engage more frequently in collaborative research (see Haynes et al., 1987; Kiselica & Pfaller, 1993; Pfeiffer et al., 1992)—is discussed in detail here because of its promise for immediately addressing the clinical-research gap as it pertains to scholarship on the subject of teenage fathers.

Professional collaboration between researchers and practitioners can enhance research on teenage fathers in several ways. First, researcher-clinician cooperation will provide researchers with better access to actual clients and thereby diminish the common practice of conducting analog studies. This will facilitate more field research that attempts to address the actual problems encountered by practitioners "on the front line," and that yields results that are more in tune with the needs of clinicians. Second, by working closely with clinicians, researchers might acquire a better understanding of the "real-world" issues that practitioners face everyday and, consequently, use research methods that are more sensitive to the constraints imposed by clinical settings. Third, Kiselica and Pfaller (1993) recommended that researchers can help practitioners to overcome common barriers that deter them from conducting research, such as a lack of time, administrative support, and funding (see Haynes et al., 1987; Pfeiffer et al., 1992), by sharing their expertise in such areas of grantsmanship, research design and methodology, and statistical analysis. Such assistance will promote more research in applied settings in which there traditionally has been a lack of support and rewards for research endeavors.

Suggestions for Collaborative
Research on Teenage Fathers

To illustrate the potential benefits of researcher-practitioner collaboration, Kiselica and Pfaller (1993) suggested a number of collaborative roles for counselor educators and school counselors for improving research on teenage parents. In this section, the recommendations of Kiselica and Pfaller (1993) are highlighted and extended. It is hoped that these recommendations will serve as examples for how helping professionals might work in concert to further our understanding of teenage fathers.

Collaboration on Applying for Grants. A common barrier encountered by practitioners who wish to provide services for adolescents are budgetary limitations. This is particularly true as school counselors and social workers attempt to increase the range of school-based services available for teenage parents (McGee, 1982). Often, funding for such services is not possible through the existing school budget.

Practitioners can hurdle financial constraints by securing grant awards specifically earmarked to support teenage parent service programs. Applying for grants can be an intimidating prospect for helpers who are unfamiliar with grant application procedures. By collaborating with academicians, mental health professionals can discover competent assistance with the grant application process. Educators commonly are encouraged, if not required, by promotion and tenure committees in academe to apply for grants related to faculty research and service. In addition, faculty interested in developing grant-supported, field-based services as part of counseling outcome studies need sites as possible bases for their studies. By working together to identify and apply for grants and by using grant funds to finance teenage parent counseling programs, clinicians and scholars can work to widen the range of pertinent services, and, in the process, conduct important outcome research.

Casas (1990) offered another consideration regarding grants and cross-cultural research. He argued that cross-cultural researchers have an obligation to give back to the community a part of what the researcher takes from it. Therefore, he recommended that scholars apply for research grants through community agencies rather than universities. Casas stated that securing grants in this manner will help community agencies to survive.

A final point related to grants is directed toward academe and the traditional promotion and tenure process. If Casas's (1990) recommendation is to become a reality, members of promotion and tenure committees in higher education must value the contribution of faculty grants writing in service to the community, even if such endeavors take away from research productivity as scholars. As Parham (1993) argued, the work of academicians who contribute positively to the well-being of troubled communities may represent a *higher* standard of faculty accountability than the traditional criteria used to measure faculty productivity, such as results that are significant at the .01 level, or publications in prestigious journals with a reputation for rejecting 70% to 80% of manuscript submissions. In short, the work of the service-minded intellectual must be afforded the same respect as the research endeavors of the laboratory scientist. Given the complex problems facing our society, such changes in the promotion and tenure process are a necessity.

Collaborative Outcome Research. Mental health professionals and academicians can combine their talents to tackle the challenges inherent in outcome research. Practitioners working in the field can contribute to research by identifying subjects, administering counseling programs, collecting data, and sharing pertinent information with counselor educators. In exchange, scholars can impart their expertise in research methodology and statistics in the development and analyses of research projects. Both parties can benefit by using Card's (1993) *Handbook of Adolescent Sexuality and Pregnancy: Research and Evaluation Instruments,* which is designed to help both researchers and practitioners to develop and assess the impact of ameliorative programs for teenage parents or adolescent pregnancy prevention projects. *Evaluation of Pregnancy Prevention Programs in the School Context* (Zabin & Hirsch, 1988) is another excellent resource on collaborative research, for it contains numerous suggestions regarding the development and implementation of school-based programs in a manner that addresses both the needs of the practitioner and those of the researcher.

Together, educators and practitioners are encouraged to present their findings at professional workshops and conferences and publish their results in scholarly journals. Collegial scholarship of this kind is likely to appeal to and inform both scientists and practitioners regarding the effectiveness of teenage parent service programs.

Collaborative Research on Counselor Biases Toward Teenage Parents. Co-operative ventures between educators and mental health professionals are needed to assess the attitudes of helpers toward teenage parents, and if necessary, to conduct training workshops designed to reduce negative atti-tudes toward pregnant and parenting teenagers.

Academicians and practitioners can contribute to these endeavors in several ways. First, educators can design national survey studies to gather data on the attitudes of counselors toward teenage parents. Mental health professionals can contribute to this effort by responding to the surveys and by making themselves available for follow-up surveys and/or interviews. The American Counseling Association, the National Association of Social Workers, the American Psychological Association, and other professional organizations can be of assistance by supplying interested researchers with membership mailing lists. Second, educators and administrators of student personnel services can develop pertinent in-service/continuing education training programs for school counselors and social workers. Ideas from other successful approaches (e.g., training counselors to work with gay and lesbian clients; Rudolph, 1989) and training paradigms (e.g., developing multicul-tural sensitivity; Pedersen, 1988) can be used to design training workshops aimed at dispelling inaccurate stereotypes and promoting knowledge about and sensitivity toward teenage parents. Research evaluating the effectiveness of such training should be conducted. Professional organizations can pro-mote these initiatives by sponsoring pertinent training workshops at their state, regional, and national conventions.

Collaborative Research on Multicultural Considerations. In this book, an attempt was made to suggest modifications in counseling processes and interventions based on the cultural backgrounds of teenage fathers. These suggestions need to be empirically evaluated. Also, to refine a multicultural approach to counseling, more empirical data about cultural variations in what motivates teenagers to become parents as adolescents is needed (Williams, 1991). In addition, much of the prior multicultural research on teenage parents was focused on the cultural variables of race and ethnicity. In this book, it was argued that such a limited view of culture ignores other key cultural variables, such as religious orientation and socioeconomic status.

Clearly, these other variables should be studied so as to broaden a multicultural perspective on teenage parenthood.

Mental health professionals and educators can play an important role in research designed to address these issues. For example, because of their access to culturally diverse students, school counselors and social workers are in the advantageous position to recruit and study this population. As with the other areas of research mentioned earlier, educators can employ the consultants and resources available in academe to design multicultural studies and conduct statistical analyses, and school counselors and social workers can apply procedures and gather data with culturally diverse teenage fathers. Academicians may need to learn and use alternative research strategies to enhance these efforts, such as the methods of qualitative and ethnographic research mentioner earlier, in studying different ethnic groups.

Ethical Issues Regarding Research With Adolescent Fathers

Counselors, psychologists, social workers, and other helping professionals are obligated to understand and abide by the ethical guidelines of their respective professions for conducting research on adolescents. Because ethical standards are general in nature, they seldom offer specific directions about what professionals should do in given situations. Therefore, in addition to learning the ethical standards of one's profession and reading this brief overview of pertinent ethical issues, researchers are encouraged to consult the works of several authors who have attempted to provide practical approaches to handling the many ethical dilemmas that might arise in conducting research on adolescents (e.g., Huey & Remley, 1988; Koocher & Keith-Spiegel, 1990; Stanley & Sieber, 1992). Also, it is recommended that researchers review Ponterotto and Casas's (1991) discussion of specific ethical issues regarding multicultural research.

Overview of Ethical Issues

In this section, the ethical issues of informed consent and confidentiality as they relate to research on teenage fathers are discussed. In addition, particular ethical considerations pertaining to multicultural research are highlighted.

Informed Consent. Ethical guidelines pertaining to research require that the informed consent of the participants be obtained prior to the initiation of a study. When children or adolescents are the subjects of study, in general, both parental permission and assent of the child are required. That is,

> the child may not participate in research without parental permission, and the parent may not "volunteer" the child without the child's approval (except in the case of possible lifesaving experimental therapy that is not available otherwise). Thus, ordinarily, research is permitted only if both agree, and the child has absolute veto power. (Tymchuk, 1992, p. 128)

In rare circumstances, the requirement of acquiring parental permission may be waived. For example, according to Grisso (1992), if the parents of a particular adolescent are judged to be incompetent, then waiver of parental permission may be allowable, provided that the researcher takes appropriate steps to protect the adolescent who will participate as a research subject. Parental permission also might be waived if the parents are competent but in a nonbeneficent posture (see Grisso, 1992). For example, a researcher investigating the decision-making strategies of adolescents using an abortion counseling service might argue that seeking parental permission could jeopardize the potential benefits of the adolescents' confidential use of the service. Under such circumstances, parental permission might be waived. As a rule of thumb, however, researchers should attempt to secure parental permission whenever possible.

Confidentiality. According to Rotheram-Borus and Koopman (1992), "The more sensitive or intimate the revealed information, the greater the responsibility for confidentiality" (p. 159). Because adolescent fatherhood involves so many sensitive issues, researchers are obligated to take great care in protecting the anonymity of their subjects.

When ethnographic studies of teenage fathers are conducted, the issue of confidentiality also might extend to the communities in which the studies occur. As Sieber (1992) noted, under such circumstances confidentiality and privacy may pertain more to the community than to the individuals within it. "Risk and harm may be more likely to be political, economic, or social consequences to the community than harm to an individual" (Sieber, 1992, p. 186). Consequently, precautions to protect the privacy of communities may be necessary. For example, Sullivan (1985) recognized that his ethnographic study of adolescent fathers in an inner-city neighborhood might result in harm to the community if the name of the neighborhood was revealed. Therefore, Sullivan decided to refer to the neighborhood as "Projectville" to protect the privacy of the community.

Ethical Issues in Multicultural Research. Many critics have charged that multicultural researchers historically have been opportunistic and self-serving in their treatment of research subjects, particularly ethnic-minority subjects (e.g., Casas, 1990; Gordon, 1973; Guthrie, 1976; Parham, 1993; Ponterotto & Casas, 1991; Zytowski, Casas, Gilbert, Lent, & Simon, 1988). The general consensus of these writers is that there are pervasive, ethical problems in the way that most multicultural research has been conducted.

Much of the problem resides in the current ethical standards of the helping professions, which do little to promote the provision of benefits to racial/ethnic-minority groups and fail to take into consideration the rich diversity of worldviews and values that are held by individuals who are members of the nonmajority culture (see Ponterotto & Casas, 1991). Consequently, research has been designed from an ethnocentric perspective that has failed to accurately perceive the realities of ethnically diverse subjects and, consequently, has provided few benefits and, at times, harm to those subjects.

Ponterotto and Casas (1991) and Parham (1993) have suggested numerous recommendations to rectify these shortcomings. These recommendations are reiterated collectively here, at times with reference to research on teenage fathers. First, more altruistic, group- and community-oriented, and action-driven philosophies and worldviews should be infused into ethical standards. This will enhance research on African American teenage fathers, for example, whose worldview may be more collectively rather than individually focused. Second, researchers need to move beyond the traditional focus of research (e.g., counselor variables, client variables, interaction of client, and counselor variables) and conduct pragmatic research, fieldwork studies, and qualitative research that addresses the tremendous sociopsychological problems that plague many cultural groups (e.g., the effects of welfare policies on the fathering roles of impoverished teenage parents). Third, more attention needs to be directed toward the identification of the strengths of particular cultural groups (e.g., What are the characteristics of Anglo teenage fathers who succeed in their marriages?) and what constitutes healthy behavior for particular cultural contexts (e.g., that single parenthood may be an adaptive form of family structure among the poor). Fourth, stronger efforts to select more representative samples of different cultural groups are needed (e.g., Hendricks's, 1988, research is one of the few projects that has targeted representative adolescent fathers from three different cultural groups). Fifth, field researchers should have an accurate and sensitive understanding of the targeted communities of their research and should involve community leaders in developing intervention programs (e.g., as L. A. Smith, 1988, did in her investigation regarding the formation of a service program for African

American teenage fathers) and interpreting findings. Sixth, as was mentioned earlier, scholars should try to apply for research grants through community agencies rather than universities so that the funding will support the agency's mission in the community (e.g., Brown, 1990, channeled funding for the Maine Young Fathers Project through several community agencies). Seventh, researchers need to acknowledge the intragroup variations of particular cultural groups (e.g., Perez & Duany, 1992, noted the tremendous diversity with the Hispanic culture in their discussion of adolescent pregnancy and parenthood within the Hispanic community). Eighth, research procedures should be those that are appropriate and acceptable to the populations targeted for study (e.g., Hendricks, 1988, used culturally sensitive interview methods with African American, Anglo American, and Hispanic American teenage fathers). Ninth, researchers should actively involve undergraduate and graduate student coresearchers who are indigenous to the cultural groups that have been targeted for study. Tenth, researchers can work to ensure that their efforts result in tangible benefits to the targeted community by making a concerted effort to inform the community of the results and of the potential social and political actions that can emanate from the results. For example, Kiselica and Sturmer conducted a study assessing services to teenage fathers throughout a midwestern state. Their findings resulted in both a journal publication (Kiselica & Sturmer, 1993b) and a resource directory (Kiselica & Sturmer, 1993a), the latter of which was contributed for free to service providers throughout the state. The providers then used the directory to network among themselves and as a supportive document in lobbying state and local policymakers to make changes regarding the status of services for teenage fathers.

Conclusion

Unwed teenage pregnancy and parenthood is one of the major societal issues of our time. Effectively responding to this crisis requires extensive efforts to prevent adolescent pregnancy and secondary prevention programs designed to address the problems of young women and men who already are unwed adolescent parents. The purpose of this book has been to sensitize the helping professionals to the often forgotten half of adolescent childbearing and parenthood, the teenage father. It was argued that the key to efficacious helping is an understanding that for each young father a complex, cultural context colors how the pregnancy is resolved, how it is viewed by his family, how he defines himself as a father, what he decides regarding his educational and career plans, and how he can be helped through counseling. It was suggested that the goal of training competent counselors requires a clarification of attitudes toward teenage fathers and the culturally different, didactic instruction in numerous subjects and supervised field experiences counseling teenage fathers from a variety of cultural backgrounds. Helping professionals and researchers are challenged to work collaboratively to develop comprehensive service programs for teenage fathers and conduct research evaluating the efficacy of such programs, assessing attitudes toward teenage fathers, and exploring pertinent multicultural issues. My earnest hope is that helpers and academicians will apply the recommendations in this book to assist teenage fathers to realize their full potential.

References

Abrahamse, A. F., Morrison, P. A., & Waite, L. J. (1988). *Beyond stereotypes: Who becomes a single teenage mother?* Santa Monica, CA: Rand.

Achatz, M., & MacAllum, C. A. (1994). *Young unwed fathers: Report from the field.* Philadelphia: Public/Private Ventures.

Alan Guttmacher Institute. (1981). *Teenage pregnancy: The problem that hasn't gone away.* New York: Author.

Allan Keith Productions (Producer). (n.d.). *A man's place* [Film]. (Available from Allan Keith Productions, 425 East 79th St., Suite 1D, New York, NY 10021)

Allen-Meares, P. (1984). Adolescent pregnancy and parenting: The forgotten adolescent father and his parents. *Journal of Social Work and Human Sexuality, 3*(1), 27-38.

Allen-Meares, P. (1989). An in-school program for adolescent parents: Implications for social work practice and multi-disciplinary teaming. In N. Cervera & L. Videka-Sherman (Eds.), *Working with pregnant and parenting teenage clients* (pp. 190-200). Milwaukee, WI: Family Service America.

Alvarez, R. (1973). The psycho-historical and socioeconomic development of the Chicano community in the United States. *Social Science Quarterly, 53,* 920-942.

American Counseling Association. (1988). *Ethical standards of the American Counseling Association.* Alexandria, VA: Author.

American Guidance Services. (1989a). *Early childhood STEP: Systematic training for effective parenting of children under six* [Film]. Circle Pines, MN: Producer.

American Guidance Services. (1989b). *Growing together* [Film]. Circle Pines, MN: Producer.

American Psychological Association. (1992). *Ethical principles of psychologists and code of conduct.* Washington, DC: Author.

Anderson, L. P., Eaddy, C. L., & Williams, E. A. (1990). Psychosocial competence: Toward a theory of understanding positive mental health among Black Americans. In D. S. Ruiz

& J. P. Comer (Eds.), *Handbook of mental health and mental disorder among Black Americans* (pp. 255-271). Westport, CT: Greenwood.

Anderson, N. L. (1990). Pregnancy resolution decisions in juvenile detention. *Archives of Psychiatric Nursing, 4,* 325-331.

Anderson-Khleif, S. (1982). *Divorced but not disastrous.* Englewood Cliffs, NJ: Prentice Hall.

Ansbacher, H. L., & Ansbacher, R. R. (Eds.). (1956). *The individual psychology of Alfred Adler: A systematic presentation in selections from his writings.* New York: Harper Torchbooks.

Arbona, C. (1990). Career counseling research and Hispanics: A review of the literature. *The Counseling Psychologist, 18,* 300-323.

Arbona, C., & Novy, D. M. (1991). Career aspirations and expectations of Black, Mexican American, and White students. *Career Development Quarterly, 39,* 231-239.

Arcana, J. (1986). *Every mother's son.* Seattle: Seal Press.

Argent, H. (1987). Progress in open adoption. *Adoption and Fostering, 11,* 22-24.

Asante, M. K. (1981). Black male and female relationships: An Afrocentric context. In G. E. Lawrence (Ed.), *Black men* (pp. 75-82). Beverly Hills, CA: Sage.

Ascher, C. (1985). *Pregnant and parenting teenagers: Statistics, characteristics, and school-based support services* (Report No. 400-82-0012). New York: Teachers College, Columbia University, Institute for Urban and Minority Education. (ERIC Document Reproduction Service No. ED 267 150)

Atkinson, D. R. (1985). Research on cross-cultural counseling and psychotherapy: A review and update of reviews. In P. B. Pedersen (Ed.), *Handbook of cross-cultural counseling and therapy* (pp. 191-197). Westport, CT: Greenwood.

Atkinson, D. R., Poston, W. C., Furlong, M. J., & Mercado, P. (1989). Ethnic group preferences for counselor characteristics. *Journal of Counseling Psychology, 36,* 68-72.

Axelson, J. A. (1993). *Counseling and development in a multicultural society* (2nd ed.). Pacific Grove, CA: Brooks/Cole.

Baker, A. (1992). *After her abortion: For parents, male partners and friends.* Granite City, IL: The Hope Clinic for Women.

Baker, S. B. (1992). *School counseling for the twenty-first century.* New York: Merrill.

Baker, S. B., & Butler, J. N. (1984). Effects of cognitive self-instruction training on adolescent attitudes, experiences, and state anxiety. *Journal of Primary Prevention, 5,* 10-14.

Baker, S. B., & Shaw, M. C. (1987). *Improving counseling through primary prevention.* Columbus, OH: Charles E. Merrill.

Ballard, C. (1993, October). Search for the lost fathers. *Guideposts,* pp. 14-17.

Balswick, J. O. (1982). Male inexpressiveness: Psychological and social aspects. In K. Solomon & N. B. Levy (Eds.), *Men in transition: Theory and therapy* (pp. 131-150). New York: Plenum.

Baly, I. (1989). Career and vocational development of Black youth. In R. L. Jones (Ed.), *Black adolescents* (pp. 249-265). Berkeley, CA: Cobb & Henry.

Baran, A., Pannor, R., & Sorosky, A. D. (1976, March). Open adoption. *Social Work,* pp. 97-100.

Barber, J., & Munn, A. (1993, March). *Male involvement.* Symposium conducted at the annual meeting of the Indiana Council on Adolescent Pregnancy, Indianapolis.

Barclay, J. (1984). Primary prevention and assessment. *Personnel & Guidance Journal, 62,* 475-478.

Barlow, D. H., Hayes, S. C., & Nelson, R. O. (1984). *The scientist practitioner research and accountability in clinical and educational settings.* Elmsford, NY: Pergamon.

Barnhill, L., Rubenstein, G., & Rocklin, N. (1979). From generation to generation: Father-to-be in transition. *The Family Coordinator, 28,* 229-235.

Barret, R. L., & Robinson, B. E. (1982). A descriptive study of teenage expectant fathers. *Family Relations, 31,* 349-352.

Barth, R. P., Claycomb, M., & Loomis, A. (1988). Services to adolescent fathers. *Health and Social Work, 13,* 277-287.

Battle, S. F. (1988/1989, Summer/Winter). African-American male responsibility in teenage pregnancy: The role of education. *Urban League Review,* pp. 71-81.

Baum, D. J. (1980). *Teenage pregnancy.* Toronto: Beaufort.

Baumrind, D. (1967). Child care practices anteceding three patterns of preschool behavior. *Genetic Psychology Monographs, 75,* 43-88.

Bedger, J. E. (1980). *Teenage pregnancy: Research related to clients and services.* Springfield, IL: Charles C Thomas.

Belsie, L. (1993, April 13). Ohio helps welfare mothers finish school. *Christian Science Monitor,* p. 4.

Belsky, J., & Miller, B. C. (1986). Adolescent fatherhood in the context of the transition to parenthood. In A. B. Elster & M. E. Lamb (Eds.), *Adolescent fatherhood* (pp. 107-122). Hillsdale, NJ: Lawrence Erlbaum.

Bennett, G. K., Seashore, H. G., & Wesman, A. G. (1972). *The differential aptitude test.* New York: The Psychological Corporation.

Berger, D. K., Kyman, W., Perez, G., Menendez, M., Bistritz, J. F., & Goon, J. M. (1991). Hispanic adolescent pregnancy testers: A comparative analysis of negative testers, child-bearers and aborters. *Adolescence, 26,* 951-962.

Bergin, J. J. (1993). Small-group counseling. In A. Vernon (Ed.), *Counseling children and adolescents* (pp. 197-234). Denver, CO: Love Publishing.

Bernal, G. (1982). Cuban families. In M. McGoldrick, J. K. Pearce, & J. Giordan (Eds.), *Ethnicity and family therapy* (pp. 187-207). New York: Guilford.

Bertocci, D. & Schechter, M. D. (1991). Adopted adults' perception of their need to search: Implications for clinical practice. *Smith Studies in Social Work, 61,* 179-196.

Beymer, L. (1995). *Meeting the guidance and counseling needs of boys.* Alexandria, VA: American Counseling Association.

Bieri, J. (1955). Cognitive complexity-simplicity and predictive behavior. *Journal of Abnormal Behavior and Social Psychology, 51,* 263-268.

Bieri, J., Atkins, A. L., Briar, S., Leaman, R. L., Miller, H., & Tripodi, T. (1966). *Clinical and social judgment: The discrimination of behavioral information.* New York: John Wiley.

Billingsley, A., & Giovannoni, J. M. (1970). *Children of the storm: Black children and American child welfare.* New York: Harcourt Brace & Jovanovich.

Black, C., Paz, H., & DeBlassie, R. R. (1991). Counseling the Hispanic male adolescent. *Adolescence, 26,* 222-232.

Blanchard, R., & Biller, H. (1971). Father availability and academic performance among third grade boys. *Developmental Psychology, 4,* 301-305.

Bloom, M. (1981). *Primary prevention: The possible science.* Englewood Cliffs, NJ: Prentice Hall.

Blustein, D. L. (1990, August). *Vocational realm of counseling psychology: Current status and future directions.* Paper presented at the annual meeting of the American Psychological Association, Boston.

Bogdan, R. C., & Biklen, S. K. (1992). *Qualitative research for education* (2nd ed.). New York: Brunner/Mazel.

Bogren, L. Y. (1986). The couvade syndrome. *International Journal of Family Psychiatry,* *7,* 123-136.

Bolton, F. G. (1987). The father in the adolescent pregnancy at risk for child maltreatment: I. Helpmate or hindrance? *Journal of Family Violence, 2,* 67-80.

Bolton, F. G., & Belsky, J. (1986). The adolescent father and child maltreatment. In A. B. Elster & M. E. Lamb (Eds.), *Adolescent fatherhood* (pp. 123-140). Hillsdale, NJ: Lawrence Erlbaum.

Bovee, T. (1991, October 11). Failure to pay child support widespread. *Muncie Star,* pp. 1, 16.

Bovee, T. (1993, January 15). Poor families more likely to break up. *Muncie Star,* p. D2.

Bowen, M. (1978). *Family therapy in clinical practice.* New York: Jason Aronson.

Bowman, P. J. (1991). Work life. In J. S. Jackson (Ed.), *Life in Black America* (pp. 124-178). Newbury Park, CA: Sage.

Boyd-Franklin, N. (1989). *Black families in therapy: A multisystems approach.* New York: Guilford.

Braver, S. L., Fitzpatrick, P. J., & Bay, R. C. (1991). Noncustodial parent's report of child support payments. *Family Relations, 40,* 180-185.

Brindis, C. D. (1990, Fall). Helping teens wait: Abstinence education. *Family Life Educator,* *9,* 11-25.

Brindis, C. D. (1991). *Adolescent pregnancy prevention: A guidebook for communities.* Palo Alto, CA: Health Promotion Resource Center.

Brindis, C. (1992). Adolescent pregnancy prevention for Hispanic youth: The role of schools, families, and communities. *Journal of School Health, 62,* 345-351.

Brindis, C. D. (1993, March). *Keynote address.* Symposium conducted at the annual meeting of the Indiana Council on Adolescent Pregnancy, Indianapolis.

Brindis, C., Barth, R. P., & Loomis, A. B. (1987). Continuous counseling: Case management with teenage parents. *Social Casework: The Journal of Contemporary Social Work, 68,* 164-172.

Bronstein, P., & Cowan, C. (1988). *Fatherhood today: Men's changing role in the family.* New York: John Wiley.

Brown, S. (1990). *If the shoes fit: Final report and program implementation guide of the Maine Young Fathers Project.* Portland: University of Southern Maine, Human Services Development Institute.

Brown, S. V. (1983). The commitment and concerns of Black adolescent parents. *Social Work Research & Abstracts, 19,* 27-34.

Bruch, M. A. (1978). Holland's typology applied to client-counselor interaction: Implications for counseling with men. *The Counseling Psychologist, 7,* 26-32.

Buchanan, M., & Robbins, C. (1990). Early adult psychological consequences for males of adolescent pregnancy and its resolution. *Journal of Youth and Adolescence, 19,* 413-424.

Burden, D., & Klerman, L. (1984). Teenage parenthood: Factors that lessen economic dependence. *Social Work, 29,* 11-16.

Burge, P. (1987). *Career development of single parents.* (Information Series No. 324). Columbus, OH: National Center for Research in Vocational Education. (ERIC Document Reproduction Service No. ED 290 934)

Burgess, L. C. (1981). *The art of adoption.* New York: Norton.

Burton, L. M. (1990). Teenage childbearing as an alternative life-course strategy in multigenerational Black families. *Human Nature, 1,* 123-143.

Burton, L. M., & Bengston, V. L. (1985). Black grandmothers: Issues of timing and continuity of roles. In V. L. Bengston & J. F. Robertson (Eds.), *Grandparenthood* (pp. 61-79). Beverly Hills, CA: Sage.

Burton, L. M., & DeVries, C. (1992). Challenges and rewards: African American grandparents as surrogate parents. *Generations, 16,* 51-54.

Butts, J. D. (1989). Adolescent sexuality and teen pregnancy from a Black perspective. In N. Cervera & L. Videka-Sherman (Eds.), *Working with pregnant and parenting teenage clients* (pp. 146-157). Milwaukee, WI: Family Service America.

Caplan, G. (1961). *An approach to community mental health.* New York: Grune & Stratton.

Card, J. J. (1993). *Handbook of adolescent sexuality and pregnancy: Research and evaluation instruments.* Newbury Park, CA: Sage.

Card, J. J., Peterson, J. L., & Greeno, C. G. (1992). Adolescent pregnancy prevention programs: Design, monitoring, and evaluations. In B. C. Miller, J. J. Card, R. L. Paikoff, & J. L. Peterson (Eds.), *Preventing adolescent pregnancy: Model programs and evaluations* (pp. 1-27). Newbury Park, CA: Sage.

Card, J. J., Reagan, R. T., & Ritter, P. E. (1988). *Sourcebook of comparison data for evaluating adolescent pregnancy and parenting programs.* Los Altos, CA: Sociometrics.

Card, J. J., & Wise, L. L. (1978). Teenage mothers and teenage fathers: The impact of early childbearing on their personal and professional lives. *Family Planning Perspectives, 10,* 199-205.

Carrera, M. A. (1992). Involving adolescent males in pregnancy and STD prevention programs. *Adolescent Medicine: State of the Art Reviews, 3,* 1-13.

Casas, J. M. (1984). Policy, training, and research in counseling psychology: The racial/ethnic minority perspective. In S. Brown & R. Lent (Eds.), *Handbook of counseling psychology* (pp. 785-831). New York: John Wiley.

Casas, J. M. (1990, August). Ethical imperatives in multicultural counseling. In J. G. Ponterotto (Chair), *The White American researcher in multicultural counseling: Significance and challenges.* Symposium conducted at the 98th Annual Convention of the American Psychological Association, Boston.

Centers for Disease Control. (1992). *Selected behaviors that increase risk for HIV infection, other sexually transmitted diseases, and unintentional pregnancy among high school students—United States, 1991.* Atlanta, GA: Author.

Centron Films. (Producer). (1980). *Me, a teen father?* [Videocassette]. (Available from Coronet Films, P.O. Box 2649, Columbus, OH 43216)

Cervera, N. (1991). Unwed teenage pregnancy: Family relationships with the father of the baby. *Families in Society, 72,* 29-37.

Chapin, S. (1991). *Within the shadow: A biblical look at suffering, death, and the process of grieving.* Wheaton, IL: Victor Books.

Cheatham, H. E. (1990a). Africentricity and career development of African-Americans. *Career Development Quarterly, 38,* 334-346.

Cheatham, H. E. (1990b). Empowering Black families. In H. E. Cheatham & J. B. Stewart (Eds.), *Black families* (pp. 373-394). New Brunswick, NJ: Transaction Books.

Cheatham, H. E. (1991). Cultural changes and career changes: The case of Mr. Ebo. *Career Development Quarterly, 40,* 31-35.

Cheung, F. K. (1991). The use of mental health services by ethnic minorities. In H. F. Myers, P. Wohlford, L. P. Guzman, & R. J. Echemendia (Eds.), *Ethnic minority perspective on clinical training and services in psychology* (pp. 23-31). Washington, DC: American Psychological Association.

Children's Defense Fund. (1985). *Black and White children in America: Key facts.* Washington, DC: Author.

Children's Defense Fund. (1986a). *Adolescent pregnancy: What the states are saying.* Washington, DC: Author.

Children's Defense Fund. (1986b). *Welfare and teen pregnancy: What do we know? What do we do?* Washington, DC: Author.

Children's Defense Fund. (1987a). *Child care: An essential service for teen parents.* Washington, DC: Author.

Children's Defense Fund. (1987b). *Childwatch manual.* Washington, DC: Author.

Children's Defense Fund. (1988a). *Adolescent and young adult fathers: Problems and solutions.* Washington, DC: Author.

Children's Defense Fund. (1988b). *Teenage pregnancy: An advocate's guide to the numbers.* Washington, DC: Author.

Children's Defense Fund. (1991a). *Child poverty in America.* Washington, DC: Author.

Children's Defense Fund. (1991b). *Teenage pregnancy in the Latino community, fact sheet.* Washington, DC: Author.

Chilman, C. S. (1979). *Adolescent sexuality in a changing American society—social and psychological perspectives.* Washington, DC: Department of Health, Education, and Welfare, Public Health Service, National Institutes of Health.

Chilman, C. S. (1983). *Adolescent sexuality in a changing American society* (2nd ed.). New York: John Wiley.

Chilman, C. S. (1988). Never-married, single, adolescent parents. In C. S. Chilman, E. W. Nunnally, & F. M. Cox (Eds.), *Variant family forms* (pp. 17-38). Newbury Park, CA: Sage.

Chrissinger, M. S. (1980). Factors affecting employment of welfare mothers. *Social Work, 25,* 52-56.

Christmon, K. (1990a). Parental responsibility of African-American unwed adolescent fathers. *Adolescence, 25,* 645-653.

Christmon, K. (1990b). The unwed adolescent father's perceptions of his family and of himself as a father. *Child and Adolescent Social Work Journal, 7,* 275-283.

Claiborn, C. D. (1987). Science and practice: Reconsidering the Pepinskys. *Journal of Counseling and Development, 65,* 286-288.

Clarke-Stewart, K. (1980). The father's contribution to children's cognitive and social development in early childhood. In F. Pedersen (Ed.), *The father-infant relationship: Observational studies in the family setting* (pp. 111-146). New York: Praeger.

Cohen, D. L. (1993, November 3). Support program for teenage fathers seeks to nurture responsibility. *Education Week,* pp. 16-17.

The Collegiate School. (n.d.). *Guide to setting up an infant care course.* New York: Author.

Connor, M. E. (1986). Some parenting attitudes of young Black fathers. In R. A. Lewis & R. E. Salt (Eds.), *Men in families* (pp. 159-168). Beverly Hills, CA: Sage.

Cook, T. D., & Campbell, D. T. (1979). *Quasi-experimentation: Design & analysis issues for field settings.* Boston: Houghton Mifflin.

Cordasco, F. (1973). *The Puerto Rican experience: A sociological sourcebook.* Totowa, NJ: Littlefield, Adams.

Corey, G., Corey, M. S., Callanan, P., & Russell, J. M. (1992). *Group techniques* (4th ed.). Pacific Grove, CA: Brooks/Cole.

Corey, M. S., & Corey, G. (1992). *Group process and practice* (4th ed.). Pacific Grove, CA: Brooks/Cole.

Cormier, W. H., & Cormier, L. S. (1991). *Interviewing strategies for helpers: Fundamental skills and cognitive behavioral interventions* (3rd ed.). Pacific Grove, CA: Brooks/Cole.

COSSMHO. (n.d.). *Strengthening families: A curriculum for Hispanic parents.* Washington, DC: Author.

Cowen, E. L. (1984). A general structural model for primary prevention program development in mental health. *Personnel & Guidance Journal, 62,* 485-490.

Coyle-Williams, M., & Wermuth, T. (1990). Boulder Valley schools teen parenting program: An exemplary vocational education program serving a population with special needs. *TASPP-Brief, 2,* 1-5.

Craighead, W. E., Kazdin, A. E., & Mahoney, M. J. (Eds.). (1981). *Behavior modification: Principles, issues, and applications* (2nd ed.). Boston: Houghton Mifflin.

Crawford, D. R., & Mannion, M. T. (1989). *Psycho-spiritual healing after abortion.* Kansas City, MO: Sheed & Ward.

Cross, W. E. (1971). The Negro-to-Black conversion experience: Toward a psychology of Black liberation. *Black World, 20,* 13-27.

Cross, W. E. (1991). *Shades of Black: Diversity in African-American identity.* Philadelphia: Temple University Press.

Cullen, J. L. (1988). Helping women make it. *Vocational Education Journal,* 33-34.

Cunningham, D. L., & Burge, P. L. (1983). Secondary counselors and vocational directors: Sex-role attitudes and attitudes toward teenage parents. *Journal of Vocational Educational Research, 8,* 31-41.

D'Andrea, M., & Daniels, J. (1992). A career development program for inner-city youth. *Career Development Quarterly, 40,* 272-280.

Danziger, S. (1986). *Breaking the chains: From teenage mothers to welfare mothers, or, can social policy increase options?* (Institute for Research on Poverty Discussion Paper No. 825-86). Madison: University of Wisconsin—Madison, Institute for Research on Poverty.

Danziger, S. (1987). *Father involvement in welfare families headed by adolescent mothers* (Institute for Research on Poverty Discussion Paper No. 856-87). Madison: University of Wisconsin—Madison, Institute for Research on Poverty.

Darling-Hammond, L. (1993, June). Reframing the school reform agenda: Developing capacity for school transformation. *Phi Delta Kappan,* pp. 753-761.

Dash, L. (1989). *When children want children: An inside look at the crisis of teenage parenthood.* New York: Penguin.

de Anda, D., & Becerra, R. M. (1989). Support networks for adolescent mothers. In N. Cervera & L. Videka-Sherman (Eds.), *Working with pregnant and parenting teenage clients* (pp. 132-145). Milwaukee, WI: Family Service America.

DeFrain, J., LeMasters, E. E., & Schroff, J. A. (1991). Environment and fatherhood: Rural and urban influences. In F. W. Bozett & S. M. H. Hanson (Eds.), *Fatherhood and families in cultural context* (pp. 162-186). New York: Springer.

De La Cancela, V., & Guzman, L. P. (1991). Latino mental health service needs: Implications for training psychologists. In H. F. Myers, P. Wohlford, L. P. Guzman, & R. J. Echemendia (Eds.), *Ethnic minority perspectives on clinical training and services in psychology* (pp. 59-64). Washington, DC: American Psychological Association.

DeLatte, J. G., Orgeron, K., & Preis, J. (1985). Project SCAN: Counseling teen-age parents in a school setting. *Journal of School Health, 55,* 24-26.

deLissovoy, V. (1973). High school marriages: A longitudinal study. *Journal of Marriage and the Family, 35,* 245-255.

Devencenzi, J., & Pendergast, S. (1988). *A guide for group facilitators: Self and social discovery for children of all ages.* San Luis Obispo, CA: Belonging.

Dewey, J. (1929). *The sources of a science of education.* New York: Horace Liveright.

DeWoody, M. (1993). Adoption and disclosure of medical and social history: A review of the law. *Child Welfare, 72,* 195-218.

Dey, I. (1993). *Qualitative data analysis: A user-friendly guide for social scientists.* New York: Routledge.

Dickman, I. R. (1981). *Teenage pregnancy—what can be done?* (Pamphlet No. 594). New York: Public Affairs Pamphlets.

Dillard, J. M. (1983). *Multicultural counseling: Toward ethnic and cultural relevance in human encounters.* Chicago: Nelson-Hall.

Doyle, D. P. (1993, April). American schools: Good bad or indifferent. *Phi Delta Kappan,* pp. 626-631.

Doyle, J. A. (1989). *The male experience* (2nd ed.). Dubuque, IA: William C. Brown.

Dryfoos, J. G. (1990). *Adolescents at risk: Prevalence and prevention.* New York: Oxford University Press.

Dryfoos, J. G. (1994). *Full-service schools: A revolution in health and social services for children, youth, and families.* San Francisco: Jossey-Bass.

Du Bois, W. E. B. (1903). *The souls of Black folk.* Chicago: McClurg.

Duggan, A. K., DeAngelis, C., & Hardy, J. B. (1991). Comprehensive versus traditional services for pregnant and parenting adolescents: A comparative analysis. In J. B. Hardy & L. S. Zabin (Eds.), *Adolescent pregnancy in an urban environment: Issues, programs and evaluation* (pp. 255-278). Washington, DC: Urban Institute Press.

Dunn, C. W., & Veltman, G. C. (1989). Addressing the restrictive career maturity patterns of minority youth: A program evaluation. *Journal of Multicultural Counseling and Development, 17,* 156-164.

Duran, L. I., & Bernard, H. R. (Eds.). (1973). *Introduction to Chicano studies.* New York: Macmillan.

Earls, F. & Siegel, B. (1980). Precocious fathers. *American Journal of Orthopsychiatry, 50,* 469-480.

Egan, G. (1990). *The skilled helper: A systematic approach to effective helping.* Pacific Grove, CA: Brooks/Cole.

Elias, M. J., & Clabby, J. F. (1982). *Social problem solving curriculum for enhancing critical thinking skills.* New Brunswick, NJ: Rutgers University Press.

Elster, A. B., & Hendricks, L. (1986). Stresses and coping strategies of adolescent fathers. In A. B. Elster & M. E. Lamb, (Eds.), *Adolescent fatherhood* (pp. 55-66). Hillsdale, NJ: Lawrence Erlbaum.

Elster, A. B., & Lamb, M. E. (Eds.). (1986). *Adolescent fatherhood.* Hillsdale, NJ: Lawrence Erlbaum.

Elster, A. B., & Panzarine, S. (1980). Unwed teenage fathers: Emotional and health educational needs. *Journal of Adolescent Health Care, 1,* 116-120.

Elster, A. B., & Panzarine, S. (1983a). Adolescent fathers. In E. R. McAnarney (Ed.), *Premature adolescent pregnancy and parenthood* (pp. 231-252). New York: Grune & Stratton.

Elster, A. B., & Panzarine, S. (1983b). Teenage fathers: Stresses during gestation and early parenthood. *Clinical Pediatrics, 22,* 700-703.

Ellwood, D., & Summers, L. H. (1986). Poverty in America: Is welfare the answer of the problem? In S. Danziger & D. Weinberg (Eds.), *Fighting poverty: What works and what doesn't* (pp. 78-105). Cambridge, MA: Harvard University Press.

Erickson, R. J., & Gecas, V. (1991). Social class and fatherhood. In F. W. Bozett, & S. M. H. Hanson (Eds.), *Fatherhood and families in cultural context* (pp. 114-137). New York: Springer.

Etter, J. (1993). Levels of cooperation and satisfaction in 56 open adoptions. *Child Welfare, 72,* 257-267.

Everett, J. E. (1985). An examination of child support enforcement issues. In H. McAdoo & T. M. J. Parham (Eds.), *Services to young families: Program review and policy recommendations* (pp. 75-112). Washington, DC: American Public Welfare Association.

Fagan, R. R., Brody, R. A., & O'Leary, T. J. (1968). *Cubans in exile: Disaffection and the revolution.* Palo Alto, CA: Stanford University Press.

Falicov, C. J. (1982). Mexican families. In M. McGoldrick, J. K. Pearce, & J. Giordan (Eds.), *Ethnicity and family therapy* (pp. 134-163). New York: Guilford.

Family Service, Inc. (Producer). (n.d.). *Fathers: today and yesterday* [Film]. Charlottesville, VA: Producer.

Feindler, E. L., Marriott, S. A., & Iwata, M. (1984). Group anger control training for junior high school delinquents. *Cognitive Therapy and Research, 8,* 299-311.

Fernandez, M., Ruch-Ross, H. S., & Montague, A. P. (1993). Ethnicity and effects of age gap between unmarried adolescent mothers and partners. *Journal of Adolescent Research, 8,* 439-466.

Field, T., Widmayer, S. M., Stringer, S., & Ignatoff, E. (1980). Teenage, lower-class Black mothers and their preterm infants: An intervention and developmental follow-up. *Child Development, 51,* 426-436.

Fine, R. (1988). *Troubled men: The psychology, emotional conflicts and therapy of men.* San Francisco: Jossey-Bass.

Finkel, M., & Finkel, D. (1975). Sexual and contraceptive knowledge, attitudes, and behavior of male adolescents. *Family Planning Perspectives, 7,* 256-260.

Fischman, S. H. (1977). Delivery or abortion in inner-city adolescents. *American Journal of Orthopsychiatry, 47,* 127-133.

Fishman, S. T. (1981). Narrowing the generalization gap in clinical research. *Behavioral Assessment, 3,* 243-248.

Fitzpatrick, J. P. (1987). *Puerto Rican Americans: The meaning of migration to the mainland.* Englewood Cliffs, NJ: Prentice Hall.

Flood, M. F., Greenspan, S., & Mundorf, N. K. (1985). School-based services for pregnant and parenting adolescents. *Special Services in the Schools, 2*(1), 27-44.

Forbush, J. B. (1979). Family involvement in adolescent parent programs. In T. Ooms (Ed.), *Teenage pregnancy and family impact: New perspectives on policy. Family impact seminar* (p. 18). Washington, DC: George Washington University's Institute for Educational Leadership.

Forbush, J. B. (1981). Adolescent parent programs and family involvement. In T. Ooms (Ed.), *Teenage pregnancy in a family context: Implications for policy* (pp. 254-276). Philadelphia: Temple University Press.

Ford Foundation. (1984). *Hispanics: Challenges and opportunities.* New York: Author.

Franco, J. N., & Levine, E. (1980). An analogue study of counselor ethnicity and client preference. *Hispanic Journal of Behavioral Sciences, 2,* 177-183.

Frankl, V. E. (1959). *Man's search for meaning.* New York: Washington Square Press.

Franklin, A. J. (1982). Therapeutic interventions with urban Black adolescents. In E. E. Jones & S. J. Korchin (Eds.), *Minority mental health* (pp. 267-295). New York: Praeger.

Franklin, A. J. (1989). Therapeutic interventions with urban Black adolescents. In R. L. Jones (Ed.), *Black adolescents* (pp. 309-337). Berkeley, CA: Cobb & Henry.

Frazier, E. F. (1966). *The Negro family in the United States* (Rev. ed.). Chicago: University of Chicago Press. (Original work published 1939)

Freeman, E. M. (1987). Interaction of pregnancy, loss, and developmental issues in adolescents. *Social Casework: The Journal of Contemporary Social Work,* 38-46.

Freeman, E. M. (1989). Adolescent fathers in urban communities: Exploring their needs and role in preventing pregnancy. *Journal of Social Work and Human Sexuality, 8,* 113-131.

Freeman, E. W., & Rickels, K. (1993). *Early childbearing: Perspectives of Black adolescents on pregnancy, abortion, and contraception.* Newbury Park, CA: Sage.

Fry, P. S., & Trifiletti, R. J. (1983). Teenage fathers: An exploration of their developmental needs and anxieties and the implications for clinical-social intervention services. *Journal of Psychiatric Treatment and Evaluation, 5,* 219-227.

Furstenberg, F. F. (1976). *Unplanned parenthood: The social consequences of teenage childbearing.* New York: Free Press.

Furstenberg, F. F. (1979). Burdens and benefits: The impact of early childbearing on the family. In T. Ooms (Ed.), *Teenage pregnancy and family impact: New perspectives on policy. Family impact seminar* (pp. 21-22). Washington, DC: George Washington University's Institute for Educational Leadership.

Furstenberg, F. F. (1981). Implicating the family: Teenage parenthood and kinship involvement. In T. Ooms (Ed.), *Teenage pregnancy in a family context: Implications for policy* (pp. 131-164). Philadelphia: Temple University Press.

Furstenberg, F. F., Brooks-Gunn, J., & Chase-Lansdale, L. (1989). Teenage pregnancy and childbearing. *American Psychologist, 44,* 313-320.

Furstenberg, F. F., Brooks-Gunn, J., & Morgan, S. P. (1987). *Adolescent mothers in later life.* New York: Cambridge University Press.

Furstenberg, F. F., & Crawford, A. G. (1989). Family support: Helping teenage mothers to cope. In N. Cervera & L. Videka-Sherman (Eds.), *Working with pregnant and parenting teenage clients* (pp. 108-133). Milwaukee, WI: Family Service America.

Futterman, S., & Livermore, J. B. (1947). Putative fathers. *Journal of Social Casework, 28,* 174-178.

Gabriel, A., & McAnarney, E. R. (1983). Parenthood in two subcultures: White, middle-class couples and Black, low-income adolescents in Rochester, New York. *Adolescence, 18,* 595-608.

Galassi, J. P., & Galassi, M. D. (1978). Preparing individuals for job interviews: Suggestions from more than 60 years of research. *Personnel and Guidance Journal, 57,* 188-192.

Garcia-Preto, N. (1982). Puerto Rican families. In M. McGoldrick, J. K. Pearce, & J. Giordan (Eds.), *Ethnicity and family therapy* (pp. 164-186). New York: Guilford.

Gard, T. L. (1993). *Reconsideration of gender bias in clinical judgment: Characteristics of gender influenced counselors.* Unpublished master's thesis, Ball State University, Muncie, IN.

Garfinkel, I. (1992). *Assuring child support: An extension of Social Security.* New York: Russell Sage.

Garner, B. (1989). *WorkWise: A career awareness course for teen parents.* Cambridge, MA: Cambridge Community Services.

Gary, L. E., Leashore, B. R., Howard, C. S., & Buckner-Dowell, R. R. (1982). *Help-seeking behavior among Black males: Final report.* Washington, DC: Howard University, Mental Health Research and Development Center, Institute for Urban Affairs and Research.

Gatley, R., & Koulack, D. (1979). *Single father's handbook.* Garden City, NY: Doubleday.

Gelso, C. J. (1993). On the making of a scientist-practitioner: A theory of research training in professional psychology. *Professional Psychology: Research and Practice, 24,* 468-476.

Gershenson, H. P. (1983). Redefining fatherhood in families with White adolescent mothers. *Journal of Marriage and the Family, 45,* 591-599.

Gibbs, J. T. (1984). Black adolescents and youth: An endangered species. *American Journal of Orthopsychiatry, 54,* 6-21.

Gibbs, J. T. (1988). *Young, Black and male in America.* Dover, MA: Auburn.

Glass, B. L. (1982). Comparing employed and unemployed welfare recipients: A discriminant analysis. *Journal of Sociology and Social Welfare, 9,* 19-36.

Glass, B. L. (1990). Child support enforcement: An implementation analysis. *Social Service Review, 64,* 542-558.

Goddard, L. L., & Cavil, W. E. (1989). Black teenage parenting: Issues and challenges. In R. L. Jones (Ed.), *Black adolescents* (pp. 373-383). Berkeley, CA: Cobb & Henry.

Golant, M., & Golant, S. (1992). *Finding time for fathering.* New York: Fawcett Columbine.

Goldstein, H., & Wallace, H. (1978). Services for and needs of pregnant teenagers in large cities in the U.S. *Public Health Reports, 93,* 46-54.

Gordon, B. (1990). Men and their fathers. In R. L. Meth & R. S. Pasick (Eds.), *Men in therapy: The challenge of change* (pp. 234-246). New York: Guilford.

Gordon, T. (1973). Notes on White and Black psychology. *Journal of Social Issues, 29,* 87-95.

Green, M. (1976). *Fathering.* New York: McGraw-Hill.

Greenberg, M. (1985). *The birth of a father.* New York: Continuum.

Greenberg, M., & Morris, N. (1974). Engrossment: The newborn's impact upon the father. *American Journal of Orthopsychiatry, 44,* 520-531.

Greif, G. L., & Pabst, M. S. (1988). *Mothers without custody.* Lexington, MA: Lexington Books.

Grisso, T. (1992). Minors' assent without parental permission. In B. Stanley & J. E. Sieber (Eds.), *Social research on children and adolescents: Ethical issues* (pp. 109-127). Newbury Park, CA: Sage.

Griswold, R. L. (1993). *Fatherhood in America: A history.* New York: Basic Books.

Gross, H. E. (1993). Open adoption: A research-based literature review and new data. *Child Welfare, 72,* 269-284.

Groth, M., Bonnardel, D., Devis, D. A., Martin, J. C., & Vousden, H. E. (1987). An agency moves toward open adoption of infants. *Child Welfare, 69,* 263-275.

Group for the Advancement of Psychiatry. (1986). *Crises of adolescence. Teenage pregnancy: Impact on adolescent development.* New York: Brunner/Mazel.

Guerney, B. G. (1982). *Relationship enhancement.* San Francisco: Jossey-Bass.

Guthrie, R. V. (1976). *Even the rat was white.* New York: Harper & Row.

Gysbers, N. (1988). *Career development: The contemporary scene and the future.* Ann Arbor: University of Michigan, ERIC/CAPS Digest, Counseling and Personnel Services Clearinghouse.

Hackett, G. (1993). Career counseling and psychotherapy: False dichotomies and recommended remedies. *Journal of Career Assessment, 1,* 105-117.

Hackford, T. (Producer and Director). (1978). *Teenage father* [Film]. (Available from Children's Home Society of California, 1300 West 4th St., Los Angeles, CA 90017-1475)

Hackney, H. (1991, Fall). Trading places. *The ASCA Counselor,* p. 3.

Hamilton, M. (1977). *Fathers' influence on children.* Chicago: Nelson-Hall.

Hanson, S. M. H. (1985). Single custodial fathers. In S. M. H. Hanson & F. W. Bozett (Eds.), *Dimensions of fatherhood* (pp. 369-392). Beverly Hills, CA: Sage.

Hardiman, R. (1982). *White identity development: A process oriented model for describing the racial consciousness of White Americans.* Unpublished doctoral dissertation, University of Massachusetts, Amherst.

Hardy, J. B., & Zabin, L. S. (1991). *Adolescent pregnancy in an urban environment: Issues, programs and evaluation.* Washington, DC: Urban Institute Press.

Hare, B. R. (1990). African-American youth at risk. In D. J. Jones & S. F. Battle (Eds.), *Teenage pregnancy: Developing strategies for change in the twenty-first century* (pp. 25-38). New Brunswick, NJ: Transaction Books.

Harris, L., & Associates. (1986). *American teens speak: Sex, myths, TV and birth control.* New York: Author.

Hatchett, S. J. (1991). Women and men. In J. S. Jackson (Ed.), *Life in Black America* (pp. 84-104). Newbury Park, CA: Sage.

Hatchett, S. J., Cochran, D. L., & Jackson, J. S. (1991). Family life. In J. S. Jackson (Ed.), *Life in Black America* (pp. 46-83). Newbury Park, CA: Sage.

Haycock, K., & Duany, L. (1991). Developing the potential of Latino students. *Principal, 70,* 25-27.

Hayes, C. D. (Ed.). (1987). *Risking the future: Adolescent sexuality, pregnancy, and child-bearing* (Vol. 1). Washington, DC: National Academy Press.

Hayes, R. L., & Cryer, N. (1988). When adolescents give birth to children: A developmental approach to the issue of teen pregnancy. In J. Carlson & J. Lewis (Eds.), *Counseling the adolescent: Individual, family, and school interventions* (pp. 21-40). Denver: Love Publishing.

Haynes, S. N., Lemsky, C., & Sexton-Radek, K. (1987). Why clinicians infrequently do research. *Professional Psychology: Research and Practice, 18,* 515-519.

Heath, T. D., & McHenry, P. C. (1993). Adult family life of men who fathered as adolescents. *Families in Society, 74,* 36-45.

Helge, D. (1990). *A national study regarding at-risk students.* Bellingham, WA: National Rural Development Institute.

Helms, J. E. (1984). Toward a theoretical model of the effects of race on counseling: A Black and White model. *The Counseling Psychologist, 12,* 153-165.

Helms, J. E. (1990). *A training manual for diagnosing racial identity in social interactions.* Topeka, KS: Content Communications.

Helms, J. E., & Carter, R. T. (1990). White Racial Identity Attitude Scale (Form WRIAS). In J. E. Helms (Ed.), *Black and White racial identity: Theory, research, and practice* (pp. 249-251). Westport, CT: Greenwood.

Helms, J. E., & Parham, T. A. (1990). Black Racial Identity Attitude Scale (Form RIAS:B). In J. E. Helms (Ed.), *Black and White racial identity: Theory, research, and practice* (pp. 245-247). Westport, CT: Greenwood.

Hendricks, L. E. (1980). Unwed adolescent fathers: Problems they face and their sources of social support. *Adolescence, 15,* 861-869.

Hendricks, L. E. (1981). Black unwed adolescent fathers. In L. E. Gary (Ed.), *Black men* (pp. 131-138). Beverly Hills, CA: Sage.

Hendricks, L. E. (1982). Unmarried Black adolescent fathers' attitudes toward abortion, contraception, and sexuality: A preliminary report. *Journal of Adolescent Health Care, 2,* 199-203.

Hendricks, L. E. (1983). Suggestions for reaching unmarried Black adolescent fathers. *Child Welfare, 62,* 141-146.

Hendricks, L. E. (1988). Outreach with teenage fathers: A preliminary report on three ethnic groups. *Adolescence, 23*(91), 711-720.

Hendricks, L. E. (1992, April). *Expanding the initiative with teenage fathers.* Symposium conducted at the annual meeting of the Indiana Council on Adolescent Pregnancy, Indianapolis.

Hendricks, L. E., Howard, C. S., & Caesar, P. P. (1981). Black unwed adolescent fathers: A comparative study of their problems and help-seeking behavior. *Journal of the National Medical Association, 73,* 863-868.

Hendricks, L. E., & Montgomery, T. (1983). A limited population of unmarried Black adolescent fathers: A preliminary report of their views on fatherhood and the relationship with the mother of their children. *Adolescence, 18*(69), 201-210.

Hendricks, L. E., & Montgomery, T., & Fullilove, R. E. (1984). Educational achievement and locus of control among Black adolescent fathers. *Journal of Negro Education, 53,* 182-188.

Hendricks, L. E., & Solomon, A. M. (1987). Reaching Black adolescent parents through nontraditional techniques. *Child and Youth Services, 9*(1), 111-124.

Henggeler, S. W. (1989). *Delinquency in adolescence.* Newbury Park, CA: Sage.

Henshaw, S. K. (1992). Abortion trends in 1987 and 1988: Age and race. *Family Planning Perspectives, 24,* 85-86, 96.

Henshaw, S. K. (1993). Teenage abortion, birth and pregnancy statistics by state, 1988. *Family Planning Perspectives, 25,* 122-126.

Henshaw, S. K., Kenney, A. M., Somberg, D., & Van Vort, J. (1989). *Teenage pregnancy in the United States: The scope of the problem and state responses.* New York: Alan Guttmacher Institute.

Henshaw, S. K., & O'Reilly, K. (1983). Characteristics of abortion patients in the United States, 1979 and 1980. *Family Planning Perspectives, 15,* 5-16.

Heppner, P. P., Kivlighan, D. M., & Wampold, B. E. (1992). *Research design in counseling.* Pacific Grove, CA: Brooks/Cole.

Herr, E. L. (1970). *Decision-making and vocational development.* Boston: Houghton Mifflin.

Herr, E. L. (1989). Career development and mental health. *Journal of Career Development, 16,* 5-18.

Herr, E. L., & Cramer, S. H. (1988). *Career guidance and counseling through the life span* (3rd ed.). Boston: Little, Brown.

Herr, E. L., & Niles, S. G. (1994). Multicultural career guidance in the schools. In P. Pedersen & J. C. Carey (Eds.), *Multicultural counseling in schools* (pp. 177-194). Boston: Allyn & Bacon.

Herzog, J. M. (1984). Boys who make babies. In M. Sugar (Ed.), *Adolescent parenthood* (pp. 65-73). New York: SP Medical and Scientific Books.

Hetherington, E. M., & Parke, R. D. (1979). *Child psychology: A contemporary viewpoint* (2nd ed.). New York: McGraw-Hill.

Hill, R. (1977). *Informal adoption among Black families.* Washington, DC: National Urban League Research Department.

Ho, M. K. (1992). *Minority children and adolescents in therapy.* Newbury Park, CA: Sage.

Hodgkinson, H. (1993, April). American education: The good, the bad and the task. *Phi Delta Kappan,* pp. 619-623.

Hofferth, S. L. (1987a). Social and economic consequences of teenage childbearing. In S. L. Hofferth & C. D. Hayes (Eds.), *Risking the future: Adolescent sexuality, pregnancy, and childbearing* (Vol. 2, pp. 123-144). Washington, DC: National Academy Press.

Hofferth, S. L. (1987b). The effects of programs and policies on adolescent pregnancy and childbearing. In S. L. Hofferth & C. D. Hayes (Eds.), *Risking the future: Adolescent sexuality, pregnancy, and childbearing* (Vol. 2, pp. 207-263). Washington, DC: National Academy Press.

Hogan, D., & Kitagawa, E. (1985). The impact of social status, family structure, and neighborhood on the fertility of Black adolescents. *American Journal of Sociology, 90,* 825-836.

Hoge, D. R., Petrillo, G., & Smith, E. I. (1982). Transmission of religious and social values from parents to teenage children. *Journal of Marriage and the Family, 44*, 569-580.

Holland, J. (1979). *The self-directed search.* Palo Alto, CA: Consulting Psychologists Press.

Holland, J. L. (1973). *Making vocational choices: A theory of careers.* Englewood Cliffs, NJ: Prentice Hall.

Holloway, E. L., & Wolleat, P. L. (1980). Relationship of counselor conceptual level to clinical hypothesis formation. *Journal of Counseling Psychology, 27*, 539-545.

Honzik, M. (1967). Environmental correlates of mental growth: Prediction from the family setting at twelve months. *Child Development, 38*, 337-364.

Horan, J. J. (1979). *Counseling for effective decision making: A cognitive-behavioral perspective.* North Scituate, MA: Duxbury.

Horie, M., & Horie, H. (1988). *Whatever became of fathering?* Downers Grove, IL: Inter-Varsity.

Horn, A., & Sager, T. (1990). *Understanding and treating conduct oppositional defiant disorders in children.* Boston: Allyn & Bacon.

Horney, K. (1937). *The neurotic personality of our time.* New York: Norton.

Horowitz, N. (1980). Impact of a second adolescent pregnancy. In J. E. Beger (Ed.), *Teenage pregnancy: Research related to clients and services* (pp. 179-192). Springfield, IL: Charles C Thomas.

Horowitz, R., & Dodson, D. (1984). *Child support: An annotated bibliography.* Washington, DC: Department of Health and Human Services.

Hoshmand, L. T., & Polkinghorne, D. E. (1992). Redefining the science-practice relationship and professional training. *American Psychologist, 47*, 55-66.

Howard, G. S. (1986). The scientist-practitioner in counseling psychology: Toward a deeper integration of theory, research, and practice. *The Counseling Psychologist, 14*, 61-105.

Howard, M. (1991). *How to help your teenager postpone sexual involvement.* New York: Continuum.

Howe, H. (1993, Winter/Spring). We need four more national education goals. *Harvard Graduate School of Education News & Views*, pp. 15-16.

Huey, W. C. (1987). Counseling teenage fathers: The "Maximizing a Life Experience" (MALE) group. *School Counselor, 35*, 40-47.

Huey, W. C., & Remley, T. P. (Eds.). (1988). *Ethical and legal issues in school counseling.* Alexandria, VA: American School Counselor Association.

Hughey, K. F., Heppner, M. J., Johnston, J. A., & Rakes, T. D. (1989). Farm families in career transitions: Descriptive characteristics and an intervention. *Journal of Counseling and Development, 67*, 475-477.

Hunter-Geboy, C. (n.d.). *Como planear mi vida* [Make a life for yourself]. Washington, DC: Center for Population Options.

Inclan, J. (1985). Variations in value orientations in mental health work with Puerto Ricans. *Psychotherapy, 22*, 324-334.

Ingrassia, M. (1993, August 30). Endangered family. *Newsweek*, pp. 17-27.

Institute of Medicine. (1985). *Preventing low birthweight.* Washington, DC: National Academy Press.

Intermedia, Inc. (1987). *It only takes once* [Film]. Seattle, WA: Producer.

Ivey, A. E., Ivey, M. B., & Simek-Morgan, L. (1993). *Counseling and psychotherapy: A multicultural perspective.* Boston: Allyn & Bacon.

Jaffe, E. D. (1983). Fathers and child welfare services: The forgotten clients? In M. E. Lamb & A. Sagi (Eds.), *Fatherhood and family policy* (pp. 129-138). Hillsdale, NJ: Lawrence Erlbaum.

James, J. W., & Cherry, F. (1988). *The grief recovery handbook.* New York: Harper & Row.

Johnson, R. L. (1985). Black adolescents: Issues critical to their survival. *Journal of the National Medical Association, 77,* 447-448.

Johnson, T. R. B. (1991). Ethical issues in the medical care of adolescents. In J. B. Hardy & L. S. Zabin (Eds.), *Adolescent pregnancy in an urban environment: Issues, programs and evaluation* (pp. 151-161). Washington, DC: Urban Institute Press.

Jones, E. E. (1985). Psychotherapy and counseling with Black clients. In P. B. Pedersen (Ed.), *Handbook of cross-cultural counseling and therapy* (pp. 173-187). Westport, CT: Greenwood.

Jones, E. F., Forrest, J. D., Goldman, N., Henshaw, S. K., Lincoln, R., Rosoff, J. I., Westoff, C. F., & Wulf, D. (1985). Teenage pregnancy in developed countries: Determinants and policy implications. *Family Planning Perspectives, 17,* 53-63.

Kahn, J. S. (1986). Personal perspectives: An interview with two teenage fathers. In C. Kort & R. Friedland (Eds.), *The father's book: Shared experiences* (pp. 192-195). Boston: G. K. Hall.

Kahn, J. S., & Bolton, F. G. (1986). Clinical issues in adolescent fatherhood. In A. B. Elster & M. E. Lamb (Eds.), *Adolescent fatherhood* (pp. 141-154). Hillsdale, NJ: Lawrence Erlbaum.

Kalish, R. A. (1985). *Death, grief, and caring relationships.* Pacific Grove, CA: Brooks/Cole.

Kanfer, F. H. (1990). The scientist-practitioner connection: A bridge in need of constant attention. *Professional Psychology: Research and Practice, 21,* 264-270.

Kaplan, R. M., & Saccuzzo, D. P. (1989). *Psychological testing: Principles, applications, and issues.* Pacific Grove, CA: Brooks/Cole.

Kasanin, J., & Handschin, S. (1941). Psychodynamic factors in illegitimacy. *American Journal of Orthopsychiatry, 11,* 66-84.

Kazdin, A. E. (1982). *Single-case research designs: Methods for clinical and applied settings.* New York: Oxford University Press.

Kazdin, A. E. (1992). *Research design in clinical psychology.* Boston: Allyn & Bacon.

Kelly, K. R., & Hall, A. S. (1992). Mental health counseling for men: A special issue. *Journal of Mental Health Counseling, 14,* 255-256.

Kerckhoff, A. C., & Parrow, A. A. (1979). The effect of early marriage on the educational attainment of young men. *Journal of Marriage and the Family, 41,* 97-107.

Kerr, B. A., Claiborn, C. D., & Dixon, D. D. (1982). Training counselors in persuasion. *Counselor Education and Supervision, 21,* 138-148.

Keshet, H., & Rosenthal, K. (1978). Fathering after marital separation. *Social Work, 23,* 11-18.

Kiesler, C. A. (1993). Poverty and public policy [Review of the book *Children in poverty: Child development and public policy*]. *Contemporary Psychology, 38,* 134-135.

King Screen Productions. (Producer). (n.d.). *Dad and me.* [Videocassette]. (Available from Phoenix Films, 2349 Chaffee Dr., St. Louis, MO 63142)

Kirby D., & Waszak, C. (1992). School-based clinics. In B. C. Miller, J. J. Card, R. L. Paikoff, & J. L. Peterson (Eds.), *Preventing adolescent pregnancy: Model programs and evaluations* (pp. 185-219). Newbury Park, CA: Sage.

Kiselica, M. S. (1991). Reflections on a multicultural internship experience. *Journal of Counseling and Development, 70,* 126-130.

Kiselica, M. S. (1992, August). Are we giving teenage fathers a mixed message? In L. Silverstein (Chair), *Transforming fatherhood in a patriarchal society.* Symposium conducted at the annual meeting of the American Psychological Society, Washington, DC.

Kiselica, M. S. (1993, March). *Male involvement in teenage pregnancy and parenthood.* Symposium conducted at the annual meeting of the Indiana Council on Adolescent Pregnancy, Indianapolis.

Kiselica, M. S. (1994, April). Adoption option for teenage parents. *The ASCA Counselor, 31*(4), 19.

Kiselica, M. S. (1995, January/February). The pros and cons of the adoption option. *The ASCA Counselor, 32*(3), 8.

Kiselica, M. S. (in press-a). Healing father-son wounds with adolescent fathers. *The Psychotherapy Bulletin.*

Kiselica, M. S. (in press-b). Parenting skills training with teenage fathers: A group psychotherapeutic approach. In M. P. Andronico (Ed.), *Men in groups: Realities and insights.* Washington, DC: American Psychological Association.

Kiselica, M. S., & Baker, S. B. (1992). Progressive muscle relaxation and cognitive restructuring: Potential problems and proposed solutions. *Journal of Mental Health Counseling, 14,* 149-165.

Kiselica, M. S., Baker, S. B., Thomas, R. N., & Reedy, S. (1994). The effects of stress inoculation training on anxiety, stress, and academic performance among adolescents. *Journal of Counseling Psychology, 41,* 335-342.

Kiselica, M. S., Changizi, J., Cureton, V., & Gridley, E. (1995). Counseling children and adolescents in schools: Salient multicultural issues. In J. Ponterotto, J. M. Casas, L. Suzuki, & C. Alexander (Eds.), *Handbook of multicultural counseling* (pp. 516-532). Thousand Oaks, CA: Sage.

Kiselica, M. S., Doms, J., & Rotzien, A. (1992, March). *Improving societal excellence through courses on fatherhood for adolescent boys.* Paper presented at the annual meeting of the American Association for Counseling and Development, Baltimore, MD.

Kiselica, M. S., & Murphy, D. K. (1994). Developmental career counseling with teenage parents. *Career Development Quarterly, 42,* 238-244.

Kiselica, M. S., & Pfaller, J. (1993). Helping teenage parents: The independent and collaborative roles of school counselors and counselor educators. *Journal of Counseling and Development, 72,* 42-48.

Kiselica, M. S., Rotzien, A., & Doms, J. (1994). Preparing teenage fathers for parenthood: A group psychoeducational approach. *Journal for Specialists in Group Work, 19,* 83-94.

Kiselica, M. S., & Scheckel, S. (in press). Teenage fathers and the couvade syndrome (sympathetic pregnancy): A brief primer for school counselors. *The School Counselor.*

Kiselica, M. S., Stroud, J. C., Stroud, J. E., & Rotzien, A. (1992). Counseling the forgotten client: The teen father. *Journal of Mental Health Counseling, 14,* 338-350.

Kiselica, M. S., & Sturmer, P. (1993a). *Adolescent pregnancy and parenting services: Indiana resource directory.* Indianapolis: Indiana Council on Adolescent Pregnancy.

Kiselica, M. S., & Sturmer, P. (1993b). Is society giving teenage fathers a mixed message? *Youth and Society, 24,* 487-501.

Kiselica, M. S., & Sturmer, P. (1995). *Outreach programs for teenage parents and the second-rate status of teenage fathers.* Manuscript submitted for publication.

Klerman, L. (1982). Teenage parents: A brief review of research. In D. L. Parron & L. Eisenberg (Eds.), *Infants at risk for developmental dysfunction* (pp. 125-132). Washington, DC: National Academy Press.

Klerman, L. (1991). The association between adolescent parenting and childhood poverty. In A. C. Huston (Ed.), *Children in poverty: Child development and public policy* (pp. 79-104). Cambridge, UK: Cambridge University Press.

Klerman, L. V., & Jekel, J. F. (1973). *School-age mothers: Problems, programs, and policy.* Hamden, CT: Shoe String Press.

Klinman, D. G., & Kohl, R. (1984). *Fatherhood U.S.A.* New York: Garland.

Klinman, D. G., & Sander, J. H. (1985). *The teen parent collaboration: Reaching and serving the teenage father.* New York: Bank Street College of Education.

Klinman, D. G., Sander, J. H., Rosen, J. L., & Longo, K. R. (1986). The teen father collaboration: A demonstration and research model. In A. B. Elster & M. E. Lamb (Eds.), *Adolescent fatherhood* (pp. 155-170). Hillsdale, NJ: Lawrence Erlbaum.

Klinman, D. G., Sander, J. H., Rosen, J. L., Longo, K. R., Martinez, L. P. (1985). *The teen parent collaboration: Reaching and serving the teenage father.* New York: Bank Street College of Education.

Koocher, G. P., & Keith-Spiegel, P. C. (1990). *Children, ethics, and the law.* Lincoln: University of Nebraska Press.

Kotelchuck, M. (1976). The infant's relationship to the father: Experimental evidence. In M. Lamb (Ed.), *The role of the father in child development* (pp. 329-344). New York: John Wiley.

Kottler, J. A. (1983). *Pragmatic group leadership.* Pacific Grove, CA: Brooks/Cole.

Kratochwill, T. R., & Levin, J. R. (1992). *Single-case research design and analysis.* Hillsdale, NJ: Lawrence Erlbaum.

Kunjufu, J. (1986). *Countering the conspiracy to destroy Black boys* (Vol. 2). Chicago: African American Images.

Ladner, J. A., & Gourdine, M. (1984, Fall). Intergenerational teenage motherhood: Some preliminary findings. *Sage: A Scholarly Journal on Black Women, 1,* 22-24.

Lamb, M. E. (1983). Fatherhood and social policy in international perspective: An introduction. In M. E. Lamb & A. Sagi (Eds.), *Fatherhood and family policy* (pp. 1-12). Hillsdale, NJ: Lawrence Erlbaum.

Lamb, M. E. (1987). Introduction: The emergent American father. In M. E. Lamb (Ed.), *The father's role: Cross-cultural perspectives* (pp. 3-26). Hillsdale, NJ: Lawrence Erlbaum.

Lamb, M. E., & Elster A. B. (1986). Parental behavior of adolescent mothers and fathers. In A. B. Elster & M. E. Lamb (Eds.), *Adolescent fatherhood* (pp. 89-106). Hillsdale, NJ: Lawrence Erlbaum.

Langelier, R. (1982). French Canadian families. In M. McGoldrick, J. K. Pearce, & J. Giordano (Eds.), *Ethnicity and family therapy* (pp. 229-246). New York: Guilford.

Lanyon, R. I., & Lanyon, B. P. (1978). *Behavior modification: A clinical introduction.* Reading, MA: Addison-Wesley.

Leavy, W. (1983, August). Is the Black male an endangered species? *Ebony,* pp. 41-42, 44, 46.

Lee, C. C. (1989). Counseling the Black adolescent: Critical roles and functions for counseling professionals. In R. L. Jones (Ed.), *Black adolescents* (pp. 293-308). Berkeley, CA: Cobb & Henry.

Lee, C. C., & Richardson, B. (1991). Promise and pitfalls of multicultural counseling. In C. C. Lee & B. L. Richardson (Eds.), *Multicultural issues in counseling: New approaches to diversity* (pp. 3-10). Alexandria, VA: American Counseling Association.

Lerman, R. I. (1985). *Who are the young absent fathers?* Paper prepared for the Department of Health and Human Services, Assistant Secretary for Policy and Evaluation. Boston: Brandeis University, Heller Graduate School.

Levant, R. F. (1988). Education for fatherhood. In P. Bronstein & C. P. Cowan (Eds.), *Fatherhood today: Men's changing role in the family* (pp. 253-275). New York: John Wiley.

Levant, R. F. (1992). Toward the reconstruction of masculinity. *Journal of Family Psychology, 5,* 379-402.

Levy, R. L. (1981). On the nature of the clinical-research gap: The problems with some solutions. *Behavioral Assessment, 3,* 235-242.

Lindner, A. F. (1988). Vocational education: Empowering teen parents. *Wisconsin Vocational Educator, 12,* 8, 17.

Lindner, A. F., & Mellen-Sullivan, D. (1987). *Career planning workbook: From astronaut to zoologist. Career survival kit for teen education and employment.* Madison: University of Wisconsin, Center on Education and Work.

Lindsay, J. W. (1990). *School-age parents: The challenge of three-generation living.* Buena Park, CA: Morning Glory Press.

Lindsay, J. W., & Rodine, S. (1989a). *Teenage pregnancy challenge. Book one: Strategies for change.* Buena Park, CA: Morning Glory Press.

Lindsay, J. W., & Rodine, S. (1989b). *Teenage pregnancy challenge. Book two: Programs for kids.* Buena Park, CA: Morning Glory Press.

Liontos, L. B. (1992). *At-risk families and schools: Becoming partners.* Eugene: University of Oregon, ERIC Clearinghouse on Educational Management, College of Education.

Locke, D. (1992). *Increasing multicultural understanding: A comprehensive model.* Newbury Park, CA: Sage.

Loewen, J. W. (1988). Visitation fatherhood. In P. Bronstein & C. P. Cowan (Eds.), *Fatherhood today: Men's changing role in the family* (pp. 195-213). New York: John Wiley.

Lopez, A., & Petras, H. (1974). *Puerto Rico and the Puerto Ricans.* New York: John Wiley.

Lum, D. (1992). *Social work practice & people of color: A process-stage approach.* Pacific Grove, CA: Brooks/Cole.

Mackey, B., & Milloy, M. (1974, January). The impact of teenage pregnancy on the professional educator. *The Family Coordinator,* 15-18.

Madhubuti, H. R. (1990). *Black men: Obsolete, single, dangerous? The Afrikan American family in transition: Essays in discovery, solution, and hope.* Chicago: Third World Press.

Magna Systems. (1991). *The developing child* [Film]. Itasca, NY: Producer.

Males, M. (1993). Schools, society and "teen" pregnancy. *Phi Delta Kappan, 74,* 566-568.

Males, M. (1994). Poverty, rape, adult/teen sex: Why "pregnancy prevention" programs won't work. *Phi Delta Kappan, 75,* 407-410.

Malveaux, J. (1989). Transitions: The Black adolescent and the labor market. In R. L. Jones (Ed.), *Black adolescents* (pp. 267-289). Berkeley, CA: Cobb & Henry.

Mannion, M. T. (1986). *Abortion and healing: A cry to be whole.* Kansas City, MO: Sheed & Ward.

Marciano, T. D. (1991). Religion and its impact on fatherhood. In F. W. Bozett & S. M. H. Hanson (Eds.), *Fatherhood and families in cultural context* (pp. 138-161). New York: Springer.

Marsella, A. J., & Higginbotham, H. N. (1984). Traditional Asian medicine: Applications to psychiatric services in developing nations. In P. B. Pedersen, N. Sartorius, & A. J. Marsella (Eds.), *Mental health services: The cross-cultural context.* Beverly Hills, CA: Sage.

Marshall, C., & Rossman, G. B. (1989). *Designing qualitative research.* Newbury Park, CA: Sage.

Marsiglio, W. (1986). Teenage fatherhood: High school completion and educational attainment. In A. B. Elster & M. E. Lamb (Eds.), *Adolescent fatherhood* (pp. 67-88). Hillsdale, NJ: Lawrence Erlbaum.

Marsiglio, W. (1987). Adolescent fathers in the United States: Their initial living arrangements, marital experience and educational outcomes. *Family Planning Perspectives, 19,* 240-251.

Marsiglio, W., & Shehan, L. L. (1993). Adolescent males abortion attitudes: Data from a national survey. *Planned Parenthood Perspectives, 25,* 162-168.

Martinez, A. L. (1979). Adolescent pregnancy: The impact on Hispanic adolescents and their families. In T. Ooms (Ed.), *Teenage pregnancy and family impact: New perspectives on policy. Family impact seminar* (pp. 22-23). Washington, DC: George Washington University's Institute for Educational Leadership.

Martinez, A. L. (1989). The impact of adolescent pregnancy on Hispanic adolescents and their families. In N. Cervera & L. Videka-Sherman (Eds.), *Working with pregnant and parenting teenage clients* (pp. 158-170). Milwaukee, WI: Family Service America.

McAdoo, J. L. (1986). Black fathers' relationships with their preschool children and the children's development of ethnic identity. In R. A. Lewis & R. E. Salt (Eds.), *Men in families* (pp. 169-180). Beverly Hills, CA: Sage.

McAdoo, J. L. (1988). Changing perspectives on the role of the Black father. In P. Bronstein & C. P. Cowan (Eds.), *Fatherhood today: Men's changing role in the family* (pp. 79-92). New York: John Wiley.

McAfee, M. L., & Geesey, M. R. (1984). Meeting the needs of the teen-age pregnant student: An in-school program that works. *Journal of School Health, 54,* 350-352.

McCord, J., & Tremblay, R. E. (Eds.). (1992). *Preventing antisocial behavior: Interventions from birth through adolescence.* New York: Guilford.

McCoy, J. E., & Tyler, F. B. (1985). Selected psychosocial characteristics of Black unwed adolescent fathers. *Journal of Adolescent Health Care, 6,* 12-16.

McGee, E. A. (1982). *Too little, too late: Services for teenage parents.* New York: Ford Foundation.

McGill, D., & Pearce, J. K. (1982). British families. In M. McGoldrick, J. K. Pearce, & J. Giordano (Eds.), *Ethnicity and family therapy* (pp. 457-479). New York: Guilford.

McGoldrick, M. (1982). Ethnicity and family therapy: An overview. In M. McGoldrick, J. K. Pearce, & J. Giordano (Eds.), *Ethnicity and family therapy* (pp. 3-30). New York: Guilford.

McGoldrick, M., & Gerson, R. (1985). *Genograms in family assessment.* New York: Norton.

McGoldrick, M., Pearce, J. K., & Giordano, J. (Eds.). (1982). *Ethnicity and family therapy* (2nd ed.). New York: Guilford.

McGovern, M. A. (1990). Sensitivity and reciprocity in the play of adolescent mothers and young fathers with their infants. *Family Relations, 39,* 427-431.

McGrath, P., & Axelson, J. A. (1993). *Accessing awareness and developing knowledge: Foundations for skill in a multicultural society.* Pacific Grove, CA: Brooks/Cole.

McGuire, J. (1991). Sons and daughters. In A. Phoenix, A. Woollett, & E. Lloyd (Eds.), *Motherhood: Meanings, practices and ideologies* (pp. 143-161). London: Sage.

McKenry, P. C., Walters, L. H., & Johnson, C. (1979). Adolescent pregnancy: A review of the literature. *Family Coordinator, 29,* 17-28.

Mead, M. (1971). *And keep your powder dry: An anthropologist looks at America.* New York: William Morrow.

Meichenbaum, D. (1977). *Cognitive-behavior modification: An integrative approach.* New York: Plenum.

Meier, M. S., & Rivera, F. (1981). *Dictionary of Mexican-American experience.* Westport, CT: Greenwood.

Meloy, J. (1994). *Writing the qualitative dissertation.* Hillsdale, NJ: Lawrence Erlbaum.

Memphis Association for Planned Parenthood. (Producer). (1980). *Wayne's decision* [Film]. (Available from Memphis Association for Planned Parenthood, 1407 Union Ave., Memphis, TN 38104)

Miller, A., Rotzien, A., Kiselica, M. S., Clark, J., & Erkis, A. (1995). *The attitudes toward teenage parents scale.* Unpublished manuscript.

Miller, B. C., Card, J. J., Paikoff, R. L., & Peterson, J. L. (Eds.). (1992). *Preventing adolescent pregnancy: Model programs and evaluations.* Newbury Park, CA: Sage.

Miller, B. C., & Moore, K. A. (1990). Adolescent sexual behavior, pregnancy, and parenting: Research through the 1980s. *Journal of Marriage and the Family, 52,* 1025-1044.

Miller, N. (1986). Unplanned adolescent pregnancy and the transitional object. *Child and Adolescent Social Work, 3,* 77-86.

Miller, S. H. (1983). *Children as parents: Final report on a study of childbearing and child rearing among 12- to 15-year-olds.* New York: Child Welfare League.

Mirande, A. (1985). *The Chicano experience: An alternative perspective.* South Bend, IN: University of Notre Dame Press.

Mirande, A. (1988). Chicano fathers: Traditional perceptions and current realities. In P. Bronstein & C. P. Cowan (Eds.), *Fatherhood today: Men's changing role in the family* (pp. 93-108). New York: John Wiley.

Mirande, A. (1991). Ethnicity and fatherhood. In F. W. Bozett & S. M. H. Hanson (Eds.), *Fatherhood and families in cultural context* (pp. 53-82). New York: Springer.

Mitchell, M. (1991). *Call for papers.* Alexandria, VA: American Association for Counseling and Development.

Mitchell-Kernan, C. (1982). Linguistic diversity in the service delivery setting: The case of Black English. In B. A. Bass, G. E. Wyatt, & G. J. Powell (Eds.), *The Afro-American family: Assessment, treatment, and research issues* (pp. 85-98). New York: Grune & Stratton.

Montemayor, R. (1986). Boys as fathers: Coping with the dilemmas of adolescence. In A. B. Elster & M. E. Lamb (Eds.), *Adolescent fatherhood* (pp. 1-18). Hillsdale, NJ: Lawrence Erlbaum.

Montijo, J. A. (1985). Therapeutic relationships with the poor: A Puerto Rican Perspective. *Psychotherapy, 22,* 436-441.

Moore, K. A. (1981). Government policies related to teenage family formation and functioning: An inventory. In T. Ooms (Ed.), *Teenage pregnancy in a family context* (pp. 165-212). Philadelphia: Temple University Press.

Moore, K. A. (1992). *Facts at a glance.* Washington, DC: Child Trends.

Moore, K. A., & Burt, M. R. (1982). *Private crisis, public cost: Policy perspectives on teenage childbearing.* Washington, DC: Urban Institute Press.

Moore, K. A., & Caldwell, S. B. (1977). The effect of government policies on out-of-wedlock sex and pregnancy. *Family Planning Perspectives, 9,* 164-169.

Moore, K. A., Hofferth, S. L., Caldwell, S. B., & Waite, L. J. (1979). *Teenage motherhood: Social and economic consequences.* Washington, DC: The Urban Institute.

Moore, K. A., & Peterson, J. (1989). *The consequences of teenage pregnancy: Final report.* Washington, DC: Child Trends.

Moore, K. A., Simms, M. C., & Betsey, C. L. (1986). *Choice and circumstance: Racial differences in adolescent sexuality and fertility.* New Brunswick, NJ: Transaction Books.

Moore, K. A., Snyder, N., & Halla, C. (1992). *Facts at a glance.* Washington, DC: Child Trends.

Moore, K. A., & Waite, L. (1981). Marital dissolution, early motherhood, and early marriage. *Social Forces, 60,* 20-40.

Moran, J. R., & Corley, M. D. (1991). Sources of sexual information and sexual attitudes and behaviors of Anglo and Hispanic adolescent males. *Adolescence, 26,* 857-864.

Mott, F. (1979). *The socioeconomic status of households headed by women* (U.S. Department of Labor, Research, and Demonstration, Monograph 72, Employment and Training Administration). Washington, DC: Government Printing Office.

Mott, F. L. (1983). *Fertility-related data in the 1982 National Longitudinal Survey of Work Experience of Youth: An evaluation of data quality and some preliminary analytical results.* Columbus: The Ohio State University, Center for Human Resource Research.

Murphy, J. (1993, April). What's in? What's out? American education in the nineties. *Phi Delta Kappan,* pp. 641-646.

Nakashima, I. I., & Camp, B. W. (1984). Fathers of infants born to adolescent mothers. *American Journal of Diseases of Children, 138,* 452-454.

Napier, R. W., & Gershenfeld, M. K. (1993). *Groups: Theory and experience* (5th ed.). Boston: Houghton Mifflin.

National Association for the Education of Young Children. (1985). *Caring for infants and toddlers* [Film]. Washington, DC: Producer.

National Association of Social Workers. (1990). *Code of ethics.* Washington, DC: Author.

National Black Child Development Institute. (1989). *Who will care when parents can't? A study of Black children in foster care.* Washington, DC: Author.

National Center for Health Statistics. (1983). Advance report of final natality statistics, 1981. *Monthly Vital Statistics Report* (Vol. 32, Suppl. 9). Hyattsville, MD: Public Health Service.

National Center for Health Statistics. (1991). Advance report of final natality statistics, 1989. *Monthly Vital Statistics Report* (Vol. 40, Suppl. 8). Hyattsville, MD: Public Health Service.

NationalNet. (1990). *A basic bibliography on adolescent sexuality, pregnancy prevention and care programs and program evaluation.* Los Altos, CA: Social Research Applications.

Neimeyer, G., & Resnikoff, A. (1982). Qualitative strategies in counseling research. *The Counseling Psychologist, 10,* 75-85.

Nevill, D. D., & Super, D. E. (1986). *Manual for the Salience Inventory.* Palo Alto, CA: Consulting Psychologists Press.

Newman, G. (1981). *101 ways to be a long-distance super-dad.* Mountain View, CA: Blossom Valley Press.

Nicholau, S., & Ramos, C. L. (1990). *Together is better: Building strong partnerships between schools and Hispanic parents* (Report No. UD 027 472). New York: Hispanic Policy Development Project. (ERIC Document Reproduction Service No. ED 325 543)

Nobles, W. W., Goddard, L. L., & Cavil, W. (1985). *Black teenage parenting and early childhood education: Basic curriculum plan.* Oakland, CA: Black Family Institute.

Nsamenang, A. B. (1987). A West African perspective. In M. E. Lamb (Ed.), *The father's role: Cross-cultural perspectives* (pp. 273-293). Hillsdale, NJ: Lawrence Erlbaum.

O'Brien, M. (1987). Patterns of kinship and friendship among lone fathers. In C. Lewis & M. O'Brien (Eds.), *Reassessing fatherhood: New observations on fathers and the modern family* (pp. 225-245). London: Sage.

O'Connell, M., & Moore, M. (1980). The legitimacy status of first births to women aged 15-24, 1939-1978. *Family Planning Perspectives, 12,* 16-25.

ODN Productions. (Producer). (n.d.). *No time soon* [Film]. (Available from Select Media, 225 Lafayette St., Suite 1102, New York, NY 10012)

Ohio State Department of Education. (1989). *Adolescent parent resource guide.* Columbus: The Ohio State University, Vocational Instructional Material Laboratory.

Ooms, T. (1979). (Ed.). *Teenage pregnancy and family impact: New perspectives on policy. Family impact seminar.* Washington, DC: George Washington University's Institute for Educational Leadership.

Ooms, T. (1981). Family involvement, notification, and responsibility: A personal essay. In T. Ooms (Ed.), *Teenage pregnancy in a family context: Implications for policy* (pp. 371-398). Philadelphia: Temple University Press.

Ooms, T. (1984). The family context of adolescent parenting. In M. Sugar (Ed.), *Adolescent parenthood* (pp. 215-228). New York: SP Medical & Scientific Books.

Orange County Public Schools. (1987). *Marketable skills and jobs for single teen parents: Final report* (Project No. 480-15170-7-1D05). Orlando, FL: Author. (ERIC Document Reproduction Service No. ED 285 986)

Osipow, S. H., & Fitzgerald, L. F. (1993). Unemployment and mental health: A neglected relationship. *Applied and Preventive Psychology, 2,* 59-63.

Padilla, A. M. (1980). The role of cultural awareness and ethnic loyalty in acculturation. In A. M. Padilla (Ed.), *Acculturation: Theory, models, and some new findings* (pp. 47-84). Boulder, CO: Westview.

Padilla, A. M., & Salgado de Snyder, N. (1985). Counseling Hispanics: Strategies for effective intervention. In P. B. Pedersen (Ed.), *Handbook of cross-cultural counseling and therapy* (pp. 157-164). Westport, CT: Greenwood.

Panzarine, S. A., & Elster, A. B. (1983). Coping in a group of expectant adolescent fathers: An exploratory study. *Journal of Adolescent Health Care, 4,* 117-120.

Parham, T. A. (1989). Cycles of psychological Nigrescence. *The Counseling Psychologist, 17,* 187-226.

Parham, T. A. (1993). White researchers conducting multicultural counseling research: Can their efforts be "mo betta"? *The Counseling Psychologist, 21,* 250-256.

Parham, T. A., & Austin, N. L. (1994). Career development and African Americans: A contextual reappraisal using the nigrescence construct. *Journal of Vocational Behavior, 44,* 139-154.

Parham, T. A., & McDavis, J. (1987). Black men, an endangered species: Who's really pulling the trigger? *Journal of Counseling and Development, 66,* 24-27.

Parke, R. (1981). *Fathers.* Cambridge, MA: Harvard University Press.

Parke, R. D., & Neville, B. (1987). Adolescent fatherhood. In S. L. Hofferth & C. D. Hayes (Eds.), *Risking the future: Adolescent sexuality, pregnancy, and childbearing* (Vol. 2, pp. 145-173). Washington, DC: National Academy Press.

Parke, R. D., Power, T. G., & Fisher, T. (1980). The adolescent father's impact on the mother and child. *Journal of Social Issues, 36,* 1, 88-106.

Parker, W. M. (1988). *Consciousness-raising: A primer for multicultural counseling.* Springfield, IL: Charles C Thomas.

Parker, W. M., & Lord, S. L. (1993). Characteristics of role models for young African-American men: An exploratory survey. *Journal of Multicultural Counseling and Development, 21,* 97-105.

Parrad, H. (1967). *Crisis disequilibrium.* New York: Basic Books.

Parrott, L. (1993, July). Counseling today's teens: How to chill with your buds and be way rad, dude—not! *Christian Counseling Today,* pp. 16-20.

Patterson, C. H. (1986). Culture and counseling in Hong Kong. *Chinese University Education Journal, 14,* 77-81.

Pedersen, F., Rubinstein, J., & Yarrow, L. (1979). Infant development in father-absent families. *Journal of Genetic Psychology, 135,* 51-61.

Pedersen, P. B. (Ed.). (1985). *Handbook of cross-cultural counseling and therapy.* Westport, CT: Greenwood.

Pedersen, P. B. (1988). *A handbook for developing multicultural awareness.* Alexandria, VA: American Association for Counseling and Development.

Pedersen, P. B. (1990). The multicultural perspective as a fourth force in counseling. *Journal of Mental Health Counseling, 12,* 93-95.

Pedersen, P. B. (1991a). Introduction to the special issue on multiculturalism as a fourth force in counseling. *Journal of Counseling and Development, 70*(1), 4.

Pedersen, P. B. (1991b). Multiculturalism as a generic approach to counseling. *Journal of Counseling and Development, 70*(1), 6-12.

Perez, S. M., & Duany, L. A. (1992). *Reducing Hispanic teenage pregnancy and family poverty: A replication guide* (Report No. UD 028 843). Washington, DC: National Council of La Raza. (ERIC Document Reproduction Service No. ED 349 353)

Pfeiffer, S. I., Burd, S., & Wright, A. (1992). Clinicians and research: Recurring obstacles and some possible solutions. *Journal of Clinical Psychology, 48,* 140-145.

Phipps-Yonas, S. (1980). Teenage pregnancy and motherhood: A review of the literature. *American Journal of Orthopsychiatry, 50,* 403-431.

Pittman, K. (1986). Teen parents: The crisis and the challenge for vocational education. *Workplace Education, 4,* 8-9.

Planned Parenthood Association of Cincinnati. (Producer). (1987). *Fathers too soon* [Videocassette]. (Available from Planned Parenthood Association of Cincinnati, the Education/Training and Video Production Dept., 2314 Auburn Ave., Cincinnati, OH 45219)

Planned Parenthood Association of Cincinnati. (Producer). (1991). *A different family . . . our teenager has a baby* [Videocassette]. (Available from Planned Parenthood Association of Cincinnati, the Education/Training and Video Production Dept., 2314 Auburn Ave., Cincinnati, OH 45219)

Planned Parenthood Association of Metropolitan Washington, DC. (Producer). (n.d.). *Men and contraception: A shared responsibility* [Film]. (Available from Planned Parenthood Association of Metropolitan Washington, 1108 16th St. NW, Washington, DC 20036)

Pleck, J. H. (1985). *Working wives/working husbands.* Beverly Hills, CA: Sage.

Polit, D. F. (1987, January-February). Routes to self-sufficiency: Teenage mothers and employment. *Children Today,* pp. 6-11.

Polit, D. F. (1989, July/August). Effects of a comprehensive program for teenage parents: Five years after project redirection. *Family Planning Perspectives, 21*(4), 164-169, 187.

Ponterotto, J. G. (1988). Racial consciousness development among White counselor trainees: A stage model. *Journal of Multicultural Counseling and Development, 16,* 146-156.

Ponterotto, J. G., & Casas, J. M. (1991). *Handbook of racial/ethnic minority counseling research.* Springfield, IL: Charles C Thomas.

Ponterotto, J. G., & Pedersen, P. B. (1993). *Preventing prejudice: A guide for counselors and educators.* Newbury Park, CA: Sage.

Poussaint, A. F. (1990). The mental health status of Black Americans, 1983. In D. S. Ruiz & J. P. Comer (Eds.), *Handbook of mental health and mental disorder among Black Americans* (pp. 17-52). Westport, CT: Greenwood.

Preto, N. G. (1988). Transformation of the family system in adolescence. In B. Carter & M. McGoldrick (Eds.), *The changing family life cycle: A framework for family therapy* (2nd ed., pp. 255-284). New York: Gardner.

Production People, Ltd. (Producer). (1990). *Not me* [Videocassette]. (Available from Office of Children & Youth Services, Michigan Department of Social Services, P.O. Box 30039, Lansing, MI 48909)

Radin, N. (1976). The role of the father in cognitive, academic, and intellectual development (pp. 237-276). New York: John Wiley.

Ramirez, M. (1991). *Psychotherapy and counseling with minorities: A cognitive approach to individual and cultural differences*. Elmsford, NY: Pergamon.

Redmond, M. A. (1985). Attitudes of adolescent males toward adolescent pregancy and fatherhood. *Family Relations, 34,* 337-342.

Reid, H. (1986). Introduction: Assaulting the mask. In W. H. Reid, D. Dorr, J. I. Walker, & J. W. Bonner, III (Eds.), *Unmasking the psychopath: Antisocial personality and related syndromes* (pp. ix-xii). New York: Norton.

Reider, N. (1948). The unmarried father. *American Journal of Orthopsychiatry, 18,* 230-237.

Reitz, M., & Watson, K. W. (1992). *Adoption and the family system: Strategies for treatment*. New York: Guilford.

Rench, J. E. (1988). *Teen sexuality: Decisions and choices*. Minneapolis, MN: Lerner.

Research Press. (1991). *The practical parenting series* [Film]. Champaign, IL: Producer.

Reynolds, W. M., & Coats, K. I. (1986). A comparison of cognitive-behavioral therapy and relaxation training for the treatment of depression in adolescents. *Journal of Consulting and Clinical Psychology, 54,* 653-660.

Rivara, F. P., Sweeney, P. J., & Henderson, B. F. (1985). A study of low, socioeconomic status, Black teenage fathers and their nonfather peers. *Pediatrics, 78,* 151-158.

Rivara, F. P., Sweeney, P. J., & Henderson, B. F. (1986). Black teenage fathers: What happens when the child is born? *Pediatrics, 78,* 151-158.

Robbins, M. B., & Lynn, D. B. (1973). The unwed fathers: Generation recidivism and attitudes about intercourse in California Youth Authority wards. *Journal of Sex Research, 9,* 334-341.

Robinson, B. E. (1988a). *Teenage fathers*. Lexington, MA: Lexington Books.

Robinson, B. E. (1988b). Teenage pregnancy from the father's perspective. *American Journal of Orthopsychiatry, 58,* 46-51.

Robinson, B. E., & Barret, R. L. (1982). Issues and problems related to the research of teenage fathers: A critical analysis. *Journal of School Health, 52,* 596-600.

Robinson, B. E., & Barret, R. L. (1985, December). Teenage fathers. *Psychology Today, 19,* 66-70.

Robinson, B. E., & Barret, R. L. (1986). *The developing father*. New York: Guilford.

Robinson, B. E., & Barret, R. L., & Skeen, P. (1983). Locus of control of unwed adolescent fathers versus adolescent nonfathers. *Perceptual and Motor Skills, 56,* 397-398.

Rodriguez, C. (1989). *Puerto Ricans born in the USA*. Winchester, MA: Unwin Hyman.

Rogel, M. J., Zuehlke, M., Petersen, A., Tobin-Richards, M., & Shelton, M. (1980). Contraceptive behavior in adolescence: A decision making perspective. *Journal of Youth and Adolescence, 9,* 491-506.

Rogg, E. M., & Cooney, R. S. (1980). *Adaptation and adjustment of Cubans: West New York, New Jersey*. New York: Hispanic Research Center.

Rogler, L. H., Malgady, R. G., & Rodriguez, O. (1989). *Hispanics and mental health: A framework for research*. Malabar, FL: Krieger.

Rompf, E. L. (1993). Open adoption: What does the "average person" think? *Child Welfare, 72,* 219-230.

Rosen, R. H. (1980). Adolescent pregnancy decision-making: Are parents important? *Adolescence, 15,* 43-54.

Rosenbaum, S. (1985). *Providing effective prenatal care programs for teenagers*. Washington, DC: Children's Defense Fund.

Ross, A. (1982). *Teenage mothers, teenage fathers*. Toronto: Personal Library Publishers.

Rotheram-Borus, M. J., & Koopman, C. (1992). Protecting children's rights in AIDS research. In B. Stanley & J. E. Sieber (Eds.), *Social research on children and adolescents: Ethical issues* (pp. 143-161). Newbury Park, CA: Sage.

Rotzien, A. (1992). *The development of a scale to assess attitudes toward teenage parents.* Unpublished master's thesis, Ball State University, Muncie, IN.

Rounds, K., Weil, M., & Thiel, K. S. (1992). Adolescent pregnancy and early intervention programs benefit from case management. *Journal of Case Management, 1,* 14-20.

Rubin, R. H. (1988). Public policies and variant family forms. In C. S. Chilman, E. W. Nunnally, & F. M. Cox (Eds.), *Variant family forms* (pp. 254-289). Newbury Park, CA: Sage.

Rubinstein, D. (1976). Beyond the cultural barriers: Observations of emotional disorders among Cuban immigrants. *International Journal of Mental Health, 5,* 69-79.

Rudolph, J. (1989). Effects of a workshop on mental health practitioners' attitudes toward homosexuality and counseling effectiveness. *Journal of Counseling and Development, 68,* 81-85.

Ruiz, D. S. (1990). Social and economic profile of Black Americans, 1989. In D. S. Ruiz & J. P. Comer (Eds.), *Handbook of mental health and mental disorder among Black Americans* (pp. 3-15). Westport, CT: Greenwood.

Ruiz, R. A. (1981). Cultural and historical perspectives in counseling Hispanics. In D. W. Sue (Ed.), *Counseling the culturally different: Theory and practice* (pp. 186-215). New York: John Wiley.

Ruiz, R. A., & Padilla, A. M. (1977). Counseling Latinos. *Personnel and Guidance Journal, 55,* 401-408.

Rus-Eft, D., Sprenger, M., & Beever, H. (1979). Antecedents of adolescent parenthood and consequences at age 30. *The Family Coordinator, 28,* 173-179.

Sabnani, H. B., Ponterotto, J. G., & Borodovsky, L. G. (1991). White racial identity development and cross-cultural counselor training: A stage model. *The Counseling Psychologist, 19,* 76-102.

Salguero, C. (1984). The role of ethnic factors in adolescent pregnancy and motherhood. In M. Sugan (Ed.), *Adolescent parenthood* (pp. 75-98). New York: SP Medical and Scientific Books.

Sanchez, G. I. (1932). Group differences and Spanish-speaking children—a critical review. *Journal of Applied Psychology, 16,* 549-558.

Sander, J. (1991). *Before their time: Four generations of teenage mothers.* New York: Harcourt Brace & Jovanovich.

Sander, J. H., & Rosen, J. L. (1987). Teenage fathers: Working with the neglected partner in adolescent childbearing. *Family Planning Perspectives, 19,* 107-110.

Sanger, M. B. (1979). *Welfare of the poor.* San Diego: Academic Press.

Savickas, M. L. (1991). The meaning of work and love: Career issues and interventions. *Career Development Quarterly, 39,* 315-324.

Scales, P. (1977). Males and morals: Teenage contraceptive behavior amid the double standard. *The Family Coordinator, 26,* 211-222.

Scales, P. (1981). Sex education and the prevention of teenage pregnancy: An overview of policies and programs in the Untied States. In T. Ooms (Ed.), *Teenage pregnancy in a family context: Implications for policy* (pp. 213-253). Philadelphia: Temple University Press.

Scher, M. (1993). Men and boys, myths and mythic proportions: A rejoinder to Kelly and Hall. *Journal of Mental Health Counseling, 15,* 290-297.

Scherman, A., Korkames-Rowe, D., & Howard, S. S. (1990). An examination of the living arrangements and needs expressed by teenage mothers. *School Counselor, 38,* 133-141.

Schilpp, P. (Ed.). (1939). *The philosophy of John Dewey.* Evanston, IL: Northwestern University Press.

Schinke, S. P. (1989). Teenage pregnancy: The need for multiple casework services. In N. Cervera & L. Videka-Sherman (Eds.), *Working with pregnant and parenting teenage clients* (pp. 60-66). Milwaukee, WI: Family Service America.

Schinke, S. P., Blythe, B. J., & Gilchrist, L. D. (1981). Cognitive-behavioral prevention of adolescent pregnancy. *Journal of Counseling Psychology, 28,* 451-454.

Schinke, S. P., Blythe, B. J., Gilchrist, L. D., & Burt, G. A. (1989). Primary prevention of adolescent pregnancy. In N. Cervera & L. Videka-Sherman (Eds.), *Working with pregnant and parenting teenage clients* (pp. 208-219). Milwaukee, WI: Family Service America.

Schwartz, L. L. (1986). Unwed fathers and adoption custody disputes. *American Journal of Family Therapy, 14,* 347-354.

Scott-Jones, D. (1993, November). Adolescent childbearing: Whose problem? What can we do? *Phi Delta Kappan,* pp. K1-K12.

Scott-Jones, D., Roland, E. J., & White, A. B. (1989). Antecedents and outcomes of pregnancy in Black adolescents. In R. L. Jones (Ed.), *Black adolescents* (pp. 341-371). Berkeley, CA: Cobb & Henry.

Sears, W. (1986). *Becoming a father: How to nurture and enjoy your family.* Franklin Park, IL: La Leche League International.

Serious Business Company. (Producer). (n.d.). *What can a guy do?* [Film]. Franklin Lakes, NJ: Author.

Seward, R. R. (1991). Determinants of family culture: Effects on fatherhood. In F. W. Bozett & S. M. H. Hanson (Eds.), *Fatherhood and families in cultural context* (pp. 218-236). New York: Springer.

Shade, B. J. (1990). Coping with color: The anatomy of positive mental health. In D. S. Ruiz & J. P. Comer (Eds.), *Handbook of mental health and mental disorder among Black Americans* (pp. 273-289). Westport, CT: Greenwood.

Shapiro, J. L. (1987). *When men are pregnant: Needs and concerns of expectant fathers.* San Luis Obispo, CA: Impact Publishers.

Shapiro, S. (1990). *Between capitalism and democracy: Educational policy and the crisis of the welfare state.* New York: Bergin & Garvey.

Shinn, M. (1978). Father absence and children's cognitive development. *Psychological Bulletin, 85,* 295-324.

Shostak, A. B. (1979). Abortion as fatherhood lost: Problems and reforms. *Family Coordinator, 24,* 569-574.

Sieber, J. E. (1992). Community intervention research on minors. In B. Stanley & J. E. Sieber (Eds.), *Social research on children and adolescents: Ethical issues* (pp. 128-130). Newbury Park, CA: Sage.

Silverberg, R. A. (1986). *Psychotherapy for men: Transcending the masculine mystique.* Springfield, IL: Charles C Thomas.

Simkins, L. (1984). Consequences of teenage pregnancy and motherhood. *Adolescence, 19,* 39-54.

Simon, S. (1972). *The Anglo-Saxon manner: The English contribution to civilization.* London: Casell.

Slaney, R. B., & MacKinnon-Slaney, F. (1990). The use of vocational card sorts in career counseling. In C. E. Watkins, Jr. & V. L. Campbell (Eds.), *Testing in counseling practice* (pp. 317-371). Hillsdale, NJ: Lawrence Erlbaum.

Slavin, R. E., & Madden, N. A. (1989, February). What works for students at risk: A research synthesis. *Educational Leadership*, pp. 4-13.

Smith, A. (1988/1989, Summer/Winter). Responsibility of the African-American church as a source of support for adolescent fathers. *Urban League Review*, pp. 83-90.

Smith, E. J. (1981). Cultural and historical perspectives in counseling Blacks. In D. W. Sue (Ed.), *Counseling the culturally different: Theory and practice* (pp. 141-185). New York: John Wiley.

Smith, L. A. (1988). Black adolescent fathers: Issues for service provision. *Social Work, 33*(3), 269-271.

Smith, L. A. (1989). *Windows on opportunities: An exploration in program development for Black adolescent fathers.* Unpublished doctoral dissertation, The City University of New York.

Smollar, J., & Ooms, T. (1987). *Young unwed fathers: Research review, policy dilemmas, and options: Summary report.* Washington, DC: Department of Health and Human Services.

Solomon, B. B. (1990). Counseling Black families at inner-city church sites. In H. E. Cheatham & J. B. Stewart (Eds.), *Black families: Interdisciplinary perspectives* (pp. 353-372). New Brunswick, NJ: Transaction Books.

Sommerfeld, M. (1992, November 25). Problems in programs for unwed fathers chronicled. *Education Week*, p. 8.

Sonenstein, F. L. (1986). Risking paternity: Sex and contraception among adolescent males. In A. B. Elster & M. E. Lamb (Eds.), *Adolescent fatherhood* (pp. 31-54). Hillsdale, NJ: Lawrence Erlbaum.

Speight, S. L., Myers, L. J., Cox, C. I., & Highlen, P. S. (1991). A redefinition of multicultural counseling. *Journal of Counseling and Development, 70,* 29-36.

Spengler, P. M., & Strohmer, D. C. (1994). Clinical judgmental bias: The moderating roles of counselor cognitive complexity and counselor client preferences. *Journal of Counseling Psychology, 41,* 8-17.

Spivack, G., Platt, J. J., & Shure, M. B. (1976). *The problem-solving approach to adjustment.* San Francisco: Jossey-Bass.

Spokane, A. (1991). *Career intervention.* Englewood Cliffs, NJ: Prentice Hall.

Sprinthall, N. (1984). Primary prevention: A road paved with a plethora of promises and procrastinations. *Personnel and Guidance Journal, 62,* 491-495.

St. Pierre, T. L. (1980). *The relationship among vocational educators' attitudes toward adolescent parents, their degree of open-mindedness, and their knowledge of the problem of adolescent parenthood.* Unpublished master's thesis, The Pennsylvania State University, University Park.

Stack, C. (1974). *All our kin: Strategies for survival in a Black community.* New York: Harper & Row.

Stanley, B., & Sieber, J. E. (Eds.). (1992). *Social research on children and adolescents: Ethical issues.* Newbury Park, CA: Sage.

Staples, R., & Johnson, L. B. (1992). *Black families at the crossroads: Challenges and prospects.* San Francisco: Jossey-Bass.

Stearns, P. N. (1991). Fatherhood in historical perspective: The role of social change. In F. W. Bozett & S. M. H. Hanson (Eds.), *Fatherhood and families in cultural context* (pp. 28-52). New York: Springer.

Steinberg, D., & Jassim, L. (Producers). (1980). *Fathers* [Film]. (Available from Churchill Films, 662 North Robertson Blvd., Los Angeles, CA 90069)

Steinfels, M. O. (1981). Ethical and legal issues in teenage pregnancies. In T. Ooms (Ed.), *Teenage pregnancy in a family context* (pp. 277-306). Philadelphia: Temple University Press.

Stengel, R. (1985, December). The missing-father myth. *Time*, p. 90.

Stevens, J., & Mathews, M. (Eds.). (1978). *Mother/child father/child relationships.* Washington, DC: National Association for the Education of Young Children.

Stevens, J. H. (1984). Black grandmothers' and Black adolescent mothers' knowledge about parenting. *Developmental Psychology, 20,* 1017-1025.

Stiffman, A. R., & Feldman, R. A. (1990). Introduction. In A. R. Stiffman & R. A. Feldman (Eds.), *Advances in adolescent mental health: Vol. 4. Contraception, pregnancy, and parenting* (pp. 1-9). London: Kingsley.

Stone, R., & Waszak, C. (1991). Adolescent knowledge and attitudes about abortion. *Family Planning Perspectives, 23,* 52-61.

Stonequist, E. V. (1937). *The marginal man.* New York: Scribner.

Strauss, A., & Corbin, J. (1990). *Basics of qualitative research: Grounded theory procedures and techniques.* Newbury Park, CA: Sage.

Streett, R. (1991). Parenting education. In J. B. Hardy & L. S. Zabin (Eds.), *Adolescent pregnancy in an urban environment: Issues, programs and evaluation* (pp. 245-254). Washington, DC: Urban Institute Press.

Stricker, G. (1992). The relationship of research to clinical practice. *American Psychologist, 47,* 543-549.

Strupp, H. H. (1981). Clinical research, practice, and the crisis of confidence. *Journal of Consulting and Clinical Psychology, 49,* 216-220.

Stumphauzer, J. S. (1986). *Helping delinquents change: A treatment manual of social learning approaches.* New York: Haworth.

Sue, D. W., & Sue, D. (1990). *Counseling the culturally different* (2nd ed.). New York: John Wiley.

Sue, S., Akutsu, P. D., & Higashi, C. (1985). Training issues in conducting therapy with ethnic-minority-group clients. In P. B. Pedersen (Ed.), *Handbook of cross-cultural counseling and therapy* (pp. 275-280). Westport, CT: Greenwood.

Sue, S., McKinney, H., Allen, D., & Hall, J. (1974). Delivery of community mental health services to Black and White clients. *Journal of Consulting and Clinical Psychology, 42,* 794-801.

Sullivan, M. (1984). *Youth, crime and employment patterns in three Brooklyn neighborhoods.* New York: Vera Institute of Justice.

Sullivan, M. L. (1985). *Teen fathers in the inner city: An exploratory ethnographic study* (Report No. UD 024 536). New York: Vera Institute of Justice. (ERIC Document Reproduction Service No. ED 264 316)

Sullivan, M. L. (1989). Absent fathers in the inner city. *Annals of the American Academy of Political and Social Science, 501,* 58.

Sunburst Communications. (1989). *Teenage father* [Film]. Los Angeles, CA: Producer.

Super, D. E. (1957). *The psychology of careers.* New York: HarperCollins.

Super, D. E. (1983). Assessment in career guidance: Toward truly developmental counseling. *Personnel and Guidance Journal, 9,* 555-562.

Super, D. E. (1985). Coming of age in Middletown: Careers in the making. *American Psychologist, 40,* 405-414.

Super, D. E., Osborne, W. L., Walsh, D. J., Brown, S. D., & Niles, S. G. (1992). Developmental career assessment and counseling: The C-DAC model. *Journal of Counseling and Development, 71,* 74-79.

Super, D. E., Starishevsky, R., Matlin, N., & Jordaan, J. P. (1963). *Career development: Self-concept theory.* New York: College Entrance Examination Board.

Super, D. E., Thompson, A. S., Lindeman, R. H., Jordaan, J. P., & Myers, R. A. (1981). *The career development inventory.* Palo Alto, CA: Consulting Psychologists Press.

Szapocznik, J., & Kurtines, W. (1980). Acculturation, biculturalation and adjustment among Cuban Americans. In A. M. Padilla (Ed.), *Acculturation: Theory, models, and some new findings* (pp. 139-159). Boulder, CO: Westview.

Szapocznik, J., Scopetta, M. A., Arnalde, M. M., & Kurtines, W. (1978). Cuban value structure: Treatment implications. *Journal of Consulting and Clinical Psychology, 46,* 961-970.

Szapocznik, J., Scopetta, M. A., & King, O. E. (1978). Theory and practice in matching treatment to the special characteristics and problems of Cuban immigrants. *Journal of Community Psychology, 6,* 112-122.

Taylor, H., Kagay, M., & Leichenko, S. (1986). *American teens speak: Sex, myths, TV, and birth control* (Project No. 864012). New York: Louis Harris Corporation.

Taylor, R. J., & Chatters, L. M. (1991). Religious life. In J. S. Jackson (Ed.), *Life in Black America* (pp. 105-123). Newbury Park, CA: Sage.

Tedder, S., & Scherman, A. (1987). Counseling single fathers. In M. Scher, M. Stevens, G. Good, & G. A. Eichenfield (Eds.), *Handbook of counseling and psychotherapy with men* (pp. 265-277). Newbury Park, CA: Sage.

Thomas, H. (1977). *The Cuban revolution.* New York: Harper & Row.

Thornberg, H. (1981, April). Adolescent sources of information on self. *Journal of School Health,* pp. 274-277.

Tischler, H. L. (1990). *Introduction to sociology* (3rd ed.). New York: Holt, Rinehart & Winston.

Tyack, D. (1992). Health and social services in public schools: Historical perspectives. *Future of Children, 2,* 19-31.

Tymchuk, A. J. (1992). Assent processes. In B. Stanley & J. E. Sieber (Eds.), *Social research on children and adolescents: Ethical issues* (pp. 128-139). Newbury Park, CA: Sage.

Unger, D. G., & Wandersman, L. P. (1985). Social support and adolescent mothers: Action research contributions to theory and application. *Journal of Social Issues, 41,* 29-45.

U.S. Bureau of the Census. (1988). *Statistical abstract of the United States, 1987* (108th ed.). Washington, DC: Government Printing Office.

U.S. Congress. (1986). *Teen pregnancy: What is being done? A report of the select committee on children, youth, and families.* Washington, DC: Government Printing Office.

U.S. Congress. (1989). *Adolescent pregnancy prevention, care, and research grants act of 1989* (Report No. 101-103). Washington, DC: Government Printing Office.

U.S. Department of Education, Office for Civil Rights. (1991). *Teenage pregnancy and parenthood issues under title IX of the education amendments of 1972.* Washington, DC: Government Printing Office.

Vacc, N., Wittmer, J., & DeVaney, S. B. (1988). *Experiencing and counseling multicultural and diverse populations.* Muncie, IN: Accelerated Development.

Vanderslice, C. (Ed.). (1980). *His baby too: Prolems of teenage pregnancy* [Filmstrip]. Pleasantville, NY: Sunburst Communications.

Vann, K. R., & Kunjufu, J. (1993, February). The importance of an Afrocentric, multicultural curriculum. *Phi Delta Kappan,* pp. 490-491.

Vaz, R., Smolen, P., & Miller, C. (1983). Adolescent pregnancy: Involvement of the male partner. *Journal of Adolescent Health Care, 4,* 246-250.

Ventura, S. J., Taffel, S. M., & Mosher, W. D. (1985). Estimates of pregnancies and pregnancy rates for the United States, 1976-81. *Public Health Rep, 100,* 31-34.

Ventura, S. J., Taffel, S. M., Mosher, W. D., & Henshaw, S. (1992). Trends in pregnancies and pregnancy rates, United States, 1980-88. *Monthly Vital Statistics Report* (Vol. 41, Suppl. 6). Hyattsville, MD: National Center for Health Statistics.

Vera Institute of Justice. (1990). *The male role in teenage pregnancy and parenting: New directions of public policy.* New York: Author.

Vogt, G. M., & Sirridge, S. T. (1991). *Like son, like father: Healing the father-son wound in men's lives.* New York: Plenum.

Vontress, C. E. (1988). An existential approach to cross-cultural counseling. *Journal of Multicultural Counseling and Development, 16,* 73-83.

Wagner, T. (1993, May). Improving high schools: The case for new goals and strategies. *Phi Delta Kappan,* pp. 695-701.

Watson, R. I., & Kelly, M. J. (1989). Targeting the at-risk male: A strategy for adolescent pregnancy prevention. *Journal of the National Medical Association, 81,* 453-456.

Watson, S. R. (1976). *Counselor complexity and the process of hypothesizing about a client: An exploratory study of counselors' information processing.* Unpublished doctoral dissertation, University of California, Santa Barbara.

Weeks, W. H., Pedersen, P., & Brislin, R. W. (Eds.). (1986). *A manual of structured experiences for cross-cultural counseling.* Yarmouth, ME: Intercultural Press.

Weissberg, R. P., Gesten, E. L., Leibenstein, N. L., Doherty-Schmid, K., & Hutton, H. (1980). *The Rochester social problem-solving (SPS) program: A training manual for teachers of 2nd-4th grade children.* Rochester, NY: University of Rochester.

Welch, L. (1992). *The complete book of sexual trivia: Everything you always wanted to know about sex . . . and more.* New York: Citadel.

Westoff, C. F. (1988). Unintended pregnancy in America and abroad. *Family Planning Perspectives, 20,* 254-261.

Westoff, C. F., Cabot, G., & Foster, A. (1983). Teenage fertility in developed nations: 1971-1980. *Family Planning Perspectives, 15,* 105-110.

Wetzel, J. (1989). *American youth: A statistical snapshot.* New York: William T. Grant Foundation.

Whipple, V. (1987). *Career orientation and preparation for teen parents curriculum.* Malta, IL: Kishwaukee College, Teen Parents Program. (ERIC Document Reproduction Service No. ED 283 566)

Whitbeck, L. B., & Gecas, V. (1988). Value attributions and value transmission between parents and children. *Journal of Marriage and the Family, 50,* 829-840.

Whitehead, B. D. (1993, April). Dan Quayle was right. *Atlantic Monthly,* pp. 47-84.

Wilcox, D. W., & Forrest, L. (1992). The problems of men and counseling: Gender bias or gender truth? *Journal of Mental Health Counseling, 14,* 291-304.

William T. Grant Foundation. (1993, January). *General information brochure.* (Available from William T. Grant Foundation, 515 Madison Avenue, New York, NY, 10022-5403)

Williams, C. W. (1991). *Black teenage mothers: Pregnancy and child rearing from their perspective.* Lexington, MA: Lexington Books.

Williams, M. W. (1990). Polygamy and the declining male to female ratio in Black communities: A social inquiry. In H. E. Cheatham & J. B. Stewart (Eds.), *Black families: Interdisciplinary perspectives* (pp. 171-193). New Brunswick, NJ: Transaction Books.

Winawer-Steiner, H., & Wetzel, N. A. (1982). German families. In M. McGoldrick, J. K. Pearce, & J. Giordano (Eds.), *Ethnicity and family therapy* (pp. 247-268). New York: Guilford.

Wodarski, J. S., & Lockhart, L. L. (1987, March/April). Teenage parents on welfare. *Society,* pp. 48-52.

Wolins, M. (1983). The gender dilemma in social welfare: Who cares for children? In M. D. Lamb & A. Sagi (Eds.), *Fatherhood and social policy* (pp. 113-128). Hillsdale, NJ: Lawrence Erlbaum.

Worden, J. W. (1982). *Grief counseling and grief therapy: A handbook for the mental health practitioner.* New York: Springer.

Worthington, E. L. (1987). *Counseling for unplanned pregnancy and infertility.* Waco, TX: Word Books.

Wyatt, G. E. (1982). Identifying stereotypes of Afro-American sexuality and their impact upon sexual behavior. In B. A. Bass, G. E. Wyatt, & G. J. Powell (Eds.), *The Afro-American family: Assessment, treatment, and research issues* (pp. 333-346). New York: Grune & Stratton.

Wynn, M. (1992). *Empowering African-American Males to succeed: A ten-step approach for parents and teachers.* South Pasadena, CA: Rising Sun.

Yarrow, L., Rubinstein, J., & Pedersen, F. (1975). *Infant and environment: Early cognitive and motivational development.* New York: Halsted.

Yin, R. K. (1989). *Case study research: Design and methods.* Newbury Park, CA: Sage.

Yogman, M. (1981). Games fathers and mothers play with their infants. *Infant Mental Health Journal, 2,* 241-248.

Young, M. (1992). *Counseling methods and techniques: An eclectic approach.* New York: Merrill.

Zabin, L. S., & Hayward, S. C. (1993). *Adolescent sexual behavior and childbearing.* Newbury Park, CA: Sage.

Zabin, L. S., & Hirsch, M. B. (1988). *Evaluation of pregnancy prevention programs in the school context.* Lexington, MA: Lexington Books.

Zabin, L. S., Hirsch, M. B., Smith, E. A., Streett, R., & Hardy, J. B. (1986). Evaluation of a pregnancy prevention program for urban teenagers. *Family Planning Perspectives, 18,* 119-126.

Zayas, L. H., Schinke, S. P., & Casareno, D. (1987). Hispanic adolescent fathers: At risk and underresearched. *Children and Youth Services Review, 9,* 235-248.

Zelnick, M., & Kantner, J. F. (1980). Sexual activity, contraceptive use and pregnancy among metropolitan-area teenagers: 1971-1979. *Family Planning Perspectives, 12,* 230-237.

Zelnick, M., & Kantner, J. F., & Ford, K. (1981). *Sex and pregnancy in adolescence.* Beverly Hills, CA: Sage.

Zelnick, M., & Shah, F. K. (1983). First intercourse among young Americans. *Family Planning Perspectives, 15,* 64-70.

Zytowski, D. G., Casas, J. M., Gilbert, L. A., Lent, R. W., & Simon, N. P. (1988). Counseling psychology's public image. *The Counseling Psychologist, 16,* 332-346.

Author Index

403

Subject Index

Abortion, 22-23, 66-81, 314
  and African American teenage fathers,
    178-180
  and Anglo American teenage fathers,
    216-218
  and Hispanic American teenage fathers,
    251-254
  and religiosity, 287-288, 291-292, 293
  counseling for, 66-81
  emotional reactions to, 67
Acculturation:
  of African Americans, 202, 234-235
  of Hispanic Americans, 238, 242-244,
    246, 250-254, 256-257, 260-261
Adolescent fathers. *See* Teenage fathers
Adolescent mothers. *See* Teenage mothers
Adoption, 22-23, 66-81, 314
  and African American teenage fathers,
    218-219
  and Anglo American teenage fathers,
    178-180
  and Hispanic American teenage fathers,
    251-254
  counseling for, 66-81
  emotional reactions to, 67, 70-73
  informal, 218-219
  open, 78-81
AFDC. *See* Welfare

African American:
  church, 204-206
  definition of, 195-196
African American teenage fathers. *See*
  Teenage fathers, African American
Africentric counseling, 210, 232-235,
  332-336
Africentric education, 232-233
Aid to Families With Dependent Children.
  See Welfare
Alternative resource theory, 247-248
Anglo American:
  conceptions of fatherhood, 191-192
  definition of, 166
  value system, 166, 183
Anglo American teenage fathers. *See*
  Teenage fathers, Anglo American
ASPIRA Association, 266

Barrier theory, 247-248
Benjiger Family Life Program, 289
Booker T. Washington Alternative School, 161
Brotherhood Program, 356

California Adolescent Family Life Program,
  284

413

About the Author

Mark S. Kiselica, PhD, is an Assistant Professor in the Department of Counseling and Personnel Services at Trenton State College. He earned his bachelor's degree in psychology from Saint Vincent College in Latrobe, Pennsylvania; his master's degree in psychology from Bucknell University in Lewisburg, Pennsylvania; and his doctorate in counseling psychology from The Pennsylvania State University. He completed his school counseling internship at Tyrone Area High School in Tyrone, Pennsylvania, and his predoctoral internship in clinical child and adolescent psychology at the University of Medicine and Dentistry of New Jersey, Community Mental Health Center in Newark, New Jersey.

Dr. Kiselica is a licensed psychologist and health services provider in psychology with nearly 20 years of experience counseling adolescents and their families. Prior to his employment at Trenton State, he worked in the following clinical settings: Fair Oaks Hospital in Summit, New Jersey; Danville State Hospital in Danville, Pennsylvania; the University of Medicine and Dentistry of New Jersey, Community Mental Health Center in Piscataway, New Jersey; the Albert C. Wagner Youth Correctional Facility in Bordentown, New Jersey; and The Back Door of Muncie, Indiana. He also is a former assistant professor and director of the master's program in counseling at Ball State University in Muncie, Indiana, and a former adjunct assistant professor of psychology at Rider College in Lawrenceville, New Jersey.

The author of two books and numerous articles and conference presentations on the subjects of teenage parents and multicultural counseling, Dr. Kiselica serves as the National Coordinator of the American School Counselor Association Professional Interest Network on Teenage Parents; is a member of the National Organization of Adolescent Pregnancy, Parenthood, and Prevention; serves on the Teen Pregnancy Task Force of Bucks County, Pennsylvania; and is a former member of the Board of Directors of the Indiana Council on Adolescent Pregnancy. He also has served on the editorial board of the *Journal of Counseling and Development* and the *Journal of Mental Health Counseling*. He also serves as the book review editor for *The School Counselor.*

DATE DUE

MAR 2 9 2002		
APR 2 0 2002		
GAYLORD		PRINTED IN U.S.A.